ESSENTIALS *of* UTILIZATION-FOCUSED EVALUATION

To
Jean K. Gornick,
my brevity muse.
The calculus she holds before me:
"Fewer words,
more readers,
more smiles,
greater utility."

ESSENTIALS *of* UTILIZATION-FOCUSED EVALUATION

MICHAEL QUINN PATTON

Utilization-Focused Evaluation, Saint Paul, Minnesota

Los Angeles | London | New Delhi
Singapore | Washington DC

Los Angeles | London | New Delhi
Singapore | Washington DC

FOR INFORMATION:

SAGE Publications, Inc.
2455 Teller Road
Thousand Oaks, California 91320
E-mail: order@sagepub.com

SAGE Publications Ltd.
1 Oliver's Yard
55 City Road
London EC1Y 1SP
United Kingdom

SAGE Publications India Pvt. Ltd.
B 1/I 1 Mohan Cooperative Industrial Area
Mathura Road, New Delhi 110 044
India

SAGE Publications Asia-Pacific Pte. Ltd.
33 Pekin Street #02-01
Far East Square
Singapore 048763

Acquisitions Editor: Vicki Knight
Associate Editor: Lauren Habib
Editorial Assistant: Kalie Koscielak
Production Editor: Astrid Virding
Copy Editor: Terri Lee Paulsen
Typesetter: C&M Digitals (P) Ltd.
Proofreader: Dennis W. Webb
Indexer: Kathleen Paparchontis
Cover Designer: Candice Harman
Marketing Manager: Helen Salmon
Permissions Editor: Adele Hutchinson

Printed in the United States of America

Library of Congress Cataloging-in-Publication Data

Patton, Michael Quinn.

Essentials of utilization-focused evaluation/Michael Quinn Patton.

p. cm.
Includes bibliographical references and index.

ISBN 978-1-4129-7741-8 (pbk.)

1. Evaluation research (Social action programs)—United States. I. Title.

H62.5.U5P3688 2012
300.72—dc23 2011019187

This book is printed on acid-free paper.

11 12 13 14 15 10 9 8 7 6 5 4 3 2 1

Contents

Detailed Contents

Preface

"Patton's book is overwhelming."

This was the lead item on a PowerPoint slide presenting some first-year lessons learned in developing utilization-focused evaluation capacity (Ramírez & Brodhead, 2010). The presenters reported that they had to work hard to turn the 667 pages of the 4th edition of *Utilization-Focused Evaluation* (Patton, 2008) into a practical set of processes they could apply to a real-world development evaluation. Others joined them in reflecting on putting the principles of utilization-focused evaluation (U-FE) into practice at the 2010 Evaluation Conclave in New Delhi (Mizumoto & Lim, 2010). I am grateful to Joaquin Navas, Ricardo Ramirez, and their colleagues for their positive feedback on what they found useful and their honest feedback about what was difficult as they worked with utilization-focused evaluation, especially the summary U-FE checklist (Patton, 2008, pp. 576–581).

They were not the first to comment on the length of the book. Jim Rugh, the 2010 recipient of the Alva and Gunnar Myrdal Evaluation Practice Award from the American Evaluation Association and coauthor of *RealWorld Evaluation: Working Under Budget, Time, Data, and Political Constraints* (Bamberger, Rugh, & Mabry, 2006), e-mailed me shortly after the book was published about his experience carrying it on a trip to India. He found himself on an overnight train in a sleeping compartment with no pillows. Jim wrote that the thickness of the 4th edition made it quite serviceable and useful as a substitute pillow. He expressed appreciation for the book's *real-world utility.* Others have written lauding its weighty value for strength training. Minnesota colleague Gene Lyle threatened to send me an invoice for the costs of hiring professional movers to lift and carry the book into his house.

The first edition of *Utilization-Focused Evaluation* in 1978 was 303 pages; the 2nd edition (1986) grew to 368 pages; and the 3rd edition (1997) came in at 431 pages. But the big jump to 667 pages in 2008 may have reached the upper threshold of what people can manage. To be sure, the increasing length reflected the huge development of the evaluation profession and the great volume of research on utilization-focused evaluation over the years, but the book was still meant to be *focused,* utilization-focused. Yet, the feedback I was getting suggested that by striving to be comprehensive, the book's utility for in-the-trenches practitioners was being cast in doubt. One reader struggling to digest the book made allusion to feeling like a python swallowing an elephant. As Karen Kirkhart observed in reviewing the book in the *American Journal of Evaluation* (2010):

> Despite its approachable writing style, the usefulness of *Utilization-Focused Evaluation* as a textbook is limited by its size. It is lengthy even for a primary text and to pair it with a more traditional introductory text makes a prohibitive reading load. . . . For general instruction, a primer-length version that could be paired with other readings would be more useful than this full volume. (p. 591)

Admittedly, brevity is not my strong suit, which is why I'm appreciative of the constant admonitions of Jean Gornick, to whom this book is dedicated, reminding me that life is short and brevity a virtue, leaving more time for experiencing life and not just reading about it. Still, I remain an intrepid member of the T. S. Eliot school of writing epitomized by his sincere apology, "If I had more time, I would have written a shorter letter." But what kind of evaluator would I be if I ignored all this feedback? So, with thanks to the many friends, colleagues, teachers, students, and readers who have urged me to produce a more focused utilization-focused book, I offer this volume on *Essentials.* (For the sake of brevity, I won't list all those who deserve acknowledgement and to whom I am thankful. See the Preface to the 4th edition for that list. However, I do want to make special mention of Terri Lee Paulsen, the copy editor for this book. Her careful corrections and attention to detail increased both the accuracy and readability of the book. My thanks to Sage for assigning the book to her.)

The Janus Challenge

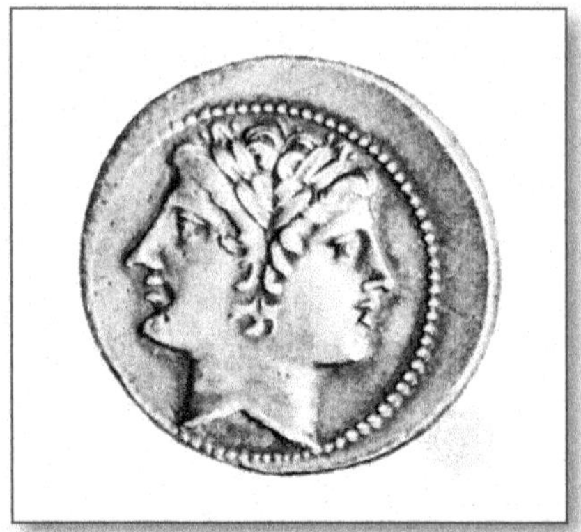

In Roman mythology, Janus is the god of gates, doors, beginnings, endings, and time. The month of January is named in his honor. He is depicted classically with two faces looking in opposite directions. One looks back at the past year while the other looks forward to the new, simultaneously peering into the future and the past. The challenge I faced in writing this book was not in looking simultaneously backwards and forward, but rather in portraying utilization-focused evaluation as a series of sequential steps while also capturing the complex nature of the utilization-focused process as nonlinear, interactive, and dynamic.

Presenting U-FE as a series of steps, *17 steps to be precise,* is driven by the necessarily linear and sequential nature of writing and, to some extent, our human thinking processes involved in figuring out how to do something: One thing comes before another. But the process is not neatly linear and sequential. There are interactions among the steps, feedback loops, recursive iterations, interrelationships, and interdependencies among those involved in the evaluation, and other complex dynamics that can be observed in any open and emergent system (Patton, 2011.) To reflect the real-world interdependencies among the steps, I periodically offer an interlude between steps (and chapters) to call attention to the importance of understanding utilization-focused evaluation as a complex dynamic process. Of course, invoking Janus and presenting two perspectives on utilization-focused evaluation made the book longer than I intended. Perhaps I should have relied more heavily on muses other than Janus, those goddesses of human inspirations who sang and danced at the parties held by the gods, inspiring poetry, music, and dance, but not, as near as I can tell, evaluation. Alas, Janus rules.

In essence, then, you're asked to operate within two perspectives at the same time; one simple, stepwise, and neatly linear, the other complexly interactive and dynamic. Is this possible? Can we walk in two worlds at once? Can we simultaneously hold two perspectives at the same time? Is this bipolar multitasking possible? Desirable?

I did an Internet search to find out what the latest brain research suggests about holding and acting on two (or more) ideas simultaneously. I found a definitive ambiguity about the matter, and some intense debate, linked to such disparate phenomena as cognitive dissonance, schizophrenia, Hegelian dialectics, and complementary pairs. One lovely metaphor that turned up was of early chamber music which often had three or four instruments each playing, simultaneously, a different simple melody. I like that: utilization-focused evaluation as simultaneously playing both simple and complex melodies, hopefully with some degree of harmony in the end. Perhaps the most insightful comments I encountered brought a gender framework to the question, essentially arguing that whether one can hold two ideas at once and/or do multiple things simultaneously is a distinctly male question, probably a function of the empty male chromosome, since from the beginning of time women have been called on to think and do many things at once. End of discussion.

The Steps

When it is obvious that the goals cannot be reached, don't adjust the goals, adjust the action steps.

Confucius (551–479 BCE)

Perhaps the number of steps caught your attention: 17, a captivating and distinct prime number. Not the usual dominant number in lists like Newton's 3 laws of motion and Asimov's 3 laws of robotics, or the 7 habits of highly effective people, or the 10 commandments, or the 12 steps to serenity (AA). No, U-FE now has an easily remembered and followed mere 17 steps. What's not to like? Well, the 4th edition had a 12-step U-FE checklist. So how did I get from 12 to 17? See the wisdom of Confucius cited above.

This book on *Essentials* is organized differently from earlier editions of *Utilization-Focused Evaluation.* The stepwise organization intertwined with complex system dynamics has led to new material, new graphics, new stories and examples, and new cartoons, for which I am especially grateful to superb cartoonist and evaluator Mark Rogers, who turned my abstract musings into concrete and, I think, humorous illustrations.

Despite a lot that is new, though presented in fewer pages, the basic message remains unchanged. *Utilization-focused evaluation* emerged from the observation that much of what has passed for program evaluation has not been very useful. The fundamental premise of the book is that *evaluations ought to be useful.* Therefore, something different must be done if evaluation is to be useful. This book illuminates what should be different. Based on research and professional experience, and integrating theory and practice, this book provides both an overall framework and concrete advice for how to conduct useful evaluations that actually get used.

Michael Quinn Patton
Saint Paul, Minnesota

Let me add a prefatory note on the icons used in the book. The between-step interludes will be identified by the Janus icon portrayed and discussed above. The book also includes numerous sidebars, like this one, meant to illustrate, illuminate, and elaborate points made in the text. These sidebars will be identified with a classic symbol of interconnectedness, shown here, connoting that while the sidebars are separate from the text, they are also part of the text. This symbol is also meant as a reminder of the interconnectedness of the steps, as elaborated in the complex systems interlude discussions between steps.

Finally, astute readers will have observed that the cover art includes a representation of the double helix evoking the *essential* structure of DNA. DNA is *essential* to life. This book is about what is essential to utilization-focused evaluation. Life, evaluation – it's all essentially interconnected. But you already knew that or you wouldn't have this book in hand.

About the Author

Michael Quinn Patton is an independent evaluation consultant with 40 years of experience conducting evaluations, training evaluators, and writing about ways to make evaluation useful. He is former president of the American Evaluation Association and recipient of both the Alva and Gunnar Myrdal Evaluation Practice Award for "outstanding contributions to evaluation use and practice" and the Paul F. Lazarsfeld Evaluation Theory Award for lifetime contributions to evaluation theory, both from the American Evaluation Association. The Society for Applied Sociology honored him with the Lester F. Ward Award for Outstanding Contributions to Applied Sociology.

In addition to *Utilization-Focused Evaluation,* he has written books on *Qualitative Research and Evaluation Methods, Creative Evaluation, Practical Evaluation,* and *Developmental Evaluation: Applying Complexity Concepts to Enhance Innovation and Use.* He has edited volumes on *Culture and Evaluation* and *Teaching Evaluation Using the Case Method.* He is coauthor of *Getting to Maybe: How the World Is Changed,* a book that applies complexity science to social innovation.

After receiving his doctorate in organizational sociology from the University of Wisconsin, Madison, he spent 18 years on the faculty of the University of Minnesota, including 5 years as director of the Minnesota Center for Social Research. He received the University's Morse-Amoco Award for outstanding teaching.

He is a regular trainer for the International Program for Development Evaluation Training (IPDET) sponsored by The World Bank each summer in Ottawa; *The Evaluators' Institute* annual courses in Washington, D.C., San Francisco, and Chicago; and the American Evaluation Association's professional development courses.

He has applied utilization-focused evaluation to a broad range of initiatives including antipoverty programs, leadership development, education at all levels, human services, the environment, public health, medical education, employment training, agricultural extension, arts, criminal justice, mental health, transportation, diversity initiatives, international development, community development, systems change, policy effectiveness, managing for results, performance indicators, and effective governance. He has worked with organizations and programs at the international, national, state, provincial, and local levels, and with philanthropic, not-for-profit, private sector, international agency, and government programs. He has worked with peoples from many different cultures and perspectives.

He has three children—a musician, an engineer, and an international development practitioner—each doing a great deal of evaluation in their own distinctive ways, but, like much of the world, seldom officially calling it that. When not evaluating, he hikes the Grand Canyon, climbs mountains in Colorado, and enjoys the woods and rivers of Minnesota—kayaking, cross-country skiing, snowshoeing, and watching the seasons change from his office overlooking the Mississippi River in Saint Paul.

Introduction, Overview, and Context

Utilization-Focused Reality Testing: Finding Out if What Is Hoped for Actually Happens

A theory must be tempered with reality.

Jawaharlal Nehru (1889–1964)
Prime Minister of India

Kiribati is an island nation in the central Pacific. The economy depends on producing coconut oil and fishing, but overfishing threatened to become an economic crisis. The Kiribati government created a program to subsidize the coconut oil industry with the goals of increasing incomes from coconut production and reducing overfishing. The idea was that if people spent more time growing coconuts, they would spend less time fishing.

On the face of it, this is a reasonable policy created by government officials who know their country and its people. The question is: Did it work? Answering that question is the job of evaluation. Lots of good ideas don't work in practice. Some do. Evaluation helps distinguish those ideas that work from those that don't. So what happened in Kiribati?

Sheila Walsh, a postdoctoral researcher at Brown University working with the Scripps Institution of Oceanography, interviewed Kiribati fishermen and helped monitor changes in fishing. She found that fishing increased by 33% and the reef fish population dropped by an estimated 17%, putting the whole ecosystem at risk. It turned out that paying people more to do coconut agriculture actually increased fishing. Why? How can that be? Walsh concluded that as people earned more money making coconut oil, they could work less to support themselves and spend more leisure time fishing. They didn't just fish for income. They fished because they liked to fish and so having more income from coconut production gave them more time to fish (Harris, 2009; Walsh, 2009).

The program aimed at reducing overfishing actually made the situation worse, a classic example of an unintended consequence. Based on the evaluation findings, Walsh began working with the government to try other interventions to reduce overfishing, like creating new jobs for fishermen by hiring them to use their boats to patrol newly created ocean preserves. Those programs will also need to be evaluated to find out if they work.

This is an example of an evaluation used to support making decisions about what works and doesn't work. We can infer several factors that made the Kiribati evaluation useful. The government officials who implemented the program had to be willing to have it evaluated. The evaluation questions needed to be relevant and meaningful to those officials. The evaluator needed to be credible and produce credible findings based on credible methods. The intervention (the program) had to be sufficiently well conceptualized and implemented that the extent to which it attained the desired goals could be determined. There needed to be sufficient resources to undertake a credible evaluation. The fishermen had to cooperate with the evaluation, answering questions about their reactions to the program and how their practices and behaviors were affected. Credible statistics about ecosystem effects (overfishing) had to be collected with agreement among those involved about how to define "overfishing"; that is, *criteria for making judgments* had to be articulated and agreed on. The findings had to be actionable. When the results proved negative, the officials had to be motivated to engage with the evaluator about the implications of the findings and, using what was learned from the evaluation, look for alternative approaches. In so doing, the government officials and evaluator formed an ongoing relationship of inquiry, evaluation, and action.

A half century of research on evaluation use has validated the importance of these factors and how they relate to each other (Patton, 2008). This book draws on that research and organizes the factors into a framework and set of steps that, taken together, increase the likelihood that evaluations will be useful—and actually used. That framework is called *utilization-focused evaluation.*

What Is Evaluation?

Before presenting the utilization-focused evaluation framework, let's begin by looking at these things called "evaluations" that we hope to see used. To evaluate something means determining its merit, worth, value, or significance. Program or project evaluations typically involve making the following kinds of judgments: How effective is the program? To what extent has the program been implemented as expected? What goals, outcomes, and results were achieved by the program? To what extent and in what ways did program participants benefit, if at all? What needs of participants were met? What unanticipated consequences resulted from the program? What are the strengths and weaknesses of the program, and how can it be improved? What worked and what didn't work? What has been learned in this program that might be useful to other programs? To what extent do the benefits of the program provide sufficient value to justify the costs of the program? Should the program's funding be maintained as is, increased, or decreased? Evaluations, then, typically describe and assess what was intended (goals and objectives), what happened that was unintended, what was actually implemented, and what outcomes and results were achieved. The evaluator will then discuss the implications of these findings, sometimes including items for future action and recommendations.

Evaluation as Defined in the *Encyclopedia of Evaluation*

Evaluation is an applied inquiry process for collecting and synthesizing evidence that culminates in conclusions about the state of affairs, value, merit, worth, significance, or quality of a program, product, person, policy, proposal, or plan. Conclusions made in evaluations encompass both an empirical aspect (that something is the case) and a normative aspect (judgment about the value of something). It is the value feature that distinguishes evaluation from other types of inquiry, such as basic science research, clinical epidemiology, investigative journalism, or public polling (Fournier, 2005, p. 140).

In the simplest terms, evaluations answer three questions: What? So what? Now what?

What? What happens in the program? What services and experiences does the program offer? What activities and processes occur? What changes in attitudes, knowledge, skills, and/or behaviors, if any, occur in participants? What outcomes and impacts result from the program? What unanticipated outcomes emerged? What are the documented costs and benefits of the program?

So what? So what do the findings *mean?* Why did the results turn out as they did? What are the implications of the findings? What judgments can be made? To what degree and in what ways can the program be considered a success? A failure? A mixed bag of positives and negatives? How does this program compare to other programs? What sense can we make of the findings?

Now what? What recommendations flow from the findings? What improvements should be made? Should its funding be continued, expanded, reduced, or ended? Should others adopt the program? Or avoid it? In short, what actions flow from the findings and interpretations of the findings?

Let's apply this framework to the Kiribati case.

What? Increased coconut production did not reduce fishing. Overfishing actually increased during the intervention.

So what? The program did not work as hoped. Fishermen don't just fish for income. They fish because they like to fish. Getting money from other sources won't reduce their fishing.

Now what? Look for alternative approaches to reduce overfishing.

Evaluation Reports—and Beyond

Often evaluation questions are answered in formal reports. Some evaluation reports are entirely internal to an organization for use by staff and administrators to support ongoing managerial decision making. Other evaluation reports are published or posted on the Internet to meet an obligation for public accountability or to share lessons learned. But producing an evaluation report is not the purpose of evaluation. Evaluation is not an end in itself. The purpose is to inform thought and action. Moving from *what,* to *so what,* to *now what* means moving from data to interpretation to action. Action flows from using evaluation findings. Getting evaluations used is what *utilization-focused evaluation* is all about.

Utilization-Focused Evaluation: Overview

Utilization-focused evaluation (U-FE) begins with the premise that evaluations should be judged by their utility and actual use; therefore, evaluators should facilitate the evaluation process and design any evaluation with careful consideration of how everything that is done, *from beginning to end,* will affect use. Use concerns how real people in the real world apply evaluation findings and experience the evaluation process. Therefore, the *focus* in utilization-focused evaluation is on *intended use by intended users.* Since no evaluation can be value-free, utilization-focused evaluation answers the question of whose values will frame the evaluation by working with clearly identified, primary intended users who have responsibility to apply evaluation findings and implement recommendations.

Utilization-focused evaluation is highly personal and situational. The evaluation facilitator develops a working relationship with intended users to help them determine what kind of evaluation they need. This requires negotiation in which the evaluator offers a menu of possibilities within the framework of established evaluation standards and principles.

Standards for Evaluation

The profession of evaluation has adopted standards to guide professional practice. Professional evaluators are challenged to take responsibility for use. If evaluations are ignored or misused, we have to look at where our own practices and processes may have been inadequate.

Utility

The Utility Standards are intended to ensure that an evaluation will serve the information needs of intended users.

Feasibility

The Feasibility Standards are intended to ensure that an evaluation will be realistic, prudent, diplomatic, and frugal.

Propriety

The Propriety Standards are intended to ensure that an evaluation will be conducted legally, ethically, and with due regard for the welfare of those involved in the evaluation, as well as those affected by its results.

Accuracy

The Accuracy Standards are intended to ensure that an evaluation will reveal and convey technically adequate information about the feature that determine worth or merit of the program being evaluated.

Accountability

The Accountability Standards aim to ensure that evaluations are conducted in accordance with standards of quality.

For the full set of detailed standards, see Joint Committee on Standards for Educational Evaluation, 2010.

Specific standards have also been adapted to various international contexts (Russon & Russon, 2004) and reviewed through the lens of cultural diversity (AEA Diversity Committee, 2004). See also the *Guiding Principles for Evaluators* (AEA, 2004).

Utilization-focused evaluation does not advocate any particular evaluation content, model, method, theory, or even use. Rather, it is a process for helping primary intended users select the most appropriate content, model, methods, theory, and uses for their particular situation. *Situational responsiveness* guides the interactive process between evaluator and primary intended users. This means that the interactions between the evaluator and the primary intended users focus on fitting the evaluation to the particular situation with special sensitivity to context. A utilization-focused evaluation can include any evaluative purpose (formative, summative, developmental), any kind of data (quantitative, qualitative, mixed), any kind of design (e.g., naturalistic, experimental), and any kind of focus (processes, outcomes, impacts, costs, and cost-benefit, among many possibilities). *Utilization-focused evaluation is a process for making decisions about these issues in collaboration with an identified group of primary users focusing on their intended uses of evaluation.*

A psychology of use undergirds and informs utilization-focused evaluation: Intended users are more likely to use evaluations if they understand and feel ownership of the evaluation process and findings; they are more likely to understand and feel ownership if they've been actively involved; by actively involving primary intended users, the evaluator is training users in use, preparing the groundwork for use, and reinforcing the intended utility of the evaluation every step along the way.

Before we begin systematically examining the utilization-focused evaluation framework in depth and detail, let's look at some of the challenges that arise when trying to conduct useful evaluations. The Kiribati overfishing situation offers a positive example of evaluation use. Let's take a moment and look at the shadow side, evaluations that aren't used. Why would people ignore and resist evaluation findings? Well, we have a lot of research on that as well. Consider the case of DARE as an example.

Resistance to Reality Testing: The Case of DARE

DARE stands for *Drug Abuse Resistance Education,* a 17-week drug education program targeted at middle school children in which police officers went into schools to teach the dangers of drug use and alcohol abuse. Launched in 1983 in Los Angeles, DARE spread rapidly, eventually being taught to fifth- or sixth-graders in 80% of the school districts across the United States, and 54 other countries around the world, reaching an estimated 36 million students annually (Eyle, 2002; Hanson, 2007). Thousands of evaluations of DARE were conducted in local districts as well as several national evaluations (GAO, 2003). These evaluations have consistently shown that the program "was not effective in actually keeping young people from using drugs" (C. H. Weiss, Murphy-Graham, & Birkeland, 2005, p. 15). However, the program did lead students to have more positive views of the police. But knowledge and attitude changes about drugs were not sustained, and DARE did not lead to lower drug use (Eyle, 2002; Hanson, 2007). I know of no program that has been so thoroughly evaluated with such consistently negative results—and yet remains widely popular. Distinguished evaluation pioneer and knowledge use scholar Carol Weiss of Harvard University has examined DARE in depth as an example of "the neglect of evaluation" and "an elegant case of nonutilization" (C. H. Weiss et al., 2005, p. 15). Indeed, DARE is still going strong (DARE, 2011), though with a revised curriculum and more comprehensive approach. Evaluation findings remain negative. And DARE remains popular. Why?

The program is popular with police, parents, school officials, and elected representatives who are quite sensitive to what constituents like. In 1997 the attorney general of Minnesota, Skip Humphrey (son of Minnesota's well-known U.S. senator and vice president, Hubert Humphrey) conducted a major review of DARE. He concluded that the program was ineffective but too popular to eliminate: "I don't think we should dump something that's got a positive aspect to it. The public feels this is an affirmation of community standards" (O'Connor, 1997, p. A1). To cut to the chase, politics trumped evidence. Parents liked the idea that at least something was being tried, even if ineffective. Police liked connecting with students to make a positive impression. School officials and elected officials showed they were being responsive to widespread concerns about drug use. So what if it doesn't work? The Minnesota Institute of Public Health conducted a statewide survey of school officials, parents, police, and student in all 80 Minnesota school districts:

- 94% agreed: "DARE is very popular in our community."
- 88% agreed: "Even if there is no scientific evidence that DARE works, I would still support it." (O'Connor, 1997, p. A5)

Economist Edward Shepard (2002) found that between $1 billion and $1.3 billion was spent annually on DARE in the United States long after negative evaluation findings were widely reported. DARE has an effective national organization that promotes DARE and attacks negative findings about outcomes by emphasizing DARE's popularity with parents and police (Hanson, 2007). The DARE case illustrates the power of belief over evidence, the sometimes-domineering role of politics in undermining science, and the resistance that can be created when powerful stakeholders with great sums of money at stake work to undermine the use of evaluation findings.

Utilization-focused evaluation, then, is informed by studies of positive evaluation use, like the Kiribati example, as well as negative examples of evaluation resistance like DARE.

And before harshly condemning DARE supporters for failing to act on evaluation evidence, ask yourselves these questions: Are you consistently following evidence-based health advice? Eating nutritious foods? Exercising regularly? Engaging in safe sex? Are you following the evidence about how to nurture positive interpersonal relationships? Are you managing your finances according to well-established principles? Are you doing the things in your life that you know you should be doing based on evidence about what works? Do you even stay up to date about such evidence and use it to guide your decisions?

You see, evaluation use is not just about making program and policy decisions. It has to do with the larger issue of how we, as human beings, make decisions and engage in reality testing in all facets of our lives. Before looking systematically at the details of and steps in conducting utilization-focused evaluation, let's look a little more deeply into the complexities of reality testing. For a commitment to evaluation use ultimately depends on a commitment to reality testing.

"If coconut subsidies don't work we can educate people to resist overfishing."

"I can visualize the campaign now: ***JUST SAY NO TO OVERFISHING."***

"Have you ever heard of DARE?

Getting Ready for Evaluation: Engendering Commitment to Engage in Reality Testing

Farmers till the soil before planting seeds. They don't scatter seeds on hard, untilled soil, for that would mean the germinated seeds wouldn't take root and grow into healthy plants. Likewise, evaluators have to prepare people in programs and organizations to undertake evaluation. Providing evaluation findings to people who are not prepared to hear and use them means that the findings will not take root and grow into action.

Evaluation aims to be logical, rational, and empirical. Evaluation tests reality. Evaluation involves asking: Is what program funders and staff hope and think is happening really happening? Are desired results being attained? But people aren't automatically inclined to welcome such questions—or reality testing generally. Quite the contrary. We are inclined to believe what we want to believe and treat our beliefs as reality.

Perception is treated as reality. Sociologist W. I. Thomas posited that what is perceived as real is real in its consequences. This has become known as the *Thomas Theorem.* It captures succinctly a great deal of what social and behavioral science has discovered about how we function as human beings. We routinely treat our perceptions as if they are reality. We act on those perceptions and our actions have consequences. In the DARE program, many parents, educators, and public officials perceived that putting a drug resistance program into schools would reduce drug use. They wanted to believe this. They did believe this. And when the evidence showed the program did not reduce drug use, they preferred their perceptions and beliefs to reality and said to themselves and each other, "It's better to do something than nothing, so DARE is good." They didn't look at negative consequences and opportunity costs (meaning that money spent on DARE was not available to support other potentially more effective interventions).

But this happens in many areas of our personal lives. Studies regularly show that people perceive themselves as being good drivers, above-average drivers, even excellent drivers when they are at best quite ordinary. People driving cars, even at high speeds, believe that they can safely talk on mobile phones or send text messages. Interestingly, most people don't think that other drivers should do these things, but they view themselves as more competent and in control. Put that together with studies that show that incompetent people don't realize how incompetent they are. Poor communicators perceive themselves as excellent communicators. Tyrannical bosses perceive themselves as excellent managers. Married men perceive themselves as sharing equally in household tasks while their wives perceive them as making only token contributions.

We like to perceive ourselves as rational and thoughtful about money, but the new field of behavior finance consistently documents that our decisions about money are irrational and highly emotional. People take pride in making their own decisions, but the evidence shows that people are heavily influenced by those around them. Following the herd and *groupthink* are common. For example, Salganik and Watts (2008), in an article titled "Leading the Herd Astray: An Experimental Study of Self-Fulfilling Prophecies in an Artificial Cultural Market," reported results of a devious experiment in an online music market in which more than 12,207 participants listened to, downloaded, and ranked songs by unknown bands. Participants could see each others' ratings, but what they didn't know was that the researchers inverted the ratings, reporting as most popular those that were actually least popular. As new listeners joined the experiment, they followed the false ratings and rated highest those songs that had initially been rated lowest. Good news for quality: Over time, a few of the songs initially rated high returned to high ratings despite the false low ratings fed to new participants, but even that process was affected by social norms about what constitutes quality.

We think that we're making autonomous decisions when, in fact, we're actually like sheep, thus the "following the herd" metaphor. It happens on Wall Street where money managers' stock recommendations and economists' market predictions notoriously manifest following the herd and groupthink patterns. It happens in mainstream media reports as when media of all kinds reported positively on the U.S. invasion of Iraq and only gradually did negative reporting emerge as the war became a quagmire and public opinion turned.

The advocates of DARE became more adamant in their belief in DARE as they shared their views with each other and took comfort from finding their perceptions reinforced by others, both other people like themselves (other parents and teachers) and people in authority (police officers and elected officials). *Groupthink.*

We are all socialized to believe that certain things are true and are discouraged from questioning those beliefs. We tend to belong to groups of people who share the same beliefs we do, so we hear the same beliefs repeated as truth and accept them as truth. This is certainly true of religious cults and fringe political groups, we all know that. But it's also true for all of us, for as social beings we seek out affinity groups of people who share our worldviews. In programs, then, staff tell each other that they're doing all they can, working hard, and making a difference—and believe that and want to believe that—and are not automatically open to some evaluator coming in and asking: What's your evidence that you're making a difference? This can be a threatening question, even a terrifying one. This is part of what evaluators face as we try to involve people in serious reality testing.

By the way, scientists are as prone to reality distortion as are ordinary people. Kevin Dunbar, director of the Laboratory for Complex Thinking and Reasoning at the University of Toronto Scarsborough, has studied extensively how scientists interpret laboratory findings. He found that when lab experiments turned out differently from what scientists hypothesized, their first instinct was to explain away the results. When the same results were replicated, they would just ignore the findings and deal with cognitive dissonance by blaming imperfect methods and measures, and set about correcting and improving their methods and measures in search of results that would confirm their hypotheses. Dunbar is among those who has documented with social experiments of his own that scientists, like nonscientists, see what they want to see and interpret research findings through selective perception and layers of preconception and strong beliefs. Scientists operate with a strong "confirmation bias," expecting to confirm their theories and beliefs. Belief, especially scientific theory-based belief, can make us blind to what is actually happening (Dunbar & Fugelsang, 2005). The good news is that over time, with many scientific experiments and many scientists struggling in a domain of inquiry, the truth gradually emerges. But beliefs and theories die hard.

The fact is, we carefully edit our reality, searching for evidence that confirms what we already believe. Although we pretend we're empiricists—our views are dictated by nothing but the facts—we're actually blinkered, especially when it comes to information that contradicts our theories. The problem with science isn't that most experiments fail—it's that most failures are ignored (Lehrer, 2010a, reporting on Dunbar's studies of scientists).

Of Paradigms, Reality Testing, and Decision Making

Substantial research has documented the limits of human rationality in decision making and reality testing. Daniel Kahneman was awarded the Nobel Prize in Economics for his pioneering work showing that how we decide what to do is far from rational. Our rationality is "bounded" by our beliefs about what is possible and our limited cognitive and emotional capacity to consider alternatives (Simon, 1957, 1978). This applies no less to well-educated professionals than to common folk. We all act out of deeply embedded heuristics, rules of thumb, standard operating procedures, long-practiced behaviors, socialized beliefs, and selective perception. We operate within and see the world through *paradigms* built on implicit assumptions, comfortable habits, values defended as truths, and beliefs projected as reality. Our paradigms tell us what is important, legitimate, and reasonable. They tell us how to think and what to do (Kuhn, 1970).

Programs are inevitably based on paradigms of belief about what constitutes a problem, how to change human behavior, what works and doesn't work, and generally how to make the world a better place. Evaluation invites those working within a program paradigm to test the assumptions of the paradigm against the realities of how the program actually works in practice. This is no small thing. It is a lot to ask. It is even more to expect that when results raise fundamental doubts about the program's effectiveness, adherents of the program will simply accept the evaluation's findings. That expectation is based on a paradigm of logic and rationality that is inconsistent with how people take in and use data. Evaluators need to understand how decision making actually occurs to work with decision makers and get them ready to undertake reality testing evaluation. Committing to serious evaluation can involve a paradigm shift among those involved, a shift from acting on belief and hope to acting on data and feedback.

Reality testing and philosophy of science

While we are discussing paradigms and reality testing, I should perhaps add that I am using the term "reality testing" in its common and ordinary connotation of finding out what is happening. While philosophers of science will rightly point out that the whole notion of "reality" is an epistemological and ontological quagmire, I find that the people I work with in the "real world"—*their* phrase—resonate to the notion of "reality testing." It is their own sense of reality I want to help them test, not some absolute, positivist construction of reality. The notion that reality is socially constructed doesn't mean it can't be tested and understood.

Evaluators are no less susceptible to treating their perceptions as reality. Evaluators, on the whole, want to have their findings used. Evaluators prefer being useful to not being useful. And when I ask evaluators whether what they do is useful, they generally respond positively, affirming their perception and belief. And when I ask what evidence they have of their utility, they report perceptions, not evidence. Just as program people do. When I ask program people how they know they're effective, they often say, "I just know." Evaluators are susceptible to the same illusion. The final step in a utilization-focused evaluation is to follow up our own evaluations and find out how they were actually used, to engage in our own reality testing and use what we learn to improve our practice.

Taken as a whole, social and behavioral sciences research shows that humans are more often reality distorters than reality testers. We operate with selective perception, social and cognitive biases, dominating worldviews, and within paradigms of perception and belief that make it hard to even ask questions about reality much less test our perceptions and beliefs against reality. When we ask people in programs to undertake evaluation, we are asking them to subject their perceptions and beliefs to empirical test: Is what they hope for and believe in actually happening? It takes some preparation to help people embrace this question. It requires tilling the metaphoric program soil so that those involved can receive the seeds of evaluation and those seeds can grow into useful findings that actually get used. That's why utilization-focused evaluation begins by assessing program and organizational readiness for evaluation—and engaging stakeholders in getting ready for evaluation, the subject of the next chapter. The principle that guides this readiness assessment, as in all of utilization-focused evaluation, is *listening before telling.* (For an insightful and provocative exploration of this principle applied to development, see Quarry and Ramírez, 2009.)

The Utilization-Focused Evaluation Checklist: Overview of the Book

Pilots use checklists for every stage of flying: preparing to fly, taking off, navigating, landing, and taxiing to the gate. Checklists are used by even the most experienced pilots to assure that everything that needs to be done is done to avoid a crash. Checklists save lives in hospital emergency, intensive care, and surgical units (Gawande, 2007, 2009). There are checklists for virtually any human activity and a website devoted to monitoring and linking people to specialized checklists (http://checklists.com).

Under the leadership of Dan Stufflebeam, the Center for Evaluation at Western Michigan University has developed checklists for evaluation on evaluation methods, management, models, capacity building, institutionalization, values, criteria, standards, and metaevaluation (evaluation of evaluations).

> A sound evaluation checklist clarifies the criteria that at least should be considered when evaluating something in a particular area; aids the evaluator not to forget important criteria; and enhances the assessment's objectivity, credibility, and reproducibility. Moreover, such a checklist is useful in planning an enterprise, monitoring and guiding its operation, and assessing its outcomes (Stufflebeam, 2000, p. 1).

This book is organized as a checklist of utilization-focused evaluation essentials. Following this introductory chapter, each subsequent chapter is an item or step in the checklist. The concluding chapter includes a complete U-FE checklist summary of primary tasks and major facilitation challenges for each step. Periodically we will pause between steps to do a *complex dynamic systems interconnections review*. Portraying the utilization-focused evaluation process as a series of steps is driven by the necessarily linear and sequential nature of writing and, to some extent, the human thinking processes involved in figuring out how to do something. But the process is not neatly linear and sequential, and certainly not mechanical. There are interconnections among the steps, feedback loops, and the complex dynamics that affect any open and emergent system (Patton, 2011). To reflect these real-world system dynamics, I will periodically offer an interlude between "steps" to call attention to the importance of examining the iterative and nonlinear dynamics of a utilization-focused evaluation process. At the end of the book and online you will find the full utilization-focused evaluation checklist (Patton, 2010). Here, then, as an overview of the book, are the major steps in the utilization-focused evaluation checklist.

Utilization-Focused Evaluation Checklist

A chapter is devoted to each of the 17 steps in the checklist below.

Step 1.	Assess and build program and organizational readiness for utilization-focused evaluation
Step 2.	Assess and enhance evaluator readiness and competence to undertake a utilization-focused evaluation
Step 3.	Identify, organize, and engage primary intended users
Step 4.	Situation analysis conducted jointly with primary intended users
Step 5.	Identify and prioritize primary intended uses by determining priority purposes
Step 6.	Consider and build in process uses if and as appropriate
Step 7.	Focus priority evaluation questions
Step 8.	Check that fundamental areas for evaluation inquiry are being adequately addressed
Step 9.	Determine what intervention model or theory of change is being evaluated
Step 10.	Negotiate appropriate methods to generate credible findings that support intended use by intended users
Step 11.	Make sure intended users understand potential methods controversies and their implications
Step 12.	Simulate use of findings
Step 13.	Gather data with ongoing attention to use

(Continued)

(Continued)

Step 14.	Organize and present the data for interpretation and use by primary intended users
Step 15.	Prepare an evaluation report to facilitate use and disseminate significant findings to expand influence
Step 16.	Follow up with primary intended users to facilitate and enhance use
Step 17.	Metaevaluation of use: Be accountable, learn, and improve

PRACTICE EXERCISES

1. This chapter includes an example of a program evaluation that was used to change the intervention (the Kiribati overfishing initiative) and an example of resistance to evaluation findings (DARE). Find your own examples, an example of evaluation use and an example of resistance to evaluation use. You'll find examples reported in the news and posted on the Internet. It's worth having your own examples that are meaningful to you.

2. Develop an "elevator speech" for both evaluation in general and utilization-focused evaluation in particular. An *elevator speech* is a short description of something presented in the time it takes an elevator to go from the top floor to the first floor, or vice versa, in a tall building. The idea is that sometimes we meet important people in our lives in elevators, waiting to board an airplane, in coffee shops, at meeting receptions, and other places where, without notice, we are asked to explain what we do or something we care about. The idea of an *elevator speech* is be ready with a prepared presentation that grabs attention and says a lot in a few words. You never know what it might lead to.

3. Search the Internet for *recent research* on the human barriers to rational decision making and reality testing. Find examples of experiments and research that are relevant to your own field of interest. For instance, if you work in health, find examples of research on how people in hospitals make mistakes; classic examples include Atul Gawande (2002) and Jerome Groopman (2007). For samples of a half-century of research on the nonrational nature of human decision making, see Gigerenzer, Todd, and the ABC Research Group, 1999; Inbar, 1979; Kahneman and Tversky, 2000a, 2000b; Kuhn, 1970; Simon, 1957, 1978; Tversky and Fox, 2000; Tversky and Kahneman, 2000.

1

Assess and Build Program and Organizational Readiness for Utilization-Focused Evaluation

Reality isn't the way you wish things to be, nor the way they appear to be, but the way they actually are.

Robert J. Ringer,
American entrepreneur and author

The phrase "reality testing" implies that being "in touch with reality" cannot simply be assumed. When individuals lose touch with reality, they become dysfunctional and, if the distortions of reality are severe, they may be referred for psychotherapy. Programs and organizations can also "lose touch with reality" in the sense that the people in those programs and organizations are operating on myths and behaving in ways that are dysfunctional to goal attainment and ineffective for accomplishing desired outcomes. As the introductory chapter emphasized, program evaluation provides a mechanism for finding out whether what's hoped for is, in fact, taking place—a form of reality testing.

Getting people ready for evaluation means helping them commit to reality testing. Research on *readiness for evaluation* has shown that "valuing evaluation" is a necessary condition for evaluation use (Patton, 2008, pp. 42–46). Valuing evaluation cannot be taken for granted. Nor does it happen naturally. Users' commitment to evaluation is typically fragile, often whimsical, and must be cultivated like a hybrid plant that has the potential for enormous yields, but only if properly cared for, nourished, and appropriately managed. When beginning a new program evaluation or entering an organization to improve an existing evaluation system, it is wise to begin with an assessment of existing attitudes toward and behaviors related to evaluation use. Here is some of what to watch for.

Naysayers. Some people seem to be naturally negative—about most everything. You probably know someone like this. Whenever an idea comes up that involves change, their instant reaction is: Won't work here.

The complacent. These people belong to the *things are okay as is* crowd. If it's not broken, why fix it? And from their perspective, nothing involving them is ever broke. They've constructed their own comfortable worlds built on untested assumptions and unexamined beliefs. Evaluation is a threat to such people. Reality testing will only upset things. "Why bother?" they ask.

The compliant. Many program administrators experience evaluation only as something mandated by funders so they've developed a compliance mentality. The compliant-oriented say: "Just tell us what we have to do and we'll do it." They don't want to think about it or engage with it, they just want to meet the mandate. They know that money comes with strings attached. They don't like it, but they accept it. Ironically, mandated evaluations can actually undercut utility. A career internal evaluator with 25 years experience once told me: "The most pervasive problem we deal with, particularly in our relations with state and federal agencies, is submitting mandated reports that no one cares about, no one reads, and we never get any feedback on. It is constantly discouraging and frustrating."

The cynics. These are the "been there, done that" folks. They have evaluation horror stories to share. Waste of time and money. Academic. Esoteric. Irrelevant. Useless. These are old-timers who take pride in having survived lots of what they consider bad evaluations—and lived to tell about it. And tell about it they do, to any and all who will listen.

The frightened and anxious. These tend to be people who confuse program evaluation with personnel evaluation and are worried that THEY are being evaluated. They also know some of the program's weaknesses but hope such blemishes will stay hidden from outside eyes. Now they fear exposure and imagine ruin.

The enthusiastic. Some people hunger for learning. They want to improve. They may even be data junkies—can't get enough of it. These can be allies, but ironically, some of the most enthusiastic adherents of evaluation are adherents of the idea but not the practice. They believe that evaluation is important and like the idea of gathering data, but they haven't thought through the possibility that findings may show a need for change.

The sophisticates. This person values data, is open to learning and feedback, understands that data must be interpreted to take action, and is prepared to engage in the evaluation process from design to interpretation and use. Sophisticates can be strong allies. They can also create conflicts by insisting on their way of doing things and acting with disdain toward those stakeholders who are less sophisticated.

The offended. These are sincere, committed, hard-working and dedicated true believers who are doing everything they know how to do to help people. They work long hours under difficult conditions with limited resources and engage daily with the afflictions that beset humanity's least privileged and most neglected: people ravaged by extreme poverty; those suffering from HIV/AIDS; the hungry and homeless; abused children; and victims of war, natural disasters, oppression, and all the many varieties of humankind's inhumanity toward fellow humans. Then some evaluator comes along and asks: "How do you know that you're doing good?" They are offended by the question. They are even more offended by the fact that resources are being spent on evaluation that could be used instead to feed the hungry, house the homeless, or comfort the afflicted: "Who the hell do you think you are coming in here with your surveys and data forms? We're dealing with life and death here. Get out of my face." At such moments it is worth remembering that they are right. Funds spent on evaluation are funds not spent on direct help to those in need. Evaluation's contribution is indirect. The justification for our inquiry is the belief and hope that we can help make them more effective. But they must join us in that belief. And we must be able to make the case that we have something to offer that will justify the costs of evaluation.

The politicos. These are folks whose attention is riveted on which way the political winds are blowing. They view data and evaluation findings like they view everything else—ammunition for political combat. They are attuned to the political power of a program's constituencies. If powerful constituents want the program, or if more is to be gained politically by support for rather than opposition to the program, then the program is judged worthwhile; no other evidence of program effectiveness is needed, though data may be sought to support this predetermined political judgment. Political vested interests are one reason it is so difficult to terminate government-funded programs and agencies. Programs develop constituencies whose vested interests lie in program continuation. The driving interest of *politicos* is to direct program funds where they count politically, not where they will be used most effectively. *Politicos* judge programs as effective as long as they serve powerful interests. Empirical evaluation findings are of interest only insofar as they can be manipulated for political and public relations purposes. Politicos emphasize findings that support their political interests and dismiss, ignore, or distort findings that run counter to their political commitments and vested interests. Evaluators have to be politically astute to deal with *politicos.*

Now, of course, these are all caricatures and stereotypes and don't do justice to the great diversity and individuality of those wonderful folks we call "stakeholders." The point is to pay attention to the characteristics of the stakeholders who will be involved with an evaluation. Program and organizational cultures consist of a mix of types of people. The blend of perspectives in any given program gives rise to an organizational culture that will affect how evaluation is undertaken. Taking time at the beginning to understand and assess the program and organizational culture is the beginning of the utilization-focused evaluation process. Methods-driven evaluators want to cut to the chase and get right to work designing the evaluation and generating instruments. Utilization-focused evaluators, in contrast, begin by figuring out the context within which the evaluation will unfold and learning about the people within that context.

Learning About and Assessing the Evaluation Context

Evaluations are funded and commissioned by someone or some group. Those who fund and commission the evaluation are the evaluator's client. However, they are not the only people who will be affected by the evaluation or use evaluation findings. A government agency or philanthropic foundation may mandate and fund an evaluation, but the people running the program may be expected to make primary use of the evaluation for program improvement. In other cases the evaluation may be done for accountability purposes or to make a major decision about future funding or expansion of the program. Program participants have a stake in how the evaluation is conducted and what is done with findings. In later chapters we'll discuss in depth and detail alternative evaluation purposes and uses. At this point, we want to begin by getting the clients' perspective on the evaluation and assessing the evaluation context.

The first step is typically reviewing important documents and meeting with the key clients. This is often followed by interviewing some other key stakeholders, either individually or sometimes in a focus group. This is a chance to meet key people (and for them to meet the evaluator), learn more about the program's history, find out about important political issues, get a sense of the organization's culture, and interact around why the evaluation is being conducted and how it is perceived. This is also a chance to assess how committed to testing reality the client and key stakeholders are.

Because evaluators have typically internalized the value of data-based reality testing, it is easy to assume that others share this perspective. But a commitment to examine beliefs and test actual goal attainment is neither natural nor widespread. Evaluators who ignore the threatening nature of reality testing and plow ahead with instrument design and data collection in the hope that knowledge will prevail are engaged in their own form of reality distortion. Utilization-focused evaluators, in contrast, work with intended evaluation users to help them understand the value of reality testing and buy into the process, thereby reducing the threat of evaluation and resistance (conscious or unconscious) to evaluation use. A common error made by novice evaluators is believing that because someone has requested an evaluation or some group has been assembled to design an evaluation, the commitment to reality testing and use is already there. Quite the contrary, these commitments must be engendered (or revitalized if once they were present) and then reinforced throughout the evaluation process. Utilization-focused evaluation makes this a priority.

Once you have met key people, started learning about the organizational and political context for the evaluation, and have a sense of the issues the evaluation will need to address, it is time to move to the next level of formal stakeholder engagement. The remainder of this chapter presents some exercises that can be used to assess readiness for evaluation and give an evaluator a feel for the people who are being asked to undertake an evaluation and the program culture within which it will take place. Strategies for engagement flow from what is learned in these opening exercises that take place at an evaluation launch workshop.

Formally Launching the Evaluation: Exercises to Help Assess and Build Readiness for Evaluation—and Get the Process Started

To begin an evaluation, I like to assemble key people for a half-day workshop (sometimes a full day) aimed at laying the groundwork (tilling the program and organizational soil) for reality testing. People invited to this opening workshop include key program and organizational leadership, staff, funders, board members, and long-time program participants or graduates who are knowledgeable about the program. I'll say a lot more about selecting and involving these various stakeholders later. Right now I want to share examples of 10 exercises that help get people ready for reality testing, that is, begin the process of creating an evaluative mindset among those who will be involved in, affected by, and use the evaluation. Menu 1.1 summarizes these 10 exercises and the situations for which each is especially appropriate. The remainder of this chapter elaborates on the rationale for and what is involved in using each exercise.

MENU 1.1

Menu of Exercises to Assess and Facilitate Stakeholder and Program Readiness for Utilization-Focused Evaluation

Exercises to assess & build readiness for utilization-focused evaluation	*Situation for which this exercise is particularly appropriate*
1. *Baseline assessment of evaluation use*: How are data currently collected being used? How have past evaluations been used?	Organizations already engaged in some evaluation and/or ongoing data collection.
2. *Baseline associations with and perceptions of evaluation*: "What comes to mind when you see the word EVALUATE?"	Use with a group of stakeholders brought together to launch a new evaluation effort; surfaces the "baggage" that people bring to the new initiative from past experiences.
3. *Create a positive vision for evaluation*: If evaluation was really useful and actually used here, what would that look like?	Use to help a group move from evaluation anxiety and resistance to focus on the potential benefits of evaluation. Creates readiness for evaluation by focusing on use and creating a shared group understanding of and commitment to use the evaluation.
4. *Assess incentives for and barriers to reality testing and evaluation use in their own program culture.*	Once a group has a general sense of evaluation's potential utility, this exercise takes the next step of getting concrete about what will need to occur with this program context to make evaluation useful.
5. *Engender commitment to reality-testing*: Are you willing to take a close look at whether what you think is happening in this program is actually happening, and whether what you hope it is accomplishing is actually being accomplished?	These questions are useful at the moment of commitment after some basic groundwork has been laid. These questions implicitly ask those involved: *Are you ready to get serious?*
6. *Grounding any specific evaluation in the professional standards of evaluation*: *utility, feasibility, propriety,* and *accuracy*. Give a copy of the	This exercise is useful for groups with little knowledge about the profession of evaluation. It helps evaluators position themselves and their work within a larger

Exercises to assess & build readiness for utilization-focused evaluation	*Situation for which this exercise is particularly appropriate*
standards to stakeholders involved with the evaluation and give them a chance to discuss what they see in the standards.	context of professional standards of excellence.
7. *Establishing project-specific evaluation norms and standards*: In addition to the evaluation profession's standards (# 6), what other values will be important in conducting this evaluation?	This exercise is useful with a group of particularly diverse stakeholders who come from different backgrounds and work in diverse professions with their own standards. This exercise offers the group a chance to articulate their own context-specific standards.
8. *Sharing good ideas that haven't worked out in practice.* This can be done in small groups where participants share their examples and how they came to see that what they thought was a good idea at the time didn't work out so well.	This exercise illustrates evaluative thinking in practice. It gives participants a chance to learn more about each other and start to create trust by sharing things about themselves and hearing each others' stories.
9. *Generate evaluation metaphors and analogies.* Have participants share some activities that they engage in (like fishing, sports, artistic creations, exercise, cooking, gardening) and look at the evaluation issues that are part of such activities. Or have them create evaluation metaphors around objects (chalkboards, light-bulbs, coffee cups).	This exercise engages participants creatively with each other while having some fun by sharing the associations they conjure up related to evaluation. This doesn't take much time to do and carries the message that everyone brings some evaluation expertise and experience to the process.
10. *Generating questions for evaluation*: What don't you know that if you did know would make a difference to your engagement with this program? What do you want to find out through this evaluation?	This is especially useful with groups that are expecting the evaluator to determine the evaluation questions. Engaging a group in this exercise sends the message that *their* questions and issues will focus the evaluation. This moves them from general evaluation principles to getting specific about the evaluation that is to be designed here and now.

1. **Baseline assessment of evaluation use**

Baseline data are critical in any evaluation. You can't tell how much participants have benefitted from a program if you don't know what their status was at the beginning. Administering a pretest before a program begins is a common way to establish baseline. Intake forms gather information when participants enter a program and are a source of baseline data. Needs assessments used to design a program typically include baseline indicators. Comparing program outcomes against an initial baseline is fundamental evaluation analysis.

The same logic applies to increasing evaluation use. What is the baseline of evaluation use in the program? Even if the program itself is new, it is likely that the people running and staffing the program have prior evaluation experiences and perspectives based on those experiences. Thus, a good place to begin a program and organizational assessment is to learn the organization's past and current evaluation and management information system practices. This can be done in interviews with key people who know the program, in focus groups, or in small-group discussions at the evaluation launch workshop. Questions to explore include: What information is currently collected and how is it used? What are examples of evaluations that you consider useful? What made them useful? What are examples of evaluations that were not used? What were the barriers to use? How would you say evaluation is viewed here? What are key factors to take into account in designing an evaluation to enhance its utility?

2. **Baseline associations with and perceptions of evaluation**

As a simple opening exercise at an evaluation launch workshop, I like to begin by asking participants to share words and feelings they associate with evaluation, then we explore how their perceptions they've brought with them may affect their expectations about the evaluation's likely utility. I write the word "EVALUATE" on a flip chart and ask those present to free-associate with the word: "What comes to mind when you see the word EVALUATE?" They typically begin slowly with synonyms or closely related terms: *assess, measure, judge, rate, compare.* Soon someone calls out *"waste of time."* Another voice from the back of the room yells: *"crap."* The energy picks up and more associations follow in rapid succession: *budget cuts, downsize, politics, demeaning, pain, fear.* And inevitably, the unkindest cut of all: "USELESS."

Clearly, evaluation can evoke strong emotions, negative associations, and genuine fear. People carry with them into new experiences the emotional baggage of past experiences. To ignore such perceptions, past experiences, and feelings people bring to an evaluation is like ignoring a smoldering dynamite fuse in the hope it will burn itself out. More likely, unless someone intervenes and extinguishes the fuse, it will burn faster and eventually explode. Many an evaluation has blown up in the face of well-intentioned evaluators because they rushed into technical details and methods decisions without establishing a solid foundation for the evaluation in clear purposes and shared understandings. To begin, both evaluators and those with whom we work need to develop a shared definition of evaluation and mutual understanding about what the process will involve, and in so doing, acknowledge anxiety and fears.

Whether evaluations are mandated or voluntary, those potentially affected by the evaluation may approach the very idea with trepidation, manifesting what has come to be recognized by experienced evaluations as "evaluation anxiety"—or what I jokingly refer to with clients as a clinical diagnosis of *pre-evaluation stress syndrome*. But the fear is often serious and needs to be acknowledged and managed. Signs of extreme evaluation anxiety include "people who are very upset by, and sometimes rendered virtually dysfunctional by, any prospect of evaluation, or who attack evaluation without regards to how well conceived it might be" (Donaldson, Gooler, & Scriven, 2002, p. 262).

Moreover, there are genuine reasons for people to fear evaluation. Evaluations are sometimes used as the rationale to cut staff, services, or entire programs. Poorly done evaluations may misrepresent what a program has done and achieved. Even when an evaluator has done a good job, what gets reported in the news may be only the negative findings—or only the positive findings—rather than the balanced picture of positives and negatives, strengths and weaknesses, that was in the full evaluation report. These things happen. There's no point in denying them. Evaluations can be well done or poorly done, useful or useless. By acknowledging these realities, we can begin the discussion of how, for this evaluation in this time and place, what do we have to do to undertake an evaluation that will be useful, credible, meaningful, and fair?

3. Creating a positive vision for evaluation

Because of bad past experiences and understandable fears about being unfairly judged, people don't necessarily or naturally think about what evaluation can offer if it is well done. So, having established a baseline of past and current evaluation practices in the program and organization, and having gotten out in the open the perceptions and concerns of those who will be involved in and affected by the evaluation, we can begin the process of creating a positive vision for evaluation. In small groups, I ask people to create scenarios in response to the questions:

If evaluation was really useful and actually used here, what would that look like?

What could take place that would tell you that the evaluation was successful?

What would evaluation success look like?

The notion here, which is true in fields as disparate as sports, politics, business, and the arts, is that people are more likely to achieve success if they can envision success in a concrete way. That's also true, by the way, for participants and staff in programs, which is another reason evaluators push for clarity about intended program outcomes. We're applying the same logic here to the evaluation: What are the positive intended outcomes for the evaluation? This exercise aims at transforming a skeptical, hostile, or dubious program culture into one that is at least open to the possibility of engaging in evaluation being a positive and useful experience.

4. Assess incentives for and barriers to reality testing and evaluation use in their own program culture

Having created together a positive vision of evaluation, the next step is to have the group identify what needs to happen to realize that vision as well as identify any barriers that will need to be overcome. As I work with intended users to agree on what we mean by evaluation and engender a commitment to use, I invite them to assess incentives for and barriers to reality testing and information use in their own program culture. Barriers typically include fear of being judged, cynicism about whether anything can really change, skepticism about the worth of evaluation, concern about the time and money costs of evaluation, and frustration from previous bad evaluation experiences, especially lack of use. As we work through these and related issues to "get ready for evaluation," the foundation for use is being built in conjunction with a commitment to serious and genuine reality testing.

Sometimes, indeed often, there are issues that people are reluctant to discuss openly. There may be huge personality conflicts with bosses or funders. There may be suspicions that key decisions have already been made and the evaluation is just a pretense to justify and put window-dressing around those already-made decisions. Some may know of irregularities, even illegalities, that the evaluation could expose. A key person who is supposed to lead the evaluation internally may be viewed as incompetent and has been assigned to lead the evaluation as punishment or because the administrator just needs to give that person something to do. How do you find out about these beneath-the-surface issues that may derail an evaluation? Here's what I do.

I give everyone the following piece of paper:

CONFIDENTIAL FEEDBACK

On this sheet of paper, please tell me anything you think I should know about what goes on in this program or organization that could affect how the evaluation is conducted and used. As an outsider, what do you want me to know that may not surface in open group discussions? This information is for **my eyes only.** Please return this to me personally. Don't put your name or any identifying information on this paper. However, if you don't want to write down your concerns but wish to talk to me confidentially, please provide your contact information.

I always alert the evaluation client and those organizing the launch workshop that I'll be doing this. Sometimes I learn little from asking for this feedback. At other times amazing, important, and disturbing things emerge. This is also a trust-building exercise and a chance to surface concerns early when strategies can still be developed to deal with issues that might derail the evaluation if they are not addressed. I typically invite this feedback just before a break or at the end of the session so that I can collect the feedback myself as people are leaving the room. Once collected, confidentiality must be protected absolutely. This is context information to help navigate the sometimes treacherous terrain of programs, organizations, and communities. As Spanish novelist Miguel de Cervantes had Don Quixote proclaim: "Forewarned, forearmed; to be prepared is half the victory."

5. Engender commitment to reality-testing

The preceding exercises have embedded within them getting a program group to begin thinking evaluatively. It gets them thinking about baselines and desired results and how to move from the baseline to desired results. The next step is to deepen the commitment to reality testing.

To do so, I like to appeal to what I presume to be a desire to be effective. I don't encounter many people who get up in the morning wanting to be ineffective. Indeed, the desire to be effective is so strong that it is often the source of evaluation anxiety. What if I've been wasting my time? What if what we've been doing isn't helping people? What then?

What then, indeed? The evaluation answer: Change the program to become more effective. So, engendering a commitment to evaluation use often involves engendering an openness to change. That openness can start with a commitment to examine reality. I ask: Are you willing to take a close look at whether what you think is happening in this program is actually happening, and whether what you hope it is accomplishing is actually being accomplished? Are you willing and ready to engage in serious reality testing?

Because evaluation use is so dependent on the commitment to reality testing, evaluators need ways to cultivate that commitment and enlarge the capacity of intended users to undertake the process. This means engaging program staff, managers, funders, and other intended users in examining how their beliefs about program effectiveness may be based on selective perception, predisposition, prejudice, rose-colored glasses, unconfirmed assertions, or simple misinformation. I often share evidence from psychology showing that we all tend to distort reality. For example, social scientist Yi-Fu Tuan (2000) has studied the human propensity toward escapism as a way of avoiding facing reality and even defines human beings as "animals congenitally indisposed to accept reality as it is" (p. 6).

One way we distort reality is through the "confirmation bias," the tendency to look for evidence to confirm our preconceptions and biases. If a program director believes his program is effective, he'll look for evidence of effectiveness and discount or ignore evidence of ineffectiveness. If a philanthropic foundation executive believes she is doing good, she'll find evidence of doing good wherever she looks. Our brains look for patterns, and once we decide there is a pattern, we quite naturally and persistently look for confirming evidence. At the same time, we tend to dismiss contradictory evidence as unreliable or invalid. Systematic and balanced evaluation aims to counter our human tendency to distort reality.

Another barrier to reality testing is overconfidence in our judgments. Study after study shows that we tend to be overconfident about our ability to make informed and objective decisions. For example, the work of Kahneman and Tversky (2000b) on "prospect theory" has established that people have an aversion to loss that is about twice the desire for gain; in essence, we fear bad news and failure twice as much as we hope for good news and success. Brain research is helping us understand these proclivities, but culture and socialization also play key roles. The research of psychologists David Dunning and Justin Kruger (1999) brings irony to this picture of human reality distortion. They found that people who perform poorly are typically quite confident about their competence. In fact, they're often more confident than those who actually perform well. The title of their research report sums up the problem quite succinctly: "Unskilled and Unaware of It: How Difficulties in Recognizing One's Own Incompetence Lead to Inflated Self-Assessments." Incompetent people also lack the skill to recognize competence in others.

A classroom experiment by behavioral economist Richard Thaler provides yet another glimpse of common reality distortion. At the beginning of his course on decision making, he asks students to anonymously write down where they'll rank in the final grading. He reports that none of his 125 MBA students thought they would finish in the bottom half of the class. "Obviously, half of them were wrong," he adds. "We all think we are pretty good at sizing things up, just the same way we all think we are good judges of character. We should know that we really are all hopeless" (quoted in Peltz, 1999, p. 105).

In addition to our tendency to deceive ourselves and distort reality, the irony of living in the information age is that we are surrounded by so much misinformation and act on so many untested assumptions. By putting intended users in touch with how little they really know, and how flimsy is the basis for much of what they think they know, we are laying the groundwork for evaluation use. We are, in fact, identifying that there are useful things to be found out, establishing that systematic inquiry processes are needed to counter our tendencies to distort reality, and creating the expectation that testing reality will be valuable, not just an academic or mandated exercise. In short, we are establishing psychological and organizational openness to and readiness for serious evaluation.

6. Grounding any specific evaluation in the professional standards of evaluation

As I work with key stakeholders toward a shared understanding of evaluation and a clear commitment to reality testing and evaluation use, I look for opportunities to review the development of program evaluation as a field of professional practice and present the standards for and principles of evaluation. (See the introductory chapter, page 5.). The *Standards* call for evaluations to be useful, practical, ethical, accurate, and accountable (Joint Committee on Standards for Educational Evaluation, 2010). Sharing the standards communicates to primary intended users that evaluation has developed into an established profession—and that those engaged in evaluation have an obligation to act in accordance with professional standards and principles, including priority attention to utility.

I always give participants in the evaluation launch meeting or workshop a copy of the standards and ask them for their reactions. What stands out to you? What comes across to you? I explain to them that these are the professional standards for which I am accountable. We begin with my accountability before dealing with theirs. We then discuss the implications of the standards for the particular evaluation we are working on.

Few nonevaluators are aware of the field's professional associations, conferences, journals, standards, and principles. By associating a particular evaluative effort with the larger profession, you can elevate the status, seriousness, and meaningfulness of the process you are facilitating, and help the primary intended users understand the sources of wisdom you are drawing on and applying as you urge them to attend carefully to utilization issues from the start.

Let me make special mention of what may well be the most challenging of all the standards: the cost-effectiveness standard. In opening this chapter, I offered caricatures of various stakeholder types one may encounter. One of those was *the offended,* people working very hard on difficult problems with limited resources. They question the value of spending scarce funds on evaluation when the resources to meet pressing human needs are so few. One of the original standards addressed this concern:

> *Cost Effectiveness*—The evaluation should be efficient and produce information of sufficient value, so that the resources expended can be justified. (Joint Committee, 1994, F3)

The justification is that the findings will be used to make improvements in programs and inform important decisions that will ultimately help more people. No standard is more important—or more challenging to meet.

7. Establishing project-specific evaluation norms and standards

Introducing the evaluation profession's standards to stakeholders can offer an opportunity to generate additional specific standards and norms for the specific program evaluation about to be undertaken. This exercise helps surface any additional concerns and deepens buy-in to and ownership of the evaluation process. For example, one evaluation group I worked with established these norms for their evaluation:

- Strive for balance, looking at both the positive and negative.
- Respect confidentiality.
- Give the evaluation process a chance. Don't bad-mouth the evaluation and try to undermine it before we see what it yields.
- Be honest with the evaluator. Being honest, even about problems, is not disloyalty to the program.
- Collect both statistics and stories. This is part of balance.

This norm-setting exercise is especially useful with a group of particularly diverse stakeholders who come from different backgrounds, work in diverse professions with their own standards, and have diverse cultural experiences. This exercise offers them an opportunity to put forward to the group what they care about regarding how the evaluation is conducted. As the group deliberates about norms for and values that will guide the evaluation, they move from considering *whether to engage* genuinely with the evaluation process to *how to engage* genuinely with the process. In making that transition, they became ready to undertake a utilization-focused evaluation.

8. Sharing good ideas that haven't worked out in practice

This next exercise is one I like to assign groups at an evaluation launch session or capacity-building workshop just before taking a morning or afternoon break. I ask them to think of "a good idea you've had that didn't work out in practice. It can be a work idea, something you tried in your personal life—anything at all. Something that seemed like a good idea at the time, but, well, things didn't quite turn out as expected. And what evidence emerged that led you to realize that it hadn't been such a good idea?" Then we take the planned 15-minute break and when they return, I ask them to share their examples in small groups. Then each small group picks one example to share with the full group. Often what they share is simple and funny. Nothing quite bonds a group together around a challenge like laughing together about life's follies. Here are classic examples.

- "I thought it would be a good idea to buy the latest Microsoft computer operating system as soon as it came out. Crashed. Had all kinds of bugs. Took over my life doing updates and patches and rebooting. Now I wait until they work out the bugs."
- "Trying to attract teenagers to a new program at our community center, we advertised free pizza. We had a great turnout and served the pizza right away to reward them for coming. But as soon as they had eaten, more than half left and didn't stay for the program, didn't even sign up for it. We learned to hold the pizza 'til near the end."
- "As a public service during the presidential campaign, we decided to sponsor a debate with local reps of the two parties. We're an employment training program, but don't have anything to do with politics. We just wanted our participants to be informed and see democracy in action. Well, the two reps got very nasty with each other. Instead of discussing issues in a thoughtful way, they attacked each other's motives and made derogatory comments about each other's candidates. It was horrible. The debaters had each invited supporters to come and the evening denigrated into shouting. We were so naïve. We had done no screening of who was coming, set no ground rules, didn't have a skilled moderator. We just thought, 'It's an election year. Let's sponsor a little debate.' Bad idea, at least the way we did it."

These stories illustrate evaluative thinking at the most basic level. People had an idea about something they wanted to have happen (a goal). They tried it out (implementation). They observed what actually happened (data collection). Then made a judgment (evaluation) and took away a lesson for the future (learning). Sharing these stories sets a context for the evaluation at hand. I follow up their stories with examples of good program ideas that didn't work out as hoped for, like the Kiribati overfishing initiative that opened the introductory chapter or the DARE example in which educating middle school students about drugs turned out not to work. They get the message: *We all have good ideas that don't work out in practice.* Utilization-focused evaluation isn't about blaming and criticizing and filling out forms and complying with funder mandates. It's about separating good ideas that work from seemingly good ideas that turn out not to work. It's about learning what works and doesn't work in order to do a better job in the future. As they absorb this message, they're getting ready to undertake their own program evaluation in a serious way—open to learning and change.

9. Generate evaluation metaphors and analogies

Key metaphors help determine what and how we perceive and how we think about our perceptions.

M. H. Abrams
Linguist and literary critic

Another way to ground evaluation in people's own experiences is to have them generate and share evaluation analogies and metaphors. For example, I'm based in Minnesota, where car license plates celebrate the *Land of 10,000 Lakes*—though the state actually has 11,842 lakes, a bit of a rounding error that, itself, raises the question of how accurate evaluation data need to be to be useful. But I digress. A lot of people in Minnesota fish—and those who don't are used to talking about fishing with those who do. So if I'm launching an evaluation in Minnesota, I'll often begin by asking: What constitutes a good day fishing? Well, it turns out that the answer depends on the purpose of fishing—whether it's with friends, or family; whether it's for food or recreation (catch and release), or some of each; and whether it's just for leisure or competitive, including high-stakes fishing contests. Different people have different criteria for what constitutes a good day fishing: number caught, size of fish caught, and type sought and reeled in, whether walleye, bluegill, northern pike, crappie, bass, or trout. Implicit in this example and discussion is that the seemingly straightforward question—What constitutes a good day fishing?—can be and will be answered differently by different people depending on their goals, values, criteria, preferences, the type of fishing they're doing, and who they're doing it with. And costs vary from very simple equipment (a pole, a line, a hook, and a lure) to very expensive fishing (a boat, a guide, fish-finding radar, high-tech poles, custom lures, and private access on exclusive lakes).

The same issues arise in program evaluation. The seemingly straightforward question—What constitutes a good program?—can be and will be answered differently by different people depending on their goals, values, criteria, preferences, the type of program being implemented, the nature of the problem addressed, the types of participants targeted by the program, and the resources available for serving them. The purpose of bringing diverse stakeholders together for the evaluation launch is to discuss and come to agreement on these issues.

Any activity common to a group can serve as an analogy that grounds the evaluation discussion in shared experience. Sports, artistic endeavors, movie and theater preferences, vacation and holiday experiences, cooking, exercising, and major purchases (computers, cars) all involve goal-setting, criteria that distinguish good from bad and better from worse, differences of values and opinion, and data to inform decision making and judgment. Discussing such familiar activities and the evaluation issues embedded in them can be a warm-up exercise before turning to evaluation of the program at hand (like stretching before jogging).

Metaphors and analogies help us make connections between seemingly unconnected things and deepen our understanding of parallel issues. The language of research and evaluation—the jargon—is alien to many laypersons, decision makers, and stakeholders. From my point of view, the burden for clear communications rests on the evaluator. It is the evaluator who must find ways of bridging the communications gap. Metaphors and analogies help because:

> Metaphor does more than adorn our thinking. It structures our thinking. It conditions our sympathies and emotional reactions. It helps us achieve situation awareness. It governs the evidence we consider salient and the outcomes we elect to pursue. (Klein, 1999, pp. 198–199)

When working with a group that I know by reputation or prior experience is relaxed together and open to a more playful and engaging process, I like to ask them to construct metaphors and similes about evaluation. The exercise helps participants discover their own values concerning evaluation while also giving them a mechanism to communicate those values to others. As with all the exercises in this chapter, it can be used with a program staff, an evaluation task force, evaluation trainees, workshop participants, or any group for whom it might be helpful to clarify and share perceptions about evaluation. The exercise opens like this.

> One of the things that we'll need to do during the process of working together is come to some basic understandings about what evaluation is and can do. In my experience, evaluation can be a very creative and energizing experience. In particular, interpreting and using evaluation findings for program improvement requires creativity and openness to a variety of possibilities. To help us get started on this creative endeavor I'm going to ask you to participate with me in a little exercise.
>
> In this box I have a bunch of toys, household articles, office supplies, tools, and other miscellaneous gadgets and thingamajigs that I've gathered from around my house. I'm going to dump these in the middle of the table and ask each of you to take one of them and use that item to make a statement about evaluation.

Evaluation is like ____________ because . . .

To illustrate what I want people to do, I offer to go first. I ask someone to pick out any object in the room that I might use for my metaphor. What follows are some examples from actual workshops.

Someone points to a coffee cup: "This cup can be used to hold a variety of things. The actual contents of the cup will vary depending on who is using it and for what purpose they're using it. Utilization-focused evaluation is a process like this cup; it provides a container but is empty until the group of people working on the evaluation fill it with focus and content and substance. The potential of the coffee cup cannot be realized until it holds some liquid. The potential of utilization-focused evaluation cannot be realized until it is given the substance of a concrete evaluation problem and situation. One of the things that I'll be doing as we work together is providing an evaluation framework like this cup. You will provide the substance."

Someone points to a chalkboard: "Evaluation is like a chalkboard because both are tools that can be used to express a variety of different things. The chalkboard itself is just an empty piece of slate until someone writes on it and provides information and meaning by filling in that space. The chalkboard can be filled up with meaningless figures, random marks, obscene words, mathematical formulas, or political graffiti—or the board can be filled with meaningful information, insights, helpful suggestions, and basic facts. The people who write on the chalkboard carry the responsibility for what it says. The people who fill in the blanks in the evaluation and determine its content and substance carry the responsibility for what the evaluation says. The evaluation process is just a tool to be used—and how it is used will depend on the people who control the process—in this case, you."

I'll typically take a break at this point and give people about 10 minutes to select an item and think about what to say. If there are more than 10 people in the group I will break the larger group into small groups of five or six for sharing analogies and metaphors so that each person is given an opportunity to make an evaluation statement. Below are some examples from actual workshops.

> This empty grocery bag symbolizes my feelings about evaluation. When I think about our program being evaluated I want to find some place to hide. I can put this empty bag over my head so that nobody can see me and I can't see anything else, and it gives me at least the feeling that I'm able to hide. (She puts the bag over her head.)

> Evaluation can be like this toothbrush. When used properly it gets out the particles between the teeth so they don't decay. If not used properly, if it just lightly goes over the teeth or doesn't cover all the teeth, then some of the gunk will stay on and cause the teeth to decay. Evaluation should help get rid of any things that are causing a program to decay.

> Evaluation is like this camera. It lets you take a picture of what's going on, but it can only capture what you point it at, and only for a particular point in time. My concern about this evaluation is that it won't give the whole picture, that an awful lot may get left out.
>
> Evaluation for me is like this empty envelope. You can use it to send a message to someone. I want to use evaluation to send a message to our funders about what we're doing in the program. They don't have any idea about what we actually do. I just hope they'll read the letter when they get it.
>
> Evaluation for me is like this adjustable wrench. You can use this wrench to tighten nuts and bolts to help hold things together. If used properly and applied with the right amount of pressure it holds things together very well. If you tighten the bolt too hard, however, you can break the bolt and the whole thing will fall apart. I'm in favor of evaluation if it's done right. My concern is that you can overdo it and the program can't handle it.

The process of sharing is usually accompanied by laughter and spontaneous elaborations of favorite metaphors. It's a fun process that offers hope the evaluation process itself may not be quite as painful as people thought it would be. In addition, participants are often surprised to find that they have something to say. They are typically quite pleased with themselves. Most important, the exercise serves to express very important thoughts and feelings that can be dealt with once they are made explicit.

Those participating are typically not even aware that they have these feelings. By providing a vehicle for discovering and expressing their concerns, it is possible to surface major issues that may later affect evaluation use. Shared metaphors can help establish a common framework for the evaluation, capturing its purpose, its possibilities, and the safeguards that need to be built into the process.

By the way, I've used this exercise with many different groups and in many different situations, including cross-cultural settings, and I've never yet encountered someone who couldn't find an object to use in saying something about evaluation. One way of guaranteeing this is to include in your box of items some things that have a pretty clear and simple message. For example, I'll always include a lock and key so that a very simple and fairly obvious analogy can be made: "Evaluation is like a lock and key, if you have the right key you can open up the lock and make it work. If you have the right information you can make the thing work." Or I'll include a lightbulb so that someone can say "evaluation is like this lightbulb, its purpose is to shed light on the situation."

10. Generating questions for evaluation

> *It is impossible for a man to learn what he thinks he already knows.*
>
> *Epictetus (CE 55–135),*
> *Greek Stoic philosopher*

One way of facilitating a program's readiness for evaluation is to take primary intended users through a process of generating meaningful evaluation questions. I find that when

I enter a new program setting as an external evaluator, the people with whom I'm working typically expect me to tell them what the focus of the evaluation will be. They're passively waiting to be told by the evaluation expert—me—what questions the evaluation will answer. But I don't come with specific evaluation questions. I come with a process for determining what questions will be meaningful and what answers will be useful given the program's situation, priorities, and decision context. Taking them through the process of formulating questions and determining evaluation priorities is aimed at engendering their commitment to data-based evaluation and use.

This exercise involves getting stakeholders to think about what they want to learn from the evaluation without the jargon of or concern about goals, criteria, or measurement. On a chalkboard, flipchart, or handout I ask them to fill in the blank in the following sentence:

I WOULD REALLY LIKE TO KNOW ____
ABOUT THIS PROGRAM.

I ask each person, individually, to complete the blank 10 times. I ask: "What are 10 things about the program that you'd like to know, things you aren't certain about, that would make a difference in what you do if you had more information? Take a shot at it, without regard to methods, measurement, design, resources, precision—just 10 basic questions, real questions about this program."

After about 10 minutes I have them work in groups of four people each and ask them to combine their lists together into a single list of 10 things that *each group* wants to know, in effect, to establish each group's priority questions. Then we pull back together, the groups report, and together we generate a single list of 10 basic evaluation questions—answers to which could make a real difference to the effectiveness of the program.

The questions generated are usually the kind an experienced evaluator could anticipate. But being generated by the group, the questions are phrased in *their* terms, incorporating important local nuances of meaning and circumstance. Most important, they discover together that they have questions they care about—not my questions, as the external evaluator, but *their* questions, as people with some relationship to and stake in the program. In the process of generating, sharing, and prioritizing evaluation questions, it becomes *their* evaluation.

Later work together will involve refining questions, further prioritizing, formalizing evaluation procedures, determining methods, and establishing evaluation measures. But they aren't ready to engage in determining those details until they know they have questions that they want answered. This exercise increases their readiness for evaluation while allowing me, by seeing them in action and hearing what they come up with, assess their readiness and determine what to do next in the evaluation process. Thus, generating a list of real and meaningful evaluation questions can play a critical part in getting key stakeholders involved in launching the evaluation process.

But generating a list of potentially useful questions is only one way to start interacting with primary users. How one begins depends on what backgrounds, experiences, preconceptions, and relationships the primary users bring to the table. If I need to get a group engaged quickly in reframing how they are thinking about my role as external evaluator, helping them discover their questions can move the focus from me to them and their stakes as stakeholders.

"I don't know what it is, but I feel like we're just not quite ready."

Initiating a Utilization-Focused Evaluation

Menu 1.1, pages 20–21, summarizes the 10 exercises we've just reviewed.

A utilization-focused evaluator begins by assessing program and organizational readiness for evaluation and using that assessment to begin strengthening the capacity to undertake a utilization-focused evaluation. Taking time at the beginning to understand and assess the program and organizational culture increases the likelihood that the evaluation can be designed to be relevant to and useful within the specific context within which it will unfold. Methods-driven evaluators often want to get right to work on designing the evaluation and generating instruments. Utilization-focused evaluators, in contrast, begin by learning about the context within which the evaluation will be conducted and, equally important, learning about the people within that context by getting them engaged in their own assessment of the evaluation context while deepening their commitment to serious reality testing.

Initial assessment and initial engagement go hand in glove. Assessing is a form of early engagement. Engaging stakeholders offers opportunities for both assessing and building the capacities of key stakeholders. The *utilization-focused checklist* in the book's concluding chapter includes a summary of the key elements of Step 1. (See pp. 406–407.)

In closing, let me evoke the wisdom of Lao-tzu (604–531 BC), the Chinese philosopher who founded Taoism. He is famously attributed with the astute observation that "A journey of a thousand miles begins with a first step." This chapter has been about that first step in utilization-focused evaluation.

However, this oft-cited quotation offers a deeper insight into the importance of understanding context when taking that first step. Michael Moncur (2004), a Chinese scholar, disputes this version of the popular quote and asserts that a more correct translation from the original Chinese would be, "The journey of a thousand miles begins beneath one's feet." He explains that rather than emphasizing the first step, Lao-tzu regarded action as something that arises naturally from stillness. Or, he goes on, another potential phrasing would be "Even the longest journey must begin where you stand."

This chapter has emphasized finding out how key stakeholders understand, relate to, and translate EVALUATION. Different stakeholders will attach different meanings to the word, both cognitively and emotionally. They will also come with varying perceptions about what the evaluation journey will entail, many fearing that it will, indeed, be a journey of a thousand miles, or 10,000 miles, or even an interminable and quite treacherous journey. Assessing readiness to undertake the evaluation journey and deepening commitment to engage in the journey in a way that leads to useful results is where utilization-focused evaluation begins. It is an essential first step.

And I quite like the translation of Lao-tzu that says "Even the longest journey must begin where you stand." We've been looking primarily at where the evaluation's clients and primary stakeholders stand at the beginning. The next chapter looks at where the evaluator stands.

PRACTICE EXERCISES

1. Look up the full set of standards for evaluation: http://www.jcsee.org/program-evaluation-standards. Select one specific standard from each of the four overall categories (utility, feasibility, propriety, and accuracy) and explain how it would apply to a specific evaluation example.
2. Come up with a good idea of your own that didn't work out in practice. (See Exercise 8 in Menu 1.1.) What was the idea? How did you try to implement it? What was the "evidence" that led you to conclude it wasn't working? What did you learn from the experience? What does this example illustrate about evaluative thinking? How would you use this example with a group to help them get ready to engage in an evaluation?
3. Based on your own interests and expertise, develop a metaphor or analogy for evaluation. (See Exercise 9, Menu 1.1.) Explain how you would use it with a group.
4. The theme for the 2009 annual conference of the American Evaluation Association was *Context and Evaluation.* This chapter has been about how context matters and offered exercises to engage stakeholders in elucidating context: for example, assessing how past evaluations have been used and identifying incentives for and barriers to evaluation use.

> Context typically refers to the setting (time and place) and broader environment in which the focus of the evaluation is located. Context also can refer to the historical context of the problem or phenomenon that the program or policy targets as well as the policy and decision-making context enveloping the evaluation. Context has multiple layers and is dynamic, changing over time (AEA, 2009).

Select a program that you are acquainted with and identify some contextual factors that would affect how an evaluation would be conducted.

2

Assess and Enhance Evaluator Readiness and Competence to Undertake a Utilization-Focused Evaluation

Never ascribe to malice that which can be adequately explained by incompetence.

Napoleon Bonaparte

The Dunning–Kruger effect describes the phenomenon of people making erroneous judgments about their competence. Those with low competence tend to rate themselves as above average, while the highly skilled tend to underrate their abilities. This means that, ironically and perversely, less competent people rate their own ability higher than more competent people (Dunning & Kruger, 1999). Or, as philosopher Bertrand Russell observed in *The Triumph of Stupidity in Mortals and Others:* "The trouble with the world is that the stupid are cocksure and the intelligent are full of doubt" (1998, p. 28).

This phenomenon was demonstrated in a series of experiments performed by Kruger and Dunning with psychology undergraduates at Cornell University. They had students assess themselves on logical reasoning skills, grammatical skills, and humor, then administered tests that measured these skills. After seeing their actual test scores, the students again assessed how they thought they would rank compared to others. The more competent students accurately ranked themselves but the incompetent students still overestimated how they would compare to peers. Kruger and Dunning (1999) called this the *unskilled–unaware hypothesis.* More than a century earlier, Charles Darwin (1871) observed this phenomenon in concluding that "Ignorance more frequently begets confidence than does knowledge" (p. 4).

The phenomenon has been substantiated in more recent research. For example, Burson, Larrick, and Klayman (2006) concluded that "People have limited insight into their skills and performance" (p. 71). One of the authors of this research commented on having spent several years leading horseback rides and being struck by "the number of incompetent riders who actually put their lives in danger by claiming that they were highly skilled" (p. 60).

But what does this have to do with evaluation in general and utilization-focused evaluation in particular?

This chapter discusses the skills required to effectively conduct utilization-focused evaluations and invites you to assess whether you have, or are willing to acquire, the requisite competence to do so. Such self-assessments being prone to error, the task appears best approached with some care. It also helps to seek, and take seriously, feedback from people who know you well. Moreover, should you choose to undertake utilization-focused evaluations, it will be important to get feedback from those with whom you work about how useful the evaluation was and your competence in facilitating the process. Indeed, this book ends with that admonition (Step 17). But for the moment, let's look at the skills required so that you can begin an upfront assessment of your readiness to undertake a utilization-focused evaluation.

Essential Competencies

Jean King, a recipient of the American Evaluation Association's prestigious Alva and Gunnar Myrdal Practice Award, has worked for a number of years with colleagues and students conducting research on and developing a framework for *Essential Competencies for Program Evaluators* (Ghere, King, Stevahn, & Minnema, 2006; King, Stevahn, Ghere, & Minnema, 2001; Stevahn, King, Ghere, & Minnema, 2005, 2006). The final product is a taxonomy of essential program evaluator competencies organized into six primary categories.

1. *Professional practice:* Knowing and observing professional norms and values, including evaluation standards and principles.
2. *Systematic inquiry:* Expertise in the technical aspects of evaluations, such as design, measurement, data analysis, interpretation, and sharing results.
3. *Situational analysis:* Understanding and attending to the contextual and political issues of an evaluation, including determining evaluability, addressing conflicts, and attending to issues of evaluation use.

4. *Project management:* The nuts and bolts of managing an evaluation from beginning to end, including negotiating contracts, budgeting, identifying and coordinating needed resources, and conducting the evaluation in a timely manner.
5. *Reflective practice:* An awareness of one's program evaluation expertise as well as the needs for professional growth.
6. *Interpersonal competence:* The people skills needed to work with diverse groups of stakeholders to conduct program evaluations, including written and oral communication, negotiation, and cross-cultural skills.

Based on these competencies and the specific context of evaluation practice in Canada, the Canadian Evaluation Society (CES) adopted a Professional Designations Program at its 2009 Annual Conference in Ottawa. The CES Credentialed Evaluator designation is designed to "define, recognize and promote the practice of ethical, high quality and competent evaluation in Canada. . . . The designation means that the holder has provided evidence of the education and experience required to be *a competent evaluator*" (CES, 2010). Attention to professional competence is so important that CES created a Vice President of Professional Designation Programs. Dr. Keiko Kuji-Shikatani, of the Ontario Ministry of Education, is the first person to hold this position and is providing important leadership for this initiative, launched officially at the 2010 annual conference of CES in Victoria.

The Aotearoa New Zealand Evaluation Association has also launched an evaluator competencies initiative focused on the particular cultural sensitivities and priorities of evaluation practice in New Zealand (McKegg, 2010). These international initiatives point to the importance of essential evaluator competencies as a foundation for designing and implementing useful evaluations. Essential evaluator competencies include *both* general evaluation knowledge capabilities as well as context-specific cultural competencies.

Questions to Ask in Selecting an Evaluator

In working with government agencies, philanthropic foundations, not-for-profit organizations, and businesses that want to hire an evaluator, these are common questions that arise in the vetting and hiring process. If you are an evaluator (or would-be evaluator), consider your answers to these questions. If you are in a position to be seeking an evaluator, consider these questions as a starting point to stimulate your thinking about what characteristics you're looking for in an evaluator.

1. What are the main reasons why you think a program should conduct an evaluation?
2. What are the main standards and guiding principles for conducting evaluations?

(Continued)

(Continued)

3. How would you determine if a program is ready to undergo an evaluation?
4. How do you estimate the resources needed to conduct an evaluation? That is, how do you compute the costs of an evaluation, both in money and time (yourself and others)?
5. What are your methodological strengths and weaknesses? What major evaluation techniques are you competent to do on your own and what techniques or methods would you need to seek from others?
6. Frequently evaluations involve various diverse stakeholders that all have different expectations for the evaluation. If you had a conflict among stakeholders in a program evaluation that could threaten the evaluation, how would you resolve the conflict? What steps might you take to proactively avoid such conflicts?
7. How does your own background and experience affect your approach to evaluation? What are your approaches to working with and gathering data from people of diverse and different backgrounds in the course of doing an evaluation?
8. Have you read any interesting articles on evaluation lately? In what journals? What was interesting about it? What other journals do you review regularly?
9. What do you consider the most significant developments in the field of evaluation in the last decade? How do you keep up with developments in the field of evaluation?
10. What would you do to ensure that an evaluation is useful–and useful in what ways?

Evaluator Credibility

Now, let's connect essential competencies directly to evaluation use. Research on use consistently shows that findings are more likely to be used if they are credible—and *evaluator credibility* is a central factor in the overall credibility of the findings. Yes, the methods and measures themselves need to be credible so that the resulting data are credible. But methods and measures derive their credibility from appropriate and competent application by the person conducting the evaluation. Methods don't just happen. Someone, namely the evaluator, has to employ methods. So the evaluator's competence in selecting and applying appropriate methods and measures, and appropriately and competently analyzing and presenting the findings, are the fundamental source of an evaluation's credibility. This premise is highlighted in the *Evaluation Standard on Evaluator Credibility,* the very first of the standards:

> Evaluations should be conducted by qualified people who establish and maintain credibility in the evaluation context. (Joint Committee, 2010, U1)

The American Evaluation Association Guiding Principles for Evaluators also emphasize competence: "Evaluators should possess (or ensure that the evaluation team possesses) the education, abilities, skills and experience appropriate to undertake the tasks proposed in the evaluation" (AEA, 2004). See Exhibit 2.1 for the full Guiding Principle on Competence.

EXHIBIT 2.1

Evaluator Competence: Guiding Principle

Evaluators provide competent performance to stakeholders.

1. Evaluators should possess (or ensure that the evaluation team possesses) the education, abilities, skills, and experience appropriate to undertake the tasks proposed in the evaluation.
2. To ensure recognition, accurate interpretation, and respect for diversity, evaluators should ensure that the members of the evaluation team collectively demonstrate cultural competence. Cultural competence would be reflected in evaluators seeking awareness of their own culturally based assumptions, their understanding of the worldviews of culturally different participants and stakeholders in the evaluation, and the use of appropriate evaluation strategies and skills in working with culturally different groups. Diversity may be in terms of race, ethnicity, gender, religion, socioeconomics, or other factors pertinent to the evaluation context.
3. Evaluators should practice within the limits of their professional training and competence, and should decline to conduct evaluations that fall substantially outside those limits. When declining the commission or request is not feasible or appropriate, evaluators should make clear any significant limitations on the evaluation that might result. Evaluators should make every effort to gain the competence directly or through the assistance of others who possess the required expertise.
4. Evaluators should continually seek to maintain and improve their competencies in order to provide the highest level of performance in their evaluations. This continuing professional development might include formal coursework and workshops, self-study, evaluations of one's own practice, and working with other evaluators to learn from their skills and expertise.

Guiding Principles for Evaluators,
American Evaluation Association (AEA, 2004)

Utilization-Focused Evaluation Competence and Credibility

The basic competencies for utilization-focused evaluation are the same as those for any evaluation based on the profession's standards and guiding principles. What utilization-focused evaluation adds is a greater emphasis on direct engagement with primary intended users of the evaluation and therefore increased attention to interpersonal and group facilitation skills. Traditionally, evaluation training and professional development have emphasized methodological competence above all else with only secondary attention, if any at all, to interpersonal skills and cultural competence. This is sometimes talked about as a contrast between "hard skills" (technical knowledge) and "soft skills" (competence to work effectively with diverse stakeholders). But, ironically, it turns out that the so-called "soft skills" are *hard* to acquire. Moreover, a narrow focus on "strong technical skills" can weaken evaluation credibility and use by failing to attend to the full range of factors and complex dynamics that determine whether an evaluation is actually credible to intended users, and therefore useful and used. The fact that an evaluator thinks that she or he has done a credible job doesn't mean that users will think so. And therein lies the rub.

The traditional emphasis on methodological competence assumes that methodological rigor is the primary determinant of evaluation credibility. But the evidence from studies of use shows that evaluator characteristics interact with methodological criteria in determining an evaluation's credibility, and that how the evaluation is facilitated with meaningful involvement of primary intended users affects those users' judgments about the evaluation's credibility and utility. For example, Alkin (1985), in a now-classic and still-influential study, identified some 50 factors associated with evaluation use. He organized them into four categories:

1. *Evaluator characteristics,* such as commitment to make use a priority, willingness to involve users, political sensitivity, and credibility
2. *User characteristics,* such as interest in the evaluation, willingness to commit time and energy, and position of influence
3. *Contextual characteristics,* such as size of organization, political climate, and existence of competing information
4. *Evaluation characteristics,* such as nature and timing of the evaluation report, relevance of evaluation information, rigor of methods, and quality of the data

In this chapter, we are examining the critical intersection of an evaluator's essential competencies with the commitment to facilitate a utilization-focused evaluation. Exhibit 2.2 summarizes how these factors interact to increase the likelihood that an evaluation will be perceived as credible and therefore more likely to be used.

EXHIBIT 2.2

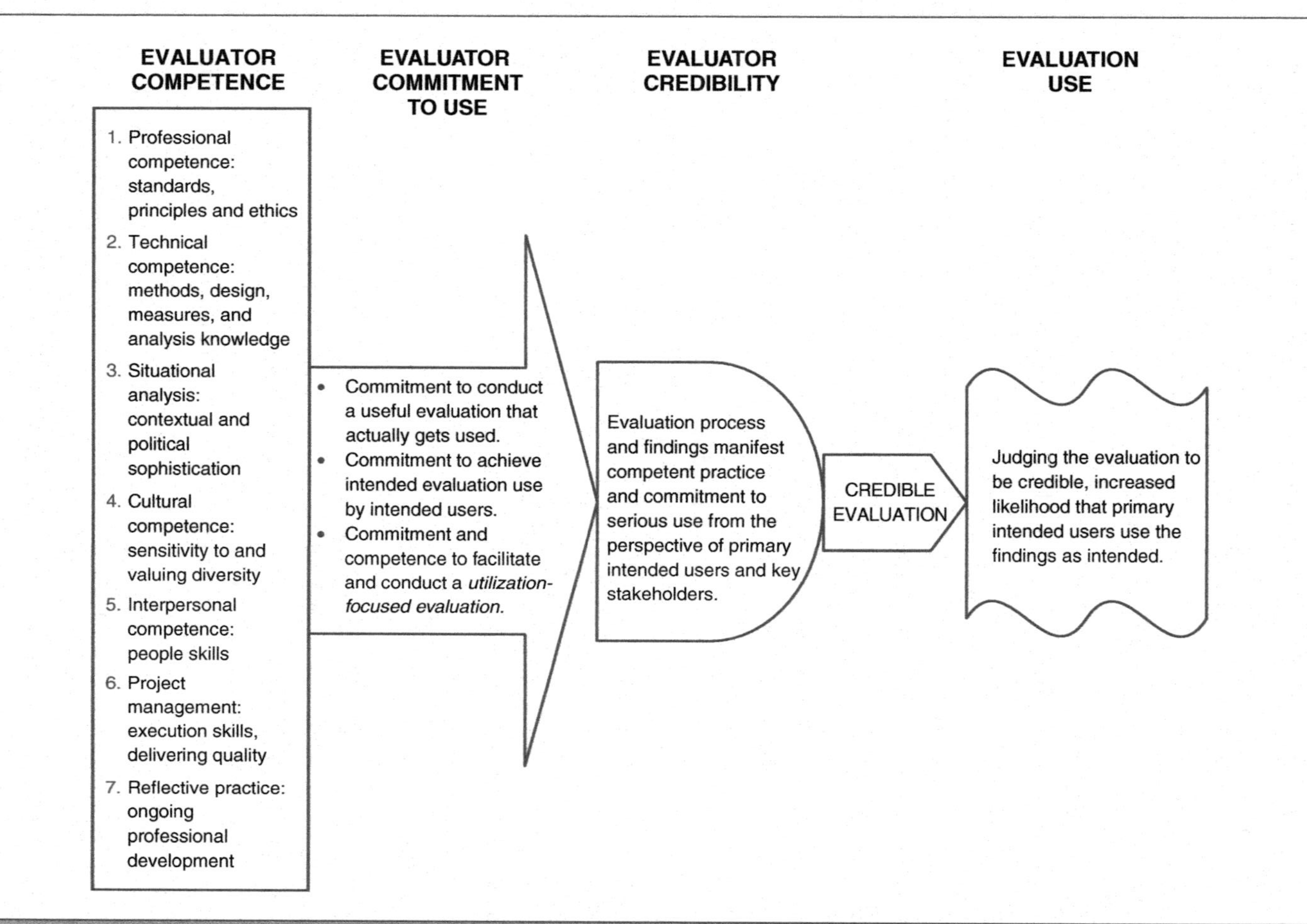

EVALUATOR COMPETENCE
1. Professional competence: standards, principles and ethics
2. Technical competence: methods, design, measures, and analysis knowledge
3. Situational analysis: contextual and political sophistication
4. Cultural competence: sensitivity to and valuing diversity
5. Interpersonal competence: people skills
6. Project management: execution skills, delivering quality
7. Reflective practice: ongoing professional development
EVALUATOR COMMITMENT TO USE
• Commitment to conduct a useful evaluation that actually gets used.
• Commitment to achieve intended evaluation use by intended users.
• Commitment and competence to facilitate and conduct a *utilization-focused evaluation.*
EVALUATOR CREDIBILITY
Evaluation process and findings manifest competent practice and commitment to serious use from the perspective of primary intended users and key stakeholders.
CREDIBLE EVALUATION
EVALUATION USE
Judging the evaluation to be credible, increased likelihood that primary intended users use the findings as intended.

Technical and Methodological Competence: Utilization-Focused Pragmatism

Let me hasten to add that methodological competence and rigor remain important factors in evaluation use. In later chapters we'll discuss methods at some length. At this point let me just say that the practical experience of utilization-focused evaluators working to improve program effectiveness has led them to become *pragmatic* in their approaches to methods issues. Pragmatism means doing what works in a given situation rather than a commitment to methodological rigor as an end in itself or in isolation from other factors that affect use. This is where the essential competencies of situation analysis and technical skill intersect. Step 4 will focus on situation analysis, and Steps 10 to 15 will discuss technical, methodological, and analytical competencies. The point here is that technical competence, as important as it is, and it is important, is not the only factor that determines use—and not even the most important factor in many cases.

Those who use evaluations experience the evaluator as a whole person, not just as a walking and talking technical manual. Utilization-focused evaluation is not about producing findings that are admired for their methodological brilliance by researchers and evaluation peers because researchers and evaluation colleagues are not the primary evaluation users. Thus, utilization-focused evaluation is about grounding findings *in the relationship* between the evaluator and primary intended users to ensure that the questions asked are relevant, the methods used are appropriate, the findings are understandable, and the entire evaluation process is credible. *That total package is what leads to use.* The issue at this stage, then, is whether you are ready to conduct a utilization-focused evaluation. That readiness means having both the competence and commitment to do so. Take another look at Exhibit 2.2 to see how competence and commitment combine to produce credible evaluations that get used.

Evaluation Negotiations

I said earlier that utilization-focused evaluation emphasizes direct engagement with primary intended users of the evaluation and therefore increased attention to interpersonal and group facilitation skills. This is because a utilization-focused evaluation is negotiated with primary intended users. Different stakeholder representatives come to an evaluation with varying perspectives about what is important. They will usually have different views about the most important questions for the evaluation to address. They may value different kinds of data. They come with political agendas. And they bring their splendidly diverse backgrounds and personalities. So guess what? Sometimes, just occasionally, just once in a while, all of this diversity leads to disagreements and conflict. That's when the negotiating begins—giving voice to varying views, hearing the case for conflicting priorities, identifying viable trade-offs, and ultimately reaching common ground through shared understandings and compromises. This means a utilization-focused evaluator must have skills in group facilitation, negotiation, conflict resolution, group problem-solving, and decision-making dynamics. Consider these situations:

- Teachers, school administrators, parents, and state education officials disagree about whether an evaluation should include data about and evaluate "school climate." They also disagree about what "school climate" is.

- Nurses, clinic administrators, physicians, insurance company representatives, and federal health officials have quite different views about how much emphasis should be placed on prevention and where in the health system accountability rests for prevention outcomes. They also are in conflict about what prevention outcomes should be measured.

- The program officer from the philanthropic foundation funding a developmental disabilities initiative is part of an evaluation task force that includes not-for-profit grantees, an advocacy organization that promotes the rights of people with disabilities, a university researcher with scholarly expertise in developmental disabilities, and the state administrator for disability services. The researcher proposes an evaluation using a randomized controlled trial. The advocates insist on consumer choice and are adamantly opposed to randomization. The grantees are concerned that the foundation's objectives overpromise what can reasonably be accomplished and want to scale back the outcome targets. The state administrator is worried that the state will be expected to pick up the initiative if it is successful and doesn't see the state having future funds to sustain such an initiative.

- A major community-based environmental initiative includes an evaluation task force with environmental activists, private sector homebuilders, the city mayor's chief of staff, and the citizens' organization representing the community where the initiative will take place. All agree that the initiative is a good idea and badly needed but they are suspicious of each other, have a long history of antagonism, and have very different priorities for the initiative. For the initiative to have any chance of succeeding they need to agree on priority outcomes and what will constitute success or failure. These are ultimately evaluation issues so the evaluator is asked to facilitate agreement to break the political and interpersonal logjam that has stopped the initiative from moving forward.

- A federal and state collaboration on reducing juvenile crime includes data management staff who use different systems with different codes. They are territorial about their own data system, and each wants the other to change forms and indicators to make the integrated system compatible with their own preferences. City, county, state, and federal data systems are incompatible. There are additional barriers to sharing data because of different data privacy procedures. And in designing a new survey aimed at high school students, some want even-numbered scales (no midpoint) while others insist on odd-numbered scales. It's hard to tell how much this is a technical debate, how much is power dynamics, and how much is just good old personality conflict. For an evaluation to get done, these issues have to be resolved without undermining the evaluation's credibility and utility.

- A state legislative committee wants an evaluation of the policy that requires women seeking abortions to attend an educational presentation on fetus development and wait 48 hours before having an abortion. For the evaluation to have credibility with political constituencies that both support and oppose access to abortion, the evaluation task force includes representatives of opposing groups. It is an understatement to say that these people do not like or much respect each other. Yet for the policy evaluation to have credibility and legislative utility, they need to agree on the evaluation criteria, design, and instruments.

- A multicountry HIV/AIDS initiative in Africa involves a major collaboration among nongovernmental organizations (NGOS), two major philanthropic foundations, the World Health Organization (WHO), health officials from participating countries, and community representatives. Each comes with their own accountability mandates from the organizations and constituencies they represent. Those mandates differ in significant ways. The initiative cannot get under way until the collaborating parties agree on evaluation indicators and accountability targets and baseline data are collected.

- The evaluation task force for a sustainable agricultural development project in Asia includes three small farmers, an agricultural extension agent, an agronomist, a soil scientist, a crop breeder, a hydrologist, an integrated pest management specialist, and a gender issues expert. They have differing views and definitions of sustainability, different priorities, and divergent areas of expertise. The evaluation must find a way to incorporate those divergent views within an overall systems change framework.

Experienced evaluators will recognize these scenarios, all of which are real, and could easily add their own. It is precisely because of the challenges of dealing with such situations that many evaluators prefer to just design and conduct the evaluation without direct stakeholder involvement. Why bother? Why go to all the trouble of trying to get these diverse people to agree? Why bother, indeed? The answer: increased credibility, user buy-in, and, ultimately, use.

Some evaluation approaches, like "responsive evaluation" (Guba & Lincoln, 1981; Stake, 1975), take a middle ground. The "responsive evaluator" interviews various constituency representatives and diverse stakeholders to surface different views and concerns, then the evaluator designs an evaluation that she or he thinks appropriately addresses and is "responsive to" stakeholder concerns. The stakeholders, however, are primarily sources of data and an audience for the evaluation, not real partners in the evaluation process. That, at least, has been the classic approach to responsive evaluation. More recent applications, for example Abma (2006), include face-to-face dialogue among stakeholders in responsive evaluation. Such direct interactions and negotiations are always core in utilization-focused evaluation.

Being Active-Reactive-Interactive-Adaptive

I use the phrase *active-reactive-interactive-adaptive* to suggest the nature of the consultative interactions that go on between evaluators and intended users. The phrase is meant to be both descriptive and prescriptive. It describes how real-world decision making actually unfolds—act, react, interact, and adapt. Yet, it is prescriptive in alerting evaluators to consciously and deliberately act, react, interact, and adapt in order to increase their effectiveness in working with intended users. Being active-reactive-interactive-adaptive is, in a nutshell, the facilitation style of utilization-focused evaluation. This approach to facilitation requires versatility, flexibility, creativity, political astuteness, and responsiveness.

Utilization-focused evaluators are, first of all, active in deliberately and calculatedly identifying intended users and focusing useful questions (Steps 3 to 7). They are reactive in listening to intended users and responding to what they learn about the particular situation in which the evaluation unfolds. They are adaptive in altering evaluation questions and designs in light of their increased understanding of the situation and changing conditions. Active-reactive-interactive-adaptive evaluators don't impose cookbook designs. They don't do the same thing time after time. They are genuinely immersed in the challenges of each new setting and authentically responsive to the intended users of each new evaluation.

It is the paradox of decision making that effective action is born of reaction. Only when organizations and people take in information from the environment and react to changing conditions can they act on that same environment to reduce uncertainty and increase discretionary flexibility. The same is true for the individual decision maker or for a problem-solving group. Action emerges through reaction and interaction and leads to adaptation. The imagery is familiar: thesis-antithesis-synthesis; stimulus-response-change. Exhibit 2.3 depicts this Adaptive Cycle.

Adaptive Management

In a rapidly changing environment, quick adaptation is one of the crucial tasks for modern management and ongoing situation analysis and responsiveness are key to successfully coping with dynamic situations. Adaptive management consultants advise observing a

EXHIBIT 2.3

Working with Primary Intended Users: The Adaptive Cycle

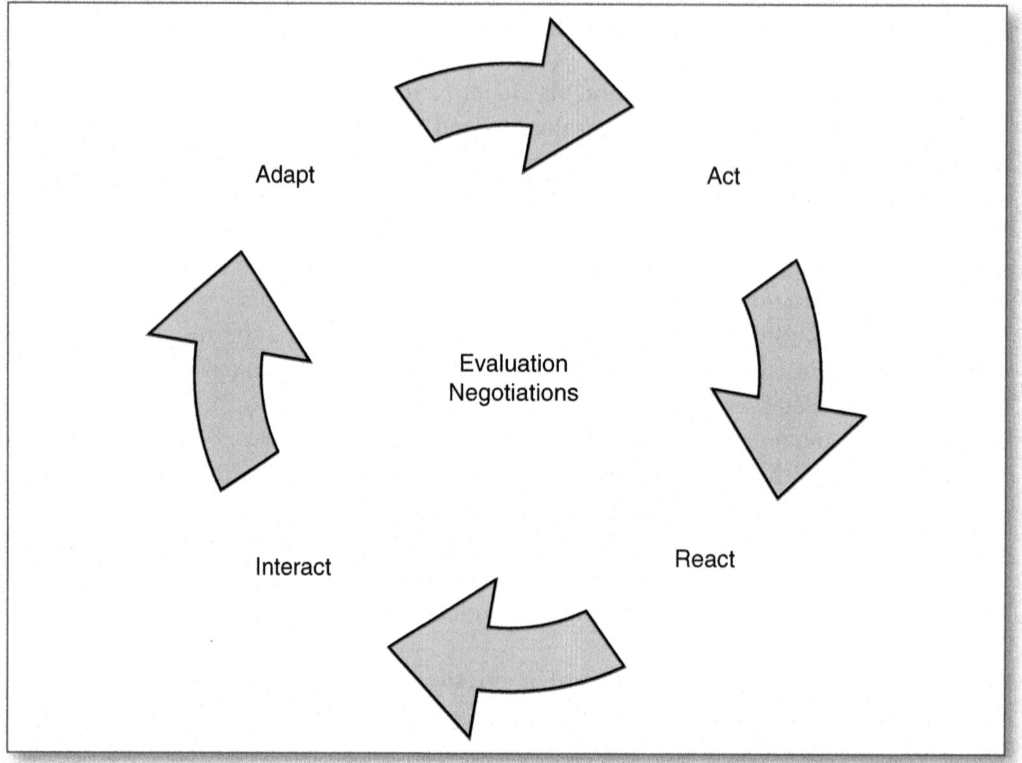

system for a while to determine its natural tendencies before intervening. They may even try out some things on a small scale to learn how the system reacts. The focus is on learning through interaction, not just standing outside the system and observing it.

This active-reactive-interactive-adaptive stance characterizes all phases of evaluator–user interactions, from initially identifying primary intended users to focusing relevant questions, choosing methods, and analyzing results. All phases involve collaborative processes of action-reaction-interaction-adaptation as evaluators and intended users consider their options. The menu of choices includes a broad range of design options, various methods, and diverse reporting possibilities—evaluation ingredients from bland to spicy. Throughout this book, we'll be looking at those options.

Multiple Evaluator Roles and Individual Style

Evaluator roles vary: collaborator, trainer, group facilitator, technician, politician, organizational analyst, internal colleague, external expert, methodologist, information broker, communicator, change agent, diplomat, problem solver, and creative consultant. Some of these roles may be combined, and the roles of evaluation and program development may be integrated. The roles played by an evaluator in any given situation will depend on the evaluation's purpose, the unique constellation of conditions with which the evaluator is faced, and the evaluator's own personal knowledge, skills, style, values, and sense of what is ethical.

The mandate to be active-reactive-interactive-adaptive in role-playing provokes protest from those evaluators and intended users who advocate only one narrow role, namely, that the evaluator renders judgment about merit or worth—*nothing else* (Scriven 1991, 1993; Stufflebeam, 1994). Clearly, I have a more expansive view of an evaluator's role possibilities and responsibilities. Keeping in mind that the idea of multiple evaluator roles is controversial, let's turn to look at what the evaluator brings to the utilization-focused negotiating table.

The evaluator as a person in his or her own right is a key part of the negotiating mix. Each evaluation will be unique, in part, because individual evaluators are unique. Evaluators bring to the negotiating table their own style, personal history, and professional experience. All of the techniques and ideas presented in this book must be adapted to the style of the individuals using them.

Being active-reactive-interactive-adaptive explicitly recognizes the importance of the individual evaluator's experience, orientation, and contribution by placing the mandate to be active first in this dynamic framework. Situational responsiveness does not mean rolling over and playing dead (or passive) in the face of stakeholder interests or perceived needs. Just as the evaluator in utilization-focused evaluation does not unilaterally impose a focus and set of methods on a program, so too the stakeholders are not set up to impose their initial predilections unilaterally or dogmatically. Arriving at the final evaluation design is *a negotiated process* that allows the values and capabilities of the evaluator to intermingle with those of intended users.

The utilization-focused evaluator, in being active-reactive-interactive-adaptive, is one among many at the negotiating table. At times there may be discord in the negotiating process; at other times harmony. Whatever the sounds, and whatever the themes, the utilization-focused evaluator does not sing alone. He or she is part of a choir made up of primary intended users. There are solo parts, to be sure, but ultimately a utilization-focused process is owned by the group that negotiated it. The focus of the negotiations and tradeoffs is driven by the commitment to producing the most useful possible evaluation within the resource and time constraints of the situation.

Evaluation Teams

This may be a good place to note that many, if not most, evaluations are conducted by teams, not individuals. Teams bring together people with diverse and complementary competencies so that no one person has to be adept at everything. The team, then, needs to have the full range of essential competencies but no single evaluator needs them all. A great way for less experienced evaluators to learn the ropes and gain experience is to be part of a team with more experienced and sophisticated evaluators.

When considering the value of experience, it's worth noting the findings of Cousins, Donohue, and Bloom (1996). They surveyed North American evaluators to find out what variables correlated with a collaborative style of practice. Organizational affiliation, gender, and primary job responsibility did not differentiate practice and opinion responses. Canadian evaluators reported greater depth of stakeholder involvement than Americans. Most telling, however, were years and depth of experience with collaborative approaches. More experienced evaluators expected and attained more use of their evaluations, and reported a greater sense of satisfaction from the collaborative process and greater impacts of the resulting evaluations. In essence, evaluators get better at the active-reactive-interactive-adaptive process the more they experience it; and the more they use it, the more they like it and the more impact they believe it has.

Teams are also a primary way of dealing with cultural competence, an issue of increasing importance and one that deserves special attention as it relates to both evaluation credibility and utility.

Cultural Competence

> Attention to the location of power and privilege in evaluation, and to community engagement and 'sense-making' processes are the conversational starting points to begin to explore what it takes to do evaluation in communities, where the language, culture, and cultural context are different from one's own. (Wehipeihana, Davidson, McKegg, & Shanker, 2010, p. 182)

Sensitivity to and sophistication about cultural issues has taken on increased importance over the last decade. A helpful starting point for considering cultural issues is to recognize that evaluation, itself, constitutes a culture, of sorts. We, as evaluators, have our own values, our own ways of thinking, our own language, and our own reward system.

When we engage other people in the evaluation process, we are providing them with a cross-cultural experience. They often experience evaluators as imperialistic: that is, as imposing the evaluation culture on top of their own values and culture—or they may find the cross-cultural experience stimulating and friendly. But in either case, it is a cross-cultural interaction. Those new to the evaluation culture may need help and facilitation in coming to view the experience as valuable. The last chapter (Step 1) offered a number of exercises to launch an evaluation by getting key people involved in thinking about evaluation, drawing on their own experiences in making evaluative judgments, and getting them more deeply engaged in thinking evaluatively. One of the ways I sometimes discuss the value of evaluation is to suggest that those involved in designing and using an evaluation may reap personal and professional benefits from learning how to operate in an evaluation culture. Many funders are immersed in that culture. Knowing how to speak the language of evaluation and conceptualize programs logically are not inherent goods, but they can be instrumentally good in helping people get the things they want, not least of all, to attract resources for their programs and make their work more effective. They may also develop skills in reality testing that have application in other areas of professional and even personal life.

This culture of evaluation that we evaluators take for granted can be quite alien to many of the folks with whom we work. Like people living daily inside any culture, our way of thinking, shaped by the research culture, seems natural and easy to us. However, to practitioners, decision makers, and policymakers, our logic can be hard to grasp and quite unnatural. I'm talking about what appear to be very simple notions that have profound effects on how one views the world. Thinking in terms of what's clear, specific, concrete, and observable does not come easily to people who thrive on, even depend on, vagueness, generalities, and untested beliefs as the basis for action. They're in the majority. Practitioners of evaluation logic are a small minority. The good news is that our way of thinking, once experienced, is often greatly valued. That's part of what creates demand for our services.

To avoid coming across as insensitive evaluation imperialists, we need to demonstrate cultural sensitivity and competence. Involvement of stakeholders and primary intended users has to be adapted to cultural and contextual factors. Clayson, Castaneda, Sanchez, and Brindis (2002) examined negotiations between evaluation stakeholders in Latino communities and found that they had to be especially attentive to power inequalities and a dynamic environment. Along the way they had to play a variety of roles including interpreters, translators, mediators, and storytellers. Relationships among people in evaluation situations are affected by larger societal issues including the challenges of involving people with disabilities, racism, sexism, and other forms of prejudice that engender conflict and misunderstandings. Moreover, the norms for and challenges to stakeholder involvement and evaluation practice vary greatly across cultures and geographies.

Culturally Competent and Responsive Evaluators

Diversity, in its many dimensions and manifestations, is increasingly acknowledged as a necessary prerequisite for excellence. . . . Diversity fires and fuels creativity, innovation, and generative engagement in all sectors of life and living. . . . Multicultural development requires moving beyond tolerance, accommodation, and pressure to fit in toward a focus on changes in policies, processes, and practices in order to genuinely invite and engage the full spectrum of diverse voices, perspectives, experiences, and peoples.

Clearly, evaluative judgments are, by their very nature, inextricably bound up with culture and context. So, where there is sociocultural diversity, there very likely is some diversity in the expected and preferred evaluative processes and practices that undergird judgments of merit, worth, value, quality, significance, congruence. Maximizing accuracy, appropriateness, respect, and excellence calls for an openness to the decentering realities and complexities of difference and diversity.

"Walking Pathways Toward Becoming a Culturally Competent Evaluator: Boundaries, Borderlands, and Border Crossings,"

Hazel Symonette (2004, pp. 96, 107)

In beginning an evaluation training program with Native Americans, I started off by asking them, as part of introducing themselves, to mention any experiences with and perceptions of evaluation they cared to share. With 15 participants I expected the process to take no more than a half hour. But deep feelings surfaced and a dialogue ensued that took over two hours. Here is some of what they said.

- "I'm frustrated that what constitutes 'success' is always imposed on us by somebody who doesn't know us, doesn't know our ways, doesn't know me."
- "By White standards I'm a failure because I'm poor, but spiritually I'm rich. Why doesn't that count?"
- "I have a hard time with evaluation. We need methods that are true to who we are."
- Said through tears by a female elder: "All my life I've worked with grant programs and evaluation has been horrible for us—horribly traumatic. Painful. Made us look bad, feel bad. We've tried to give the funders what they want in numbers but we know that those numbers don't capture what is happening. It's been demeaning. It's taken a toll. I didn't want to come here today."
- Spoken in his native language by a spiritual leader who had opened the session with a smudge ceremony and blessing, translated by his son: "Everything I do is connected to who

I am as an Oglala Lakota elder, to our way as a people, to what you call our culture. Everything is connected. Evaluation will have to be connected if it is to have meaning. That's why I brought my son, and my neighbor, and my friend, and my granddaughter. They aren't signed up for this thing we're here to do. But they are connected, so they are here."

Respecting and honoring culture is a significant dimension of effective stakeholder involvement and group facilitation. As these quotations show, culture is personal. Everyone who comes to the evaluation table brings culture with them. To ignore it is to disrespect those present and imperil use.

Respect for Intended Users

Cultural competence is one dimension of a more central value that should undergird the evaluator's active-reactive-interactive-adaptive role: respect for all those with a stake in a program or evaluation. In their classic article on evaluation use, Davis and Salasin (1975) asserted that evaluators were involved inevitably in facilitating change and that "any change model should . . . generally *accommodate* rather than *manipulate* the view of the persons involved" (p. 652). Respectful utilization-focused evaluators do not use their expertise to intimidate or manipulate intended users. Egon Guba, one of evaluation's pioneers, in a keynote presentation on evaluation described in powerful language an archetype that is the antithesis of the utilization-focused evaluator:

> It is my experience that evaluators sometimes adopt a very supercilious attitude with respect to their clients; their presumptuousness and arrogance are sometimes overwhelming. We treat the client as a 'childlike' person who needs to be taken in hand; as an ignoramus who cannot possibly understand the tactics and strategies that we will bring to bear; as someone who doesn't appreciate the questions he *ought* to ask until we tell him—and what we tell him often reflects our own biases and interests rather than the problems with which the client is actually beset. The phrase 'Ugly American' has emerged in international settings to describe the person who enters into a new culture, immediately knows what is wrong with it, and proceeds to foist his own solutions onto the locals. In some ways I have come to think of evaluators as 'Ugly Americans.' And if what we are looking for are ways to manipulate clients so that they will fall in with *our* wishes and cease to resist our blandishments, I for one will have none of it. (Guba, 1977, p. 3)

The utilization-focused evaluation process is aimed at building mutual respect between evaluators and intended users.

Balancing Attention to Tasks and Relationships in Group Facilitation

One of the most fundamental and oft-replicated findings from early research on group effectiveness is that high-performing groups attend to both task completion and relationship building. In an evaluation context, *the task focus* concerns the primary intended uses of the evaluation and how those uses will be achieved. *The relationship focus* concerns how the evaluator works with and relates to primary intended users to enhance the likelihood of use. Embedded in the utilization-focused evaluation goal of *intended use by intended users* is attention to both task and relationship. This is sometimes talked about as attending to both process and outcomes, or getting things done while oiling the gears of relationships to keep things running smoothly in order to get things done.

Some evaluators focus only on getting the evaluation designed, the data collected and analyzed, and the report written. They are entirely task-focused and want no part of relationship building. Indeed, they wear their independence as a badge of pride, justifying their inattention to relationships and process as fundamental to their credibility. In this approach to evaluation, independence, neutrality, distance, and autonomy are the cornerstones of credibility and utility.

At the other end of the continuum are utilization-focused evaluators who make regular interaction with primary intended users a priority and give at least as much attention to relationship building as getting the technical work done *because building and maintaining relationships is part of the work.*

"Just to be on the safe side, let's look into evaluation models that don't involve working with people."

Reflexivity

"Reflexivity" has entered the evaluation lexicon as a way of emphasizing the importance of self-awareness, political/cultural consciousness, and ownership of one's own perspective. Being reflexive involves self-questioning and self-understanding. It refers to "the process of critical self-reflection on one's biases, theoretical predispositions, preferences and so forth" (Schwandt, 2001, p. 224). To be reflexive, then, is to undertake an ongoing examination of *what I know* and *how I know it.* Reflexivity reminds the evaluator to be attentive to and conscious of the cultural, political, social, economic, linguistic, and ideological origins of one's own perspective as well as the perspective and voices of those you gather data from and those to whom you present findings. Exhibit 2.4 depicts

EXHIBIT 2.4

Reflexive Questions: Triangulated Inquiry

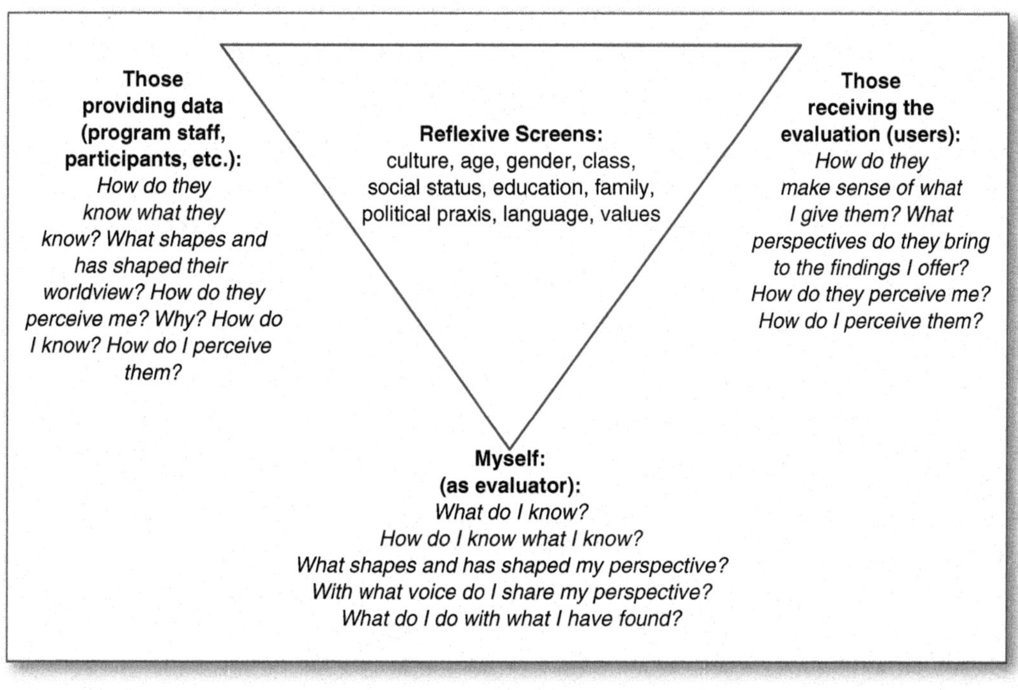

this reflexive triangulation and offers reflexive questions to sensitize you to the varying perspectives that come into play in an evaluation.

This chapter opened by citing research that people tend to make erroneous judgments about their competence. Those with low competence tend to rate themselves as above average, while the highly skilled tend to underrate their abilities. The good news in this research is that, with practice and feedback, people can get better at assessing their competence and, in so doing, can increase their competence. The premise of this chapter, this second U-FE step, is that utilization-focused evaluators need to know their strengths and limitations and develop the skills needed to facilitate utilization-focused evaluations. The *Utilization-Focused Checklist* in the book's concluding chapter includes a summary of the key elements of Step 2. (See pp. 407–408.)

Self-Knowledge: Beyond Narcissism

The ancient Greek myth of Narcissus tells of an exquisitely handsome young man, son of a god, who attracted the love of women and admiration of men wherever he went. As Narcissus experienced the infatuations of others, he became infatuated with himself. One day while walking in the woods alone he came upon a pond with a smooth, mirror-like surface. He saw his reflection in the water and became entranced with his own image. He fell in love with himself. In his self-absorption, he ceased to eat or drink. He stayed on that spot until he died. A flower grew in that spot, a flower the Greeks called Narcissus.

In modern times, Narcissus has a different legacy. The myth of Narcissus gave us the word ***narcissism,*** defined as excessive love or admiration of oneself. In the extreme this can become pathological, what psychologists call *narcissistic personality disorder* (NPD):

> A pattern of traits and behaviors characterized by infatuation and obsession with one's self to the exclusion of all others and the egotistic and ruthless pursuit of one's gratification, dominance and ambition. Some psychological researchers believe modern society may be generating a *narcissism epidemic.* (Twenge & Campbell, 2009)

Narcissists, let me assert, make lousy evaluators. They are inept at both knowing themselves and understanding others (Ames & Kammrath, 2004). People who manifest the Dunning–Kruger effect of making erroneous judgments about their own competence also make lousy evaluators. One of the essential competencies for program evaluators (Ghere et al., 2006) reviewed at the beginning of this chapter is *reflective practice.* In-depth reflective practice would include an enhanced capacity for authentic and genuine *reflexivity* which, we would hope, would increase one's capacity for and competence in assessing one's own strengths and weaknesses.

In this regard, it is worth highlighting the findings of distinguished Australian researcher John Hattie whose important book, *Visible Learning: A Synthesis of Over 800 Meta-Analyses Relating to Achievement* (2008), analyzed the results of 50,000 educational studies covering 83 million students around the world. Hattie concluded that many of the concerns that dominate political debates about education, including class size, amount of homework, and which school a child attends, have little effect on children's learning. The most important factor is students' ability to assess for themselves how well they are doing and to discuss with the teacher what they need to do next to improve. This in turn depends on the level and quality of feedback students receive from teachers. He found that most students do not get nearly enough quality feedback. Moreover, feedback requires a classroom culture of trust in which students can admit out loud that they don't understand something.

In essence, we can learn to be better at reflecting on and assessing our competence. Those who learned to do so in school and at home through the experience of receiving high-quality feedback are ahead of the game. Those unfortunates who didn't will have a lot of make-up to do, but the evidence is that one can get better with practice. Making a realistic assessment of and getting feedback about one's competence is important to being an effective utilization-focused evaluator. Utilization-focused evaluation is not for everyone and not everyone is good at it. The point of this chapter has been to highlight the qualities and skills that make for successful utilization-focused evaluation practice and to push you to do a serious reality-testing assessment of your readiness to undertake this approach—and, if not ready, have you assess your willingness to undertake the professional development and gain the experience that will get you ready. Narcissists need not apply.

The rest of this book will give you an ever deeper perspective on how to engage in utilization-focused evaluation beginning, in the next chapter, with identifying the primary intended users with whom you will work to design and implement a useful evaluation.

PRACTICE EXERCISES

1. *Conduct your own readiness assessment.* Being active-reactive-interactive-adaptive explicitly recognizes the importance of the individual evaluator's experience, orientation, and contribution. Assess your readiness to engage in utilization-focused evaluation. What assets and strengths do you bring to this approach to evaluation? What are your weaknesses? To what extent are your values and philosophy congruent with utilization-focused evaluation?

(Continued)

(Continued)

2. *Demonstrating knowledge and readiness.* On pages 39–40 are a sidebar feature on "Questions to Ask in Selecting an Evaluator." Answer these questions.

3. *Cultural competence.* In January 2010, distinguished evaluation author E. Jane Davidson (2005) hosted the American Evaluation Association President's Thought Leaders Forum, engaging in dialogue with evaluation professionals from around the world. Cultural competence emerged as an important concern. Davidson noted that she had reviewed a draft graduate student proposal to evaluate a smoking cessation program aimed at Pasifika communities in New Zealand where she lives.

> A mixed method design was duly trotted out. The student had spotted that there would be a language issue involved (many of our Pacific people in New Zealand are island-born and have English as a second language). The student "solved" this problem by writing into the budget a couple of $15/hour "Pacific Assistants."

What's wrong with this picture?

[In answering], focus in particular on the language, culture, and context issues; how the student addressed them; what was missing; and any options for improving the proposal even if the budget is quite low (Davidson, 2010a).

After constructing your own response, you may want to consider the responses of professional evaluators available online (Wehipeihana et al., 2010).

INTERLUDE, STEPS 1 AND 2. COMPLEX DYNAMIC SYSTEMS INTERCONNECTIONS

Assessing the Match Between the Program and Evaluator, the Interrelationship Between Steps 1 and 2

One perspective on the *Essentials of Utilization-Focused Evaluation* is captured by the checklist of sequential steps, Step 1, then Step 2. But the process is not nearly so linear and sequential. There are interconnections among the steps, feedback loops, and the complex dynamics that affect any emergent system. To reflect these real-world dynamics, I will periodically offer an interlude between "steps" to call attention to the importance of doing what I'm calling a "complex systems interconnections check." This is where you look at, reflect on, and consider the implications of the dynamic and interconnected relationship among the steps.

We've now discussed the first two steps of a utilization-focused evaluation:

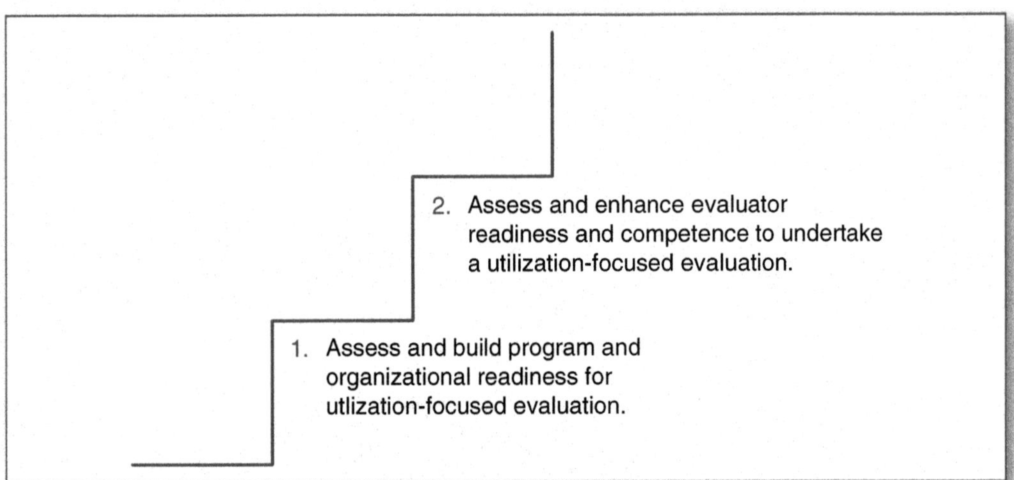

Details about what is involved in each step are provided in the summary *U-FE Checklist* in the concluding chapter. (See pages 406–408.)

These two steps typically occur simultaneously and together. Sometimes Step 2 precedes Step 1; that is, finding an appropriate evaluator is necessary before the organization can assess its readiness for evaluation. Whatever the sequence, at the end of these two processes, the point is to have a good match between the organization's evaluation needs and the evaluator's capacity to meet those needs. Both the program and the evaluator are on the same page, so to speak. Both understand what it means to undertake a utilization-focused evaluation. Both are committed to doing so. The program has the resources to do so and the evaluator has the competence to do so. Those are the outcomes that we're looking for at this stage.

Another caution: The U-FE steps don't just get completed and then you move on. Readiness is dynamic and layered as is capacity and competence. Each subsequent step in the U-FE process will involve another aspect of readiness and require more capacity and competence. So it's not a matter of checking these first two steps off a "to do" list, considering them done, and forgetting them. The issue is one of sufficiency. Is the program *sufficiently ready* to move into the process of actually engaging in the next steps? Is the evaluator *sufficiently ready* to move into facilitating the next steps in the utilization-focused process? In essence, has a basic foundation of understanding and commitment been established enough to proceed? This foundation is necessary but not sufficient. The foundation will be strengthened as the process unfolds.

This Interlude between chapters offers a Complex Dynamic Systems Graphic to portray the dynamic interconnection between Steps 1 and 2.

Complex Dynamic Systems Graphic for Steps 1 and 2

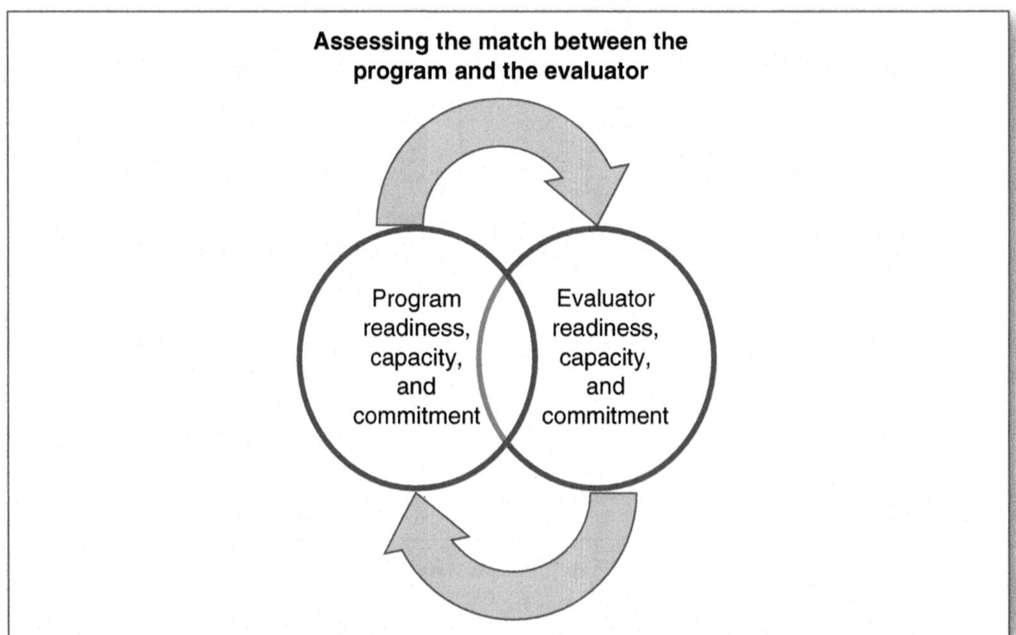

Examine interconnections between Steps 1 and 2.

- To what extent is there a good match between the organization's evaluation needs and the evaluator's capacity to meet those needs?
- To what extent does the program have the resources, capacity, and commitment to undertake a utilization-focused evaluation, and to what extent does the evaluator have the competence and commitment to facilitate the process?

3

Identify, Organize, and Engage Primary Intended Users

The Personal Factor

There are five key variables that are absolutely critical in evaluation use. They are, in order of importance: people, people, people, people, and people.

Halcolm's Persona Grata

Asking Users About Use

In 1976, as evaluation was just emerging as a distinct field of professional practice, I was directing an interdisciplinary doctoral program in evaluation methodology at the University of Minnesota. We decided to study evaluation use. How do decision makers who receive evaluation reports think about use? What do they do with the findings they receive? What factors affect whether an evaluation is used? What can be done to enhance use? What are barriers to use?

We selected 20 federal evaluations of major U.S. health programs. The sample included four mental health evaluations, two national assessments of laboratory proficiency, two evaluations of neighborhood health centers, two health services delivery systems, a health regulatory program, a federal loan forgiveness program for health professionals, two evaluations of specialized health facilities, and six training program evaluations. The types of evaluations ranged from a three-week program review carried out by a single internal evaluator to a 4-year evaluation that cost $1.5 million. Six of the cases were internal evaluations and 14 were conducted by external evaluators.

We identified and interviewed three key informants who had been involved with each evaluation: (1) the government's internal project officer (PO) for the study, (2) the person identified by the project officer as being either the decision maker for the program evaluated or the person most knowledgeable about the study's impact, and (3) the evaluator who had major responsibility for the study. We conducted 54 interviews. Most of the federal decision makers interviewed were senior managers, division heads, or bureau chiefs. Overall, these decision makers represented over 250 years of experience in the federal government; the evaluators collectively represented over 225 years of experience in conducting evaluation research.

In the interviews we asked about the purpose of the evaluation, how it was designed, and how the findings were presented. We had copies of the evaluation reports so we asked about reactions to particular findings and recommendations in the reports. After getting these details for each case, we asked the people we were interviewing what factors they thought had affected the way the evaluation was used. We asked respondents to comment on how, if at all, each of 11 factors extracted from the evaluation literature had affected use: methodological quality, methodological appropriateness, timeliness, lateness of report, positive or negative findings, surprise of findings, central or peripheral program objectives evaluated, presence or absence of related studies, political factors, decision maker/evaluator interactions, and resources available for the study. Finally, we asked respondents to "pick out the single factor you feel had the greatest effect on how this study was used."

From these in-depth interviews only two factors emerged as consistently important in explaining use: (1) political considerations, which we'll be discussing throughout this book, and (2) a factor we called the *personal factor*. This latter factor was unexpected, and its clear importance to our respondents had, we believed, substantial implications for the use of program evaluation. None of the other specific literature factors about which we asked questions emerged as important with any consistency. Moreover, when these specific factors were important in explaining the use or nonuse of a particular study, it was virtually always in the context of a larger set of circumstances and conditions related to either political considerations or the personal factor. That study (Patton, 1978; Patton et al., 1977) marked the beginning formulation of utilization-focused evaluation.

The Personal Factor

The personal factor is the presence of an identifiable individual or group of people who personally care about the evaluation and the findings it generates. Where such a person or group was present, evaluations were used; where the personal factor was absent, there was a correspondingly marked absence of evaluation impact. The personal factor represents the leadership, interest, enthusiasm, determination, commitment, assertiveness, and caring of specific, individual people. These are people who actively seek information to learn, make judgments, get better at what they do, and reduce decision uncertainties. They want to increase their ability to predict the outcomes of programmatic activity and thereby enhance their own discretion as decision makers, policymakers, consumers, program participants, funders, or whatever roles they play. These are the primary users of evaluation.

Data on the Importance of the Personal Factor

The personal factor emerged most dramatically in our interviews when we asked interviewees to identify the single factor that was most important in explaining the impact or lack of impact of that particular study.

- I would rank as the most important factor this division director's interest in evaluation. Not all managers are that motivated toward evaluation.
- The principal investigator [made the difference]. If I have to pick a single factor, I'll pick people any time.
- That it came from the Office of the Director—that's the most important factor. . . . It had his attention and he was interested in it.
- Probably the single factor that had the greatest effect on how it was used was the insistence of the person responsible for initiating the study that the director become familiar with its findings and arrive at judgment on it.
- [The most important factor was] the real involvement of the top decision makers in the conceptualization and design of the study, and their commitment to the study.

While these comments concern the importance of interested and committed individuals in studies that were actually used, studies that were not used stand out in that there was often a clear absence of the personal factor. One evaluator, who was not sure how his study was used, but suspected it had not been, remarked:

> I think that since the client wasn't terribly interested and the whole issue had shifted to other topics. . . . Nobody was interested.

Another highly experienced evaluator was particularly adamant and articulate about the one factor that is most important in whether an evaluation gets used:

> The most important factor is desire on the part of the managers, both the central federal managers and the site managers. I don't think there's [any doubt], you know, that evaluation should be responsive to their needs, and if they have a real desire to get on with whatever it is they're supposed to do, they'll apply it. And if the evaluations don't meet their needs, they won't. About as simple as you can get.

Our sample included another adamant articulation of this premise. An evaluation of a pilot program was undertaken at the instigation of the program administrator. He made a special effort to make sure that his question was answered: Were the pilot projects capable of being extended and generalized? He participated in designing the evaluation. He started out with a favorable view of the pilot, but the evaluation findings were, in fact, negative. The program was subsequently ended, with the evaluation carrying "considerable weight" the decision maker said. Why was this study used in such a dramatic way? The decision maker's answer was emphatic:

> Look, we designed the project with an evaluation component in it, so we were committed to use it and we did. It's not just the fact that evaluation was built in, but the fact that *we* built it in on purpose. The agency head and myself had broad responsibilities for this, wanted the evaluation study results and we expected to use them. Therefore, they were used. That's my point.

The evaluator independently corroborated the decision maker's explanation:

> The principal reason [for use] was that the decision maker was the guy who requested the evaluation and used its results. That's the most important reason it had an impact. . . . The guy who was asking the question was the guy who was going to make use of the answer.

Here, then, is a case in which a decision maker commissioned an evaluation knowing what information he needed; the evaluator was committed to answering the decision maker's questions; and the decision maker was committed to using the findings. The result was a high level of use in making a decision contrary to the director's initial personal hopes.

One highly placed and widely experienced administrator offered the following advice at the end of a four-hour interview:

> Win over the program people. Make sure you're hooked into the people who're going to make the decision in six months from the time you're doing the study, and make sure that they feel it's their study, that these are their ideas, and that it's focused on their values.

Though the specifics vary from case to case, the pattern is markedly clear: Where the personal factor emerges, where some individuals take direct, personal responsibility for assuring that high-priority questions are asked and the findings get to the right people, evaluations have an impact. Where the personal factor is absent, there is a marked absence of impact. Use is not simply determined by some configuration of abstract factors; it is determined in large part by real, live, involved human beings.

The Personal Factor

The personal factor is the presence of an identifiable individual or group of people who personally care about the evaluation and the findings it generates. Where such a person or group is present, evaluations are more likely to be used; where the personal factor is absent, there is a correspondingly lower probability of evaluation impact.

Research on use supports the influential insights of the Stanford Evaluation Consortium, one of the leading places of ferment and reform in evaluation's early days. Participants in the Consortium published a provocative set of 95 theses, following the precedent of Martin Luther. Among them was this gem:

"Nothing makes a larger difference in the use of evaluations than *the personal factor*—the interest of officials in learning from the evaluation and the desire of the evaluator to get attention for what he knows" (Cronbach & Associates, 1980, p. 6).

Supporting Research on the Personal Factor

Hofstetter and Alkin (2003) conducted a comprehensive review of research on evaluation use. They concluded that while many factors can influence use, the personal factor appeared to be the most important determinant of an evaluation's impact. Based on the evidence from studies of use, they offered the following recommendation:

> The evaluator could enhance use by engaging and involving intended users early in the evaluation, ensuring strong communications between the producers and users of evaluations, reporting evaluation findings effectively so users can understand and use them for their purposes, and maintaining credibility with the potential users. (p. 216)

Marvin Alkin, founder and former director of the Center for the Study of Evaluation at UCLA, and an evaluator with more than 40 years experience, emphasizes the personal factor in his book on *Evaluation Essentials: From A to Z* (2011):

> I focus more directly on those *individuals* within the system who have a *strong interest* in seeing the evaluation conducted and who might potentially have the power to use, or influence the use, of results. . . . I pay special attention to the information needs designated by these individuals. . . . It is impossible to attend to too vast a group of stakeholders. I want to focus on those who care and who will likely want to use, and be able to use, evaluation findings as a basis for considering potential program improvements. (p. 43; emphasis in the original)

For four decades, evaluation researchers have been studying how interactions with primary intended users affect actual use. Over that time the evaluation literature has generated substantial evidence that attention to the personal factor—involving key stakeholders and working with intended users—can increase use. (For a comprehensive review of the evidence, see Cousins and Shulha, 2006; Patton, 2008, Chapter 3).

"Don't know where she learned it, but she can find an evaluation user anywhere. Freddy you might as well come out now and get started on that plan of action."

Identifying and Working With Primary Intended Users

Many decisions must be made in any evaluation. The purpose of the evaluation must be determined. Concrete evaluative criteria for judging program success will usually have to be established. Methods will have to be selected and time lines agreed on. All of these are important issues in any evaluation. The question is: Who will decide these issues? The utilization-focused answer is: *primary intended users of the evaluation.*

Clearly and explicitly identifying people who can benefit from an evaluation is so important that evaluators have adopted a special term for potential evaluation users: *stakeholders*. Evaluation stakeholders are people who have a stake—a vested interest—in evaluation findings. For any evaluation there are multiple possible stakeholders: program funders, staff, administrators, and clients or program participants. Greene (2006) clusters stakeholders into four groups:

> (a) people who have decision authority over the program, including other policy makers, funders, and advisory boards; (b) people who have direct responsibility for the program, including program developers, administrators in the organization implementing the program, program managers, and direct service staff; (c) people who are the intended beneficiaries of the program, their families, and their communities; and (d) people disadvantaged by the program, as in lost funding opportunities (pp. 397–398).

Others with a direct, or even indirect, interest in program effectiveness may be considered stakeholders, including journalists and members of the general public, or, more specifically, taxpayers, in the case of public programs. Ordinary people of all kinds who are affected by programs and policies can be thought of as stakeholders. Stakeholders include anyone who makes decisions or desires information about a program. However, stakeholders typically have diverse and often competing interests. No evaluation can answer all potential questions equally well. This means that some process is necessary for narrowing the range of possible questions to focus the evaluation. In utilization-focused evaluation, this process begins by narrowing the list of potential stakeholders to a much shorter, more specific group of primary intended users. Their information needs, that is, their intended uses, focus the evaluation. They are the people the evaluator works with, negotiates with, and engages with throughout the evaluation to assure relevance, credibility, and use.

Primary Intended Users of an Evaluation

Primary intended users of an evaluation are those specific stakeholders selected to work with the evaluator throughout the evaluation to focus the evaluation, participate in making design and methods decisions, and interpret results to assure that the evaluation is useful, meaningful, relevant, and credible. Primary intended users represent key and diverse stakeholder constituencies and have responsibility for transmitting evaluation findings to those constituencies for use.

Intended Users at Different Levels: From Local to National and International Engagement

In local program settings it's fairly easy to imagine the personal factor at work. For example, in Minnesota I met with 15 people gathered to discuss evaluation of a county welfare-to-work program. The primary intended users were the county commissioner who chaired the human services committee and another commissioner on the committee; state legislators from the county who served on the House and Senate welfare committees; the county administrator for human services and his deputy; an associate director from the state welfare office; two citizen advisory board representatives, one of whom had once been on welfare; the director of a welfare rights advocacy organization; the director of a local employment training program; a university public policy scholar; and the internal county evaluator. These people knew each other and, although they came with varying political perspectives and values, they could be counted on to behave in a congenial manner. The network and influence of these 15 people extended to a broad range of stakeholder constituencies.

But does the personal factor work in larger, more complex settings like the federal government, international agencies, and national organizations? Can targeting and working with key stakeholders enhance use in these broader contexts? Let's look at the evidence.

Wargo (1995), in a classic study, analyzed three unusually successful federal evaluations in a search for "characteristics of successful program evaluations." He found that active involvement of key stakeholders was critical at every stage: during planning, while conducting the evaluation, and in dissemination of findings (p. 77).

In 1995 the U.S. General Accounting Office (since renamed the Government Accountability Office) studied the flow of evaluative information to Congress (GAO, 1995) by following up on three major federal programs: the Comprehensive Child Development Program, the Community Health Centers program, and the Chapter 1 Elementary and Secondary Education Act aimed at providing compensatory education services to low-income students. Analysts concluded that underutilization of evaluative information was a direct function of poor communications between intended users (members of the Senate Committee on Labor and Human Resources) and responsible staff in the three programs. They observed that communication between the Committee and key agency staff was limited to one-way communications (from the Committee to the agency or the reverse) rather than joint discussion. The result was little opportunity to build a shared understanding about the Committee's needs and how to meet them (p. 40). The GAO report recommended "increased communication with agency program and evaluation staff to help ensure that information needs are understood and that requests and reports are suitably framed and are adapted as needs evolve" (GAO, p. 41).

Patrick Grasso has been a federal-level and international agency evaluator with extensive experience dealing with large-scale program contexts at the GAO and The World Bank. He has written about the importance of moving from vague and general audiences to "priority" and "key" evaluation users. He has observed that, even in broad evaluations with multiple potential audiences, evaluation "efforts can be made more successful through up-front consultations with prospective users of the evaluation. Where possible, it is helpful to solicit from the identified potential users indications of what information they need and when they need to have it to meet any pending decision points." But how is this done? He tells of the evaluation of a World Bank forestry policy that began with a "kick-off workshop for interested parties to define the appropriate evaluation questions for the study and frequent communications with this group throughout the evaluation helped to ensure that it would meet the needs of these often-competing interests." He concluded that an important benefit was that "the final report was accepted by virtually all the parties involved in this contentious area of Bank development work" (all quotes from Grasso, 2003, p. 510).

George Grob (2003), another highly experienced evaluator at the federal level, has laid out how to get evaluations used at that level by actively engaging "gate-keepers" and "thought leaders" on the program or policy of interest. *Thought leaders* form a "community of experts" on a topic. Grob advises:

> Once you start engaging the thought leaders in a field of interest to you, listen to them. They know what they are talking about. Answer their questions. Make practical recommendations. Tell them something they don't already know. Treat them with respect. (p. 503)

In essence, attending to the personal factor is a smart and effective utilization-focused strategy regardless of the context—local, national, or international.

Evaluation Use Exemplars

Another place to learn what works in large, complex contexts is to examine evaluation exemplars. Each year the Awards Committee of the American Evaluation Association gives an Outstanding Evaluation Award. In 1998 the outstanding evaluation was the Council for School Performance's "School and System Performance Reports" for the state of Georgia. The reports and reporting process garnered high accolades for their utility. Obviously, schools have a multitude of stakeholders and a statewide education system magnifies the number and diversity of vested interests and competing perspectives. There are lots of potential "audiences." Were there any primary intended users actually involved in the evaluation's design and use? In an interview for the *American Journal of Evaluation*, Gary Henry described how the evaluation unfolded.

> We knew that it would be important to engage superintendents, school board members, teachers, and principals. Our work was overseen by six Council members who were appointed by the Governor, Lieutenant Governor, the Speaker of the Georgia House of representatives and an ex-officio member, the State Superintendent of Schools. Members of the Council were emphatic about extending stakeholder status to members of the community in a highly inclusive way—including parents and others in the community. It took almost a year working with these groups to create the architecture of the accountability system. . . . Once we all got on the same page, there was a great deal of creativity and excitement. The process focused on

> identifying what indicators we would use. We met in four separate groups—principals, superintendents, teachers, and community members—to reduce the influence of pre-existing power relationships on the deliberations. At three points during the process and twice after the system was being implemented we brought all four groups together. Turnout at the meetings was very high. (Henry quoted in Fitzpatrick, 2000, p. 109)

Another exemplar and the 2002 Outstanding Evaluation Award recipient was the evaluation of the Colorado Healthy Communities Initiative. This was an 8-year study that involved community-based health promotion projects in 29 communities across the state. Ross Connor (2005), former president of the American Evaluation Association and overall program evaluator, used what he called a "collaborative, community-based approach" that "involved a lot of different stakeholders" to design the evaluation and interpret findings. The evaluation brought together key stakeholders from different communities at various times to prioritize evaluation questions—people called the "primary question askers." Key stakeholders also participated in designing instruments (the evaluation used a variety of methods), overseeing implementation, and interpreting findings. Connor spent a lot of time in communities, and community people spent a lot of time working collaboratively on the evaluation. With so many people involved over a number of years, managing the stakeholder involvement process was a major activity of the evaluation—and that included managing inevitable conflicts. Lest we give the impression that involving primary intended users in evaluation is always a love-fest, consider this incident in the Colorado evaluation. In the process of involving community people in designing a survey, Connor reports:

> [T]he discussion got so heated that I actually ended up having the sheriff come to the parking lot. . . . There was a religious right segment of the community that was invited to participate. They attended, but they did not come to participate. They came to collect information to send to their attorney, they said, to sue these people because they were spending blood money—money that came from abortionists. (Quoted in Christie, 2005, p. 374)

The situation got resolved, but that group dropped out of the process. And this makes an important point about identifying primary intended users. Not everyone is interested in data for decision making. Not everyone is an information user. Not everyone will buy into evaluation. Some may participate for ulterior motives. Later in this chapter we'll discuss how to locate and involve those who make good primary intended users.

Jody Fitzpatrick (2004) analyzed patterns in evaluations chosen as exemplary by the Awards Committee of AEA and subsequently featured in the *American Journal of Evaluation.* She examined case studies of eight exemplary evaluations and found that, regardless of the evaluation model, methods, or theories guiding the evaluation, "stakeholder involvement is a central component in these exemplary evaluators' practice" (p. 552).

Evaluation's Premier Lesson

The importance of the personal factor in explaining and predicting evaluation use leads directly to the emphasis in utilization-focused evaluation on working with intended users to specify priority intended uses. (Specifying intended uses is Step 5.) The personal factor directs us to attend to specific people who understand, value, and care about evaluation, and further directs us to attend to their interests to assure the evaluation's relevance. This is the primary lesson the profession has learned about enhancing use. It is wisdom now widely acknowledged by practicing evaluators, as evidenced by research on evaluators' beliefs and practices.

Preskill and Caracelli (1997) conducted a survey of members of the American Evaluation Association Topical Interest Group on Use. They found that 85% rated as extremely or greatly important "identifying and prioritizing intended users of the evaluation" (p. 216). The only item eliciting higher agreement (90%) was the importance of "planning for use at the beginning of the evaluation." Preskill and Caracelli also found that 80% of survey respondents agreed that *evaluators should take responsibility for involving stakeholders in the evaluation processes.* Fleischer (2007) asked the same question on a replication survey of AEA members in 2006 and found that *98% agreed with this assertion.* In rating the importance of eight different evaluation approaches, "user-focused" evaluation was rated highest. Primary intended user involvement in evaluations has become accepted practice.

Evaluators' Responsibility for Intended Use by Intended Users

In a 2006 online survey of members of the American Evaluation Association, 77% of 1,047 respondents agreed or strongly agreed with the following statement:

Evaluators should take responsibility for:
Being accountable to intended users of the evaluation for intended uses of the evaluation.

SOURCE: Fleischer, 2007.

UCLA evaluation scholar Christina Christie (2003) examined the "practice-theory relationship in evaluation" by conducting research on the actual practices of prominent and influential evaluation theorists. She found:

> Regardless of the extent to which theorists discuss stakeholder involvement in their writing, results from this study show that all theorists involve stakeholders in the evaluation process. . . . This revelation is interesting, because not all theorists have traditionally been proponents of

> stakeholder involvement. . . . I offer as a plausible explanation of this finding that, in practice, the trend has turned toward increased stakeholder involvement, even across a broad theoretical spectrum. (Christie, 2003, p. 30)

Attending to the personal factor also applies cross-culturally and internationally. Long-time New Zealand evaluator Bob Williams (2003) has conducted his own research on what he elegantly calls "getting the stuff used," uncovered the importance of "the personal effect," and has related it to how things work in New Zealand.

> In the interviews I conducted . . . most people stressed the importance of personal relationships within and between government agencies. There are close and often personal relationships between ministers, policy advisors, politicians, programme providers, and clients of programmes. . . . Things happen here in New Zealand because of who knows whom and their particular reputations. Process matters—a lot. Evaluations and evaluation processes that sustain or improve these relationships are inevitably more welcome than those that undermine them. (pp. 198–199)

Given widespread agreement about the personal factor in evaluation use, let's now examine some of the practical implications of this finding.

Practical Implications of the Personal Factor: Selecting and Working With Primary Intended Users

Here are 10 tips for selecting and engaging primary intended users.

1. *Find and involve the right people, those with both interest and influence.*

It can be helpful to conduct a stakeholder analysis to distinguish different degrees of potential involvement for different stakeholders based on personal factor considerations: their interest, influence, importance, availability, connections, and capacity for contributing to the evaluation and its use. For example, it can be helpful to sort stakeholders by degree of interest and amount of power. Those with high interest and considerable power can be excellent candidates to become primary intended users. Those with high power but low interest may become obstacles to use and will need to be cultivated. Those with high interest but relatively little power may provide connections to those with power. Those with low interest and little power, for example, the program's intended beneficiaries, are often in this category, may require extra attention and support to generate interest and enhance their capacity to participate in the evaluation. Exhibit 3.1 presents the "Power Versus Interest" grid (Eden & Ackermann, 1998, p. 122).

EXHIBIT 3.1

Stakeholder Analysis: Power Versus Interest Grid

	Low-power stakeholders	*High-power stakeholders*
High-interest stakeholders	Support and enhance their capacity to be involved, especially when they may be affected by findings, as in the case of program participants. Their involvement increases the diversity of the evaluation.	High potential as primary intended users. These are often key "players" who are in a prime position to affect use, including using it themselves as well as drawing the attention of others.
Low-interest stakeholders	Inform them about the evaluation and its findings. Controversy can quickly turn this amorphous "crowd" of general public stakeholders into a very interested mob.	Need to cultivate their interest and be alert in case they pose barriers to use through their disinterest. They are "context setters" (Eden & Ackermann, 1998, p. 122).

Politically and realistically, an evaluator does not have complete control over selection of primary intended users. Those who fund or commission an evaluation are typically self-selected primary intended users, though it is important to check out and assess their genuine interest. They may just be doing the job of getting the evaluation started and will prefer not to be personally involved, though they may expect to be consulted on who will be involved. Indeed, it is wise to strategize with them and help them understand why primary intended users need to be identified and involved to enhance use. They may want to play the role of "gatekeepers," controlling access to who the evaluator involves (Alkin, 2011, section D). Make them allies and, in the end, make it clear that the evaluation's credibility and use will depend in part on a credible and transparent approach to identifying and involving primary intended users.

2. *Recruit primary intended users who represent important stakeholder constituencies.*

The evaluator will work with the primary intended users to design a credible, relevant, rigorous, practical, and useful evaluation. All of these criteria, but especially credibility, are enhanced by involving people who are well positioned by temperament and contacts to represent key stakeholder constituencies. This is where political sophistication and savvy come into play as expressed by the evaluation standard on *attention to stakeholders*:

> Evaluations should devote attention to the full range of individuals and groups invested in the program and affected by its evaluation. (Joint Committee on Standards, 2010, U2)

While stakeholders' points of view may vary on any number of issues, what primary intended users should share is a genuine interest in using evaluation, an interest manifest in a willingness to take the time and effort to work through diverse information needs and interests. Their role as primary intended users will include representing the larger stakeholder constituency of which they are a member, which can involve checking out priorities and preferred options with important and influential people in those constituencies.

3. *Find tipping point connectors.*

Formal position and authority are only partial guides in identifying primary intended users. Evaluators must find strategically located people who are enthusiastic, committed, competent, interested, and connected—*tipping point connectors,* people who are looked to by others for information. People who are connectors are especially influential in drawing attention to evaluation findings. *Connectors* are widely networked and know who is influential. Best-selling author Malcolm Gladwell (2002) in *The Tipping Point: How Little Things Can Make a Big Difference* called the influence of connectors the *Law of the Few.* When connectors are the primary intended users, they get the evaluation findings out to a broad range of people. They are hubs connected to spokes, and they make the wheels of change turn.

Our studies of use suggest that sometimes more may be accomplished by working with a lower-level person displaying these characteristics than by working with a passive, disinterested person in a higher position. However, the lower-level person needs to be able to connect to, have credibility with, and be able to influence higher-level people. Evaluation use is clearly facilitated by having genuine support from the program and organizational leadership, but those people are not always the best for detailed, hands-on engagement along the way. Reaching them with findings remains critical to use.

4. *Facilitate high-quality interactions among and with primary intended users.*

Quality, quantity, and timing of interactions with intended users are all important—but quality is most important. A large amount of interaction between evaluators and users with little substance may backfire and actually reduce stakeholder interest. Evaluators must be strategic and sensitive in asking for time and involvement from busy people, and be sure they're interacting with the right people around relevant issues. Increased contact by itself is likely to accomplish little. Nor will interaction with the wrong persons (i.e., people who are not oriented toward use) help much. It is the nature and quality of interactions between evaluators and decision makers that is at issue. My own experience suggests that where the right people are involved, the amount of direct contact can sometimes be reduced because the interactions that do occur are of such high quality.

5. *Nurture interest and develop capacity to engage in evaluation.*

Evaluators will typically have to work to build and sustain interest in evaluation use. Identifying intended users is part selection, part nurturance, and part capacity-building. Potential users with low opinions of or little interest in evaluation may have had bad prior experiences or just not have given much thought to the benefits of evaluation. In Step 1, assess and build program and organizational readiness, I presented ways of cultivating interest in evaluation and building commitment to use. Even people initially inclined to value evaluation will still often need support and encouragement to become effective information users. The exercises in Menu 1.1 (Step 1, pp. 20–21) are all aimed at nurturing interest and developing capacity to engage in evaluation.

Some primary intended users will come to the evaluation with backgrounds and experiences that make them ready to fully engage. Others will need help, which means training and support to understand evaluation options, make methods choices, and interpret findings. This is usually a learn-by-doing experience in which the evaluator is both facilitating the evaluation decision process while also teaching primary intended users about evaluation. This teaching is often subtle and implicit, or may be overt and formal. However it is done, and to whatever extent it is done, involving primary intended users typically requires some attention to increasing their capacity to be effective evaluation users. There are things to learn. That learning is actually one of the benefits that those involved get from their involvement. I treat every session with intended users as both an engagement opportunity to get work done on the evaluation and as a capacity-building opportunity to increase user competence. This increased competence serves both the immediate evaluation being worked on as well as future evaluations in which they may become involved.

Use as a Two-Way Interaction

Far from being a one-way process of knowledge flow, . . . evaluation utilization needs to be understood as a complex, dynamic transaction. The stakeholders or users cannot be construed as passive receptacles of information. Evaluation utilization is an active process in terms of which meaning is shaped by both the evaluator and those involved in evaluation.

Kate McKegg (2003, p. 222),
New Zealand evaluator

6. *Develop facilitation and training skills.*

Evaluators need skills in building relationships, facilitating groups, managing conflict, walking political tight-ropes, and effective interpersonal communications to capitalize on the importance of the personal factor. Technical skills and social science knowledge aren't sufficient to get evaluations used. People skills are critical. Assessing the evaluator's readiness for undertaking a utilization-focused evaluation (Step 2) involves both self-assessment and assessment by those hiring the evaluator and commissioning the evaluation. Ideals of rational decision making in modern organizations notwithstanding, personal and political dynamics affect what really happens. Evaluators without the savvy and skills to deal with people and politics will find their work largely ignored or, worse yet, used inappropriately. Moreover, people skills aren't static. Each new situation and group of people provides new challenges. I've been at this more than 40 years and I'm still learning.

7. *Demonstrate cultural competence and sensitivity.*

In Step 2, I discussed cultural sensitivity and competence as an important characteristic of evaluator readiness. Involvement of stakeholders and primary intended users has to be adapted to cultural and contextual factors. For example, as reported earlier, Clayson, Castaneda, Sanchez, and Brindis (2002) examined negotiations between evaluation stakeholders in Latino communities and found that in designing and conducting the evaluation they had to play a variety of roles including interpreters, translators, mediators, and storytellers. Relationships among people in evaluation situations are affected by larger societal issues including the challenges of involving people with disabilities, racism, sexism, and other forms of prejudice that engender conflict and misunderstandings (Hopson, 1999, 2000; House, 1999; Kirkhart, 2005). "Inclusive evaluation" (Mertens, 2005) means making a special effort to reach out to, recruit, and include diverse people and perspectives among primary intended users, and in so doing being especially attentive to ways in which social injustices make such inclusion difficult and atypical, which is all the more reason to do it. Nor is there some recipe for doing cultural sensitivity and inclusion. The norms for and challenges to stakeholder involvement and evaluation practice vary greatly across ethnic groups, cultures, and geographies. E. Jane Davidson (2010b) has offered an example from New Zealand of how cultural norms can affect an evaluator's credibility beyond just having people skills and displaying sensitivity:

> Here in Aotearoa New Zealand, we've had some very interesting conversations about the relationships among credibility, objectivity, and connectedness. Particularly in Maori communities, an evaluator has near-zero credibility unless they can demonstrate some connection with the community. I'm not talking about interpersonal skills and being able to "connect" with people here; I am talking about knowing, having worked with, or being related to someone who has some connection with the community.

> Let me try and explain why. . . . When engaging with a community or a service/program provider, finding that connection creates trust—not only do we know someone who knows you (and has positive things to say), but we now know you have something serious to lose if you botch this job, so we feel you are more motivated to do it well than someone who has no connections that could be broken/damaged.

8. *Strategize about appropriate involvement to enhance use—and stay focused on use.*

A particular evaluation may have multiple levels of stakeholders and therefore need multiple levels of stakeholder involvement. For example, funders, chief executives, and senior officials may constitute the primary users for overall effectiveness results while lower-level staff and participant stakeholder groups may be involved in using implementation and monitoring data for program improvement. Exhibit 3.2 provides an example of such a multiple-level structure for different levels of stakeholder involvement in support of different kinds of evaluation use.

In thinking and acting strategically, stay focused on use. Don't get distracted by personality conflicts, power plays, side issues, petty grievances, personal agendas, and organizational politics. Take these things in stride, deal with them as needed, but keep your eye on the prize: evaluation use. Stay strategically focused on use.

9. *Work with a manageable number of primary intended users.*

The number may vary from one prime user to a fairly large group representing several constituencies: for example, a task force of program staff, clients, funders, administrators, board members, community representatives, and officials or policymakers. Cousins, Donohue, and Bloom (1996) surveyed evaluators and found that they reported six stakeholders as the median number typically involved in a project. Different types and degrees of involvement may vary for various stakeholder groups (as Exhibit 3.2 illustrates), but the core group that is most heavily involved in designing the evaluation, setting priorities, negotiating trade-offs, and interpreting findings needs to be a manageable number, which usually means fewer than 15, and is often closer to 6 to 10, enough for diversity of perspectives but still manageable.

10. *Anticipate turnover of intended users.*

One implication of the personal factor concerns the problem of turnover. An experienced, utilization-focused evaluator recently wrote me:

> I've very nearly finished all the revisions to the final reports for a 4-year national evaluation and none of the people I'm now working with were involved in the evaluation design. During the project, there were SEVEN different people in the position of signing-off on critical stages of the evaluation. This is quite a typical experience and has obvious effects on utilization. How can evaluators deal with the more usual turnover issue, apart from trying to do more rapid cycles of planning, implementing and reporting evaluations before the next round of musical chairs?

EXHIBIT 3.2

A Multi-Level Stakeholder Structure and Process

The Saint Paul Foundation formed a Donor Review Board of several philanthropic foundations in Minnesota to fund a project "Supporting Diversity in Schools" (SDS). The project established local school-community partnerships with communities of color: African Americans, Hispanics, Native Americans, and Southeast Asians. The evaluation had three layers based on different levels of stakeholder involvement and responsibility.

Stakeholder group	*Evaluation focus*	*Nature of involvement*
1. *Donor Review Board:* executives and program officers from contributing foundations, and the school superintendent	Overall program effectiveness; policy implications; sustainability	Twice-a-year meetings to review the design and interim evaluation results; final report directed to this group
2. *District-Level Evaluation Group:* representatives from participating schools, social service agencies, community organizations, and project staff	Implementation monitoring in early years; district level outcomes in later years	An initial full-day retreat with 40 people from diverse groups; annual retreat sessions to update, refocus, and interpret interim findings.
3. *Partnership-Level Evaluation Teams:* each school formed a partnership of teachers, parents, community members, staff liaisons, and an evaluator.	Documenting activities and outcomes at the local partnership level; findings for improvement	Develop annual partnership evaluation plan; generate data for major activities; quarterly review of progress to use

Turnover among primary intended users can be the Achilles' heel of utilization-focused evaluation unless evaluators watch for, anticipate, and plan for turnover. The longer the time frame for the evaluation, the more important it is to engage with multiple intended users, build in some overlap, and, when turnover happens, bring the new people up to speed quickly. This will sometimes involve making some later stage design changes, if possible, to get their buy-in and increase their sense of ownership of the evaluation.

Exhibit 3.3 summarizes these 10 tips for selecting and working with primary intended users.

EXHIBIT 3.3

10 Tips for Selecting and Working With Primary Intended Users

1. Find and involve the right people, those with both interest and influence.
2. Recruit primary intended users who represent important stakeholder constituencies.
3. Find tipping point connectors.
4. Facilitate high-quality interactions among and with primary intended users.
5. Nurture users' interest and develop their capacity to engage in evaluation.
6. Develop facilitation and training skills.
7. Demonstrate cultural competence and sensitivity.
8. Strategize about appropriate involvement to enhance use—and stay focused on use.
9. Work with a manageable number of primary intended users.
10. Anticipate turnover of intended users.

Temptations Away From Engaging Primary Intended Users

To appreciate some of the subtleties of the admonition to focus on intended use by intended users, let's consider a few of the temptations evaluators face that lure them away from identifying and working with primary intended users.

First, and most common, evaluators are tempted to make themselves the major decision makers for the evaluation. This can happen by default (no one else is willing to do it), by intimidation (clearly, the evaluator is the expert), or simply by failing to think about or seek primary users (Why make life difficult?). The tip-off that evaluators have become the primary intended users (either by intention or default) is that the evaluators are answering their own questions according to their own interests, needs, and priorities. Others may have occasional input here and there, but what emerges is an evaluation by the evaluators, for the evaluators, and of the evaluators. Such studies are seldom of use to other stakeholders, whose reactions are likely to be, "Great study. Really well done. Shows lots of work, but, honestly, it doesn't tell us anything *we* want to know."

A less innocent version of this scenario occurs when academics pursue their basic research agendas under the guise of evaluation research. The tip-off here is that the evaluators insist on designing the study in such a way as to test some theory they think is particularly important, whether or not people involved in the program see any relevance to such a test.

A second temptation is to fall prey to an *audience-oriented* approach. Early in evaluation's history there was a lot of advice about targeting audiences. But audiences are amorphous, largely anonymous entities. Audience connotes passive reception rather than the active engagement of specific users. If specific individuals are not identified from these audiences and organized in a manner that permits meaningful involvement in the evaluation process, then, by default, the evaluator becomes the real decision maker and stakeholder ownership suffers, with a corresponding threat to utility.

The 1994 revision of the Joint Committee Standards for Evaluation moved to language about "intended users" in place of earlier references to "audiences." In the revised version, the "Utility Standards are intended to ensure that an evaluation will serve the information needs of *intended users,*" as opposed to "given audiences" in the original 1981 version. Such changes in language are far from trivial. They indicate how the knowledge base of the profession has evolved. The language we use shapes how we think. The nuances and connotations reflected in these language changes are fundamental to the philosophy of utilization-focused evaluation.

A third diversion from intended users occurs when evaluators target organizations rather than specific individuals. Targeting an organization appears to be more specific than targeting general audiences, but really isn't. "The evaluation is for the 'Feds.'" Or: "The evaluation is for funders." Such statements ignore the personal factor. Organizations and amorphous groups are an impersonal collection of hierarchical positions. Organizations do not consume information; people do—individual, idiosyncratic, caring, uncertain, searching people. To target evaluations at organizations is to target them at nobody in particular—and, in effect, not to really target them at all. To ignore the personal factor is to diminish utilization potential from the outset.

A fourth diversion away from intended users is to focus on decisions instead of on decision makers. The decision-focused approach makes the first step in an evaluation identification of the decision for which information is required. The question of who will make the decision remains implicit. But people make decisions and, it turns out, most "decisions" accrete gradually and incrementally over time rather than get made at some concrete, decisive moment (Weiss, 1977, 1980). It can be helpful, even crucial, to orient evaluations toward future decisions, but identification of such decisions, and the implications of those decisions for the evaluation, are best made in conjunction with intended users who come together to decide what data will be needed for what purposes, including, but not limited to, decisions. For example, an evaluation may lead to a judgment of merit or worth, or new understandings about strengths and weaknesses, without being used directly and immediately to make a decision. This important nuance means that *utilization-focused evaluation is always user-oriented but only sometimes decision-oriented.*

A fifth temptation is to assume that the funders of the evaluation are the primary intended users, that is, those who pay the fiddler call the tune. In some cases this is accurate. Funders are hopefully among those most interested in using evaluation. But there may be additional important users. Moreover, evaluations are funded for reasons other than their perceived utility, for example, wanting to give the appearance of supporting evaluation, because legislation or licensing requires evaluation, or because someone thought it had to be written into the budget. Those who control evaluation purse strings may not have any specific evaluation questions. Often, they simply believe that evaluation is a good thing that keeps people on their toes. They do not care about the content of a specific evaluation, they only care that evaluation—any evaluation—takes place. They mandate the process but not the substance. Under such conditions (which are not unusual) there is considerable opportunity for identifying and working with additional interested stakeholders to formulate relevant evaluation questions and a correspondingly appropriate design.

A sixth temptation is to put off attending to and planning for use from the beginning. It's tempting to wait until findings are in to worry about use. But as experienced evaluator Bob Williams (2003) warns: "Evaluation use is not something to think about at the end of an evaluation. The initial conditions, the negotiations, the development of the evaluation design, the implementation of the reporting phases all influence the use of an evaluation" (p. 212).

A seventh temptation is to convince oneself that it is unseemly to enter the fray and thereby run the risks that come with being engaged. I've heard academic evaluators insist that their responsibility is to assure data quality and design rigor in the belief that the scientific validity of the findings will carry the day. The evidence suggests this seldom happens. An academic stance that justifies the evaluator standing above the messy fray of people and politics is more likely to yield scholarly publications than improvements in programs. Fostering use requires becoming engaged in building relationships and sorting through the politics that enmesh any program. In so doing, the evaluator runs the risks of getting entangled in changing power dynamics, having the rug pulled out by the departure of a key intended user, having relationships go bad, and/or being accused of bias. These are certainly risks, but the only way I know to avoid them altogether is to stand aloof. That may provide safety but at the high cost of relevance and utility.

An eighth temptation is to allow oneself to be co-opted by acquiescing to powerful stakeholders who ask for or demand subtle or significant changes in the evaluation after it is underway (this can happen up front during design but it's easier to deal with then), or who become gradually more resistant as time goes by as it becomes apparent that they will not be able to control findings. Particularly powerful stakeholders will sometimes act in ways that undermine the involvement of less powerful stakeholders. This is a particular danger for less experienced evaluators or those who lack the skill to deal with powerful stakeholders. Being politically attentive and astute comes with the territory for utilization-focused evaluators.

A ninth temptation is letting concerns about methodological rigor become more important than facilitating use. Methodological rigor is not an end in itself; it is a means to establish credibility and support use. Methods decisions inevitably involve trade-offs, often because of limited resources and tight time lines, that affect use. Users need to be involved in negotiating methodological trade-offs. These are not purely technical issues. Moreover, user involvement and responsiveness should not mean a sacrifice of technical quality. Later steps will discuss in detail the utilization-focused approach to ensuring technical quality. A beginning point is to recognize that standards of technical quality vary for different users and varying situations. The issue is not meeting some absolute research standard of technical quality but, rather, making sure that methods and measures are *appropriate* to the validity and credibility needs of a particular evaluation purpose and specific intended users.

Jennifer Greene (1990) examined in depth the debate about technical quality versus user responsiveness. She found general agreement that both are important but disagreement about the relative priority of each. She concluded that the debate is really about how much to recognize and deal with evaluation's political inherency:

> Evaluators should recognize that tension and conflict in evaluation practice are virtually inevitable, that the demands imposed by most if not all definitions of responsiveness and technical quality (not to mention feasibility and propriety) will characteristically reflect the competing politics and values of the setting. (p. 273)

She then recommended that evaluators "explicate the politics and values" that undergird decisions about purpose, audience, design, and methods. Her recommendation is consistent with utilization-focused evaluation.

The tenth and final temptation is identifying primary intended users but not involving them meaningfully in evaluation decision making. We identify intended users to involve them in design decision, establishing priorities, negotiating trade-offs, and interpreting data, not as an end in itself. Don't bother identifying them if you're not going to engage them. The remaining U-FE steps in this book all involve engaging with primary intended users to enhance use.

Exhibit 3.4 summarizes these 10 use-deadly temptations that divert evaluators from clearly specifying and working with intended users.

Throughout all the steps in this book, we'll be guided by attention to the essence of utilization-focused evaluation: *focusing to achieve intended uses by specific intended users.* Focus and specificity are ways of coming to grip with the fact that no evaluation can serve all potential stakeholders' interests equally well. As Spanish baroque philosopher Baltasar Gracian observed in 1647 in *The Art of Worldly Wisdom:*

> It is a great misfortune to be of use to nobody;
> scarcely less to be of use to everybody.

Think about it. There's a lot there, philosophically and pragmatically.

EXHIBIT 3.4

Temptations Away From Being User-Focused: Use-Deadly Sins

Temptation	*Why and how to avoid temptation*
1. Evaluators make themselves the primary decision makers and, therefore, the primary users.	The evaluator has a stake in the evaluation, but that stake is to generate credible and relevant findings, and facilitate use. The evaluator is not the user.
2. Identifying general audiences as targets for findings instead of specific people who are identifiably users.	Audiences connote passivity. Users are active and engaged. Findings will likely be disseminated to larger audiences, but the priority focus is on use by specific intended users.
3. Targeting organizations as users (e.g., "the Feds") instead of specific persons.	People use information, not organizations. An organization can't come to the table and negotiate a design, only people can. Users will typically represent an organization or constituency, and being a credible representative is a criterion in selection. But it comes down to having specific people to work with throughout the evaluation process.
4. Focusing on decisions instead of decision makers.	Informing major decisions can be one important use of evaluation, but there are other uses as well, like deepening understanding of the program, making incremental improvements, and learning lessons. When there are decisions, people make decisions. Stay focused on them.
5. Assuming the evaluation's funder is automatically the primary stakeholder.	Those who fund and commission evaluations are important stakeholders, but may—or may not—be the primary intended users. Their role and stake in the evaluation is a question not a given.
6. Waiting until the findings are in to identify intended users and intended uses.	The groundwork for use gets laid at the beginning of an evaluation. That's when priorities get established and relevance is determined.
7. Taking a stance of staying above the fray of people and politics.	Staying above the fray risks irrelevance and makes the evaluator the decision maker (see the first temptation above) instead of the primary intended users. Evaluation is action-oriented and action is in the fray.

(Continued)

(Continued)

Temptation	*Why and how to avoid temptation*
8. Being co-opted by powerful stakeholders.	Knowledge is power. Evaluation generates knowledge. Thus, evaluation is inherently political. The challenge is being skilled in dealing with inevitable political dynamics rather than avoiding them.
9. Letting concerns about methodological rigor become more important than facilitating use.	Methodological rigor is not an end in itself; it is a means to establish credibility and support use. Methods decisions inevitably involve trade-offs, often because of limited resources and tight time lines, that affect use. Users need to be involved in negotiating methodological trade-offs. These are not purely technical issues.
10. Identifying primary intended users but not involving them meaningfully in evaluation decision making.	We identify intended users to involve them in design decisions, establishing priorities, negotiating trade-offs, and interpreting data, not as an end in itself. Don't bother identifying them if you're not going to engage them.

PRACTICE EXERCISES

1. Find a published evaluation. Does the report identify the primary intended users? If so, can you identify their degree of participation in the evaluation? If intended users are not identified, what can you infer about who determined the focus and methods of the evaluation?
2. Conduct a stakeholder analysis for a program or policy issue. Identify any well-known program, or a program with which you are personally familiar. List the various stakeholder groups in a one column and next to each stakeholder group, identify as best you can what you think the priority evaluation issues would be given their "stake" in the program.
3. Interview a program director in your area about his or her views about and uses of evaluation. Conduct your own utilization study of a particular agency or a specific evaluation that has been done. Who were the primary intended users? What factors affected use?

INTERLUDE, STEPS 1, 2, AND 3. COMPLEX DYNAMIC SYSTEMS INTERCONNECTIONS

Assessing the Readiness of Primary Intended Users to Engage

Step 3 has emphasized that, having established that the program and evaluation are ready (Steps 1 and 2), utilization-focused evaluation moves into high gear by identifying, organizing, and engaging primary intended evaluation users. All subsequent steps involve interacting with these primary users throughout the evaluation to nurture and sustain the commitment to use.

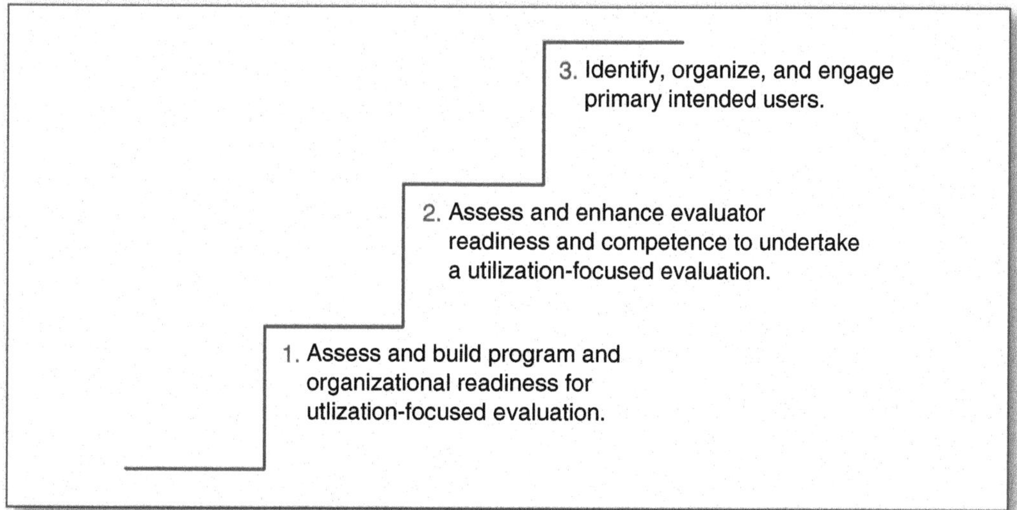

Details about what is involved in each step are provided in the summary *U-FE Checklist* in the concluding chapter. (See pages 406–409.)

These steps typically overlap considerably. Sometimes Step 3 precedes Steps 1 and 2; that is, the process begins by identifying primary intended users and working with them to do the readiness assessments. Thus, Complex Dynamic System Graphic 1-2-3 reminds us that these steps are not simply linear and sequential. Even if Steps 1 and 2 are done in order, during those steps, while assessing organization and evaluator readiness, the third step of identifying primary intended users is already being anticipated. Indeed, those first two steps aimed at laying the groundwork and getting ready, if well done, will generate a natural and rapid flow into the third step. As primary intended users are identified, the evaluator assesses their readiness to engage in making evaluation decisions and decides what, if any, capacity-building exercises will need to be offered.

As just noted, sometimes Step 3 comes first. I was recently involved in consulting on an evaluation in which the first step was identifying the primary intended users and engaging them in identifying what kind of evaluator they needed. I then helped them with the process of interviewing potential evaluators and selecting the evaluator they would work with. In this case, Step 3 came first (identifying and engaging intended users), then Step 2 (assessing evaluator readiness by selecting the evaluator) and then Step 1 (assessing program readiness to undertake the evaluation and building capacity as part of the assessment process). Complex Dynamic System Interconnections Graphic 1-2-3 depicts the interrelationships among the first three U-FE steps.

Complex Dynamic System Interconnections Among U-FE Steps 1-2-3

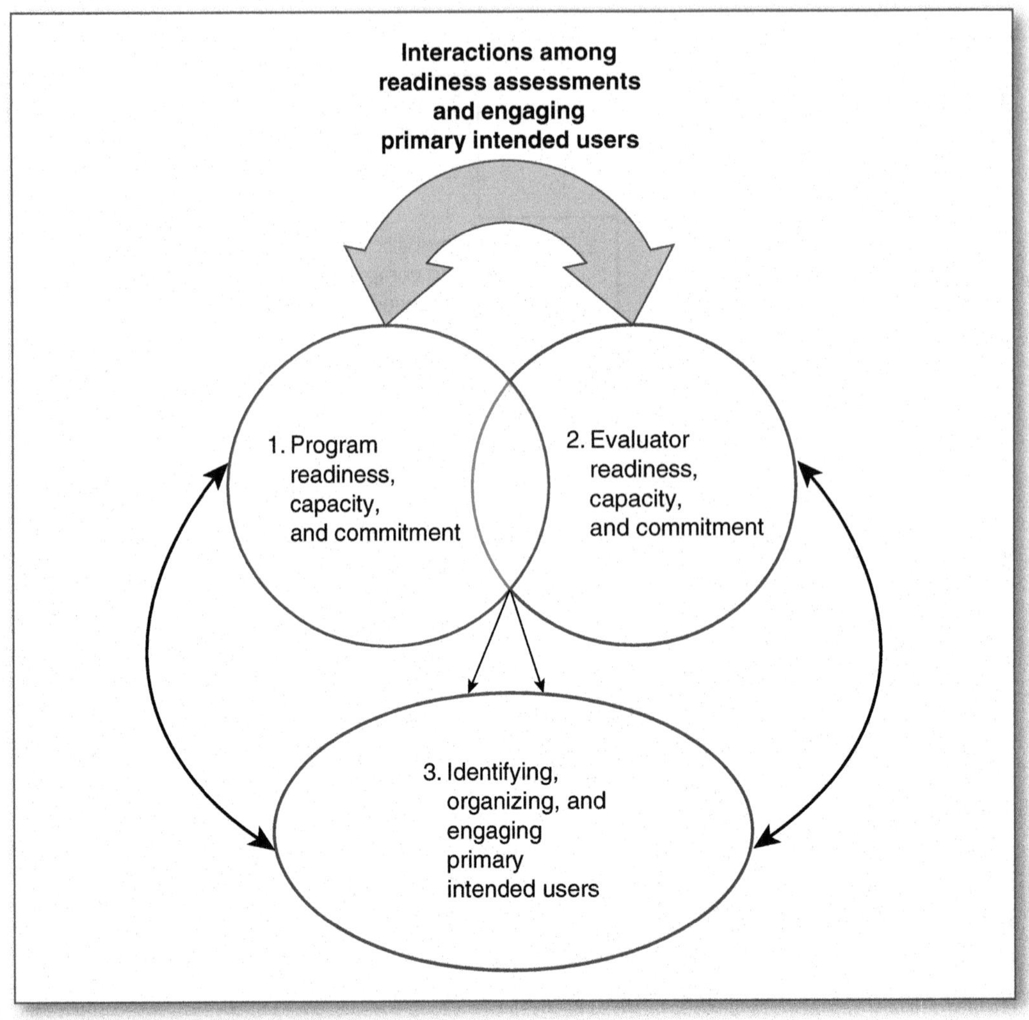

4

Situation Analysis Conducted Jointly With Primary Intended Users

Situations come and situations go.
Situations change and situations endure.
Situations get better and situations get worse.
Situations emerge and situations abate.
All of which begs the question:
What damn situation are we talking about?

Halcolm's Treatise on Situation Analysis

Situation analysis is ongoing. It's not something you do once, congratulate yourself on nailing it, check it off as done, and move on, never to pass that way again. The first three utilization-focused evaluation (U-FE) steps involve situation analysis:

Step 1. Assessing program and organizational readiness for utilization-focused evaluation, essentially analyzing the program situation.

Step 2. Assessing evaluator readiness and competence to undertake a utilization-focused evaluation, essentially analyzing the evaluator's situation.

Step 3. Identifying primary intended users and assessing their readiness to engage in utilization-focused evaluation, essentially analyzing the stakeholder situation.

As the Complex Systems Interconnections Graphic 1-2-3 (p. 86) shows, these steps—and situations—are interdependent. So why is Step 4 situation analysis? I'm glad you asked.

We're working within the constraint of a step-by-step and chapter-by-chapter framework, which is inherently linear, taking one thing at a time. Simultaneously, we're trying to recognize and call attention to the nonlinear, interactive, and iterative nature of utilization-focused evaluation as it unfolds in the real world with actual primary intended users. So Step 4 calls for a focused, intentional, and systematic situation analysis undertaken *with primary intended users* while at the same time reminding you that you've been engaged in situation analysis from the very beginning, and admonishing you to keep analyzing the situation as you move forward.

Step 4 focuses on bringing the primary intended users fully into the situation analysis. Exhibit 4.1 presents some questions for beginning situation analysis aimed at assuring understanding of the program, appreciating stakeholders' interests and potential areas of conflict, understanding the program's prior history and experiences with evaluation, and making explicit the decision context that will affect use, namely: What decisions, if any, will the evaluation findings inform? From these basic situation analysis questions, we can move to a more in-depth understanding of the evaluation use situation by identifying and examining factors that may contribute to use and those that may be barriers. First, let's look more closely at the Herculean challenges of situation analysis.

Context Matters: The Challenge of Situation Analysis in Designing and Conducting Evaluations

Every evaluation situation is unique. A successful evaluation (one that is useful, practical, ethical, accurate, and accountable) emerges from the special characteristics and conditions of a particular situation—a mixture of people, politics, history, context, resources, constraints, values, needs, interests, and chance. The standards and principles of evaluation provide overall direction, a foundation of ethical guidance, and a commitment to professional competence and integrity, but there are no absolute rules an evaluator can follow to know exactly what to do with specific users in a particular situation. As an evaluation unfolds, evaluators and primary intended users must work together to identify the evaluation that best fits their information needs and the program's context and situation. This means *negotiating* the evaluation's intended and desired uses, and adapting the design to financial, political, timing, and methodological constraints and opportunities.

To appreciate how complicated it can be to design an evaluation to fit the program's situation, let's use playing chess as an analogy. Bruce Pandolfini (1998), a world-class chess master, consults with major corporate leaders to teach them the mindset of a chess master so that they can become more skilled at strategic analysis and thinking. He points out that there are some 85 billion ways of playing just the first four moves in a game of chess (that's 85, with 9 zeros—85,000,000,000). Deciding what moves to make requires both strategy

EXHIBIT 4.1

Beginning Situation Analysis

Understand the program

What is the program's history? What situation gave rise to the program?

What are the program's primary goals? To what extent are these goals clear, specific, and measurable?

What are the strategies for attaining these goals?

Who are the intended beneficiaries of the program's intervention? What are their characteristics?

What are staff characteristics?

What's the program's budget?

For existing programs, how has the program changed overtime? What led to those changes?

Identify primary stakeholders and their interests

Where do stakeholders' interests align?

Where do their interests conflict?

What's the political context for the evaluation?

Who will be the primary intended users of the evaluation?

Evaluation history

What prior experiences, if any, has the program had with evaluation?

What are current monitoring and evaluation approaches, if any? How are monitoring and evaluation data currently used, if at all? What factors affect current uses?

What capacities does the program have to engage in evaluation (staff skills, budget for evaluation, information systems, a culture of inquiry, data management, and interpretation capacity)?

Decision and action context

What's the primary intended purpose of the evaluation?

What decisions, if any, is the program facing? What are the time lines for any such decisions?

What uncertainties does the program face? Externally? Internally?

---

and tactics grounded in an analysis of the situation presented by a particular game and opponent within an overall framework of fundamental chess ideas and concepts, understanding what the different pieces do, how they can be moved, and how they relate to each other. Once the game starts, subsequent moves are contingent on and must be adapted to what one's opponent does and the unfolding situation.

So how does one play the game of evaluation? And to successfully play the game, what is the focus of situation analysis in evaluation? The challenge is to identify factors and forces that will support and enhance evaluation use versus those factors and forces that may constitute barriers and become sources of resistance to use. Playing the evaluation use game successfully means marshalling powerful forces in support of use to overcome resistance to use. Force field analysis helps conceptualize the forces at play in the real-world utilization game.

Force Field Analysis

The idea of force field analysis was developed by eminent social psychologist Kurt Lewin in the 1940s. For any decision, he posited that there are forces that affect movement toward a goal—helping forces versus hindering forces. He applied force field analysis to such issues as behavior change, learning outcomes, group conflict resolution, and organizational morale. We're going to apply it to evaluation use. Exhibit 4.2 shows such a force field analysis.

The factors and forces identified along the top are those deemed likely to support and enhance use. Those listed along the bottom are predicted to constrain or undermine evaluation use. The length of each arrow represents the relative strength of the force, with longer arrows representing stronger forces. Broader arrows will have broad effects, while narrower arrows narrower effects on use. Dotted lines are less powerful than solid lines. The estimates of strength, breadth, and power do not have to be accurate. They are relative estimates, allowing rough comparisons of factors. Question marks may be inserted where a factor has been identified but the group is uncertain about its direction or strength. For example, a program may have many staff new to evaluation. Will that be a supporting or constraining factor, or manifest aspects of both? Not sure? Insert a question mark. Then monitor how that factor plays out over time. The force field analysis offers a framework for engaging with primary intended users in thinking strategically about use. At the beginning of the evaluation it is a baseline. When periodically updated, perhaps quarterly or annually, it provides a map of which factors and forces are actually unfolding as likely to affect evaluation use.

Once the overall force field analysis has been constructed as a baseline situation analysis, Exhibit 4.3 shows a template that can be used to engage primary intended users in considering ways of reinforcing and strengthening factors that will enhance use and counter forces that may undermine use.

Identifying Factors and Forces

With the overall framework of force field analysis in mind, let's turn to the task of identifying and distinguishing positive and negative factors and forces. Then we'll look at an example that applies these factors in a force field situation analysis.

EXHIBIT 4.2

Template for Force Field Analysis: Factors Supporting and Constraining Evaluation Use

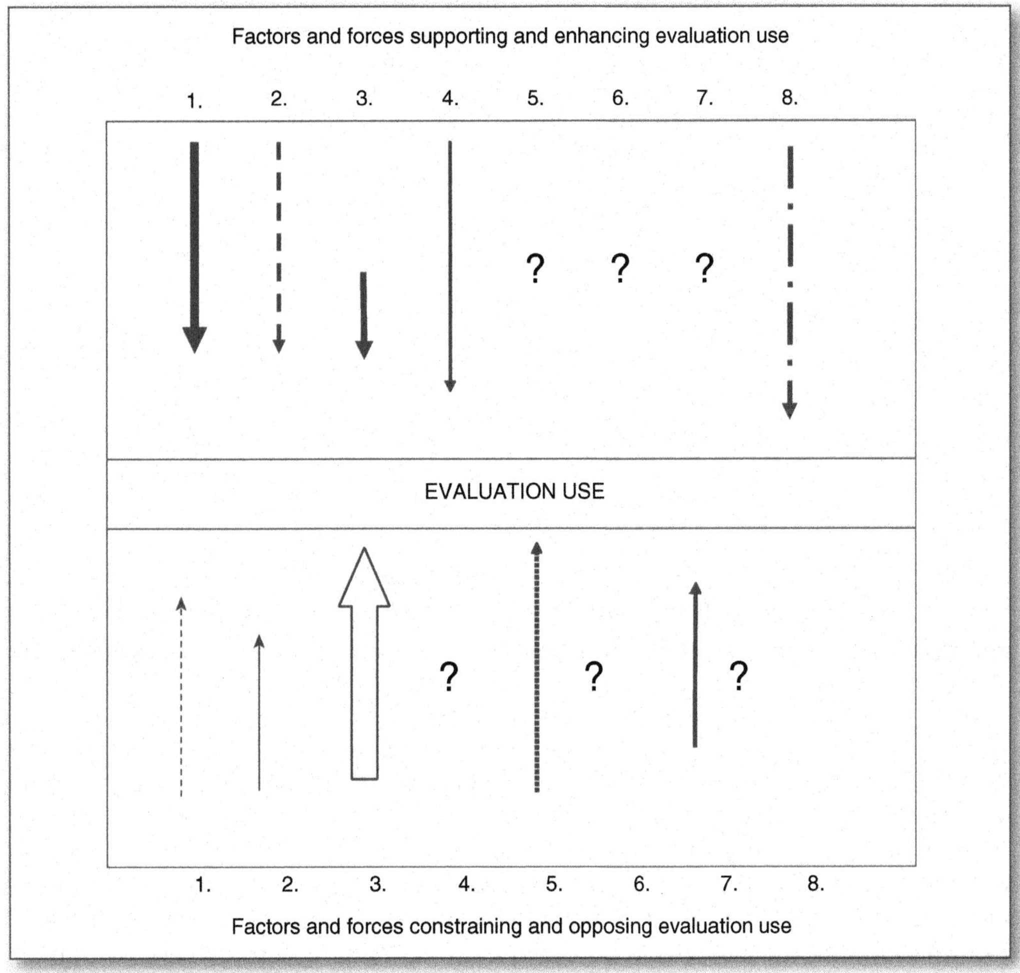

The length of each arrow represents the relative strength of the force, with longer arrows representing stronger forces. Broader arrows are expected to have broad effects, while narrower arrows will have somewhat less effect on use. Dotted lines are less powerful than solid lines. These are relative estimates, allowing rough comparisons of factors. Question marks may be inserted where a factor has been identified but the group is uncertain about its direction or strength.

EXHIBIT 4.3

Strategic Engagement for Evaluation Use

Factors and forces that support evaluation use:	*What can be done to reinforce and strengthen positive factors and forces?*
1.	1.
2.	2.
3.	3.
4.	4.
5.	5.
Factors and forces that may constrain or undermine evaluation use:	*What can be done to reduce or redirect negative factors and forces?*
1.	1.
2.	2.
3.	3.
4.	4.
5.	5.

Exhibit 4.4 (pp. 93–94) lists just 20 of the situational variables that can affect how an evaluation is designed and conducted, things like number of stakeholders to be dealt with, the evaluation's purpose, staff attitudes toward evaluation, the budget and time line for evaluation, and the program's prior experience with evaluation. These variables are presented in no particular order. Most of them could be broken down into several additional dimensions. If we conceive of just three points (or situations) on each of these dimensions—the two endpoints and a midpoint: for example, low budget, moderate budget, substantial budget—then the possible combinations of these 20 dimensions represent 8,000 unique situational configurations for evaluation.

Nor are these static situations. The program you thought was new at the first session turns out to have been created out of and to be a continuation of another program; only the name has been changed to protect the guilty. You thought you were dealing with only

EXHIBIT 4.4

Examples of Situational Factors in Evaluation That Can Affect Users' Participation and Use

One primary decision maker	1. *Number of stakeholders to be dealt with*	Large number
Formative purpose (improvement)	2. *Purpose of the evaluation*	Summative purpose (funding decision)
New program	3. *History of the program*	Long history
Enthusiasm	4. *Staff attitude toward evaluation*	Resistance
Knows virtually nothing	5. *Staff knowledge about evaluation*	Highly knowledgeable
Cooperative	6. *Program interaction patterns (administration-staff, staff-staff, staff-client)*	Conflict laden
First time ever	7. *Program's prior evaluation experience*	Seemingly endless experience
High	8. *Staff and participants education levels*	Low
Homogeneous groups	9. *Staff and/or participants' characteristics (pick any 10 you want)*	Heterogeneous groups
One site	10. *Program location*	Multiple sites
No money to speak of	11. *Resources available for evaluation*	Substantial funding
One funding source	12. *Number of sources of program funding*	Multiple funding sources

(Continued)

(Continued)

Simple and singular	13. *Nature of the program treatment*	Complex and multidimensional
Highly standardized and routine	14. *Standardization of treatment*	Highly individualized and nonroutine
Horizontal, little hierarchy, little stratification	15. *Program organizational decision-making structure*	Hierarchical, long chain of command, stratified
Well articulated, specifically defined	16. *Clarity about evaluation purpose and function*	Ambiguous, broadly defined
Operating information system	17. *Existing data on program*	No existing data
External	18. *Evaluator(s)' relationship to the program*	Internal
Voluntary, self-initiated	19. *Impetus for the evaluation*	Required, forced on program
Long time line, open	20. *Time available for the evaluation*	Short time line, fixed deadline

one primary decision maker at the outset, and suddenly you have stakeholders coming out your ears, or vice versa. With some programs, I've felt like I've been through all 8,000 situations in the first month of design negotiations.

Now, just in case 8,000 situations to analyze, be sensitive to, and design evaluations for doesn't seem challenging enough, add two more points to each dimension—a point between each endpoint and the midpoint. Now, combinations of the five points on all 20 dimensions yield 3,200,000 potentially different situations. Perhaps such complexity helps explain why the slogan that won the hearts of evaluators in attendance at the pioneering 1978 Evaluation Network conference in Aspen, Colorado, was the lament:

Evaluators do IT under difficult circumstances.

The point of this analysis is to raise a fundamental question: How can evaluators prepare themselves to deal with a lot of different people and a huge variety of situations? The research on decision making says we can't systematically consider every possible variable, or even 50 variables, or even 20 variables. What we need is a framework for making sense of situations, for telling us what factors deserve priority based on research and desired results. Such a framework, rather than providing narrow, specific prescriptions, should offer questions to force us to think about and analyze the situation. This is essential and reminds us of the title of this book: *Essentials of Utilization-Focused Evaluation*. The *utilization-focused* advice for managing situational complexity in evaluation is to *stay focused on use*. For every issue that surfaces in evaluation negotiations, for every design decision, for every budget allocation, and for every choice among alternatives, keep asking: How will what we do affect use in this situation? Here are some actual situations I've faced.

- The program has a new director. The previous director, much admired and trusted, retired after 15 years of service. The new director was hired after a national search and brought in from the outside although there were two internal candidates for the position. The evaluation process is scheduled to begin after the new director has been on the job for only a month. How might this affect the evaluation and its use? What are the elements of the situation that might support evaluation use? What are the potential pitfalls and barriers to use? How can these be acknowledged and managed?
- In another situation, the evaluation will focus on a major new initiative considered very innovative and risky because it involves a creative approach to poverty reduction that hasn't been tried in this community before. The program implementing the new initiative has a long history of solid performance delivering basic community services to people in poverty. The program's stellar reputation flows from effectively implementing government and United Way services in accordance with established procedures and rules. However, the agency leadership and staff are not known for being innovative or creative. They have been asked to take on this innovative community engagement program because of their reputation for meeting expectations. Their past approaches to evaluation have been modest and centered on delivering outputs (low-cost services) but with little attention to outcomes (no follow-up on the effects of services). The new initiative includes lots of rhetoric about being outcomes-focused. How might this situation affect the evaluation and its use? What are the elements of the situation that might support evaluation use? What are the potential pitfalls and barriers to use? How can these be acknowledged and managed? What evaluation capacity-building will need to occur?
- A few months after the devastating earthquake in Haiti, the international agencies involved in relief work were asked to cooperate in a collaborative evaluation of lessons learned that might improve future disaster relief efforts. Cooperation and collaboration are important so that the evaluation data collection does not become redundant and intrusive on continuing relief efforts as it surely would if every agency conducted its own evaluation and had to seek data from the

> same few, already-overworked Haitian sources. But such a collaborative and comprehensive evaluation has not been undertaken before. The cooperating relief agencies traditionally compete for resources and media attention. Time is short and resources for the evaluation will be limited, but the stakes are high for the agencies and the people of Haiti, as well as future victims of natural disaster. How might this context affect the evaluation and its use? What are the elements of the situation that might support evaluation use? What are the potential pitfalls and barriers to use?

These are just three brief examples of the millions of situations evaluators face. They are meant to give a hint of the challenges of situation awareness. Exhibit 4.5 provides an overview of some common situations that require special evaluator skills.

Internal and External Evaluators

Internal and external evaluators face quite different situations. Internal evaluators are employed by the program, project, or organization being evaluated. External evaluators work as independent contractors. This raises a fundamental situational issue regarding the location of the evaluator inside or outside the entity being evaluated, what is sometimes called the "in-house" versus "outhouse" issue. Let's take a closer look at internal versus external evaluation situations.

External evaluators come from universities, consulting firms, and research organizations or work as independent consultants. The defining characteristic of external evaluators is that they have no long-term, ongoing position within the program or organization being evaluated. They are therefore not subordinated to someone in the organization and not directly dependent on the organization for their job and career. External evaluators are valuable precisely because they are outside the organization. It is typically assumed that their external status permits them to be more independent, objective, and credible than internal evaluators. Internal evaluations are suspect because, it is presumed, they can be manipulated more easily by administrators to justify decisions or pressured to present positive findings for public relations purposes. Of course, external evaluators who want future evaluation contracts are also subject to pressure to produce positive findings. In addition, external evaluators are also typically more costly, less knowledgeable about the nuances and particulars of the local situation, and less able to follow through to facilitate the implementation of recommendations. When external evaluators complete their contract, they may take with them a great deal of knowledge and insight that is lost to the program. That knowledge stays "in-house" with internal evaluators. External evaluators have also been known to cause difficulties in a program through insensitivity to organizational relationships and norms, one of the reasons the work of external evaluators is sometimes called "outhouse" work.

EXHIBIT 4.5

Examples of Situations That Pose Special Challenges to Evaluation Use and the Evaluator's Role

Situation	*Challenge*	*Special Evaluator Skills Needed*
1. Highly controversial issue	Facilitating different points of view	Conflict resolution skills
2. Highly visible program	Dealing with publicity about the program; reporting findings in a media-circus atmosphere	Public presentation skills Graphic skills Media-handling skills
3. Highly volatile program environment	Rapid change in context, issues, and focus	Tolerance for ambiguity Being a "quick study" Rapid responsiveness Flexibility
4. Cross-cultural or international	Including different perspectives. Being aware of cultural blinders and biases	Cross-culture sensitivity Skills in understanding and incorporating different perspectives
5. Team effort	Managing people	Identifying and using individual skills of team members; team-building skills
6. Evaluation attacked	Preserving credibility	Calm; staying focused on evidence and conclusions
7. Corrupt program	Resolving ethical issues/ upholding standards	Integrity Clear ethical sense Honesty

Most federal, state, local, and international agencies have internal evaluation units to fulfill accountability mandates. It has become clear that internal evaluators can produce evaluations of high quality and high impact while still performing useful service to administrators if they work diligently to establish an image of an independent but active voice in the organizational structure and take a pragmatic approach to helping solve management problems. Ongoing performance monitoring has become a major activity of internal evaluation systems, and internal evaluation units now support both accountability and learning.

Over the years, I have had extensive contact with internal evaluators through training and consulting, working closely with several of them to design internal monitoring and evaluation systems. I interviewed 10 internal evaluators who I knew used a utilization-focused approach. Their comments about how they have applied utilization-focused principles offer insights into the world of the internal evaluator and illuminate research findings about effective approaches to internal evaluation.

Themes From Internal Evaluators

1. Actively involving stakeholders within the organization can be difficult because evaluation is often perceived by both superiors and subordinates as the job of the evaluator. The internal evaluator is typically expected to *do* evaluations, not facilitate an evaluation process involving others. Internal evaluators who have had success involving others have had to work hard at finding special incentives to attract participation in the evaluation process. One internal evaluator commented,

> My director told me he doesn't want to spend time thinking about evaluations. That's why he hired me. He wants me to "anticipate his information needs." I've had to find ways to talk with him about his interests and information needs without explicitly telling him he's helping me focus the evaluation. I guess you could say I kind of involve him without his really knowing he's involved.

2. Internal evaluators are often asked by superiors for public relations information rather than evaluation. The internal evaluator may be told, "I want a report for the legislature proving our program is effective." It takes clear conviction, subtle diplomacy, and an astute understanding of how to help superiors appreciate evaluation to keep internal evaluation responsibilities from degenerating into public relations. One mechanism used by several internal evaluators to increase support for real evaluation rather than public relations is establishing an evaluation advisory committee, including influential people from outside the organization, to provide independent checks on the integrity of internal evaluations.

3. Internal evaluators get asked to do lots of little data-gathering and report-writing tasks that are quite time consuming but too minor to be considered meaningful evaluation. For example, if someone in the agency wants a quick review of what other states are doing about some problem, the internal evaluator is an easy target for the task. Such assignments can become so pervasive that it's difficult to have time for longer-term, more meaningful evaluation efforts.

4. **Internal evaluators are often excluded from major decisions** or so far removed from critical information networks that they don't know about new initiatives or developments in time to build in an evaluation perspective up front. One internal evaluator explained,

> We have separate people doing planning and evaluation. I'm not included in the planning process and usually don't even see the plan until it's approved. Then they expect me to add on an evaluation. It's a real bitch to take a plan done without any thought of evaluation and add an evaluation without changing the plan. They think evaluation is something you do at the end rather than think about from the start. It's damn hard to break through these perceptions. Besides, I don't want to do the planners' job, and they don't want to do my job, but we've got to find better ways of making the whole thing work together. That's my frustration. . . . It takes me constantly bugging them, and sometimes they think I'm encroaching on their turf. Some days I think, "Who needs the hassle?" even though I know it's not as useful just to tack on the evaluation at the end.

5. **Getting evaluation used takes a lot of follow-through.** One internal evaluator explained that her job was defined as data gathering and report writing without consideration of following up to see if report recommendations were adopted (Step 16 in this book). That's not part of her job description, and it takes time and some authority. She mused:

> How do I get managers to use a report if my job is just to write the report? They're above me. I don't have the authority to ask them in 6 months what they've done. I wrote a follow-up memo once reminding managers about recommendations in an evaluation and some of them didn't like it at all, although a couple of the good ones said they were glad I reminded them.

Another internal evaluator told me he had learned how to follow up informally. He has 7 years' experience as an internal human services evaluator. He said,

> At first I just wrote a report and figured my job was done. Now, I tell them when we review the initial report that I'll check back in a few months to see how things are going. I find I have to keep pushing, keep reminding, or they get busy and just file the report. We're gradually getting some understanding that our job should include some follow-up. Mostly it's on a few things that we decide are really important. You can't do it all.

Internal Role Definitions

The themes from internal evaluators indicate the importance of carefully defining the job to include attention to use. When and if the internal evaluation job is defined primarily as writing a report and filling out routine reporting forms, the ability of the evaluator to influence use is quite limited. When and if the internal evaluator is organizationally separated from managers and planners, it is difficult to establish collaborative arrangements that facilitate use. Thus, a utilization-focused approach to internal evaluation will often require a redefinition of the position to include responsibility for working with intended users to develop strategies for acting on findings.

One increasingly important role for internal evaluators is as a resource for infusing evaluative thinking into and throughout the entire organization. This means that rather than only or primarily conducting evaluations, the internal evaluator becomes a trainer, a resource to other units, a facilitator of meetings where evaluative thinking is needed, and an evaluator of the organization's progress in learning and applying those learnings to its work. In this role the internal evaluator works to build evaluation into the organizational culture.

Internal-External Evaluation Combinations

It is important to note that internal *and* external approaches are not mutually exclusive. Actually, there are a good many possible combinations of internal and external evaluations that may be more desirable and more cost-effective than either a purely internal *or* purely external evaluation. Exhibit 4.6 describes some of the points along the external-internal continuum. These constitute varying situation-specific arrangements for locating the evaluation function.

EXHIBIT 4.6

A Continuum of Internal/External Evaluation Relationships

1. *Entirely External.* None of the evaluations of the organization's programs or projects are being completed by internal staff members. No other evaluation activities (e.g., developing program logic models, or evaluation plans) are performed by staff. When evaluation occurs in the organization, it is in response to funders' demands for accountability and is conducted by external evaluation consultants.

2. *Minimal Ad Hoc Internal Evaluation.* Program staff have conducted the evaluation of only a minority of the organization's programs and projects. Those evaluations were ad hoc; that is, they occurred in response to requests from individual managers or funders. Usually, the focus and questions for these evaluations were set by external stakeholders (e.g., providing required performance indicators to funders' accreditation demands).

3. *Occasional Internal Evaluation.* When staff perform evaluations of programs or projects, they usually focus on questions about outputs and processes (e.g., What services were delivered to which clients?). These internal evaluations are conducted by managers or staff who are temporarily given evaluation responsibilities. Core evaluation activities such as having staff create logic models only occur rarely.

4. *Part-Time Internal Evaluator.* The organization has assigned one staff member to perform evaluation tasks on a part-time basis. This person gets their assignments from the Executive Director (or a similar senior manager). Internal evaluations often focus on whether or not the program or project is doing what both the organization and its funders want it to do (e.g., Is the program meeting the goals stated in the program proposal?).

5. *Full-Time Internal Evaluator.* Evaluations performed by internal staff are fairly common in the organization with at least one staff member assigned to evaluation duties on an ongoing basis. Program managers participate in identifying priority evaluation questions and planning evaluations. These internal evaluations often include questions about program outcomes (e.g., How effective was the program? Did clients benefit? To what extent did the program produce its intended outcomes?).

6. *Routine Internal Evaluation.* Evaluation occurs on a regular basis. Several internal staff members have evaluation skills and plan/manage internal evaluations on a regular basis. The organization has policies that require that certain evaluation tasks must occur throughout the organization (e.g., all programs must have a logic model, all programs must collect data on client satisfaction). Results from internal evaluations are routinely reported to managers and staff. These evaluation results are used to inform decisions about the development of the program that was evaluated. Internal evaluations often focus on issues of program costs. Program managers decide which evaluation questions will get asked. The organization has an Evaluation Coordinator or Manager and several staff who have evaluation responsibilities.

7. *Fully Integrated and Highly Valued Internal Evaluation.* Evaluation of all programs and projects is an organizational requirement. An Evaluation Manager leads an internal Evaluation Team. Evaluation staff provide evaluation training and coaching to managers and staff, including how to use findings in their work. Findings are used to improve both individual programs and the entire organization's structures and processes in an ongoing way. Results from internal evaluations are shared with the Board, with partners, and with key stakeholders. Summaries of evaluation findings appear in the newsletter and Annual Report. Evaluation is viewed as central to organizational effectiveness and is an integral part of the organization's culture.

SOURCE: Adapted from Shea and Love (2007).

Accreditation processes are a good example of an internal-external combination. The internal group collects the data and arranges them so that the external group can come in, inspect the data collected by the internal group, sometimes collect additional information on their own, and pass judgment on the program.

There are many ways in which an evaluation can be set up so that some external group of respected professionals and evaluators guarantees the validity and fairness of the evaluation process while the people internal to the program actually collect and/or analyze the evaluation data. The cost savings of such an approach can be substantial while still allowing the evaluation to have basic credibility and legitimacy through the blessing of the external review committee.

I worked for several years with one of the leading chemical dependency treatment centers in the country, the Hazelden Foundation of Minnesota. The foundation has established a rigorous evaluation process that involves data collection at the point of entry into the program and then follow-up questionnaires 6 months, 12 months, and 24 months after leaving the program. Hazelden's own research and evaluation department collects all of the data. My responsibility as an external evaluator was to monitor that data collection periodically to make sure that the established procedures were being followed correctly. I then worked with the program decision makers to identify the kind of data analysis that was desirable. They performed the data analysis with their own computer resources. They sent the data to me, and I wrote the annual evaluation report. They participated in analyzing, interpreting, and making judgments about the data, but for purposes of legitimacy and credibility, the actual writing of the final report was done by me.

When orchestrating an internal-external combination, one danger to watch for is that the external group may impose unmanageable and overwhelming data collection procedures on the internal people. I saw this happen in an internal-external model with a group of school districts in Canada. The external committee set as the standard doing "comprehensive" data collection at the local school level, including data on learning outcomes, staff morale, facilities, curriculum, the school lunch program, the library, parent reactions, the perceptions of local businesspeople, analysis of the school bus system, and so on. After listening to all of the things the external committee thought should be done, the internal folks dubbed it the Internal-External-*Eternal* model of evaluation.

The point is that a variety of internal-external combinations are possible to combine the lower costs of internal data collection with the higher credibility of external review. In working out the details of internal-external combinations, care will need to be taken to achieve an appropriate and mutually rewarding balance based on a collaborative commitment to the standards of utility, feasibility, propriety, and accuracy.

Evaluation as a Leadership Function

Most writings about internal evaluation assume a separate unit or specialized position with responsibility to conduct evaluations. An important new direction in evaluation is to treat evaluation as a leadership function of all managers and program directors in the organization, including, especially, the executive director. The person responsible for internal evaluation then plays a facilitative, resource, and training function in support of managers and leaders rather than spending time actually conducting evaluations. The best example of this approach I've worked with and observed up close was the position of associate administrator for Performance Measurement and Evaluation in a county government. The county had no internal evaluation office. Rather, this senior position, as part of the County Executive team, had responsibility to infuse evaluation thinking and systems throughout the county, in every department and program. Every manager in the county received training in how to build outcomes evaluation into ongoing program processes and use data for decision making and budgeting. What made this approach to internal evaluation work, in my judgment, was three-fold:

1. Results-oriented evaluation was defined as a leadership function of every county manager, not just a technical reporting function delegated to data nerds.
2. The overall responsibility for evaluation resided at the highest level of the organization, in the executive team, with direct access to the County Board of Commissioners backed up by public commitments to use evaluation for decision making and budgeting.
3. Because of the prior two commitments, a person of great competence and dedication was selected to fill the position of associate administrator for Performance Measurement and Evaluation, after a national search.

These patterns of effectiveness stand out because so often internal evaluation is delegated to the lowest level in an organization and treated as a clerical or technical function. Indeed, being given an evaluation assignment is often a form of punishment, or a way of giving deadwood staff something meaningless to occupy themselves with. It is clear that, for internal evaluators to be useful and credible, they must have high status in the organization and real power to make evaluation meaningful. And even when this occurs, as in the case just reviewed, it can be difficult to sustain. After less than 2 years, when the county executive changed, the associate administrator for Performance Measurement and Evaluation was lost in a reorganization and the system reverted to treating evaluation as a separate support unit and function.

Elevating the status of evaluation to that of a leadership function may require leadership development. Indeed, as an example of reaching primary intended users, I participated in developing a leadership development workshop that focused on evaluative thinking and practice. We didn't promote it as an evaluation workshop because leaders would not come to such a workshop; they would send lower-level technical staff. To reach the leadership level of organizations with the message and promise of evaluation use, we had to promote the effort as leadership development and embed the evaluation training in that framework. Exhibit 4.7 presents the four functions of results-oriented, reality-testing, learning-focused leadership we used for the leadership training workshop. In this framework, evaluation becomes *an executive leadership responsibility* focused on decision-oriented use rather than a data-collection task focused on routine internal reporting.

EXHIBIT 4.7

Four Functions of Results-Oriented, Reality-Testing, Learning-Focused Leadership

- Create and nurture a results-oriented, reality-testing, learning-focused culture.
- Lead in deciding what outcomes to commit to and hold yourselves accountable for.
- Make measurement of outcomes thoughtful, meaningful, and credible.
- Use the results—and model for others serious use of results.

Evaluation Team Composition Analysis

Evaluations of much size or scope move us from the individual evaluator to a team of evaluators. Team situations raise questions about team composition. This typically involves calculating what combination of skills, knowledge, and experience are needed to conduct the evaluation. The primary intended users can be involved in establishing the diversity criteria for team composition that they believe will lend credibility to the team and ensure that the team has both the skills and diverse perspectives needed to do high-quality work. Here's an example of a diverse, multi-dimensional team of five people that could be assembled to evaluate an environmental initiative:

- An experienced lead evaluator able to coordinate the team and work with diverse intended users;
- A team member with expertise in environmental science;
- One or more culturally competent evaluators who could bring to the team the perspectives of any specific cultural group involved in the initiative: for example, a Native American if the initiative includes American Indian reservations, a Maori evaluator in New Zealand;
- A younger evaluator, newer to the work, who can bring fresh ideas and new technology applications to the team while being mentored professionally in evaluation by more experienced team members; and
- Gender balance to assure that the evaluation addresses and is sensitive to gender issues.

Most larger scale evaluations involve teams: for example, external site visit teams that visit projects for evaluation data collection purposes. Team composition includes calculations about the appropriate mix of expertise, experience, background, and perspective. In a 10-country evaluation of an agricultural extension initiative in the Caribbean, we assembled an evaluation task force of primary intended users that included the international funders, the chief agricultural extension officers of the participating countries, and representatives of the American universities and the University of the West Indies that were providing technical assistance. The five-member evaluation team reflected this stakeholder diversity. In each country, a farmer and local extension agent joined the team for the work in that country.

Thus, part of situation analysis is determining the appropriate team composition that will bring evaluation expertise, subject matter expertise, cultural competence, methodological expertise, and political credibility to the team.

Balancing Task and Relationship Demands

One of the most fundamental and oft-replicated findings from early research on group effectiveness is that high-performing groups attend to both task completion and relationship-building. In an evaluation context, *the task focus* concerns the primary intended uses of the evaluation and how those uses will be achieved. *The relationship focus* concerns how the evaluator works with and relates to primary intended users to enhance the likelihood of use. Embedded in the utilization-focused evaluation goal of intended use by intended users is attention to both tasks and relationships. Situation analysis and responsiveness involve ongoing assessment of the balance between task completion and facilitating good working relationships. While internal and external evaluators may face different dynamics in this regard, what they share is a need to analyze the situation they face to determine what kind of relationship and process for conducting the evaluation will support task completion and lead to use. It is worth reiterating these challenges in the context of situation analysis.

Some evaluators focus only on getting the evaluation designed, the data collected and analyzed, and the report written. They are entirely task focused and want no part of relationship-building. Indeed, they wear their independence as a badge of pride, justifying their inattention to relationships and process as fundamental to their credibility. In this approach to evaluation, independence, neutrality, distance, and credibility are the cornerstones of utility.

At the other end of the continuum are evaluation consultants who make regular interaction with clients a priority and give at least as much attention to relationship-building as getting the work done. Such a consultant once told me, "Building a strong relationship with the client is the task." This evaluator viewed trust, in-depth knowledge, shared values, and close connection to the client as the pillars that support utility.

These two evaluators defined the situational challenge differently. For our purposes, these examples raise questions that can only be answered within the context of a particular situation.

- What kind of relationship to specific intended users will enhance use given the purpose of the evaluation?
- How much distance is needed to establish credibility? How much closeness is appropriate to assure relevance and trust?

- How much ongoing interaction with intended users supports mutual understanding and keeping everyone informed? When does regular communication become burdensome and overdone? What constitutes too little communication to maintain an appropriate degree of interest and engagement?
- How does the relationship with intended users change over the course of an evaluation as the tasks change (from design to data collection, to analysis, to reporting, to use of findings)?
- To what extent is it appropriate for an evaluator to have different relationships with different intended users? Some stakeholders are likely to be more interested in both task and process while others are less so. How does an evaluator deal with these variations, by having different relationships with different intended users, without creating conflicts and distrust in the group as a whole?

There can be no standardized, recipe-like answers to these questions. The answers flow from the situation analysis, including stakeholders' concerns and perspectives, which inform the entire evaluation process. Answering these questions means asking them—seriously, thoughtfully, astutely, and pragmatically—and then letting what you come to understand guide your engagement. And, of course, you don't just ask these questions once at the beginning. As the evaluation unfolds, it's important to evaluate how well the tasks are getting done (quality of work being completed) and how the relationships are unfolding. Feedback from intended users along the way provides critical guidance about whether more or less interaction and communication is needed to enhance use.

Risk Assessment and Contingency Thinking

Contingency thinking for situational responsiveness inevitably involves some degree of risk. Designing an evaluation involves an informal cost-benefit analysis in which potential benefits—for example, using results to improve the program—are considered in relationship to costs, which include financial resources, evaluator and staff time, and opportunity costs (what else could have been done with the money spent on evaluation). Introducing the notion of risk into evaluation design and relationship decisions is a way of acknowledging that things seldom turn out exactly the way they are planned. Calculating risk involves asking the following kinds of questions:

1. What can go wrong in this evaluation?
2. What is the likelihood that it would go wrong?
3. What are the consequences and how bad would they be if things go badly?

The intent of such front-end risk assessment, done with primary intended users, is *not* to deepen the illusion that one can anticipate and thereby prevent all difficulties. Rather, it is to lay the foundation for contingency thinking as a basis for evaluator-user negotiations and revisions as the evaluation unfolds. Risk analysis should push evaluators and intended users to be prepared for contingencies. Contingency thinking and planning acknowledges the reality that every design will run into execution problems. What distinguishes one evaluation from another is not the absence of problems but the preparation for and ability to solve them. Examining what can go wrong should include thoughtful consideration of what can really be accomplished with available resources.

Risk analysis requires evaluators and stakeholders to become explicit about different scenarios and how they might behave in each.

Three Types of Risk

Risk is traditionally defined as the probability of an occurrence multiplied by the severity of the consequences associated with the hazard. In dialogues with intended users, it can be helpful to break the "what can go wrong?" question into three interdependent categories: idea risk, implementation risk, and evidence risk. Idea risk increases when new, untested, and innovative ideas are being tried out. Implementation risk increases when new organizations or inexperienced staff are implementing a program, and where the environment in which implementation is occurring is turbulent (for example, politically unstable or an arena of conflict). Evidence risk increases when data will be hard to collect or access to needed data is problematic. Two of these three types of risk—idea risk and implementation risk—derive from classic program design risk analysis. The premise is that the more risky the intervention (either because of idea risk or implementation risk, or both), the more uncertain may be the evaluation situation and therefore the more risk that could be entailed in conducting the evaluation due to those uncertainties. The third type of risk, evidence risk, is a fundamental evaluation issue. However, this is a risk shared by the program and the evaluation because the harder it is to evaluate a program, the more that program may be at risk of losing funding or other support. Exhibit 4.8 compares the three kinds of risk for programs and evaluations.

The process of risk analysis should reveal instances in which what is at risk is not just wasted money or useless findings but includes the relationship between the evaluator and intended users by failing to converse openly and honestly about actual and potential problems.

What's Worth Knowing

Focusing an evaluation involves figuring what's worth knowing *in this situation*. Situation analysis, conducted jointly by the evaluator and primary intended users, involves strategic contingency thinking and learning to be active-reactive-interactive-adaptive as a foundation for ongoing situational responsiveness.

EXHIBIT 4.8

Risk Assessment

Nature of Risk	*Program Risk Assessment*	*Evaluation Risk Assessment*
Idea/design risk	How clear, well tested, and logical is the intervention idea?	How routine is the evaluation design? How accepted and valid are the measurement approaches?
Implementation risk	What are the challenges to implementing the idea?	What are the challenges to implementing the evaluation design?
Evidence risk	How difficult will it be to evaluate the effectiveness of the idea and/or its implementation?	What are the threats to the evaluation's credibility, utility, feasibility, accuracy, and propriety?

You can't know everything about a situation—and you can't figure it all out at the beginning. Perfect knowledge is not the goal. Situational and contextual sensitivity is. You work with primary intended users to learn the most important things that are likely to affect evaluation use. That's the focus.

Distinguishing informational wheat from chaff requires determining what's important. The challenge of making such a distinction is nicely illustrated by a story about the founder of the Ford Motor Company. A visitor to Ford's factory encountered the famous Henry Ford himself while being a given a tour of the factory. Looking at a car being built, Ford told the visitor authoritatively: "There are exactly 4,719 parts in that model." The visitor was subsequently introduced to the engineer who oversaw production and, having been impressed that the president had a grasp of such details, reported what Henry Ford had said. The engineer shrugged, clearly unimpressed, and said, "I don't know if that's true, but I can't think of a more useless piece of information" (Fadiman & Bernard, 2000, p. 210).

Figuring out what information will be useful and then delivering that information to the people who can use it is the challenge of utilization-focused evaluation. Having developed a deeper understanding of the situation and context, the next step involves determining the priority purpose of the evaluation.

"Juggling four pins at once is easy with practice. The hard part is all the other stuff you have to watch out for."

PRACTICE EXERCISES

1. *Practice conducting a situation analysis.* Identify a program for which you might design an evaluation. Use Exhibits 4.1 and 4.4 to conduct a beginning situation analysis. Use Exhibit 4.5 to identify any special conditions for the evaluation.

2. *Conduct a utilization force field analysis.* Use Exhibits 4.2 and 4.3 to undertake a force field analysis of an evaluation. What factors are likely to be positive forces that support and enhance evaluation use? What factors are likely to create resistance or barriers to use? How might the positive forces be used to minimize the negative forces?

(Continued)

(Continued)

3. *Write a job description for an internal evaluator.* First, describe an organization that you know (or fabricate an organization). Specify the organization's mission, staff size, organizational structure (e.g., different units or program areas), and the challenges the organization is currently facing. Now, write a job description for an internal evaluator in this organization. Include specification of where the internal evaluator will be located, what the evaluation priorities will be, what relationship qualities will be important, and what tasks must get done. Give a rationale for your job description by explaining how the job description is attuned to and appropriate for the organizational situation.

4. *Evaluation risk assessment.* Identify an example of an innovative program that has been evaluated or that has an evaluation design. Use Exhibit 4.8 to discuss evaluation risks in relation to program risks. Elucidate the relationship between program risks and evaluation risks using a concrete program example.

INTERLUDE, STEPS 1 THROUGH 4. COMPLEX DYNAMIC SYSTEMS INTERCONNECTIONS:

Assessing the Alignment Among the Steps and Integrating the Situation Analysis From Steps 1 Through 4

The steps in the checklist are necessarily linear and sequential.

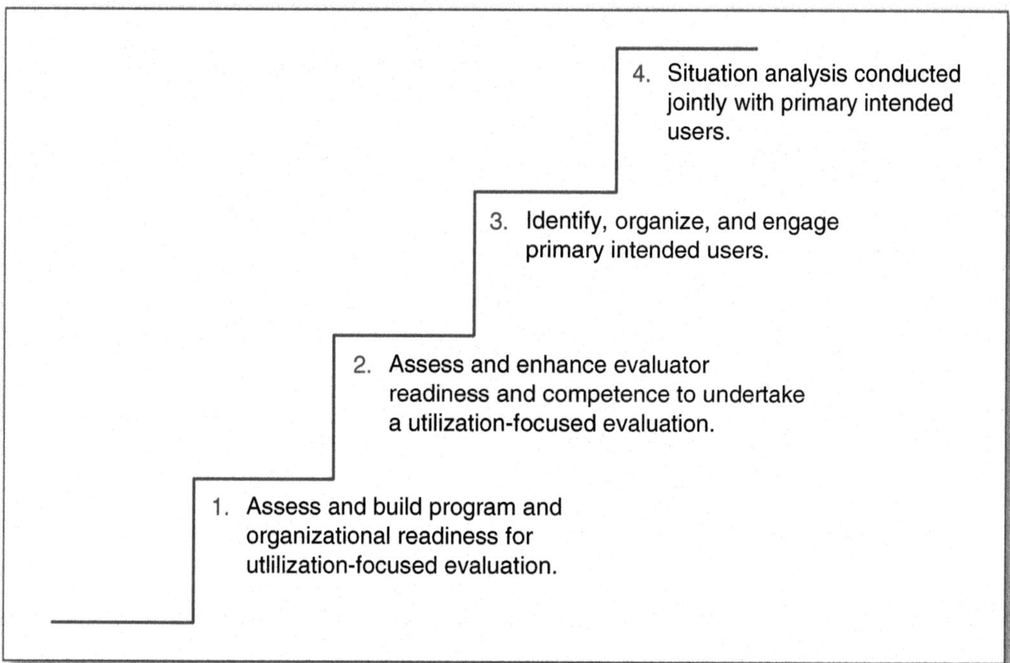

Details about what is involved in each step are provided in the summary *U-FE Checklist* in the concluding chapter. (See pages 406–411.)

But to depict utilization-focused evaluation as a complex adaptive system, each new step in the checklist also becomes another element in the complex dynamic system graphic that is emerging as we proceed through the steps of the checklist. This graphic attempts to portray the interdependence of and interactions among the steps.

Complex Dynamic System
Interactions Among U-FE Steps 1 Through 4

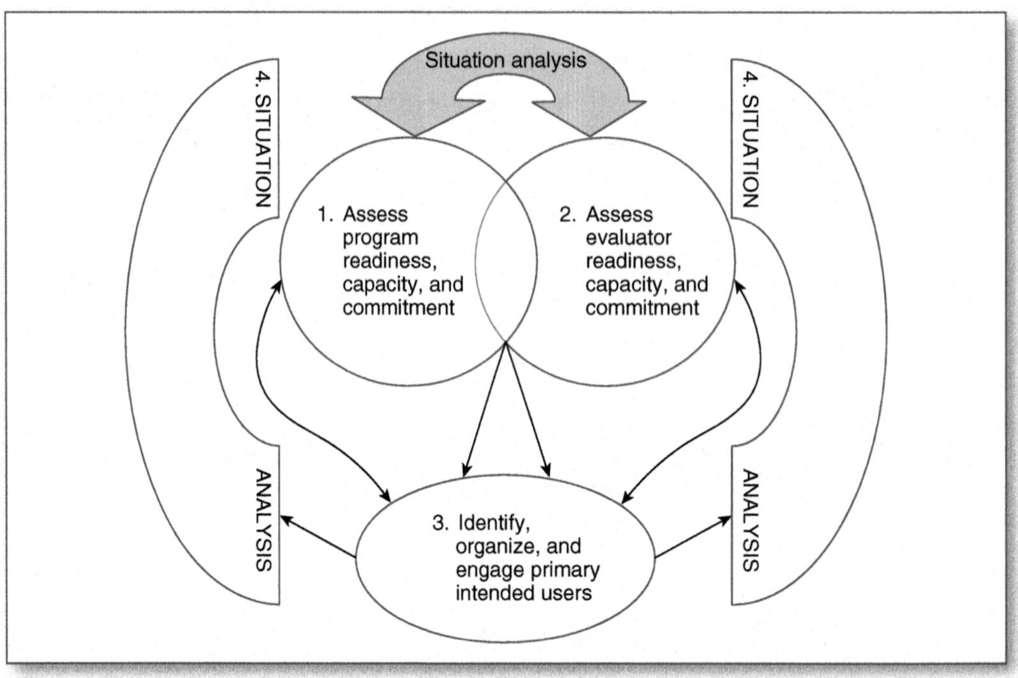

5

Identify and Prioritize Primary Intended Uses by Determining Priority Purposes

Purpose. Everything flows from purpose. Everything.

Halcolm's Exegesis of Purpose

The telephone rings. I answer. "Are you the Dr. Patton who does evaluations?"

"I am," I acknowledge.

"We need one," the caller says.

"What kind do you need?" I ask.

"Kind?"

"What's the purpose of the evaluation?"

"Purpose? I don't know. To get one done."

And thus begins the process of considering alternative purposes and making distinctions among different kinds of evaluations. I explain that if you are going to buy a car, you have lots of choices and have to narrow the options to what kind you seek. How will the car be used? What features are critical? A good car salesperson will help you find a vehicle that matches your core needs and fits your budget given your priority uses of the car. The same process holds for any major purchase, like getting a new computer or buying a house, or, for that matter, any important decision, like what courses to take in college or what apartment to rent. The priority-setting process even applies to simple things like going out to eat. You'll have to decide what kind of food you want and what restaurant offers the combination of things you want considering menu options, price, ambiance, and quality. The world is filled with options and menus. And so is evaluation. This chapter is about how to work with primary intended users to determine the primary purposes of an evaluation. The evaluator's facilitation task is to present and explain the primary purpose options and their implications for use. The primary intended users determine which purposes are primary. Choices have to be made. No evaluation can serve all possible purposes equally well. Priorities have to be established.

Purpose Decisions Connected to Situation Analysis

The situation analysis (Step 4) will have established the foundation for making purpose decisions and establishing priority uses. Indeed, all the previous steps will have foreshadowed the evaluation's purpose. Steps 1 and 2 involved assessing organizational and evaluator readiness for evaluation. Already, in those first steps, the issue of purpose will have surfaced. Ready for what kind of evaluation? Different evaluation purposes require different kinds of readiness. Readiness to do a survey of participants to get some feedback about ways of improving a program is quite different from readiness to undertake a randomized control trial to definitively test whether observed outcomes can be attributed to the intervention. So it would have been quite reasonable to make determining the evaluation's purpose the first step. But the evaluator doesn't determine the purpose. The primary intended users do. So identifying and engaging primary intended users (Step 3) has to precede determining the evaluation's purpose, except that certain primary intended users will only be interested in participating in certain types of evaluations. The primary intended user who is worried about and focused on accountability is likely to be different in important ways from one concerned about program improvement, while another may think that identifying best practices and taking a program model to scale (expanding and replicating the model) is most important. These predilections will likely be part of the conversations that occur as primary intended users are recruited to participate in the evaluation. Therefore, some sense of evaluation purpose will have framed issues of readiness, identifying primary intended users, and situation analysis. This fifth step, then, is certainly not the first time that the question of purpose will have arisen. In some cases the priority purpose will have been discussed with the first primary intended user, perhaps the evaluation funder or the program director, as part of the initial readiness assessment, and then primary intended users are recruited with that purpose in mind.

So, there are contingencies, iterations, interconnections, and context considerations that lead to important variations in how the utilization-focused process unfolds, in what order, with what speed, and with whose involvement along the way. Sometimes the process proceeds quite smoothly through the steps identified here in the order identified here. More often, the process involves some aspects of all five initial steps being juggled at the same time. However it unfolds, you'll have to deal with purpose distinctions and priorities—so let's get on with the task of making such distinctions.

Overall Utilization-Focused Evaluation Purpose: Intended Use by Intended Users

Six Alternative Evaluation Purposes

Prioritizing evaluation's purpose and intended uses is evaluation's equivalent of program goal-setting. We expect programs to articulate priority goals. When we come upon a program whose goals are muddled, conflicting, or vague, we often facilitate goals clarification. Likewise, the goals of an evaluation need to be made explicit and prioritized. Different purposes constitute distinct evaluation goals and uses. We're going to review and discuss six distinct purposes:

1. Summative, judgment-oriented evaluation
2. Improvement-oriented formative evaluation
3. Evaluation for accountability
4. Monitoring
5. Knowledge-generating evaluation
6. Developmental evaluation

Summative, Judgment-Oriented Evaluation

Summative evaluation constitutes an important purpose distinction in any menu of intended purposes. Summative evaluations judge the *overall effectiveness of a program* and are particularly important in making decisions about continuing or terminating an experimental program or demonstration project. As such, summative evaluations are often requested by funders.

Evaluations aimed at determining the overall merit, worth, significance, or value of something are *judgment-oriented.* Merit refers to the intrinsic value of a program: for example, how effective it is in meeting the needs of those it is intended help. Worth refers to extrinsic value to those outside the program: for example: to the larger community or society.

A welfare program that gets jobs for recipients has *merit* for those who move out of poverty and *worth* to society by reducing welfare costs. Judgment-oriented evaluation approaches include summative evaluations aimed at deciding if a program is sufficiently effective to be continued or replicated, and comparative ratings or rankings of products as done by *Consumer Reports.* These judgments are used to inform decisions. In the case of consumer products, the judgments inform decisions about whether to purchase a particular item. In the case of programs, the decisions concern whether to continue a program, expand it, or change it in some major way. Exhibit 5.1 presents questions to ask of intended users to establish an evaluation's intended influence on major forthcoming decisions.

EXHIBIT 5.1

Questions to Ask of Intended Users to Establish an Evaluation's Intended Influence on Forthcoming Decisions

What decisions, if any, are the evaluation findings expected to influence?

(There may not be any, in which case the evaluation's purpose may be simply to generate knowledge for conceptual use and future enlightenment. If, however, the evaluation is expected to influence decisions, clearly distinguish summative decisions about program funding, continuation or expansion from formative decisions about program improvement, and ongoing development.)

When will decisions be made? By whom? When, then, must the evaluation findings be presented to be timely and influential?

What is at stake in the decisions? For whom? What controversies or issues surround the decisions? What's the history and context of the decision-making process?

What other factors (values, politics, personalities, promises already made) will affect the decision making? What might happen to make the decision irrelevant or keep it from being made? In other words, how volatile is the decision-making environment?

How much influence do you expect the evaluation to have— *realistically*?

To what extent has the outcome of the decision already been determined?

What needs to be done to achieve that level of influence?

(Include special attention to which stakeholders to involve for the evaluation to have the expected degree of influence.)

What data and findings are needed to support decision making?

How will we know afterwards if the evaluation was used as intended?

(In effect, how can use be measured?)

The first clue that intended users are seeking an overall summative judgment is when you hear the following kinds of questions: Did the program work? Did it attain its goals? Should the program be continued, ended, or expanded to other sites? Did the program provide good value for money? Can the outcomes measured be attributed to the program? Answering these kinds of evaluative questions requires a data-based judgment that some need has been met, some goal attained, or some standard achieved. Here are two examples of summative evaluations.

- The David and Lucile Packard Foundation funded home visitation programs to support child development over many years. These programs provided education to parents about effective interaction with their children for learning and developmental screening for children in the first 3 years of life. The Foundation commissioned a rigorous external evaluation of the home visitation model conducted by a prestigious and independent national research organization. The evaluation found consistent and strong beneficial effects on virtually all measures included in the evaluation and concluded that the model was an effective intervention for improving parenting knowledge, attitudes, and behaviors and for supporting positive child development. Based on this summative evaluation, the Foundation decided to go forward with more program funding and more evaluation (Sherwood, 2005).
- The Technology for Literacy Center (TLC) was established as a 3-year demonstration project to pilot test the effectiveness of an innovative, computer-based approach to adult literacy. The pilot project was funded by six Minnesota philanthropic foundations and the Saint Paul Public Schools at a cost of $1.3 million. The primary intended users of the evaluation were the school superintendent, senior school officials, and school board directors who would determine whether to continue and integrate the project into the district's ongoing community education program. School officials and foundation donors participated actively in designing the evaluation. The summative evaluation began by validating that the model was being implemented as specified. Outcomes were measured using the Test of Adult Basic Education administered on a pre-post basis to participant and control groups. Test scores were analyzed for all students over a 3-month period. Results were compared to data on other adult literacy programs. Retention and attrition data were also analyzed and compared with programs nationally. A cost analysis was also conducted by a university economist. The report was completed 6 months prior to the end of the demonstration, in time for decision makers to use the results to determine the future of the program. Comparisons showed significant gains in reading comprehension and math for the participant group versus no gains for the control group. Based on the positive findings from the summative evaluation, the Saint Paul Public Schools moved the project from pilot to permanent status.

In summative evaluations, "the logic of valuing" rules (Scriven, 1980). Four steps are necessary in working with primary intended users: (1) facilitate selection of criteria for rendering summative judgment, (2) set standards of performance that must be met for the program to be considered successful, (3) measure performance and compare the actual results with the performance targets, and (4) synthesize the results into a summative judgment of value.

Improvement-Oriented, Formative Evaluation

Summative evaluation contrasts with *formative evaluation,* which focuses on ways of improving and enhancing programs rather than rendering definitive judgment about their effectiveness. Michael Scriven (1967, pp. 40–43) introduced the summative-formative distinction in discussing evaluation of educational curriculum. The distinction has since become a fundamental evaluation typology.

Using evaluation to improve a program is quite different from rendering judgment about its overall effectiveness, merit, and worth. Improvement-oriented forms of evaluation include formative evaluation, quality enhancement, learning organization approaches, and *continuous quality improvement* (CQI) initiatives, among others. What these approaches share is a focus on making the intervention better. Improvement-oriented approaches gather data about strengths and weaknesses with the expectation that both will be found and each can be used to inform improvements. Evaluation questions include: What are the program's strengths and weaknesses? To what extent are participants progressing toward the desired outcomes? Which types of participants are making good progress and which aren't doing so well? What kinds of implementation problems have emerged and how are they being addressed? What's happening that wasn't expected? How are staff and clients interacting? What are staff and participant perceptions of the program? What do they like? Dislike? Want to change? What are perceptions of the program's culture and climate? How are funds being used compared to initial expectations? How is the program's external environment affecting internal operations? Where can efficiencies be realized? What new ideas are emerging that can be tried out and tested? The flavor of these questions communicate improvement rather than overall summative judgment.

Bob Stake's metaphor explaining the difference between summative and formative evaluation can be adapted more generally to the distinction between judgmental evaluation and improvement-oriented evaluation: "When the cook tastes the soup, that's formative; when the guests taste the soup, that's summative" (quoted in Scriven, 1991, p. 169). More generally, anything done to the soup during preparation in the kitchen is improvement-oriented; when the soup is served, judgment is rendered, including judgment rendered by the cook that the soup was ready for serving (or at least that preparation time had run out).

Formative evaluation typically connotes collecting data for a specific period of time, usually during the start-up or pilot phase of a project, to improve implementation, solve unanticipated problems, and make sure that participants are progressing toward desired outcomes. Often the purpose of formative evaluation is to get ready for summative evaluation, that is, to get the program's early implementation bugs worked out and the model stabilized so that it can be evaluated summatively to judge merit and worth. Here are examples of formative evaluation.

- The Technology for Literacy Center (TLC), described earlier, engaged in 16 months of formative evaluation before doing the summative evaluation. The internal formative evaluator gathered extensive feedback from the adult learners about their experiences with the program and solicited their recommendations for improvements. The evaluation looked at participation levels and student progress. Student and staff feedback guided staff development activities. The formative evaluator worked with staff to conceptualize the TLC model and bring implementation to a point of stability and clarity where it was ready for summative evaluation.

- The Center for Effective Philanthropy has developed Grantee Perception Reports® (GPR) that solicit feedback from grantees of philanthropic foundations. The results can be used to improve grantee communications, enhance interactions, revise grant-making processes, and adjust grant characteristics (Center for Effective Philanthropy, 2010).
- An employment program was experiencing a high drop-out rate. Follow-up interviews with dropouts revealed areas of participant dissatisfaction that could be corrected. When those improvements were made, the number dropping out deceased significantly.

Accountability

Accountability is a state of, or process for, holding someone to account to someone else for something—that is, being required to justify or explain what has been done. Although accountability is frequently given as a rationale for doing evaluation, there is considerable variation in who is required to answer to whom, concerning what, through what means, and with what consequences. (Rogers, 2005, p. 2)

The accountability function includes *oversight and compliance,* which typically includes assessing the extent to which a program uses funds appropriately, follows mandated processes and regulations, and meets contract obligations. Accountability questions include: To what extent has the program been implemented as planned? Is implementation on schedule? Do actual participants' characteristics match eligibility criteria specifying who was supposed to be in the program? Do staff have necessary credentials and training? Are services being provided in accordance with plans and applicable rules? Are quality control mechanisms in place and being used? To what extent are performance targets being met?

Answering these questions serves the important purpose of informing funders, decision makers, and the general public whether the program is operating in accordance with expectations and mandates. Accountability as a priority purpose is appropriate when the focus of the evaluation is to determine that program compliance has been adequate.

> [A]ccountability systems focus on reporting discrepancies between targets and performance to funders, the assumption being that they will use this information in future funding and policy decisions. However, accountability systems rarely provide sufficient information to make it possible for funders to decide if such discrepancies should be followed by decreased funding (as a sanction), increased funding (to improve the quality or quantity of services being provided) clock, or termination of the function. (Rogers, 2005, pp. 3–4)

This astute conclusion by Australian Patricia Rogers, the first international recipient of the American Evaluation Association's prestigious Myrdal Award for contributions to evaluation use, frames the challenge of bringing a utilization focus to accountability. In other words, accountability findings (compliance with mandates) become problematic when the purpose includes making summative decisions. This is why it is so important to be clear with intended users about purpose. Accountability assessments are different from summative evaluations based on judgments of merit and worthy or formative feedback aimed at improvement. Performance measurement, for example, is a common approach to oversight, compliance, and accountability. Burt Perrin (1998, 2007) has long been a leader in studying the "effective use and misuse of performance measurement." He has been especially adamant about the limitations of performance indicator approaches for evaluation asserting that such data are "useless for decision making and resource allocation" (1998, p. 374). Why? Because a performance indicator alone doesn't tell a decision maker why the results are at a certain level and without knowing why, informed action is problematic. In essence, accountability systems serve the purpose of providing *an account of how things are going* but not enough information to inform decisions or solve problems. Those actions require deeper evaluative data than accountability systems usually provide.

The Utility of an Accountability System

The utility of an accountability system depends on who is held accountable, by whom, for what—and how they are held accountable: that is, the extent to which results can be determined and explained, and that there are consequences for failure and rewards for success. The credibility of an accountability system, which greatly affects its utility, depends on the extent to which those held accountable actually have the capacity to achieve those things over which they are held accountable, within the time frames expected, and that the consequences are proportionately and reasonably aligned with that capacity and those time frames.

A *comprehensive* accountability approach involves both description—What was achieved?—and explanation—How and why was it achieved at the levels attained? To describe is not to explain, and to explain is not to excuse or diminish responsibility. Ideally, description, explanation, and responsibility can be combined to produce an effective and useful accountability system. Description, however, comes first. Having an accurate account of how things are going, including what results are being attained, is essential. Explaining those results and assigning responsibility follow. And that's where it can become very political.

Accountability is like a red cape in front of a bull in the political arena where politicians fancy themselves as matadors braving the horns of waste and corruption. Funders and politicians issue shrill calls for accountability (notably for others, not for themselves), and *managing for accountability* has become a rallying cry in both private and public sectors. Program and financial audits are aimed at assuring compliance with intended purposes and mandated procedures. The program evaluation units of legislative audit offices, offices of comptrollers and inspectors, and federal agencies like the U.S. Office of Management and Budget (OMB) have government oversight responsibilities to make sure programs are properly implemented and effective. Reflecting the increased emphasis on accountability in government, in 2004, the legal name of the Congressional oversight agency, GAO, changed its name to the Government Accountability Office instead of the General Accounting Office, a designation it had had for 83 years. The U.S. Government Performance and Results Act of 1993 requires annual performance measurement to "justify" program decisions and budgets. Political leaders worldwide are vocal in attempting to link performance measurement to budgeting for purposes of accountability

The varying contexts within which such questions are asked matter a great deal. In government, accountability issues inevitably find their way into debates between those in power and those out of power. In philanthropy, accountability focuses on the fiduciary responsibility of a foundation to oversee the use of money and ensure that grant funds are spent in ways consistent with donor intent and the foundation's mission. For not-for-profit agencies and nongovernmental organizations, accountability is part of good management. In all these contexts, accountability-oriented evaluation serves an audit purpose, not just in the traditional auditing of financial accounts but in auditing compliance with program mandates, regulations, procedures, and performance data.

One of my favorite examples comes from a program audit of a weatherization program in Kansas as reported in the newsletter of Legislative Program Evaluators.

> . . . Kansas auditors visited several homes that had been weatherized. At one home, workers had installed 14 storm windows to cut down on air filtration in the house. However, one could literally see through the house because some of the siding had rotted and either pulled away from or fallen off the house. The auditors also found that the agency had nearly 200 extra storm windows in stock. Part of the problem was that the supervisor responsible for measuring storm windows was afraid of heights; he would "eyeball" the size of second-story windows from the ground. . . . If these storm windows did not fit, he ordered new ones. (Hinton, 1988, p. 3)

The auditors also found fraud. The program bought windows at inflated prices from a company secretly owned by a program employee. A kickback scheme was uncovered. "The workmanship on most homes was shoddy, bordering on criminal. . . . [For example], workers installing a roof vent used an axe to chop a hole in the roof." Some 20% of beneficiaries didn't meet eligibility criteria. Findings like these are thankfully rare, but they grab headlines when they become public, and they illustrate why accountability will remain a central purpose of many evaluations.

Rogers has identified the critical characteristics of what she calls a *smart accountability* system: "The acid test of a good accountability system is that it encourages responsibility and promotes better performance" (Rogers, 2005, p. 4).

SOURCE: Terry Smutylo and Daniel Morales-Gomez, cartoonists.

Monitoring: Evaluation's Global Partner

Monitoring as a distinct purpose focuses on data for program management, typically in the form of a management information system. Monitoring data inform managers on a weekly, monthly, or quarterly basis how critical indicators are moving. Is the targeted number of new participants coming into the program, attending regularly, making progress, and completing the program? The data are typically reported comparing one time period to another and yielding participation numbers, drop-out rates, completion rates, and indicators for interim outcomes (for example, the percentage of people in an employment training program that have completed a work internship). Sometimes monitoring is subsumed under accountability since both use performance indicators. But that's like treating formative and summative evaluation as the same because they both use data. In fact, performance indicators can serve different purposes, and this is a discussion of purpose distinctions, so it seems worth noting that (1) performance indicators can be used for either accountability or ongoing management purposes and (2) these purposes are often in conflict because they involve different primary intended users. Accountability is driven by attention to external stakeholders, those to whom the program is responsible and those who have funded it. Ongoing monitoring serves managers, providing those internal to the program with the information they need to determine where their managerial attention is needed.

The other reason for highlighting monitoring as a distinct purpose is that this has become the international norm. In the United States we talk about evaluation and performance measurement as virtually distinct endeavors. But in developing countries, the standard reference is to "M&E"—monitoring *and* evaluation. These are close siblings, always found together.

But there are different approaches to M&E. Traditional M&E has focused on monitoring inputs, activities, and outputs: that is, on project or program implementation. Governments install management information (monitoring) systems to track their expenditures and revenues, staffing levels and resources, program and project activities, numbers of participants, goods produced, services delivered, and so forth. *Results-based M&E* combines the traditional approach of monitoring implementation with the assessment of results (Imas & Rist, 2009; Kusek & Rist, 2004).

> It is this linking of implementation progress (performance) with progress in achieving desired objectives or goals (results) of government policies and programs that makes results-based M&E most useful as a tool for public management. (Rist, 2006, p. 5)

Most approaches to designing M&E systems intend them to serve both accountability and managerial functions. And therein lies the rub. Policymakers and funders want global, big-picture data, what is sometimes called the view from 40,000 feet. Managers need detailed data, the view from 1,000 feet. Aggregating detailed indicators into big-picture patterns is one of the major challenges of a performance monitoring system that tries to serve both sets of stakeholders equally well. Some evaluators emphasize blending M&E purposes and minimize the distinction between managerial use and accountability purposes:

> Performance monitoring systems . . . provide objective information to managers and policy makers in an effort to improve decision making and thereby strengthen performance, as well as to provide accountability to a range of stakeholders, such as higher-level management, central executive agencies, governing bodies, funding agencies, accrediting associations, clients and customers, advocacy groups, and the public at large. (Poister, 2004, p. 99)

A utilization-focused approach to M&E is less cavalier about such laundry lists of stakeholders and multiple intended uses. Any system will have to set priorities for intended uses by intended users at some point, or risk serving everyone poorly.

The phrase M&E makes the marriage of monitoring and evaluation explicit. In particular, findings from monitoring data can generate questions to be answered by evaluation through more in-depth inquiry, helping to focus and increase the utility of scare evaluation resources. Kusek and Rist emphasize the integration of monitoring and evaluation in a well-designed, well-implemented, and results-oriented M&E system.

> We want to stress the complementarities of evaluation to monitoring. Each supports the other even as each asks different questions and will likely make different uses of information and analyses. The immediate implication is that moving to a result-based M&E system requires building an information and analysis system with two components—monitoring and evaluation. Either alone, in the end, is not sufficient. (Kusek & Rist, 2004, p. 114)

Rist (2006) argues that we are moving from "studies to streams," by which he means that organizations are increasingly relying on data systems, not individual evaluators, to produce evaluative findings. Episodic and stand-alone evaluations, which dominated the early days of the profession, are becoming a thing of the past, he argues. He sees monitoring and evaluation as merging, with evaluations increasingly integrating multiple streams of information, using databases that are continuous and virtual. He foresees partnerships being dominant in collecting, analyzing, and sharing evaluative findings (rather than evaluators acting alone and controlling the evaluation process) and the Internet becoming the new information glue in support of increased transparency of evaluative knowledge. M&E can then support continuous organizational adaptation and improvement (Rist & Stame, 2006). In this vision of M&E, monitoring systems will generate evaluation questions which, as they are answered with specific inquiries, will feed back into and improve monitoring, yielding a continuous cycle of improvements, the results of which can be documented to meet accountability needs and demands.

It's an inspiring vision. Thus far, as I read the evidence and listen to evaluators describe their experiences from around the world, it's a vision that is far from being realized. More often, as soon as accountability mandates are introduced, and they're introduced early and authoritatively, the tail wags the dog, and everyone focuses on meeting accountability demands, effectively undercutting the learning and improvement agenda, and limiting managerial willingness and capability to take risks that might attract opposition or resistance. It's not enough to create results-oriented monitoring systems. An organizational culture and climate must be created to support the appropriate and effective use of such systems.

As always we return to the issue of use. Ongoing and continuous monitoring systems, like all useful evaluation approaches, must be designed to meet the specifiable information needs of identifiable users. A system designed by software, technology, and data experts with little or no serious input and pilot-testing with intended users can be a wonderful system—for the experts who designed it, but not for the intended users.

Knowledge-Generating Evaluation

In the knowledge age, what could be more useful than contributing to knowledge? The instrumental uses of summative and formative evaluation concern judgments about and improvements for specific programs. Accountability and monitoring focus on performance indicators for a particular program. Knowledge generation, however, changes the unit of analysis as evaluators look across findings from different programs to identify *general patterns of effectiveness* and lessons for use in future initiatives.

As the field of evaluation has matured and a vast number of evaluations has accumulated, the opportunity has arisen to look beyond and across findings about specific programs to formulate generalizations about processes and interventions that make a difference. An excellent and important example of such synthesis evaluation is Schorr's classic *Within Our Reach: Breaking the Cycle of Disadvantage* (1988), a study of programs aimed at breaking the cycle of poverty. She identified "the lessons of successful programs" as follows (pp. 256–283):

- Offering a broad spectrum of services;
- Regularly crossing traditional professional and bureaucratic boundaries, i.e., organizational flexibility;
- Seeing the child in the context of family and the family in the context of its surroundings, i.e., holistic approaches;
- Coherent and easy-to-use services;
- Committed, caring, results-oriented staff;
- Finding ways to adapt or circumvent traditional professional and bureaucratic limitations to meet client needs;
- Professionals redefining their roles to respond to severe needs; and
- Overall, intensive, comprehensive, responsive and flexible programming.

These kinds of "lessons" constitute accumulated wisdom—principles of effectiveness—that can be adapted, indeed, must be adapted, to specific programs, or even entire organizations.

In the philanthropic world, the strategy of synthesizing results from several studies is sometimes called "cluster evaluation." A cluster evaluation team visits a number of different grantee projects with a similar focus (e.g., grassroots leadership development) and draws on individual grant evaluations to identify patterns and lessons across the whole cluster. The McKnight Foundation commissioned a cluster evaluation of 34 separate grants aimed at aiding families in poverty. One lesson learned was that *effective programs have developed processes and strategies for learning about the strengths as well as the needs of families in poverty.* This "lesson" took on added meaning when connected with the finding of Independent Sector's review of "Common Barriers to Effectiveness in the Independent Sector":

> The deficits model holds that distressed people and communities are "needy"; they're a collection of problems, pathologies and handicaps; they need doctoring, rehabilitation and fixing of the kind that professionalized services are intended to provide.
>
> The assets model holds that even the most distressed person or community has strengths, abilities and capacities; with investment, their strengths, abilities and capacities can increase. This view is only barely allowed to exist in the independent sector, where organizations are made to compete for funds on the basis of "needs" rather than on the basis of "can-do."
>
> The deficit model—seeing the glass half empty—is a barrier to effectiveness in the independent sector (Mayer, 1993, pp. 7–8).

The McKnight Foundation cluster evaluation and the Independent Sector study reached similar conclusions concurrently and independently. Such triangulated evaluation findings about principles of effective programming have become the knowledge base of the evaluation profession. Being knowledgeable about patterns of program effectiveness allows evaluators to provide guidance about development of new initiatives, policies, and strategies for implementation. Such contributions constitute the conceptual use of evaluation findings. Efforts of this kind may be considered research rather than evaluation, but such research is ultimately evaluative in nature and important to the profession.

Some synthesis evaluations look at large numbers of cases. The World Bank's report on *Reducing Poverty on a Global Scale: Learning and Innovating for Development* draws on more than 100 case studies of poverty reduction worldwide. World Bank analysts identified the main factors that help or hurt in reducing poverty at scale. A whole chapter of the report assesses China's experiences in promoting economic growth and reducing poverty over the last 25 years, noting that China has achieved the most rapid large-scale poverty reduction in human history (World Bank, 2006).

Synthesis evaluations also help us generate knowledge about conducting useful evaluations. The premises of utilization-focused evaluation featured in this book originally emerged from studying the use of 20 federal evaluations as described in the chapter on Step 3. Those premises have been affirmed by a great many subsequent studies of use (Patton, 2008, Chapter 3). For example, The Council on Foundations commissioned a synthesis evaluation based on nine case studies of major foundation evaluations to learn lessons about "effective evaluating." Among the Council's 35 key lessons learned was this utilization-focused evaluation premise:

> Key 6. Make sure the people who can make the most use of the evaluation are involved as stakeholders in planning and carrying out the evaluation." (Council on Foundations, 1993, p. 255)

One of the challenges facing the profession of evaluation going forward will be to bring some degree of rigor to such popular notions as "lessons learned" and "best practices." Such rigor takes on added importance as, increasingly, the substantive contribution of evaluation includes not only how to conduct high-quality evaluations but also generating knowledge based on having learned how to synthesize cross-program findings about patterns of effective interventions: that is, better practices in program design and lessons learned about effective programming generally. The future status and utility of evaluation may depend on the rigor and integrity we bring to these challenges.

Developmental Evaluation

The last of the six purposes for evaluation is program and organizational development. Improvement-oriented, formative evaluation focuses on making an intervention or model better. Developmental evaluation, in contrast, involves changing the model by adapting it to changed circumstances and emergent conditions. Developmental evaluation is designed to be congruent with and nurture developmental, emergent, innovative, and transformative processes.

Summative judgment about overall effectiveness of a model requires a stable and fixed program intervention. Common criteria in summative evaluations include efficiency of goal attainment, replicability of the model, clarity of causal specificity, and generalizability. But none of these traditional criteria are appropriate or even meaningful for highly volatile environments, systems-change-oriented interventions, and emergent social innovations. Developmentally oriented leaders in organizations and programs don't expect (or even want) to reach the state of "stabilization" required for summative evaluation. Staff in such efforts don't aim for a steady state of programming because they're constantly tinkering as participants, conditions, learnings, and context change. They don't aspire to arrive at a fixed model that can be generalized and disseminated. At most, they may discover and articulate principles of intervention and development, but not a replicable model that says "do X and you'll get Y." Rather, they aspire to continuous development, ongoing adaptation, and rapid responsiveness. No sooner do they articulate and clarify some aspect of the process than that very awareness becomes an intervention and acts to change what they do. They don't value traditional characteristics of summative excellence such as standardization of inputs, consistency of treatment, uniformity of outcomes, and clarity of causal linkages. They assume a world of multiple causes, diversity of outcomes, inconsistency of interventions, interactive effects at every level—and they find such a world exciting and desirable. They never expect to conduct a summative evaluation because they don't expect the change initiative—or world—to hold still long enough for summative review. They expect to be forever developing and changing—and they want an evaluation approach that supports development and change. That approach is developmental evaluation. Here is an example.

- A leadership development program provided rural leaders with an intensive, week-long retreat experience in which they learned and practiced communication skills, strategy planning, using community indicators, and working together as teams. The program was continuously changed as the rural economy prospered or declined, as government policies and programs affecting rural people changed, as new technologies like cell phones and the Internet emerged with implications for leadership approaches, and as immigrants from around the world moved into rural communities. The program had to be regularly updated and adapted as new issues and challenges emerged. Rapid and ongoing evaluation feedback informed these changes. The program wasn't just improving its model. It was developing the model, thus the appropriateness of development evaluation (Patton, 2011).

Formative evaluation (improvement-oriented evaluation) is ultimately meant to lead to summative evaluation. Formative evaluation aims to make a program model better rather than making it different. In contrast, using a developmental perspective informed by complexity science and systems thinking, you do something different because something has changed—your understanding, the characteristics of participants, technology, or the world (think global climate change, the worldwide financial melt-down of 2008–2009, or the long-term effects of the 9/11 attack on The World Trade Center). Change is adaptation. Assessing the cold reality of change, social innovators can be heard to say:

> At each stage we did the best we could with what we knew and the resources we had. Now we're at a different place in our development—doing and thinking different things. *That's development.* That's change. That's more than just making a few improvements.
>
> Jean Gornick, former director of Damiano, a nonprofit working on poverty alleviation in Duluth, Minnesota (Quoted in Westley, Zimmerman, & Patton, 2006, p. 179)

The purpose of developmental evaluation is to bring evaluative thinking and data to program, organizational, and model *development.*

Applying Purpose and Use Distinctions

The six distinct purposes of evaluation are summarized in Menu 5.1. For each distinct purpose, this menu shows the priority questions asked, common evaluation approaches

MENU 5.1

Primary Uses of Evaluation Findings

Purpose	*Priority Questions*	*Common Evaluation Approaches*	*Key Factors Affecting Use*
Judgment of *overall* value to inform and support major decision making: Determine the value and future of the program or model.	Does the program meet participants' needs? To what extent does the program have merit? Worth? Does it add value for money? How do outcomes and costs compare with other options? To what extent can outcomes be attributed to the intervention? Is the program theory clear and supported by findings? Is this an especially effective practice that should be funded and disseminated as a model program?	–Summative evaluation –Impact evaluation –Cost-benefit analysis –Theory-driven evaluation	Independence and credibility of the evaluator. Rigor of the design: validity, generalizability. Significance of the findings to decision makers. Timeliness.
Learning: Improve the program.	What works and what doesn't? Strengths and weaknesses? Participant reactions? How do different subgroups respond; that is, what works for whom in what ways and under what conditions? How can outcomes and impacts be increased? How can costs be reduced? How can quality be enhanced?	–Formative evaluation –Quality enhancement –Learning reviews –Reflective practice –Participant feedback –Capacity-building –Appreciative inquiry	Creating a learning climate, openness to feedback and change. Trust. Evaluator's skill in facilitating learning. Relevance of findings; actionable.
Accountability: Demonstrate that resources are well-managed and efficiently attain desired results.	Are funds being used for intended purposes? Are goals and targets being met? Are indicators showing improvement? Are resources being efficiently allocated? Are problems being	–Government and funder mandated reporting –Program audits and inspections –Performance measurement and monitoring	Transparency. Validity of indicators. Integrity and credibility of the system and those reporting.

(Continued)

(Continued)

Purpose	*Priority Questions*	*Common Evaluation Approaches*	*Key Factors Affecting Use*
	handled? Are staff qualified? Are only eligible participants being accepted into the program? Is implementation following the approved plan? Are quality control mechanisms in place and being used?	–Accreditation and licensing –End of project reports –Scorecards	Balance. Consistency of reporting. Fairness of comparisons.
Monitoring: Manage the program, routine reporting, early identification of problems.	Are inputs and processes flowing smoothly? What are participation and drop-out rates? Are these changing? Are outputs being produced as anticipated and scheduled? Where are bottlenecks occurring? What are variations across subgroups or sites?	–Management information systems –Quality control systems and CQI (continuous quality improvement) –Routine reporting and record keeping –Performance indicators	Timeliness, regularity, relevance, and consistency of reporting; incentives to input data at field levels and incentives to use the data at management levels; capacity and resources to maintain the system. Appropriate links to accountability system.
Development: Adaptation in complex, emergent, and dynamic conditions.	What's happening at the interface between what the program is doing/ accomplishing and what's going on in the larger world around it? How is the program as an intervention system connected to and affected by larger systems in its environment? What are the trends in those larger systems? What does feedback show about	–Developmental evaluation –Complexity systems –Emergent evaluation –Real-time evaluation –Rapid assessment, rapid feedback –Environmental scanning	Openness. Adaptive capacity. Tolerance for ambiguity and uncertainty ("getting to maybe"). Balancing quality and speed of feedback.

Purpose	*Priority Questions*	*Common Evaluation Approaches*	*Key Factors Affecting Use*
	progress in desired directions? What can we control and not control, predict and not predict, measure and not measure, and how do we respond and adapt to what we cannot control, predict, or measure? How do we distinguish signal from noise to determine what to attend to?		Nimble. Integrate and synthesize multiple and conflicting data sources.
Knowledge generation: Enhance general understandings and identify generic principles about effectiveness.	What are general patterns and principles of effectiveness across programs, projects, and sites? What lessons are being learned? How do evaluation findings *triangulate* with research results, social science theory, expert opinion, practitioner wisdom, and participant feedback? What principles can be extracted across results to inform practice?	–Cluster evaluation –Meta-analyses –Synthesis evaluation –Lessons learned –Effective practices studies	Quality and comparability of sources used; quality of synthesis; capacity to extrapolate. Rigor of triangulation. Identifying principles that can inform practice.

associated with that purpose, and key factors affecting evaluation use. Menu 5.2 identifies the primary intended users and political stakes for each purpose. These exhibits are presented and labeled as "menus" to make explicit that they constitute choices.

Conceptually, the six different purposes we've examined—making summative judgments, offering formative improvements, accountability reporting, monitoring, generating generic knowledge, and developmental evaluation—can be distinguished fairly clearly. In practice, these purposes can become interrelated, parallel, and simultaneous processes as when internal government evaluators are engaged in ongoing monitoring while also preparing periodic summative reports for annual budget decisions. Or internal evaluators may be working on formative evaluation while external evaluators are conducting a summative evaluation. Many such combinations occur in real-world practice, some of them appropriate, but some of them entangling and confusing what should be distinct purposes, and those

MENU 5.2

Evaluation Purpose	*Primary Intended Users*	*What's at Stake?*
Overall Summative Judgment	Funders; those charged with making major decisions about the program's future (e.g., a board of directors); policymakers; those interested in adopting the model.	*Very high stakes*—the future of the program can be at stake, though evaluation findings are rarely the only or even primary basis for such decisions.
Formative Improvement and Learning	Program administrators, staff, and participants; those immediately involved day-to-day in the program.	*Moderate stakes*—make adjustments, act on participant feedback; enhance implementation and outcomes. Small changes involve low stakes; major improvements increase the stakes.
Accountability	Those with executive, managerial, legislative, and funding authority and responsibility to make sure that scarce resources are well-managed,	*High stakes*—the more visible the program, the more political the environment, and the more controversial the intervention, the higher the stakes.
Monitoring	Program managers as primary users for a management information system: internal accountability as the priority.	*Low stakes*—ongoing, routine management, alert for bottlenecks and blips in indicators that require attention. *Becomes high stakes* when used for external accountability.
Developmental	Social innovators: those involved in bringing about major systems change in dynamic environments.	*Low stakes day-to-day* as tactical, incremental changes are made; *high stakes longer term* and strategically because social innovators aspire to have major impacts.
Knowledge generating	Program designers, planners, modelers, theorists, scholars, and policymakers.	*Moderate to low stakes*—knowledge is accumulated incrementally and cumulatively over time; no single study carries great weight; lessons learned are often principles to inform general practice and design rather than concrete recommendations to be implemented immediately.

entanglements and confusions can affect use. The utilization-focused evaluator works with primary intended users to get clarity and agreement about priority purposes aimed at achieving the goal of utilization-focused evaluation: *intended use by intended users.*

So by way of review, let's take a look at the how six purposes lead to different kinds of data collection and different uses. Formative and summative evaluations involve significantly different data collection foci. Summative evaluation aims to produce rigorous findings about whether the program produced desired outcomes, which means gathering credible data on program outcomes and having a design that addresses attribution: Is the level of outcomes attainment sufficient to meet criteria of merit and worth, and can the documented outcomes be attributed to the intervention? Formative evaluation, in contrast, collects feedback from participants and staff about what's working well and what needs to be improved. Developmental evaluation provides rapid feedback about immediate effects of innovative initiatives to guide emergent changes and inform responsive and adaptive development in dynamic environments. Specific formative, summative, or developmental evaluations will not necessarily yield generic knowledge (lessons learned) that can be applied to effective programming in the future. Management information systems collect routine data to monitor program implementation and performance for internal managers and ongoing decision making. Such data may be insufficient to answer external accountability questions so some form of external review and validation is typically needed for the purpose of accountability. The evaluator, understanding these distinctions, works with primary intended users to identify which purposes are primary. Is an overall summative judgment of merit or worth expected? Given the program's situation, is improvement the priority? Or is the program in a dynamic situation in which further model adaptation and development is where evaluation can make the greatest contribution? Is a management information system needed? Is accountability reporting required? To what extent is generating knowledge about patterns of effectiveness and learning general lessons a priority? In posing these questions and making purpose distinctions, decisions about what to do in the evaluation can then be made in accordance with how best to support the evaluation's primary purpose. But this is easier said than done. One frequent reaction to posing alternatives is: "We want to do it all." A comprehensive evaluation, conducted over time and at different levels, may include variations on all six purposes, but for any given evaluation activity, or any particular stage of evaluation, it's critical to have clarity about the priority use of findings.

Consider the evaluation of a leadership program run by a private philanthropic foundation. The original evaluation contract called for 3 years of formative evaluation followed by 2 years of summative evaluation. The program staff and evaluators agreed that the formative evaluation would be for staff and participant use; however, the summative evaluation would be addressed to the foundation's board of directors. The formative evaluation helped shape the curriculum, brought focus to intended outcomes, and became the basis for the redesign of follow-up activities and workshops. As time came to make the transition

"So many possible evaluation uses! Couldn't we get the sampler plate with a little bit of each one?"

from formative to summative evaluation, the foundation's president got cold feet about having the evaluators meet directly with the board of directors. The evaluators insisted on interacting directly with these primary users to lay the groundwork for genuinely summative decision making. Senior staff decided that no summative decision was imminent, so the evaluation continued in a formative mode and the design was changed accordingly. As a matter of ethics, the evaluators made sure that the chair of the board was involved in these negotiations and that the board agreed to the change in focus. There really was no summative decision on the horizon because the foundation had a long-term commitment to the leadership program. However, the program was facing some major new challenges in dealing with a large influx of immigrants in the area it served and needed to adapt the program to major economic and political trends that affected the training leaders needed. Thus, the program moved from formative to developmental evaluation to create a substantially new approach based on changing conditions.

Now, consider a different case, the evaluation of an innovative school, the Saturn School, in Saint Paul, Minnesota. Again, the original evaluation design called for 3 years of formative evaluation followed by 2, final years with a summative focus. The formative evaluation revealed some implementation and outcome problems, including lower than desired scores on district-mandated standardized tests. The formative evaluation report, meant only for internal discussion to support program improvement, got into the newspapers with glaring headlines about problems and low test scores. The evaluation's visibility and public reporting put pressure on senior district officials to make summative decisions about the program despite earlier assurances that the program would have a full 5 years before such decisions were made. The formative evaluation essentially became summative when it hit the newspapers and district decision makers felt a need to make major decisions to show they were on top of things (accountability thus coming to the fore). Much to the chagrin of staff and program supporters, including many parents, the shift in purpose led to personnel changes and top-down, forced program changes. Many of those involved in openly and honestly sharing concerns in what they thought was an internal, formative process felt betrayed by the changed use from formative to summative, with heavy accountability overtones.

Sometimes, however, program staff like such a reversal of intended use as when, for example, evaluators produce a formative report that is largely positive and staff wants to disseminate the results as if they were summative, even though the methods of the formative evaluation were aimed only at capturing initial perceptions of program progress, not at rendering an overall judgment of merit or worth. Keeping formative evaluations formative, and summative evaluations summative, is an ongoing challenge, not a one-time decision. When contextual conditions merit or mandate a shift in focus, evaluators need to work with intended users to fully understand the consequences of such a change.

A knowledge-generating evaluation can also experience tugs and pulls into other purposes. A national foundation funded a cluster evaluation in which a team of evaluators would assemble data from some 30 different projects and identify lessons for effective community-based health programming—essentially a knowledge-generating evaluation. The cluster evaluation team had no responsibility to gather data to improve specific programs nor make summative judgments. Each separate project had its own evaluation for those purposes. The cluster evaluation was intended to look for patterns of effectiveness (and barriers to same) across projects. Yet, during site visits, individual grantees were hungry for feedback and comparative insights about how well they were doing and ways they might improve, and project leaders provided cluster evaluators with a great deal of formative feedback that they wanted communicated to the foundation about how the foundation could better support their efforts. Moreover, grantees were suspicious that the cluster evaluation was really an accountability exercise just posing as knowledge-generating, and their fears in this regard had to be addressed. As the cluster evaluators approached time for a final report, senior foundation officials and trustees asked for summative conclusions about the overall effectiveness of the entire program area as part of rethinking funding priorities and strategies. They also asked the evaluators to design a routine reporting and monitoring system for the cluster grantees. Thus, a knowledge-generating evaluation got caught up in pressures to adapt to meet demands for formative, summative, accountability, and monitoring uses.

Evaluation Use and Decision Making

When decisions are informed by evaluation findings, other considerations also come into play including political priorities, decision makers' values, available resources, public support, and management preferences. Evaluation findings are usually one piece of the decision-making pie, not the whole pie. Rhetoric about "data-based decision making" and "evidence-based practice" can give the impression that one simply looks at evaluation results and a straightforward decision follows. *Erase that image from your mind.* That is seldom, if ever, the case. Evaluation findings typically have technical and methodological weaknesses; data must be interpreted; other contextual factors must be taken into consideration. In short, evaluation use is a complex process. Utilization-focused evaluation acknowledges and deals with those complexities to increase the likelihood that evaluation findings are appropriately and meaningfully used.

Making Menu Selections: Connecting Decisions to Uses

The six options I've presented are by no means inherently conflicting purposes, and some evaluations strive to incorporate aspects of different approaches, as in M&E. But, in my experience, one purpose is likely to become the dominant motif and prevail as the *primary* purpose informing design decisions and priority uses; or else, different aspects of an evaluation are designed, compartmentalized, and sequenced to address these contrasting purposes: for example, doing formative evaluation to get ready for summative evaluation. I also find that confusion among these quite different purposes, or failure to prioritize them, is often the source of problems and misunderstandings along the way, and can become disastrous at the end when it turns out that different intended users had different expectations and priorities.

In helping intended users select from the evaluation purposes menu, and thereby focus the evaluation, evaluators may encounter some reluctance to make a commitment. I worked with one director who proudly displayed this sign on his desk: "My decision is maybe—and that's final." Unfortunately, the sign was all too accurate. He wanted me to decide what kind of evaluation should be done. After several frustrating attempts to narrow the evaluation's focus, I presented what I labeled a "MAYBE DESIGN." I laid out cost estimates for an all-encompassing evaluation that included formative, summative, knowledge-generating, accountability, monitoring, and developmental components looking at all aspects of the program. Putting dollars and time lines to the choices before him expedited his decision making. He decided not to undertake any evaluation "at this time."

I was relieved. I had become skeptical about the potential for doing anything useful. Had I succumbed to the temptation to become the decision maker, an evaluation would have been done, but it would have been my evaluation, not his. I'm convinced he would have waffled over using the findings as he waffled over deciding what kind of evaluation to do.

Thus, in utilization-focused evaluation, the choice of not dining at all is always on the menu. It's better to find out before preparing the meal that those invited to the banquet are not really hungry. Take your feast elsewhere, where it will be savored.

PRACTICE EXERCISES

1. Search the news, the Internet, evaluation journals, and other sources to find a case study or example of an actual evaluation that has been done. How explicit was the purpose of the evaluation? To what extent and in what ways were the methods used and findings generated aligned with the priority purpose?

2. Identify an actual program. Describe the program and its context. Specify the specific primary evaluation questions that could guide an evaluation endeavor under each of the six purposes in Menu 5.1.

3. For the program identified in question No. 1, or another program, use Menu 5.2 to identify the specific intended users by name and position in the center column, "primary intended users." Then, assess the stakes (column 3) for those intended users. How do the stakes for the intended users you've identified compare to the norms described in column 3 of Menu 5.2?

4. Use Exhibit 5.1, *Questions to ask of intended users to establish an evaluation's intended influence on forthcoming decisions,* to interact with a real-life program manager. Approach that manager as a simulation of a real evaluation consultation in which you will be assisting in designing a decision-oriented evaluation. Record the highlights of the interaction and comment on what it reveals about decision-oriented, instrumental use.

INTERLUDE, STEPS 1 THROUGH 5. COMPLEX DYNAMIC SYSTEMS INTERCONNECTIONS

Focusing on Intended Uses by Intended Users

The steps in the checklist are necessarily linear and sequential.

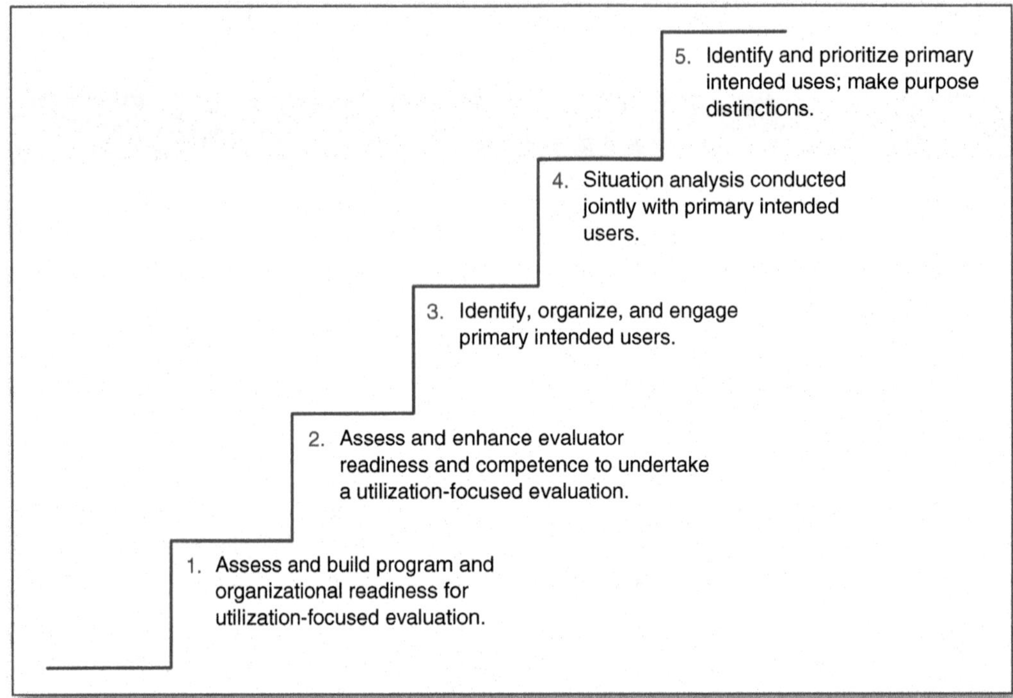

Details about what is involved in each step are provided in the summary *U-FE Checklist* in the concluding chapter. (See pages 406–412.)

Though we can think of and depict U-FE as a series of steps, it can also be thought about and portrayed as a complex adaptive system. In so doing, each new step also becomes another element in the complex systems graphic that is emerging as we proceed through the steps. Purposes distinctions (Step 5) will already have emerged and affect the assessments and situation analyses done in Steps 1 and 2, as well as decisions about who to select and engage as primary intended users. These processes go on simultaneously as much as sequentially as depicted in graphic below.

Complex Interconnections and Adaptive Interactions Among U-FE Steps 1 Through 5

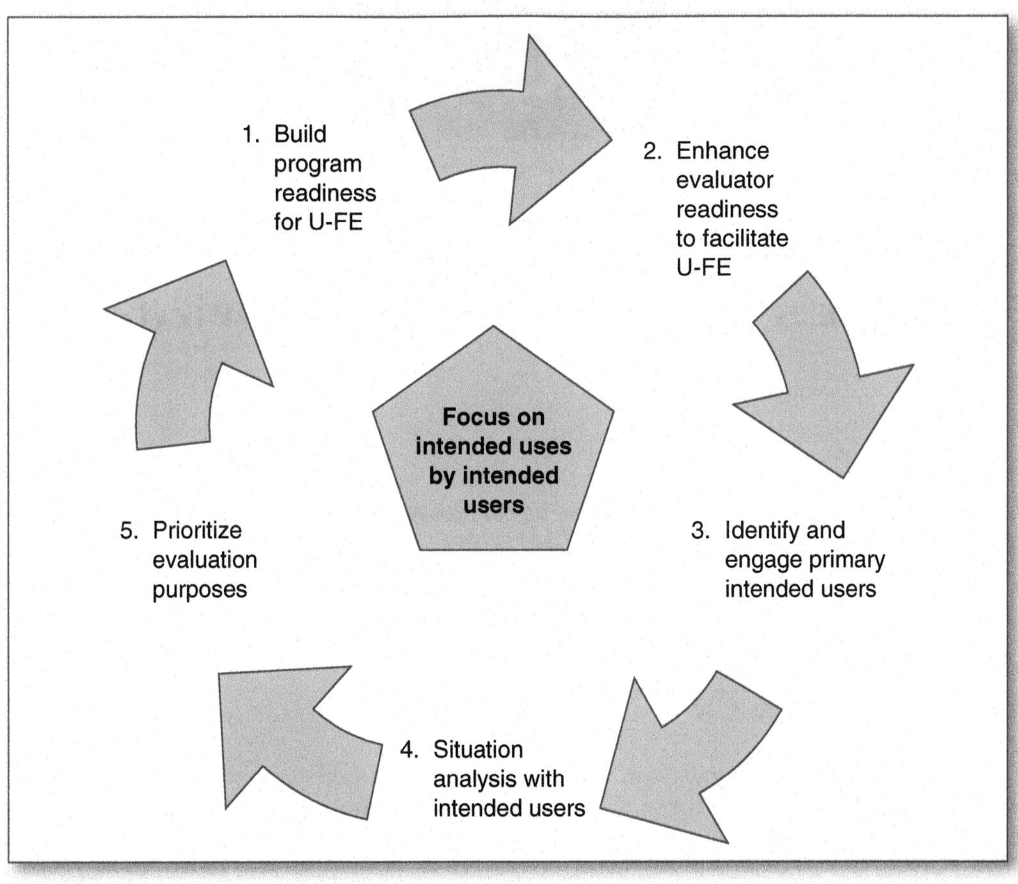

6

Consider and Build in Process Uses if and as Appropriate

Process matters. It's not just where you end up but how you get there. Things happen along the way. Important things. Pay attention. The most significant impacts may not be found at the end of the journey but along the way.

Halcolm's Ruminations on the Journey

Beyond Just Findings Use

Step 6 involves considering ways in which being engaged in the processes of evaluation can be useful quite apart from the findings that may emerge from those processes. *Process use* refers to the things that people involved in an evaluation learn from the evaluation, like using the logic of evaluation, employing the systematic reasoning processes involved in analysis, and being guided by the standards that inform evaluation practice. When primary intended users reason like an evaluator and operate according to an evaluation's values, their knowledge, attitudes, and behaviors can be affected before findings are reported and in ways that go beyond the findings.

Process use also includes the impacts on programs of getting ready for evaluation. When program staff engages in goals clarification or identifies measures for outcomes, those processes can have an impact on program operations and outcomes *before* data are ever gathered. Staff becomes more focused as goals get clarified and *what gets measured gets done.*

An old Sufi story about border guards searching for a smuggler's contraband illustrates the challenge of identifying potential process uses. Nasrudin used to take his donkey across a frontier every day, the panniers loaded with straw. Since he admitted to being a smuggler, when he trudged home every night, the frontier guards searched his person, sifted the straw, steeped it in water, and even burned it sometimes. Meanwhile, he was becoming visibly more prosperous.

Eventually, he retired to another country, very wealthy. One of the customs officials encountered him there. "You can tell me now, Nasrudin," he said. "Whatever was it that you were smuggling, that we could never catch you at?"

"Donkeys," replied Nasrudin grinning (adapted from Shah, 1964, p. 59).

Process as Outcome

Process use is distinct from use of findings. It's equivalent to the difference between learning how to learn versus learning substantive knowledge about something. Learning how to think evaluatively is learning how to value evidence and think more critically, and those who become involved in an evaluation learn by doing. Facilitating evaluative thinking opens up new possibilities for impact that organizations and funders are coming to value because the capacity to engage in this kind of thinking can have enduring value. This especially resonates for organizations interested in becoming what has come to be called popularly "learning organizations."

Findings have a very short "half-life"—to use a physical science metaphor; they lose relevance quickly. Specific findings typically have a small window of applicability. In contrast, learning to think and act evaluatively can have ongoing relevance. The experience of being involved in an evaluation, then, for those actually involved, can have a lasting impact on how they think, on their openness to reality testing, and on how they view the things they do.

How do I know this? Because that's often what intended users tell me when I follow up the evaluations I conduct. Months after an evaluation, I'll talk with clients (intended users) to get their assessments of whether the evaluation achieved its intended uses and to find out what other impacts may have resulted (Step 16). They often say some version of the following, a response from an experienced and wise program director:

> We used the findings to make some changes in our intake process and improvements in the treatment program. We reorganized parts of the program and connected them together better. But, you know, the big change is in our staff's attitude. They're paying more attention to participant reactions on a daily basis. Our staff meetings are more outcomes-oriented and reflective. Staff exchanges about results are more specific and data based. We're more focused. And the fear of evaluation is gone. Doing the evaluation had a profound impact on our program culture. It really did.

Any evaluation can have these kinds of effects. What's different about utilization-focused evaluation is that the process of actively involving intended users increases these kinds of evaluation impacts. Furthermore, the possibility and desirability of building an organization's capacity to learn from evaluation processes as well as findings can be made intentional and purposeful. In other words, instead of treating process use as an informal offshoot, explicit and up-front attention to the potential impacts of evaluation logic and processes can increase those impacts and make them a planned purpose for undertaking the evaluation. In that way, the evaluation's overall utility is increased. Exhibit 6.1 provides a formal definition of process use.

EXHIBIT 6.1

Process Use Defined

Process use occurs when those involved in the evaluation learn from the evaluation process itself or make program changes based on the evaluation process rather than just the evaluation's findings. Process use, then, includes cognitive, attitudinal, and behavior changes in individuals, and program or organizational changes resulting, either directly or indirectly, from engagement in the evaluation process and learning to think evaluatively (e.g., increased evaluation capacity, integrating evaluation into the program, goals clarification, conceptualizing the program's logic model, setting evaluation priorities, and improving outcomes measurement). An example of or evidence for process use is when those involved in the evaluation later say something like this: "The impact on our program came not just from the findings but also from going through the thinking process that the evaluation required."

As always, the most convincing evidence that learning has occurred is subsequent translation into action. Process use includes the effects of evaluation procedures and operations, for example, the premise that "what gets measured gets done," so establishing measurements and setting targets affects program operations and management focus. These are uses of evaluation processes that affect programs, different from use of specific findings generated by an evaluation.

Process Use as a Usefulism

Process use is best understood and used as a sensitizing concept, or "usefulism" (Safire, 2007)—an idea or concept that calls our attention to something useful, but that something takes its meaning from and must be defined within a particular context, like being "middle aged" (the definition of which varies over time and in different places). A sensitizing concept, in the tradition of qualitative research (Patton, 2002), raises consciousness about a possibility and alerts us to watch out for it within a specific context. That's what the concept of *process use* does. The concept of *process use* says, things are happening to people and changes are taking place in programs and organizations as evaluation takes place, especially when stakeholders are involved in the process. Watch out for those things. Pay attention. Something important may be happening. The process may be producing outcomes quite apart from findings. Think about what's going on. Help the people in the situation pay attention to what's going on, if that seems appropriate and useful. In that way, *process use* can become a matter of intention (Patton, 2007). (For variations in operationalizing and studying process use in research on evaluation, see Cousins, 2007).

Valuing Process Use

In working with intended users, it's important to help them think about the potential and desired impacts of how the evaluation will be conducted. Questions about who will be involved take on a different degree of importance when it's understood that those most directly involved will not only play a critical role in determining the focus of the evaluation, but they also will be most affected by exposure to evaluation logic and processes. The degree of internal involvement, engagement, and ownership will affect the nature and degree of impact on the program's culture, as will the capacity of the program or organization to engage in evaluation for ongoing learning.

How funders and users of evaluation think about and calculate the costs and benefits of evaluation are also affected. The cost-benefit ratio changes on both sides of the equation when the evaluation produces not only findings but also serves immediate programmatic needs like organizational capacity-building, staff development, or participant empowerment.

Varieties of Process Use

To help primary intended users consider process use opportunities and options, I differentiate six primary uses of evaluation processes: (1) infusing evaluative thinking into an organization's culture; (2) enhancing shared understandings; (3) supporting and reinforcing the program through intervention-oriented evaluation; (4) instrumentation effects (what gets measured gets done); (5) increasing participants' engagement, sense of ownership, and self-determination (participatory and empowerment evaluation); and (6) program or organizational development. Menu 6.1 summarizes these six types of process use. Again, the menu metaphor is aimed at framing these different types of process uses as choices. I'll elaborate each, with examples, then consider the challenges and controversies engendered by using evaluation in these ways.

1. Infusing evaluative thinking into organizational culture: Building evaluation capacity

Building the evaluation capacity of an organization to support staff in thinking *evaluatively* means integrating evaluation into the organization's culture. The arena of organizational culture involves looking at how decision makers and staff incorporate evaluative thinking into everything they do as part of ongoing attention to mission fulfillment and continuous improvement. Integrating evaluation into organizational culture means "mainstreaming evaluation":

> Mainstreaming refers to the process of making evaluation an integral part of an organization's everyday operations. Instead of being put aside in the margins of work, evaluation becomes a routine part of the organization's work ethic if it is mainstreamed. It is part of the culture and job responsibilities at all levels of the organization. . . . Mainstreaming depends on evaluation being internalized as a value throughout the organization and on an infrastructure that supports and maintains evaluation. (Sanders, 2002, p. 254)

MENU 6.1

Process Uses

Uses that derive from engaging in an evaluation process in contrast to using evaluation findings

Uses	*Examples*
Infusing evaluative thinking into the organizational culture	Becoming an authentic learning organization Incorporating evaluative questioning into routine decision making Integrating monitoring and evaluation, and linking both to budget and planning cycles Incentives and rewards for evaluation use Building support for evaluation throughout the organization, ongoing capacity development and training in evaluation
Enhancing shared understandings	Agreeing on the program's model and expected outcomes as a result of evaluation questions and determining evaluation priorities *Evaluability assessment,* in which the program gets ready for evaluation by clarifying goals and the program's logic model Managing staff meetings or the program's plan of work around evaluation issues and explicit outcomes Giving voice to different perspectives and valuing diverse experiences
Supporting and reinforcing the program intervention	Building evaluation into program delivery processes in such a way that desired program outcomes are achieved in part through the effects of data collection Participants monitoring their own progress Specifying and monitoring outcomes as integral to working with program participants
Instrumentation effects and reactivity	What gets measured gets done so resources and staff efforts are aligned with performance measures and evaluation priorities Using interview protocols to enhance reflection Data collection processes affect program participants and staff intentionally or unintentionally Participants learn from and are affected by evaluation tests, surveys, and interviews Using the data collection process to enhance organizational communications

(Continued)

(Continued)

Uses	*Examples*
Increasing engagement, self-determination, and ownership	Participatory and collaborative evaluation Empowerment evaluation Reflective practice Self-evaluation Building evaluation capacity Learning evaluation by doing evaluation
Program and organizational development	Developmental evaluation (Patton, 2011) Making the organization the unit of analysis and organizational effectiveness the focus Looking at the connections between program effectiveness and organizational effectiveness to enhance understanding and support realignment Evaluability assessment and logic modeling used for program design

An excellent example of mainstreaming is illustrated by the International Development Research Centre (IDRC) headquartered in Ottawa, Canada. IDRC helps developing countries use science and technology to find practical, long-term solutions to the social, economic, and environmental problems they face. In 2001, IDRC's senior management expanded the organization's evaluation commitment to include a framework for mission assessment at the overall corporate level. This involved the systematic collection of performance data regarding IDRC's strategic goals and operating principles. This is where it gets interesting from our point of view because one of those operating principles was evaluative thinking. This was the first organization I had encountered that made infusing evaluative thinking into the organizational culture an explicit dimension for performance measurement. In essence, senior management committed not only to supporting the conduct and use of specific high-quality evaluation studies and management information system data, they made evaluative thinking a fundamental way of doing business, infused throughout the culture. What did they mean? Here are examples of what they committed to:

- Evaluative thinking permeates our work so that we consciously and constantly reflect on project, program, regional, and corporate experience with a view to implementing improvements based on what is learned.

- Evaluative thinking is demonstrated in the implementation of well-focused programs and in the use of high-quality evaluations that feed into program and project decision making. Time and resources are allocated for reflection on evaluation findings and for documenting use of the findings.

Evaluative Thinking in Practice

Having observed that routine program reporting had become boring, tedious, and not-much-used, IDRC evaluation staff helped create an innovative reporting process dubbed the "Rolling Project Completion Report" (rPCR). The new system emphasized learning rather than paperwork accountability. Early in the life of a project, a junior staff member interviews a project officer to gather data about project design, start-up lessons, and issues that will need attention going forward. In the middle of a project, team leaders interview project officers to capture lessons about implementation and interim outcomes, as well as update work on key issues. After the end of a project, senior managers interview project officers to complete the project reports, identify results, and capture any final learnings. Major learnings are highlighted at an Annual Learning Forum. This new rPCR process replaced the old paperwork requirement with an interview process that has people at different levels in the organization talking to each other, learning about each other's work, and sharing lessons. The process was designed so that interview responses are entered into the learning system in real time, as the interview takes place, with subsequent opportunities for project managers to make corrections and append supporting documentation and cross-reference information sources (Carden & Earl, 2007). The old project completion reports, long disdained, were replaced by this new interactive reporting process. It became a source of energy and enlightenment, and a manifestation of evaluative thinking infused into the organizational culture.

2. Using evaluation to enhance shared understandings

Evaluation both depends on and facilitates clear communications. Shared understandings emerge as evaluation logic pushes the senders of messages to be as specific as possible and challenges listeners to reflect on and provide feedback to senders what they think they've heard. Shared understandings are especially important with regard to expected results. For example, board members and program staff often have different notions of what an agency or program is supposed to accomplish. The processes of clarifying desired ends and focusing staff efforts on accomplishing those ends by evaluating actual accomplishments ought to be primary board functions, but few boards fulfill these functions effectively.

I'm often asked to facilitate board or staff retreats to help them apply the logic and discipline of evaluation to formulating the organization's mission and goals. The feedback I get is that the questions I pose as an evaluator (e.g., What *specific* results are you committed to achieving and how would you know if you accomplished them? What would success look like?) are different from what they are asked by nonevaluators. It's not so much that other facilitators don't ask these questions, but they don't ask them with the same seriousness and pursue the answers with the same rigor and intensity. The very process of formulating a mission and goals *so they can be evaluated* will usually have an impact on how people think about what they're trying to accomplish, long before data are actually collected to measure results.

A parallel use of evaluation is to increase shared understandings between program managers and line staff. Managers can work with staff under the guidance of an evaluator to establish a monitoring system to help everyone involved stay focused on desired outcomes. While the data from such a system may ultimately support decision making, in the short run, the impact is to focus staff attention and energy on priority outcomes. The process needs to be facilitated in such a way that staff can speak openly about whether board and administrative expectations are meaningful, realistic, and attainable. Done properly, evaluation facilitates shared commitments to results from top to bottom *and* bottom to top for enhanced communication between staff at different levels of program implementation.

The logic and principles of evaluation also can be useful in negotiations between parties with different perspectives. For example, a major foundation was interested in funding an effort to make schools more racially equitable through a process that would engage the community. The school district expressed great interest in such funding but resisted committing to involving community people in schools in any ways that might undermine building-level autonomy or intrude into personnel evaluations of principals. Over a period of several months, the funder and school officials negotiated the project. The negotiations centered on defining what was meant by "greater racial equity"—which is basically an evaluation question. Was the only criterion closing the gap in test scores between students of different races? Should other criteria, like parental involvement, attendance rates, and graduation rates, be included? The funder and school district eventually agreed to focus the project and evaluation on community-based, school-specific action plans, activities, and outcomes rather than a standardized and prescribed set of districtwide, uniform indicators. Part of the reason was to increase the buy-in of teachers and community people on a school-by-school basis since different schools had quite different racial profiles and varying equity challenges. The design of the entire project was changed and made more focused as a result of these evaluation-focused negotiations. Applying the logic of evaluation had a major impact on the project's design *before* any data collection was done, or before findings and a report were produced. Everyone came out of the negotiations clear about what was to happen in the project and how it would be evaluated.

Another form of process use involves *giving voice* to the disenfranchised, underprivileged, poor, and others outside the mainstream (H. B. Weiss & Greene, 1992, p. 145). In the evaluation of a diversity project in the Saint Paul Public Schools, a major part of the design included capturing and reporting the experiences of people of color. Providing a way for African American, Native American, Chicano-Latino, and Hmong (from Laos) parents to tell their stories to mostly White, corporate funders was an intentional purpose of the design, one approved by those same White corporate funders. The final report was a multivocal, multicultural presentation of different experiences with and perceptions of the program's impacts (Stockdill, Duhon-Sells, Olson, & Patton, 1992). *Being heard was an end in itself, quite separate from use of the findings.*

3. Evaluation as integral to the program intervention

Consider the case of a one-day workshop. A traditional evaluation design would typically include a pretest and posttest to assess changes in participants' knowledge, skills, and attitudes. As the workshop opens, participants are asked to complete a pretest. At the end of the day, they are given the same instrument as a posttest. The pretest and posttest are clearly separate from the workshop intervention.

Let us now tweak this standard approach to fully integrate the evaluation data collection into the workshop. The session begins as follows:

> The first part of the workshop involves your completing a self-assessment of your knowledge, skills, and attitudes. This will help you prepare for and get into thinking about the things we will be covering today in your training.

The workshop then proceeds. At the end of the day, the workshop presenter closes as follows:

> Now the final workshop activity is for you to assess what you have learned today. To that end, we are going to have you retake the self-assessment you took this morning. This will serve as a review of today and let you see how much you've learned.

In this second scenario, the word evaluation is never mentioned. The pre- and post-assessments are explicitly and intentionally part of the workshop in accordance with adult learning principles. We know, for example, that when participants are told what they will learn, they become prepared for the learning; learning is further enhanced when it is reinforced both immediately and over the long term. In the second scenario, the self-assessment instrument serves both the function of preparing people for learning and as baseline data. The posttest serves the dual functions of learning reinforcement and evaluation. Likewise, a 6-month follow-up to assess retention can serve the dual functions of learning reinforcement and longitudinal evaluation.

The methodological specialist will note that the second scenario is fraught with threats to validity. However, the purpose of data collection in this second scenario is not only assessment of the extent to which change has occurred, but increasing the likelihood that change will occur. It does not matter *to these particular intended users (the workshop instructors)* how much of the measured change is due to pretest sensitization versus actual learning activities, or both, as long as the instrument items are valid indicators of desired outcomes and the desired outcomes are being attained. Moreover, in the second scenario, the data collection is so well integrated into the program that there are no separate evaluation costs except for the data analysis itself. Under the second scenario, the administration of the pretest and posttest is a part of the program such that *even if the data were not analyzed for evaluation purposes, the data collection would still take place,* making evaluation data collection highly cost-effective. This enhances the sustainability of evaluation because, when it's built in rather than added on, it's not viewed as a temporary effort or luxury that can be easily dispensed with when cuts are necessary.

Principles of Intervention-Oriented Evaluation

I have called this process *intervention-oriented evaluation* to make explicit the direct and integral connection between data collection and program results. An evaluation becomes part of the programmatic intervention to the extent that the way it is conducted supports and reinforces accomplishing desired program goals. The primary principle of *intervention-oriented evaluation* is to build a program delivery model that logically and meaningfully interjects data collection in ways that enhance achievement of program outcomes, while also meeting evaluation information needs. I followed this principle in evaluating a wilderness program that aimed to transform traditional college administrators (presidents, college deans, and department heads) into leaders in *experiential education.* They engaged in a variety of outdoor activities—hiking, mountain climbing, and river rafting. Participants kept journals for reflection. The program's philosophy was, "One doesn't just learn from experience; one learns from *reflection* on experience." The process of journaling was part of the program intervention, but it was also a prime source of qualitative evaluation data capturing how participants reacted to and were changed by project participation. In addition, participants were paired together to interview each other before, during, and after each wilderness experience. These interviews were part of the project's reflection process but also were a source of case data for evaluation. The evaluation process thus became part of the intervention in providing participants with experiences in *reflective practice* (Patton, 2011, Chapter 9). Such personal, intensive, and reflective data collection is an intervention. In intervention-oriented evaluation, such data collection is designed to reinforce and strengthen the program's impact.

In my experience, program funders, managers, and staff can become enthused about the creative possibilities for integrating evaluation to support and reinforce the program intervention. This can make the evaluation more relevant, meaningful, accessible, and useful. Yet this approach can be controversial because the evaluation's credibility may be undercut by concerns about whether the data are sufficiently independent of the treatment to be meaningful and trustworthy; the evaluator's independence may be suspect when the relations with staff and/or participants become quite close; and the capacity to render an independent, summative judgment may be diminished. These are considerations to discuss with intended users and evaluation funders in deciding the relative priority of different potential uses of evaluation and in reviewing the principles of intervention-oriented evaluation (see Exhibit 6.2).

4. **Instrumentation effects and reactivity**

The assertion that *what gets measured gets done* is an example of how measuring something can have an impact. Instrumentation effects, or reactivity, call attention to the ways in which people are affected by taking tests, completing surveys, or being interviewed. For example, a probing interview invites program participants to share their experiences and perspectives. The process of being taken through an in-depth, directed, and reflective process can affect interviewees' opinions, feelings, and even behaviors. Such changes are *instrumentation effects*—the effect of the interview process and experience.

The purpose of an evaluation interview is first and foremost to gather data, not change people. Skilled interviewers take a nonjudgmental stance and communicate neutrality so

EXHIBIT 6.2

Principles of Intervention-Oriented Evaluation

1. The evaluation is designed to support, reinforce, and enhance attainment of desired program outcomes.
2. Evaluation data collection and use are integrated into program delivery and management. Rather than being separate from and independent of program processes, the evaluation is an integral part of those processes.
3. Program staff and participants know what is being evaluated and know the criteria for judging success.
4. Feedback of evaluation findings is used to increase individual participant goal attainment as well as overall program goal attainment.
5. There are no or only incidental add-on costs for data collection because data collection is part of program design, delivery, and implementation.
6. Evaluation data collection, feedback, and use are part of the program model; that is, evaluation is a component of the intervention.

that the person being interviewed feels comfortable saying what they really think and feel. An evaluation interviewer is not a therapist. Staying focused on the data-gathering purpose of the interview is critical to gathering high-quality data. Still, those being interviewed may be affected, either negatively or positively. Interviews, by stimulating memories, can reopen old wounds, which may be painful, healing, or both. When interviewing families who had experienced child sexual abuse, we found that most mothers appreciated the opportunity to tell their stories, vent their rage against the system, and share their feelings with a neutral, but interested listener. Our interviews with elderly residents participating in a program to help them stay in their homes and avoid nursing home institutionalization typically lasted much longer than planned because the elderly interviewees longed to have company and talk. All these are *reactions to the process of being interviewed.*

People being interviewed can learn things from the questions asked. If you ask a mother in an early childhood education program whether she is interacting with other mothers outside the formal sessions, she may respond, as one quite shy mother once did to me, "No, but that's a good idea. I'd like to do that." Then, looking quizzical, "Are we supposed to be doing that? I get it. Is that why we all exchanged phone numbers?" She was learning about the program from the evaluation interview.

Learning from being interviewed or taking a test is an instrumentation effect. Questionnaires can also affect people, solidifying attitudes about a program or stimulating discussions among those who complete the questionnaires: "How did you answer that question about how the program can be improved?" Such exchanges of views can affect how participants engage with staff going forward.

The performance measurement mantra, "What gets measured gets done," is a recognition of process use and measurement reactivity. When a teacher announces a test and says, "Here's what will be on the test and here's what I'll be looking for," that teacher is manifesting the performance measurement principle that *what gets measured gets done.* Some weight loss programs have participants set goals and then weigh in weekly in front of other participants as a way of increasing commitment to losing weight. Weighing oneself is a measurement. It is also feedback about progress aimed at encouraging goal achievement. Weighing oneself in front of other participants increases the likelihood of reacting to the measurement process. That's why it is done, to harness the desire to avoid shame and embarrassment in service of goal attainment. Such regular monitoring becomes part of the intervention.

In performance monitoring, what gets measured gets done means that program resources and staff efforts are meant to be focused on moving the indicators. Staff, therefore, is expected to react to what is being measured. In summary, process use occurs when the measurement process itself affects what people do and when the evaluation data collection instruments—tests, questionnaires, interviews, journals—affect how participants experience a program and what outcomes they attain.

5. Supporting engagement: Participatory, collaborative, and empowerment evaluation

Early in my career, I was commissioned by a provincial deputy minister in Canada to undertake an evaluation in a school division he considered mediocre. I asked what he wanted the evaluation to focus on. "I don't care what the focus is," he replied. "I just want to get the people engaged in some way. Education has no life there. Parents aren't involved. Teachers are just putting in time. Administrators aren't leading. Kids are bored. I'm hoping evaluation can stir things up and get people involved again."

Getting people involved—participation, collaboration, engagement—has an impact on those who participate beyond whatever tasks they may accomplish together. In the *process* of participating in an evaluation, participants are exposed to and have the opportunity to learn evaluation reasoning. Skills are acquired in problem identification, criteria specification, and data collection, analysis, and interpretation. Acquisition of such skills and ways of thinking can have a long-term impact beyond the use of findings from a particular evaluation.

Participants and collaborators can be staff and/or program participants (e.g., clients, students, community members). Sometimes administrators, funders, and others also participate, but the usual connotation is that the primary participants are "lower down" in the hierarchy.

Evaluators interested in "Collaborative, Participatory, and Empowerment Evaluation" have formed a Topical Interest Group within the AEA. What these approaches have in common is a style of evaluation in which the evaluator becomes a facilitator, collaborator, and teacher in support of program participants and staff engaging in their own evaluation. While the findings from such a participatory process are intended to be used for program improvement, the more immediate impact is to use the evaluation process to increase participants' sense of being in control of, deliberative about, and reflective on their own lives and situations.

Grassroots development organizations use participatory evaluation as one of the tools for community leadership training. Participation is a basic development strategy because it supports gaining and enhancing skills. Thus, in developing countries, participatory monitoring and evaluation (M&E) has been used for community development, capacity building, and collaborative learning (Salmen & Kane, 2006; Vernooy, 2010; Wageningen International UR, 2006). Whitmore (1998) worked with a community-based team and found that, through the evaluation process, participants gained not only new knowledge and skills but also created a support network among themselves and gained a greater sense of self-efficacy. Norman Uphoff (1991) reviewed a number of participatory evaluations and concluded:

> If the process of self-evaluation is carried out regularly and openly, with all group members participating, the answers they arrive at are in themselves not so important as what is learned from the discussion and from the process of reaching consensus on what questions should be used to evaluate group performance and capacity, and on what answers best describe their group's present status. (p. 272)

Here is clear support for the central premise of this chapter: The process of engaging in evaluation can have as much or more impact than the findings generated. It was not a group's specific questions or answers that Uphoff found most affected the groups he observed. It was the process of reaching consensus about questions and engaging with each other about the meanings of the answers turned up. The process of participatory self-evaluation provided useful learning experiences for participants. Exhibit 6.3 presents principles of participatory evaluation. This list can be a starting point for working with potential participants to decide what principles they want to adopt for their own process.

Cousins (2001) has studied the effects of collaborative evaluation when primary users of evaluation data participate directly in technical activities like instrument development, data collection, interpreting findings, and reporting results. He found that "engagement in such activities engenders deep levels of understanding, by evaluators and program practitioners alike" (p. 115).

EXHIBIT 6.3

Principles of Participatory Evaluation

1. The evaluation process involves participants in learning evaluation logic and skills, for example, goal setting, establishing priorities, focusing questions, interpreting data, data-based decision making, and connecting processes to outcomes.
2. Participants in the process *own* the evaluation. They make the major focus and design decisions. They draw and apply conclusions. Participation is real, not token.
3. Participants focus the evaluation on process and outcomes they consider important and to which they are committed.
4. Participants work together as a group, and the evaluation facilitator supports group cohesion and collective inquiry.
5. All aspects of the evaluation, including the data, are understandable and meaningful to participants.
6. Internal, self-accountability is highly valued. The evaluation, therefore, supports participants' accountability to themselves and their community first, and external accountability secondarily, if at all.
7. The evaluator is a facilitator, collaborator, and learning resource; participants are decision makers and evaluators.
8. The evaluation facilitator recognizes and values participants' perspectives and expertise and works to help participants recognize and value their own and each other's expertise.
9. Status differences between the evaluation facilitator and participants are minimized.

Participatory evaluation involves a partnership between the evaluator and those who participate in the evaluation. Establishing a well-functioning evaluation partnership can be challenging in part because of underlying fears, bad past experiences with evaluation, resistance to reality testing, and cultural norms that undercut openness and questioning. Facilitating participatory processes adds layers of complexity to the already complex tasks of evaluation. Nor do all evaluators have the skills and temperament to successfully engage in and facilitate a participatory evaluation (see Step 2). Some evaluators can't imagine anything more horrific than spending time with a group of untrained, nonresearch-oriented laypeople designing an evaluation. "Why would I want to do that?" a colleague once asked me after a panel on the topic, his face filled with disdain. "I can't imagine a bigger waste of time."

Utilization-focused evaluation is inherently participatory and collaborative in actively involving primary intended users in all aspects of the evaluation. Evidence shows the effectiveness of this strategy for increasing use of findings (Patton, 2008). The added emphasis we're exploring here is how participation and collaboration can lead to an ongoing, longer-term commitment to using evaluation logic and building a culture of learning in a program or organization. Making this kind of *process use* explicit enlarges the menu of potential evaluation uses. How important this use of evaluation should be in any given evaluation is a matter for negotiation with intended users. The practical implication of an explicit emphasis on creating a learning culture as part of the process will mean building into the evaluation attention to and training in evaluation logic and skills.

Factors Affecting Learning From an Evaluation

The theme chosen by President Hallie Preskill for the 2007 Annual Conference of the American Evaluation Association was "Learning to evaluate . . . evaluating to learn." Several factors appear to influence the likelihood that those involved in evaluation processes will learn from their participation. These include factors related to the following:

1. *How evaluation meetings are facilitated.* This involves the intentionality of learning from the evaluation process, the amount and quality of dialogue and reflection, the meeting facilitators' group process skills, the degree of trust among participants, and how much time is given to discussing various issues.
2. *The extent to which, and the ways in which, management and leadership support participants' involvement in the evaluation process.* This involves expectations managers have for participants to share their learning with others in the organization or community, and how they are rewarded for sharing and using what they have learned.

(Continued)

(Continued)

3. *Participants' personal characteristics and experiences with evaluation in the program being evaluated.* These include participants' motivation to engage in the evaluation process, their position, their rank, their previous training in evaluation, and the belief that evaluation findings will be used.
4. *The frequency, methods, and quality of communications between and among stakeholder participants.*
5. *Organizational characteristics.* These include the extant degree of organizational stability, external demands, constraints, and threats in the extent to which the organization supports evaluation work.

If process use is supported, nurtured, and studied, it may lead not only to individual learning but also to team and organizational learning.

SOURCE: Preskill, H. (2007).

Approaches That Support Users' Engagement in the Process

- Capacity-building is a common emphasis of participatory and collaborative approaches. Preskill and Russ-Eft (2005) have described 72 activities that can be used in *Building Evaluation Capacity.*
- *Empowerment evaluation* (Fetterman & Wandersman, 2005) is an approach that makes capacity-building, ownership by those involved, and ongoing learning the focus of engagement.
- Focusing evaluation on issues of social justice was theme of the 1994 annual conference of the American Evaluation Association under President Karen Kirkhart. The first prominent evaluation theorist to advocate evaluation based on principles of social justice was Ernest House (1980, 2005b) as he analyzed the ways in which evaluation inevitably becomes a political tool in that it affects "who gets what" (distributive justice). Evaluation can enhance fair and just distribution of benefits and responsibilities, or it can distort such distributions and contribute to inequality. In rendering judgments on programs, the social justice evaluator is guided by principles such as equality, fairness, and concern for the common welfare.
- "Deliberative democratic evaluation" is an approach that attends to social justice by engaging the full range of stakeholder perspectives (the principle of inclusion) in dialogue and deliberation (House & Howe, 1999, 2000). House has emphasized that such an inclusive and deliberative process reduces bias in findings:

  > To be unbiased, evaluators might obtain stakeholder opinions from all relevant parties and process these values, views, and interests in systematic ways, thus balancing bias against bias in arriving at (relatively) unbiased conclusions. The process is analogous to enlisting different perspectives on panels to secure a balanced outcome or collecting diverse facts to obtain a correct perspective. (House, 2004, p. 222)

Those stakeholders who participate in such deliberative and dialogic processes are learning to think evaluatively.

- Feminist evaluation emphasizes participatory, empowering, and social justice agendas (Bamberger & Podems, 2002; Podems, 2010; Seigart & Brisolara, 2002).

The approaches listed above change the role of the evaluator from the traditional independent judge of merit or worth to a social change agent—or advocate. Thus, these approaches are controversial (Cousins, Donohue, & Bloom, 1996). Certainly, evaluators undertaking such an approach need to be comfortable with and committed to it, and *such an activist agenda must be explicitly recognized by, negotiated with, and formally approved by primary intended users and those funding the evaluation.*

The Power of Group Processes

Participatory evaluations often involve forming groups for collective action and reflection. For example, social isolation is a common characteristic of families in poverty. Isolation breeds a host of other problems, including family violence, despair, and alienation. Bringing participants together to establish mutual goals of support and identifying ways of evaluating (reality testing) goal attainment is a process of community development. The very process of working together on an evaluation has an impact on the group's collective identity and skills in collaborating and supporting each other. One poverty program director explained to me the impact of such a process as she observed it:

> It's hard to explain how important it is to get people connected. It doesn't sound like a lot to busy, middle-class people who feel their problem is too many connections to too many things. But it's really critical for the people we work with. They're isolated. They don't know how the system works. They're discouraged. They're intimidated by the system's jargon. They don't know where to begin. It's just so critical that they get connected, take action, and start to feel effective. I don't know how else to say it. I wish I could communicate what a difference it makes for a group of poor people who haven't had many years of formal education to share the responsibility to evaluate their own program experiences, learn the language of evaluation, deal with data, and report results. It's very empowering.

6. Evaluation for program and organization development: Developmental evaluation

The profession of evaluation has developed parallel to the professions of management consulting and organizational development (OD). Management and OD consultants advise on and facilitate a variety of change processes including solving communications problems, conflict resolution, strategic planning, leadership development, organizational learning, teamwork, human resources development, shaping organizational culture, and defining mission, to name but a few OD arenas of practice. Sometimes their methods include organizational surveys and field observations, and they may facilitate *action research* as a basis for problem solving.

Program evaluation can be viewed as one approach on the extensive menu of organization and program development approaches. Capacity-building in evaluation can be a core part of more general organizational development initiatives and processes. For example, *evaluability assessment* (M. F. Smith, 2005) has emerged as a process for evaluators to work with program managers to help them get ready for evaluation (see Step 1). It involves clarifying goals, finding out various stakeholders' views of important issues, and specifying the model or intervention to be assessed. Time and time again, evaluators are asked to undertake an evaluation only to find that goals are muddled, key stakeholders have vastly different expectations of the program, and the model that the program supposedly represents, that is, its intervention, is vague at best. In other words, the program has been poorly designed, conceptualized, or developed. To do an evaluation, the evaluator has to make up for these deficiencies. Thus, by default, the evaluator becomes a program or organizational developer. Rog (1985) studied the use of evaluability assessments and found that many of them precipitated substantial program change but did not lead to a formal evaluation. The programs realized through the process of evaluability assessment that they had a lot more development to do before they could or should undertake a formal evaluation, especially a summative evaluation. In such cases, the processes and logic of evaluation have impact on program staff quite beyond the use of findings from the assessment.

The Organization as the Unit of Analysis

The evaluation situation typically becomes more complex at the organizational level. There may be more stakeholders to deal with, more levels of stakeholders, and therefore greater challenges in sorting through various interests, interpersonal dynamics, and organizational politics. The environment surrounding and influencing an organization may also be more complex and dynamic compared with the environment of a single program. On the other hand, operating at the organizational level may increase the possibility of having impact by being able to deal directly with those who have the power to make changes. Moreover, at the organizational level, leaders may be especially interested in *evaluating overall strategy* (Patrizi & Patton, 2010).

Because programs and projects are usually embedded in larger organizational contexts and strategies, improving programs and projects may be linked to and even dependent on changing the organizations of which they are a part. For example, when evaluating the effectiveness of government programs, evaluators may need to examine, understand, and assess the ways in which being part of larger bureaucracies affects program and project effectiveness. Factors that can affect effectiveness include staff motivation, efficiency of program processes, and incentives to achieve outcomes, all of which are more determined at the organizational level than at the program or project level. Thus, improving programs may mean developing greater organizational effectiveness. This point deserves elaboration through an example and review of supporting data.

Here's an example of how organizational context affects program effectiveness. In synthesizing patterns across our evaluation of 34 Aid to Families in Poverty (FIP) programs supported by The McKnight Foundation in Minneapolis, we found that effective projects shared some common characteristics, including the following:

- Effective projects support staff responsiveness by being *flexible* and giving staff discretion to take whatever actions assist participants to climb out of poverty.
- Flexible, responsive projects affect the larger systems of which they are a part by *pushing against boundaries,* arrangements, rules, procedures, and attitudes that hinder their capability to work flexibly and responsively—and therefore effectively—with participants.

What is of interest for our purposes here is the extent to which we found an interconnectedness of these patterns at project, program, and organizational levels. An important breakthrough in our synthesis came when we understood that project and agency-wide organizational cultures were systemically interrelated. In examining FIP patterns across projects and host agencies, we found that how people are treated affects how they treat others:

responsiveness reinforces responsiveness,

flexibility supports individualization, and

empowerment breeds empowerment.

Effective projects emphasized the importance of individualized, responsive, and respectful work with families in poverty. But we also found that staff generally could not (or would not) be individually responsive and supportive if they were part of organizational environments that were rigid and bureaucratic. We found that staff tended to treat participants the way they were treated as professionals within their organizations. If the program administration and environment was rigid, rules oriented, and punitive, the staff tended to be rigid, rules oriented, and blaming with participants. If the program environment and administration were flexible, responsive, nurturing, and supportive, the staff in that environment was more likely to interact with participants in ways that were responsive, nurturing, and supportive.

The evaluation synthesis, by highlighting these interconnections, led to further organizational development efforts. As our findings emerged in collaboration with leadership from these different organizations, their discussions, interactions, and reflections led many of them to change how they managed programs and projects. Well before we had produced formal findings and written a report, the processes of being engaged in the evaluation synthesis led those involved to begin thinking in different ways about how projects and programs related to their overall organizational cultures. Being involved in the evaluation process, especially interpreting findings through interaction with leaders from other organizations, stimulated organizational development—a *process use* of the synthesis evaluation.

Developmental Evaluation

The explicit purpose of a *developmental evaluation* is to help develop the intervention or program (Patton, 1994, 2011). In Step 5, I presented developmental evaluation as a purpose option emphasizing the difference between improving versus developing a program. The developmental option reappears as a process use menu option because the nature of the team approach to developmental evaluation can affect team processes and effectiveness. In developmental evaluation the evaluator becomes part of the innovation implementation team, not apart from the team or just reporting to the team, but facilitating discussion about how to evaluate whatever happens. All team members, together, engage in evaluation questioning, interpreting emergent findings, analyzing implications, and applying results to the next stage of development. The evaluator's function in the team is to facilitate and elucidate team discussions by infusing evaluative questioning, data, and logic into decision making throughout the developmental process.

Developmental evaluation enlarges the role of the evaluator from just facilitating evaluation to also facilitating program or organizational development. There are sound arguments for defining evaluation narrowly in order to distinguish genuinely evaluative efforts from other kinds of organizational engagement. However, on a comprehensive menu of possible evaluation uses, organizational development is a legitimate use of evaluation processes. What is lost in conceptual clarity and purity with regard to a narrow definition of evaluation that focuses only on judging merit or worth is made up for with a gain in appreciation for evaluation expertise. When evaluation theorists caution against crossing the line from rendering judgments to offering advice, they may underestimate the valuable role evaluators can play in intervention design and innovation based on cumulative knowledge. Part of the value of an evaluator to a design team is bringing a reservoir of knowledge (based on many years of practice and having read a great many evaluation reports) about what kinds of things tend to work and where to anticipate problems. Young and novice evaluators may be well advised to stick fairly close to the data. However, experienced evaluators have typically accumulated a great deal of knowledge and wisdom about what works and doesn't work. More generally, as a profession, the field of evaluation has generated a great deal of knowledge about patterns of effectiveness. That knowledge makes evaluators valuable partners in the design process. Crossing that line, however, can reduce independence of judgment. The costs and benefits of such a role change must be openly acknowledged and carefully assessed with primary intended users.

Intentional and Planned Process Use as a Menu Option in Utilization-Focused Evaluations

Menu 6.1, presented earlier, summarizes the six primary uses of evaluation processes just reviewed: (1) infusing evaluative thinking into organizational culture, (2) enhancing shared understandings, (3) reinforcing interventions, (4) instrumentation effects and reactivity, (5) supporting participant engagement, and (6) developing programs and organizations. In Step 6, the evaluator works with primary intended users to consider which, if any, process uses to build into the evaluation. Any evaluation can, and often does, have these kinds of effects unintentionally or as an offshoot of using findings. What's different about utilization-focused evaluation is that the possibility and desirability of using and learning from evaluation processes, as well as from findings, can be made intentional and purposeful—an option for intended users to consider building in from the beginning. Instead of treating process use as an informal ripple effect, explicit and up-front attention to the potential impacts of using evaluation logic and processes can increase those impacts and make them a planned purpose for undertaking the evaluation. In this way, the evaluation's overall utility is increased.

Concerns, Caveats, and Controversies: Objections to and Abuses of Process Use

Just as evaluation findings can be misused, so too evaluation processes can be misused. Evaluation can help make interventions more effective, but it can also interfere with programs, as when so many forms have to be filled out or so much testing is done that time for direct work with those in need is significantly reduced. Resources and staff time devoted to evaluation are resources and staff time not available for working with clients (as staff, in frustration, will often readily point out). Indeed, evaluation can become its own source of goal displacement in which an organization becomes so enamored with its evaluation system that its attention to data collection diverts attention from meeting client needs. One major foundation invited me in to look at its sophisticated process for capturing lessons. The foundation was, indeed, seriously engaged in analyzing and reflecting on what was working and not working; evaluative thinking clearly permeated the foundation's documents, plans, staff meetings, and governance sessions. The problem was that it was all thinking and no doing. They were congratulating themselves for openly acknowledging failures, but they had been documenting the same failures over and over again for several years and nothing seemed to have significantly changed. They were heavy into process use—but had neglected findings use. They were thinking and talking a lot about evaluation, but, in fact, they weren't adept at actually using findings. All the attention to and rhetoric about evaluation, and their precious status as a knowledge-generating learning organization, had disguised the fact that they were quite ineffective in actually using evaluation findings. Process use is no substitute for findings use. Process use should enhance findings use.

When working with primary intended users, it is important to alert them that certain types of process use have provoked controversy primarily because of the changed role for evaluators when process use becomes intentional. Six objections—closely interrelated, but conceptually distinct—arise most consistently when process use is proposed as an evaluation option.

1. *Definitional objection.* Evaluation should be narrowly and consistently defined in accordance with the "common sense meaning of evaluation," namely, "the systematic investigation of the merit or worth of an object" (Stufflebeam, 1994, p. 323). Adding empowerment or collaboration outcomes to evaluation undermines the essential job rendering judgment.

2. *Goals confusion objection.* "While . . . 'helping people help themselves' is a worthy goal, it is not the fundamental goal of evaluation" (Stufflebeam, 1994, p. 323). Goals such as organizational development, evaluation capacity building, and infusing evaluative thinking into the organization's culture are worthy undertakings, but are not evaluation.

3. *Role confusion objection.* Evaluators as people may play various roles beyond being an evaluator, such as training clients or helping staff develop a program, but in taking on such roles, one moves beyond being an evaluator and should call the role what it is, for example, trainer or developer, not evaluator.

> While one might appropriately assist clients in these ways, such services are not evaluation. . . . The evaluator must not confuse or substitute helping and advocacy roles with rendering of assessments of the merit and/or worth of objects that he/she has agreed to evaluate. (Stufflebeam, 1994, p. 324)

4. *Threat to data validity objection.* Quantitative measurement specialists teach that data collection, for the results to be valid, reliable, and credible, should be separate from the program being evaluated. Integrating data collection in such a way that it becomes part of the intervention contaminates both the data and the program. Designing instruments to contribute to learning and reflection undercut their validity to measure program processes and outcomes accurately.

5. *Loss of independence objection.* Approaches that depend on close relationships between evaluators and other stakeholders can undermine the evaluator's neutrality and independence. Overly close relationships, it is feared, can lead to overly favorable findings and an inability to give direct, negative feedback when merited.

6. *Corruption and misuse objection.* Evaluators who identify with and support program goals, and develop close relationships with staff and/or participants, can be inadvertently co-opted into serving public relations functions or succumb to pressure to distort or manipulate data, hide negative findings, and exaggerate positive results. Even if they manage to avoid corruption, they may be suspected of it, thus undermining the credibility of the entire profession. Or these approaches may actually serve intentional misuse and foster corruption, as Stufflebeam (1994) worries.

> What worries me most about . . . empowerment evaluation is that it could be used as a cloak of legitimacy to cover up highly corrupt or incompetent evaluation activity. Anyone who has been in the evaluation business for very long knows that many potential clients are willing to pay much money for a "good, empowering evaluation," one that conveys the particular message, positive or negative, that the client/interest group hopes to present, irrespective of the data, or one that promotes constructive, ongoing, and nonthreatening group process. . . . Many administrators caught in political conflicts would likely pay handsomely for such friendly, nonthreatening, empowering evaluation service. Unfortunately, there are many persons who call themselves evaluators who would be glad to sell such service. (p. 325)

Exhibit 6.4 summarizes contributions and concerns about different kinds of process use. For the purpose of concluding this discussion of Step 6, it is sufficient to note that the utilization-focused evaluator who presents to intended users options that go beyond narrow and traditional uses of findings has an obligation to disclose and discuss objections to such approaches. As evaluators explore new and innovative options, they must be clear that dishonesty, corruption, data distortion, and selling out are *not* on the menu. Where primary intended users want and need an independent, summative evaluation, that is what they should get. Where they want the evaluator to act independently in bringing forward improvement-oriented findings for formative evaluation, that is what they should get. But those are no longer the only options on the menu of evaluation uses. New participatory, collaborative, intervention-oriented, and developmental approaches are already being used. The utilization-focused issue is not whether such approaches should exist. They already do. The issues are understanding when such approaches are appropriate and helping intended users make informed decisions about their appropriateness.

EXHIBIT 6.4

Process Use Contributions and Concerns

Type of process use	*Contributions*	*Concerns, challenges, and caveats*
1. Infusing *evaluative thinking* into the organizational culture	Evaluation becomes part of the organization's way of doing business, contributing to all aspects of organizational effectiveness. People speak the same language, and share meanings and priorities. Reduces resistance to evaluation.	Requires consistent leadership, ongoing training, and reinforcement (rewards). The rhetoric is easy, but actually internalizing evaluative thinking is difficult. Can increase conflict between those who "get it" and those who don't.
2. Enhancing shared understandings	Gets everyone on the same page; supports alignment of resources with program priorities.	Can force premature closure before alternatives are fully considered; those with the most power may impose their perspective on the less powerful.
3. Supporting and reinforcing the program intervention	Enhances outcomes and increases impact; increases the value of evaluation.	Complicates attribution; the effects of the program become intertwined with the effects of the evaluation, in effect making the evaluation part of the intervention.
4. Instrumentation effects	What gets measured gets done. Focuses program resources on priorities. Measurement contributes to participant learning.	Measure the wrong things, the wrong things gets done. Goal displacement, where what can be measured becomes the program's goals. Corruption of indicators, especially where the stakes become high.
5. Increasing engagement, self-determination, and ownership	Makes evaluation especially meaningful and understandable to participants; empowering.	Can reduce the credibility of the evaluation to external stakeholders; co-mingles evaluation purposes with empowerment agendas, potentially undermining both.
6. Program and organizational development	Capacity-building; long-term contribution beyond specific findings; enhances ongoing adaptability.	Evaluator serves multiple purposes and plays multiple roles, potentially confusing the evaluation role; evaluator develops a close relationship with program decision makers, raising questions about the evaluator's independence.

PRACTICE EXERCISES

1. Identify a real program. Choose one kind of *process use* from Menu 6.1 and describe how that process could be applied to an evaluation of this program. What would be the benefits of such process use? What disadvantages or difficulties can be anticipated?
2. Interview someone who has experienced a powerful learning experience. Ask about any major change experienced in behaviors, attitudes, feelings, and priorities. Probe about the nature of the learning experience, the context, and the factors that affected what happened. At the end of the interview, ask about the experience of being interviewed. Did the person come to any new understandings about the learning experience during the interview? Probe for reactions to the questions asked. Analyze those reactions as instrumentation effects and discuss this kind of reactivity as an example of process use.
3. Conduct an Internet search of the term *participatory evaluation*. Examine the variations in what is meant by and described as "participatory evaluation." Discuss the implications of these variations for evaluation practice. How does utilization-focused evaluation deal with such variations in definition, meaning, and practice?

INTERLUDE, STEPS 1 THROUGH 6. COMPLEX DYNAMIC SYSTEMS INTERCONNECTIONS

Integrating Findings Uses and Process Uses

The steps in the checklist are necessarily linear and sequential.

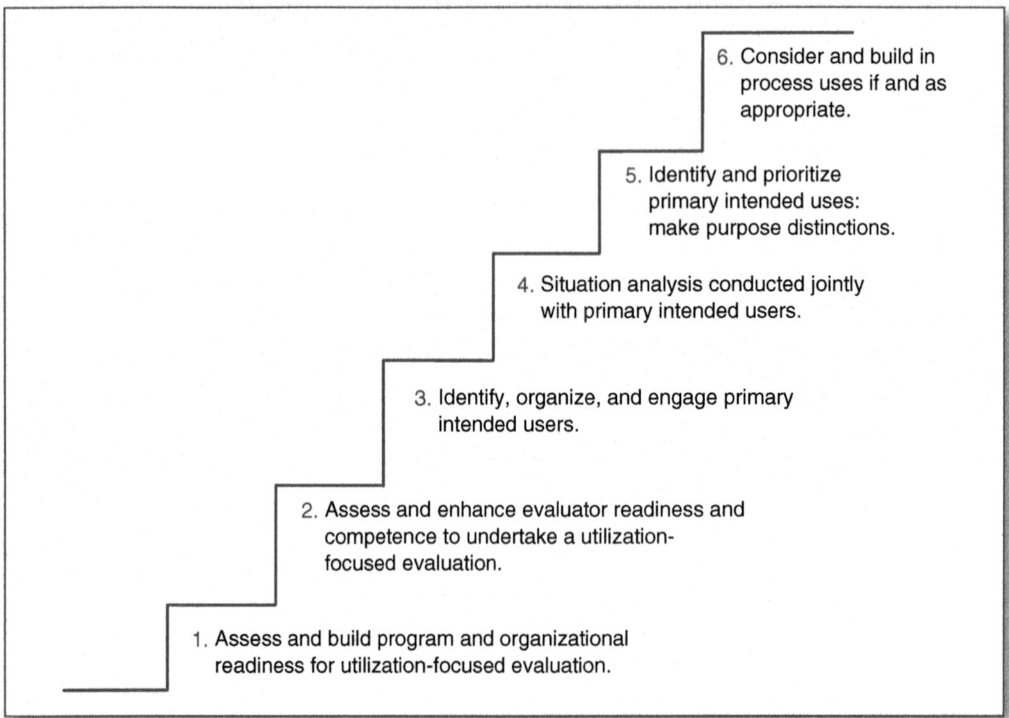

Details about what is involved in each step are provided in the summary *U-FE Checklist* in the concluding chapter. (See pages 406–413.)

We turn now to a graphic depiction of the interconnection between Steps 5 and 6 in relation to the other U-FE steps. While Step 5 focuses on clarifying and agreeing on the primary intended uses of the evaluation and Step 6 focuses on discussing and deciding on process uses, these discussions and decisions are not necessarily or even typically linear and sequential. Indeed, they are quite interconnected and may take place together, or back-and-forth, because each has implications for the other. For example, using a participatory evaluation approach will affect how findings are generated and used. I have presented Steps 5 and 6 as sequential because findings use is more familiar and expected, so it's easier to deal with it first. Process use is a newer idea and can be harder to grasp. But before findings use decisions are finalized, potential process uses should be considered. In the end, the two kinds of uses are highly interdependent and interactive.

In working with primary intended users, it's helpful to have examples and metaphors that illustrate and explain the connection between findings use and process use. Here's an example that has worked for me. Consider exercise for health and wellness. The purpose is greater fitness. You set a target, perhaps a desired weight loss or running five miles three times a week. You monitor your workouts to see how well you're doing. Improving your workouts with advice from a coach, trainer, or friend is formative evaluation. Judging whether you've met your target and deciding whether to continue your exercise regimen as a way of life is a summative evaluation, generalizing the results into your future. Now we add process use options. How do you want to go about exercising? Alone? With friends? In formal groups? Some people exercise at a gym or club because, in addition to exercising, they want to meet people. Some exercise with a friend or spouse to make relationship-building part of the process. Some exercise with someone else to keep up their motivation and reduce what they experience as the drudgery of exercise. Still others use exercise as alone time, to reflect or just clear their heads. These are uses of the exercise process that go beyond the physical health and wellness purposes, but they are clearly related. Physical health is related to psychological health, and vice versa. How you go about exercising is integrally related to the outcomes you achieve through exercise. Indeed, in some cases, the *how* becomes more important than the *what,* as when exercising as part of a relationship takes on more importance than the fitness purpose of the exercise. That's equivalent to a process use like capacity-building through participatory evaluation becoming more important than the specific findings from a particular evaluation. The learning and organizational processes that come through participation can have more lasting effects than the short-term findings generated.

Essentially, then, findings use and process use are interconnected. What's an example from your own life and work where *how you do something* is interconnected with *what you do and accomplish?* Sharing your own example is an excellent way to communicate the differences between findings use and process use as well as their interconnections. Coming up with your own example moves from theory to practice. In doing so, keep in mind the wisdom of New York Yankees baseball coaching sage Yogi Berra:

In theory there is no difference between theory and practice.

In practice there is.

Complex Interconnections and Adaptive Interactions Among U-FE Steps 1 Through 6

Integrating findings uses and process uses

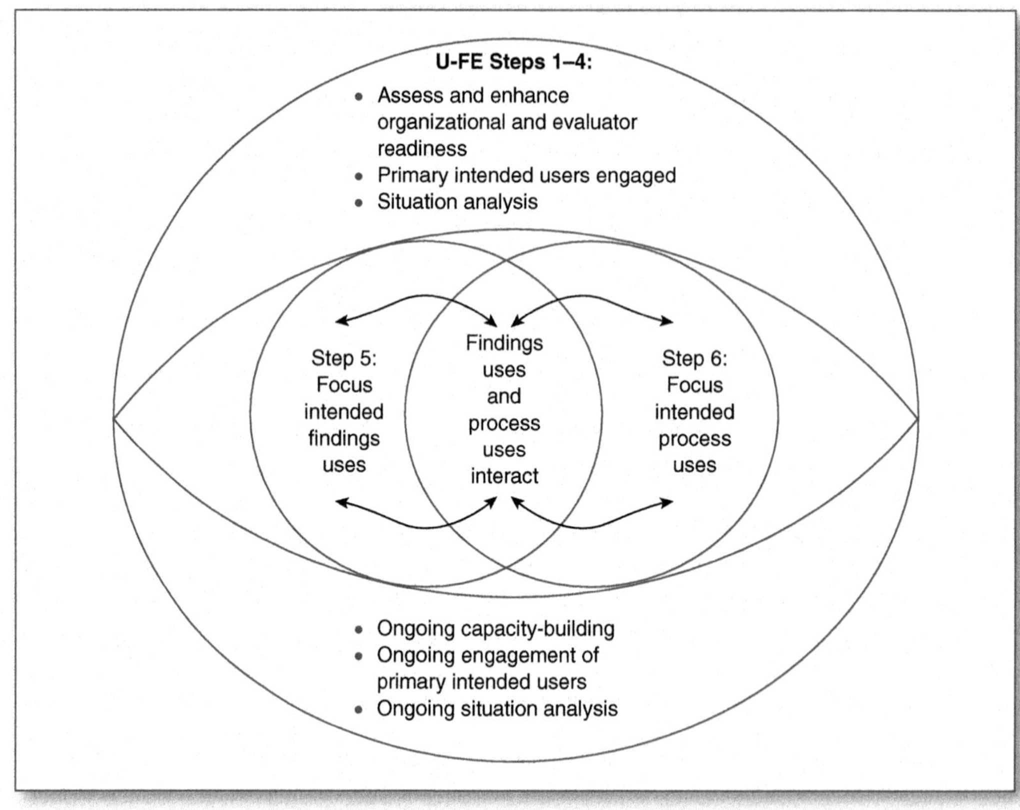

Focus Priority Evaluation Questions

Human propensities in the face of evaluation; feline curiosity; stultifying fear; beguiling distortion of reality; ingratiating public acclamation; inscrutable selective perception; profuse rationalization; and apocalyptic anticipation. In other words, the usual run-of-the-mill human reactions to uncertainty.

Once past these necessary initial indulgences, it's possible to get on to the real evaluation issues: What's worth knowing? How will we get it? How will it be used?

Meaningful evaluation answers begin with meaningful questions.

Halcolm's Guide to Questioning

No evaluation can look at everything. Priorities have to be determined, questions focused. All of life involves prioritizing and focusing, for example, deciding how we spend time and money, what work tasks get done, what leisure activities to engage in, and what we eat. Despite widespread attention deficient disorder in modern society, or perhaps because of it, knowing how to focus is a key to success. So, too, evaluation questions have to be focused. No evaluation, no matter how comprehensive, can look at everything.

How are evaluation questions prioritized? In utilization-focused evaluation, focus flows from intended use by intended users. That's what it means to be *utilization-focused.*

Of course, we're not just starting to focus here in Step 7 when we focus priority evaluation questions. Each step involves focusing. Steps 1 and 2 involved focusing on organization and evaluator readiness. That led to identifying and engaging primary intended users, and from that third step on, we have been focusing on *their* understanding of the situation (Step 4) and *their* primary intended uses, which involved establishing the evaluation's priority purposes (Step 5). Step 6 considered process use options and priorities. So every step in utilization-focused evaluation (U-FE) brings sharper, clearer, and narrower focus to the evaluation, always guided by and attentive to how the focusing decisions made will affect evaluation use. Now we move to the next level of focusing, from overall purpose to specific evaluation questions.

Actionable Evaluation Questions

There's a deceptively simple logic involved in asking evaluation questions. It goes like this: Ask questions. Get answers. Take action based on those answers.

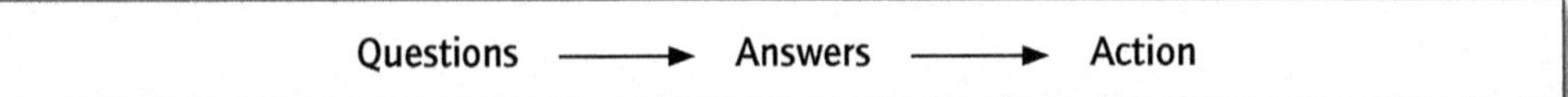

When we inquire more deeply into these connections, as we will in this chapter, we start to generate criteria for what constitutes good questions, good answers, and appropriate actions.

Let's start simple with questions: *Good questions are those that can be answered.* Will middle school students who participate in drug abuse resistance education (DARE) eschew drug use in 20 years? Or even 10 years? That question, if it could be answered at all, certainly can't be answered within an actionable time frame. Decisions about whether to continue funding DARE will have to be made within a year or 2 or 3, certainly well before a 10-year follow-up study has been completed. An evaluation, however, can answer the following question: To what extent do students who completed DARE use drugs less in high school than students without DARE experience? As I noted in the opening chapter, that evaluation question has been asked widely and often with a consistently negative answer. DARE has been found to be ineffective in reducing drug use among students. So, what does that mean for action? Well, there's the rub, as also discussed in the opening chapter. Proponents of DARE have resisted the overwhelming and consistent evidence that the program doesn't work. The link between answers and action hasn't been made for those who insist that, despite the negative evidence, they want to do something about student drug use and DARE offers something to do. In fact, proponents of DARE were not really interested in the answer to the evaluation question, unless it provided political fuel to support their already-made-up minds. In contrast, Step 7 of U-FE involves working with primary intended users to identify questions that will yield both answers *and* action. This means making sure that questions are relevant, answerable, and actionable so that answers are useful and lead to actual use.

Another criterion for good questions is that data can yield answers. Many important questions are primarily philosophical or religious in nature: that is, matters of belief and opinion that can't be answered with data. Consider evaluating a program to educate high school students about sex. Someone on the evaluation advisory team says, "I have some questions I'd like us to ask. Is sex education moral? Is teenage sex moral?" Data can't answer these questions. Data can be gathered through questionnaires or interviews about what participants in the program believe about these matters. Whether sex education is moral can be discussed and debated, but it can't be answered empirically. The evaluation facilitator, working with primary intended users, may have to diplomatically help people learn to distinguish between answerable and unanswerable questions.

Thus, part of the facilitation challenge in working with stakeholders is clarifying questions to make them clear and answerable. I was working with a task force evaluating an employment training program. One person proposed the question: "Do dropouts stop coming to the program?" I was confused. The definition of a *dropout* is someone who stops coming to the program. So I probed. "Say more. What are you trying to find out with that question?" It turned out that the issue was voluntary versus forced dropouts. How many dropped out by choice versus getting kicked out? The program reported the drop-out rate quarterly but didn't make this distinction. What constituted a dropout and why participants were dropping out were important and answerable questions, especially because the program had a high drop-out rate.

From a utilization-focused evaluation perspective, good questions are those that the primary intended users want answered and can indicate how they would use the answer; that is, they can specify the relevance of an answer for future action. Some questions are interesting but not particularly actionable. In an evaluation of an adult literacy program, a question arose about what proportion of participants were men. It's almost automatic to ask gender as a background question. But why in this case? How would gender data be used? Was the program supposed to be gender-balanced? Were there targets for a certain number of men versus women? Was there reason to believe that men and women had different success rates or drop-out rates? And suppose that turned out to be true. What would the program do about gender differences? What would make exploring gender differences a *priority* question? Discussing the potential utility of gender data opened up concerns about how males and females were recruited and treated that were both important and actionable. Finding that out meant probing into the purpose of collecting and analyzing data by gender.

The point is to get beyond knee-jerk questions that people are used to seeing on questionnaires, like gender and age, and ask: What would we do with that information? What's the actionable issue? Why is gender or age important?

You see that what drives the utilization-focused question formulation process is ongoing attention to utility. The evaluation facilitator is establishing a pattern of probing into potential utility and making discernible and intended use of findings a priority. Exhibit 7.1

EXHIBIT 7.1

Criteria for Utilization-Focused Evaluation Questions

1. The questions can be answered sufficiently well to inform understanding and support action.
2. Questions can be answered in a reasonable time frame and at reasonable cost.
3. Data can be brought to bear on the questions; that is, they aren't philosophical, religious, or moral questions.
4. The answer is not biased or predetermined by the phrasing of the question.
5. The primary intended users want the question answered; they have identified it as important and can say why.
6. The answer is actionable; intended users can indicate how they would use the answer to the question for future decision making and action.

summarizes the criteria for good utilization-focused evaluation questions. For a practical online guide to engaging stakeholders in developing evaluation questions, see Preskill and Jones (2009). Let's turn then to some of the specific kinds of questions that can provide focus to an evaluation.

Generating Questions

In the chapter on Step 1, assessing and building program and organizational readiness for evaluation, I described a questions-generating exercise for focusing an evaluation in which primary intended users generate questions that they want answered—without regard to methods, measurement, design, resources, precision, goals—just basic questions, real questions that they consider important (Menu 1.1, option 10, p. 21, pp. 32–34). Those involved are asked to generate questions the answers to which could make a real difference to the program's operations. The questions are phrased in ways that are meaningful to those involved: that is, in *their* terms, incorporating important local nuances of meaning and circumstance. In this way, primary intended users discover together that they have questions they care about—not the evaluator's questions but their own questions. Here are examples of questions that came from such an exercise.

- An evaluation of city services began with a focus on resident satisfaction: What are residents satisfied with? What are they dissatisfied with? Why?

- An evaluation of a private school cut to the chase in seeking evaluative feedback from parents: What are you worried about in your child's education? What keeps you awake at night about your child's school experiences?

Matching Questions to the Evaluation's Purpose

The process of working with primary intended users to identify priority questions varies depending on the evaluation's overall purpose, any decisions pending about the program's future, and myriad situational factors. Menu 5.1 in Step 5 (pp. 129–130) highlighted questions for different evaluation purposes. Here's a quick review.

Summative evaluation questions that lead to overall judgments of merit, worth, and significance:

- To what extent and in what ways does the program meet participants' needs?
- To what extent have intended outcomes been attained?
- What have been the larger impacts of the program?
- To what extent can documented outcomes be attributed to the intervention?
- Is this an especially effective practice that should be funded and disseminated elsewhere as a model program?
- How do outcomes and the costs of achieving them compare to other intervention or program options? Does the program add value for money?
- What are unanticipated outcomes and impacts, if any?

Formative, program improvement-oriented questions:

- What are the program's strengths and weaknesses? What works and what doesn't?
- What implementation processes need to be improved, if any?
- How are participants reacting to the program? What do they like and dislike? What do they find valuable? What do they resist? What factors seem to be affecting program completion?
- How do different subgroups in the program respond; that is, what works for whom in what ways and under what conditions?
- What are program staff reactions? What are their perceptions of what could be improved?
- Where are opportunities for improvement? How can outcomes and impacts be increased? How can costs be reduced? How can quality be enhanced?

Accountability questions:

- Are funds being used for intended purposes?
- Are resources being efficiently allocated?
- Is implementation following the approved plan?

- Are staff qualified? Are only eligible participants being accepted into the program? Are partners performing as promised and expected?
- Are quality control mechanisms in place and being used?
- Are goals, targets, and key performance indicators being met?
- Are problems being handled?

Ongoing monitoring questions:

- To what extent are inputs and processes flowing smoothly and according to plan?
- What are entry, participation, completion, and drop-out rates? Are these changing?
- Are outputs being produced as anticipated and scheduled?
- Where are bottlenecks occurring, if at all?
- What are variations across subgroups or sites?
- Are funds coming in and expenditures going out in accordance with the approved budget?
- What, if anything, is changing in the program's context that is or could affect operations?

Developmental evaluation questions for innovative interventions in complex systems:

- What is being developed?
- How is the intervention adapting to complex, emergent, and dynamic conditions?
- What innovations are emerging and developing, with what effects?
- What's happening at the interface between what the program is doing and accomplishing and what's going on the larger world around it?
- What complex systems changes are occurring?

Knowledge-generation questions:

- What are general patterns and principles of effectiveness across programs, projects, and sites?
- What lessons are being learned?
- How do evaluation findings *triangulate* with research results, social science theory, expert opinion, practitioner wisdom, and participant feedback?
- What principles can be extracted across results to inform practices and models in new settings?

Evolving Questions Over Time: Stage Models of Evaluation

Evaluate no program until it is proud.

Donald Campbell (1983)

An important consideration in focusing an evaluation involves matching the evaluation to the program's stage of development. Evaluation priorities can vary at the *initiation stage* (when resources are being sought), the *contact stage* (when the program is just getting under way), and the full implementation stage. Jacobs (1988), for example, conceptualized a "five-tier" approach:

Tier 1: Pre-implementation phase focused on needs assessment and design issues

Tier 2: Documenting basic functioning to funders to demonstrate accountability

Tier 3: Program model clarification, improvement, and feedback to staff

Tier 4: Assessing progress toward objectives with focus on immediate, short-term outcomes and differential effectiveness among clients

Tier 5: Evaluating program impact to make overall judgments of effectiveness, knowledge about what works, and model specification for replication.

The logic of a staged or phased approach to evaluation is that, not only do the questions evolve as a program develops, but the stakes go up. When a program begins, all kinds of things can go wrong, and, as we'll see in the next chapter, which looks more closely at implementation evaluation, all kinds of things typically do go wrong. It is rare that a program smoothly unfolds as planned. Before committing major resources to overall effectiveness evaluation, then, a stage model begins by making sure the groundwork was carefully laid during the needs assessment phase; then basic implementation issues are examined and formative evaluation for improvement becomes the focus; if the early results are promising, then *and only then,* are the stakes raised by conducting rigorous summative evaluation. It was to this kind of staging of evaluation that Donald Campbell, one of the most distinguished social scientists of the twentieth century, was referring when he implored that *no program should be evaluated before it is "proud."* Only when program staff has reached a point where they and others close to the program believe that they're on to something, "something special that we know works here and we think others ought to borrow," should rigorous summative evaluation be done to assess the program's overall merit and worth (Campbell quoted in Schorr, 1988, pp. 269–270).

An example may help clarify why it's so important to take into account a program's stage of development. The Minnesota State Department of Education funded a "human liberation" course in the Minneapolis public schools aimed at enhancing communication skills around issues of sexism and racism. Funding was guaranteed for 3 years, but a renewal application with evaluation findings had to be filed each year. To ensure rigorous evaluation, an external, out-of-state evaluator was hired. When the evaluator arrived on the scene, virtually everything about the program was uncertain: curriculum content, student reaction, staffing, funding, relationship to the school system, and parent support. The evaluator insisted on beginning at what Jacobs (1988) called the fourth of five tiers: assessing progress toward objectives. He forced staff, who were just beginning course development (so they were at the initiation or pre-implementation stage, tier 1), to articulate clear, specific, and measurable goals in behavioral terms. The staff had no previous experience writing behavioral objectives, nor was program conceptualization sufficiently advanced to concretize goals, so the evaluator formulated the objectives for the evaluation.

To the evaluator, the program seemed chaotic. How can a program operate if it doesn't know where it's going? How can it be evaluated if there are no operational objectives? His first-year evaluation rendered a negative judgment with special emphasis on what he perceived as the staff's failure to seriously attend to the behavioral objectives he had formulated. The teaching staff reacted by dismissing the evaluation as irrelevant. State education officials were also disappointed because they understood the problems of first-year programs and found the evaluation flawed in failing to help staff deal with those problems. The program staff refused to work with the same evaluator the second year and faced the prospect of a new evaluator with suspicion and hostility.

When a colleague and I became involved the second year, staff made it clear that they wanted nothing to do with behavioral objectives. The funders and school officials agreed to a developmental evaluation with staff as primary users. The evaluation focused on the staff's need for information to inform ongoing, adaptive decisions aimed at program development. This meant confidential interviews with students about strengths and weaknesses of the course, observations of classes to describe interracial dynamics and student reactions, and beginning work on measures of racism and sexism. On this latter point, program staff was undecided as to whether they were really trying to change student attitudes and behaviors or just make students more "aware." They needed time and feedback to work out satisfactory approaches to the problems of racism and sexism, which would include concrete objectives, possibly even behavioral ones.

By the third year, uncertainties about student reaction and school system support had been reduced by the evaluation. Initial findings indicated support for the program. Staff had become more confident and experienced. They decided to focus on instruments to measure student changes. They were ready to deal with program outcomes as long as they were viewed as experimental and flexible.

The results of the third-year evaluation showed that students' attitudes became more racist and sexist because the course experience inadvertently reinforced students' prejudices and stereotypes. Because they helped design and administer the tests used, teachers accepted the negative findings. They abandoned the existing curriculum and initiated a whole new approach to dealing with the issues involved. By working back and forth between specific information needs, contextual goals, and focused evaluation questions, it was possible to conduct an evaluation that was used for continuous development of the program. The key to use was matching the evaluation to the program's stage of development and the information needs of designated users as those needs changed over time.

Momma bear was the first to suspect that Goldilocks might have a future as an evaluator.

A Menu Approach to Focusing Evaluations

The field of evaluation has become a many-splendored thing, rich with options, alternatives, models, and approaches. There are a variety of ways of focusing evaluations. Menu 7.1 at the end of this chapter offers an extensive list of alternative ways of focusing an evaluation based on different priority questions. The challenge is to match the evaluation to the situation, which in utilization-focused evaluation is determined by the information needs and intended evaluation uses of primary intended users. I'll elaborate on only a few of these here.

Focusing on Future Decisions

An evaluation can be focused on information needed to inform future decisions. Proponents and opponents of school busing for desegregation may never agree on educational goals, but they may well agree on what information is needed to inform future debate, for example, data about who is bused, at what distances, from what neighborhoods, and with what effects.

Focusing on Critical Issues or Concerns

When the Minnesota Legislature first initiated Early Childhood Family Education programs, some legislators were concerned about what advice was being given to parents. The evaluation focused on this issue, and the evaluators became the eyes and ears for the legislature and general public at a time of conflict about "family values" and anxiety about values indoctrination. The evaluation, based on descriptions of what actually occurred and data on parent reactions, helped put this issue to rest. Over time new issues arose. For example, universal access became a matter of contentious debate. Should the program be targeted to low-income parents or continue to be available to all parents, regardless of income? What are the effects on parents of a program that integrates people of different socioeconomic backgrounds? An evaluation was commissioned to inform that policy debate and examine programming implications. These Early Childhood and Parent Education program evaluations, done for the state legislature, were issue-based more than goals-based, although attention to differential parent outcomes was subsumed within the issues.

Testing Assumptions

The Greek Stoic philosopher Epictetus observed: "It is impossible for a man to learn what he thinks he already knows." Assumptions are the things that typically go unquestioned, which is why they're called *assumptions.* Evaluations can open up new understandings by opening up assumptions. International development agencies typically assume that their efforts will be credited to them. An evaluation of new water and sewer services in rural Iraq included this question: Who do villagers credit with building the new water and sewer system? It turned out that the Taliban insurgents were taking credit for the work of international development assistance agencies.

Discussing Undiscussables

With a group that has some trust and is willing to dig deeply into tougher issues, the evaluation can draw on organizational development and action research techniques for surfacing "undiscussables"—what is sometimes called naming the elephant in the organization (Hammond & Mayfield, 2004). Much of evaluation is framed as finding out what is not known or filling the knowledge gap. But deeper problems go beyond what is not known to what is known but not true (false assumptions) or known to be untrue, at least by some, but not openly talked about (undiscussable). In doing a cluster evaluation for a group of antipoverty programs, the undiscussable was that the staff was almost all White while the clients were virtually all African American. The unexamined assumptions were that not enough "qualified" Black staff could be found and that clients didn't care about the race of staff. In fact, racism was an *undiscussable.* It wasn't until the third year of the evaluation, after trust had been built, some appreciation of evaluative thinking had been established, and those involved were ready to dig more deeply into tougher issues that the group made the effects of racial differences an issue for evaluative inquiry.

When I offer a group the option of testing assumptions and examining undiscussables, I ask them if they're ready to take on the evaluation challenge of American humorist Mark Twain, who famously observed: "*It ain't what you don't know that gets you into trouble. It's what you know for sure that just ain't so.*" This is hard-core reality testing. I'm not inclined to start there with a group.

I find it's better to start a new group off with less threatening issues and strengthen capacity for evaluative inquiry before taking on more challenging and threatening questions.

The IT *Question*

Perhaps the most basic evaluation question asked by policymakers, philanthropic funders, and journalists is: Does it work? But what's the *IT?* There's the rub. What is this *IT* that works or doesn't work? The evaluation jargon for the *IT* is *evaluand:* "any object of an evaluation . . . , a person, program, idea, policy, product, object, performance, or any other entity being evaluation" (Mathison, 2005, p. 139). *Evaluand* works well enough in academic encyclopedia explanations of evaluation's focus, but it's not exactly user-friendly language. People don't ask, "Does the evaluand work?" They ask, "Does *IT* work?"

Answering the *IT* question is deceptively challenging. Getting an answer requires, first, defining what it means for the program to *work:* that is, defining and measuring what desired goals and outcomes were achieved. The second part of unpacking the question is the *IT* itself: that is, what was the program or intervention? This requires implementation and process evaluation to find out what happened to participants in the program. What did they experience? The final and most difficult aspect of answering "Does *IT* work?" is connecting implementation with outcomes. Can the outcomes observed (the results of what worked) be attributed to the program or intervention (the *IT*). This involves identifying the program's logic model and testing its theory of change. A logic model depicts the connections and linkages between inputs, activities, outputs, and outcomes. A theory of change specifies the causal mechanisms that explain how experiences and processes in the program lead to desired outcomes.

These three elements constitute the most fundamental ways of approaching evaluation:

1. The implementation question: *What happened in the program?*
2. The outcomes question: *What resulted?*
3. The attribution question: *Can what resulted be attributed to what was implemented?*

Because they are so important, it is essential to be sure that these ways of focusing an evaluation are reviewed with primary intended users. Implementation evaluation, outcomes evaluation, and attribution evaluation involve additional focus options and degrees of depth of inquiry. Because these issues and options are so central to evaluation, Step 8 involves checking to make sure that these fundamental issues have been sufficiently addressed as intended users finalize the evaluation's priorities and focus. Thus, I've devoted the whole next chapter (Step 8), to examining these questions in depth.

Focusing an Evaluation

Focusing an evaluation is an interactive process between evaluators and the primary intended users of the evaluation. It can be a difficult process because deciding what will be evaluated means deciding what will not be evaluated. Programs are so complex and have so many levels, goals, and functions that there are always more potential study foci than there are resources to examine them. Moreover, as human beings, we have a limited capacity to take in data and juggle complexities. We can deal effectively with only so much at one time. The alternatives have to be narrowed and decisions made about which way to go. That's why I've emphasized the menu metaphor throughout this book and offer Menu 7.1 in this chapter to show the great variety of ways an evaluation can be focused. The utilization-focused evaluation facilitator is a chef offering a rich variety of choices, from full seven-course feasts to fast-food preparation (*but never junk*). The stage approach to evaluation involves figuring out whether, in the life of the program, it's time for breakfast, lunch, a snack, a light dinner, or a full banquet.

This problem of focus is by no means unique to program evaluation. Management consultants find that a major problem for executives is focusing their energies on priorities. The trick in meditation is learning to focus on a single mantra, koan, or image. Professors have trouble getting graduate students to analyze less than the whole of human experience in their dissertations. Time-management specialists find that people have trouble setting and sticking with priorities in both their work and personal lives. And evaluators have trouble getting intended users to focus evaluation questions.

The challenge is to find those *vital few facts* among the *trivial many* that are high in payoff and add real value to decision making and program improvement efforts. The 20–80 rule expresses the importance of focusing on the right information. The 20–80 rule states that, in general, 20% of the facts account for 80% of what's worth knowing. The trick is identifying and focusing on that critical 20%.

Because of limited time and limited resources, it is never possible to look at everything in great depth. Decisions have to be made about what's worth looking at. Choosing to look at one area in depth is also a decision not to look at something else in depth. Making use the focus of evaluation enhances the evaluation's relevance. Ensuring relevance reinforces user engagement and deepens interest in getting quality and actionable answers. That's why it's worth taking the time to carefully focus an evaluation for optimum utility.

In closing, it is worth reiterating that formulating appropriate and meaningful questions demands considerable skill and insight. How one poses a question frames the answer one gets—and its utility. In her novel, *The Left Hand of Darkness,* science fiction author Ursula K. Le Guin (1969) reminds us that questions and answers are precious resources, not to be squandered or treated casually. In the novel, the character Herbor makes an arduous journey to fortune tellers who convene rarely and, when they do, permit the asking of only a single question. His mate is obsessed with death, so Herbor asks them how long his mate will live. Herbor returns home to tell his mate the answer, that Herbor will die before his mate. His mate is enraged: "You fool! You had a question of the Foretellers, and did not ask them when I am to die, what day, month, year, how many days are left to me—you asked *how long?* Oh you fool, you staring fool, longer than you, yes, longer than you!" And with that his mate struck him with a great stone and killed him, fulfilling the prophecy and driving the mate into madness (pp. 45–46).

Formulate evaluation questions thoughtfully and carefully. The stakes can be quite high.

PRACTICE EXERCISES

1. Review the section on matching evaluation to the stage of a program's development (pp. 174–176). Use an example of an actual program that has been in existence for some time. Learn about the stages of that program's development and match evaluation questions and data to those different stages.
2. Review Menu 7.1 on pages 182–187. Select three quite different approaches, types, or areas of focus. Compare and contrast them, emphasizing what factors, circumstances, and contingencies would lead you, as an evaluator, to recommend each one because of its particular suitability and utility for an evaluation situation and challenge you describe.

MENU 7.1

Alternative Ways of Focusing Evaluations

Different types of evaluations ask different questions and focus on different purposes. This menu is meant to be illustrative of the many alternatives available. These options by no means exhaust all possibilities. Various options can be and often are used together within the same evaluation, or options can be implemented in sequence over a period of time, for example, doing implementation evaluation before doing outcomes evaluation, or formative evaluation before summative evaluation.

Focus or type of evaluation	*Defining question or approach*
Accountability focus	How have resources been appropriately used to accomplish intended results? Key issue: Who is accountable to whom for what?
Accreditation focus	Does the program meet minimum standards for accreditation or licensing?
Appreciative inquiry	What is best about the program? (Preskill, 2005)
Attribution focus (also causal focus)	Use rigorous social science methods to determine the relationship between the program (as a treatment) and resulting outcomes.
Capacity-building focus	Doing evaluation in a way that enhances the long-term capacity to engage in evaluation more systematically.
CIPP Model	Evaluation of an entity's context, inputs, processes, and products (Stufflebeam, 2005).
Cluster evaluation	Synthesizing overarching lessons and/or impacts from a number of projects within a common initiative or framework (Russon, 2005).
Collaborative approach	Evaluators and intended users work together on the evaluation.
Comparative focus	How do two or more programs rank on specific indicators, outcomes, or criteria?
Compliance focus	Are rules and regulations being followed?
Connoisseurship approach	Specialists or experts apply their own criteria and judgment, as with a wine or antiques connoisseur (Donmoyer, 2005).

Focus or type of evaluation	*Defining question or approach*
Context focus	What is the environment within which the program operates politically, socially, economically, culturally, and scientifically? How does this context affect program effectiveness?
Cost-benefit analysis	What is the relationship between program costs and program outcomes (benefits) expressed in dollars?
Cost-effectiveness analysis	What is the relationship between program costs and outcomes where outcomes are *not* measured in dollars?
Criterion-focused	By what criteria (e.g., quality, cost, client satisfaction) shall the program be evaluated?
Critical issues focus	Critical issues and concerns of primary intended users focus the evaluation.
Culturally responsive	Focusing on the influences of cultural context and factors on program processes and outcomes (Kirkhart, 2005).
Decisions focus	What information is needed to inform specific future decisions?
Deliberative democratic approach	Uses concepts and procedures from democracy to arrive at justifiable conclusions through inclusion, dialogue, and deliberation (House, 2005a; House & Howe, 2000).
Descriptive focus	What happened in the program? (No "why" question or cause/effect analyses.)
Developmental evaluation	The purpose is program or organizational development and rapid response to emergent realities in highly dynamic and complex systems under conditions of uncertainty (Patton, 2011).
Diversity focus	The evaluation gives voice to different perspectives on and illuminates various experiences with the program. No single conclusion or summary judgment is considered appropriate.
Effectiveness focus	To what extent is the program effective in attaining its goals? How can the program be more effective?
Efficiency focus	Can inputs be reduced and still obtain the same level of output or can greater output be obtained with no increase in inputs?
Effort focus	What are the inputs into the program in terms of number of personnel, staff/client ratios, and other descriptors of levels of activity and effort in the program?

(Continued)

(Continued)

Focus or type of evaluation	*Defining question or approach*
Empowerment evaluation	The evaluation is conducted in a way that affirms participants' self-determination and political agenda (Fetterman & Wandersman, 2005).
Equity focus	Are participants treated fairly and justly?
Ethnographic focus	What is the program's culture?
Evaluability assessment	Is the program ready for formal evaluation? What is the feasibility of various evaluation approaches and methods? (Smith, 2005)
Extensiveness focus	To what extent is the program able to deal with the total problem? How does the present level of services and impacts compare to the needed level of services and impacts?
External evaluation	The evaluation is conducted by specialists outside the program and independent of it to increase credibility.
Feminist evaluation	Evaluations conducted for the explicit purpose of addressing gender issues, highlighting the needs of women, and promoting change through increased social justice (Seigart & Brisolara, 2002).
Formative evaluation	How can the program be improved?
Goals-based focus	To what extent have program goals and intended outcomes been attained?
Goal-free evaluation	To what extent are actual needs of program participants being met (without regard to stated program goals)? (Scriven,1972b).
Inclusive evaluation	Emphasizes stakeholder inclusiveness, dialogical data collection methods, social justice, cultural pluralism, and transformation (Mertens, 2005).
Impact evaluation	What are the direct and indirect program impacts, over time, not only on participants, but also on larger systems and the community? Impact evaluation often includes a focus on determining the extent to which results can be attributed to the intervention.
Implementation focus	To what extent was the program implemented as designed? What issues surfaced during implementation that need attention in the future?

Focus or type of evaluation	*Defining question or approach*
Inputs focus	What resources (money, staff, facilities, technology, etc.) are available and/or necessary?
Internal evaluation	Program employees conduct the evaluation.
Intervention-oriented evaluation	Design the evaluation to support and reinforce the program's desired results.
Judgment focus	Make an overall judgment about the program's merit, worth, and/or significance. (See also summative evaluation.)
Judicial model	Two evaluation teams present opposing views of whether the program was effective, like a legal trial (Datta, 2005).
Knowledge focus (or lessons learned)	What can be learned from this program's experiences and results to inform future efforts?
Logical framework	Specify goals, purposes, outputs, and activities, and connecting assumptions: For each, specify indicators and means of verification.
Longitudinal focus	What happens to the program and to participants over time?
Metaevaluation	Evaluation of evaluations: Was the evaluation well done? Is it worth using? Did the evaluation meet professional standards and principles?
Mission focus	To what extent is the program or organization achieving its overall mission? How well do outcomes of departments or programs within an agency support the overall mission?
Monitoring focus	Routine data collected and analyzed routinely on an ongoing basis, often through a management information system.
M&E (Monitoring & Evaluation)	M&E: Integrating monitoring and evaluation (Kusek & Rist, 2004).
Needs assessment	What do clients need and how can those needs be met? (Altschuld & Kumar, 2005)

(Continued)

(Continued)

Focus or type of evaluation	*Defining question or approach*
Needs-based evaluation	See goal-free evaluation.
Norm-referenced approach	How does this program population compare to some specific norm or reference group on selected variables?
Outcomes evaluation	To what extent are desired client/participant outcomes being attained? What are the effects of the program on clients or participants?
Participatory evaluation	Intended users, usually including community members, program participants, and/or staff, are directly involved in the evaluation (King, 2005).
Personalizing evaluation	Portrayal of people's lives and work as contexts within which to understand a program (Kushner, 2000).
Personnel evaluation	How effective are staff in carrying out their assigned tasks and in accomplishing their assigned or negotiated goals?
Process focus	Evaluating the activities and events that occur as part of implementation: What do participants experience in the program? What are strengths and weaknesses of day-to-day operations? How can these processes be improved?
Product evaluation	What are the costs, benefits, and market for a specific product?
Quality assurance	Are minimum and accepted standards of care being routinely and systematically provided to patients and clients?
Questions focus	What do primary intended users want to know that would make a difference to what they do? The evaluation answers questions instead of making judgments.
Realist Evaluation (also realistic evaluation)	What are the underlying mechanisms (possible mediators) of program effects? What values inform the application of findings for social betterment? What works for whom in what circumstances and in what respects, and how? The result is a context-mechanism-outcome configuration (Mark, Henry, & Julnes, 2000; Pawson & Tilley 2005).
RealWorld evaluation	How can evaluation be done under budget, time, data, and political constraints? (Bamberger, Rugh, & Mabry, 2006)

Focus or type of evaluation	*Defining question or approach*
Reputation focus	How the program is perceived by key knowledgeables and influentials; ratings of the quality of universities are often based on reputation among peers.
Responsive evaluation	What are the various points of view of different constituency groups and stakeholders? The responsive evaluator works to capture, represent, and interpret these varying perspectives under the assumption each is valid and valuable (Stake & Abma, 2005).
Social and community indicators	What routine social and economic data should be monitored to assess the impacts of this program? What is the connection between program outcomes and larger-scale social indicators, for example, crime rates?
Social justice focus	How effectively does the program address social justice concerns?
Success case method	Compares highly successful participants with unsuccessful ones to determine primary factors of success (Brinkerhoff, 2003, 2005).
Summative evaluation	Should the program be continued? If so, at what level? What is the overall merit and worth of the programs?
Systems focus	Using systems thinking, concepts, perspectives, and approaches as the framework for evaluation (Williams, 2005; Williams & Iman, 2006).
Theory-driven evaluation	On what theoretical assumptions and model is the program based? What social scientific theory is the program a test of and to what extent does the program confirm the theory? (Chen, 2005)
Theory of change approach	What are the linkages and connections between inputs, activities, immediate outcomes, intermediate outcomes, and ultimate impacts? (Funnell & Rogers, 2011)
Transformative evaluation	Diverse people are included in the evaluation in a way that is genuinely and ethically respectful of their culture, perspectives, political and economic realities, language, and community priorities (Mertens, 2007).
Utilization-focused evaluation	What information is needed and wanted by primary intended users that will actually be used for program improvement and decision making? (Utilization-focused evaluation can include any of the other types above.)

INTERLUDE, STEPS 1 THROUGH 7. COMPLEX DYNAMIC SYSTEMS INTERCONNECTIONS

Questioning and Focusing as Part of Each Step Throughout the U-FE Process

The depiction of the utilization-focused process as a series of steps denotes a linear sequence in which one step comes after another as the process unfolds. We have now reviewed 7 of the 17 steps in this book.

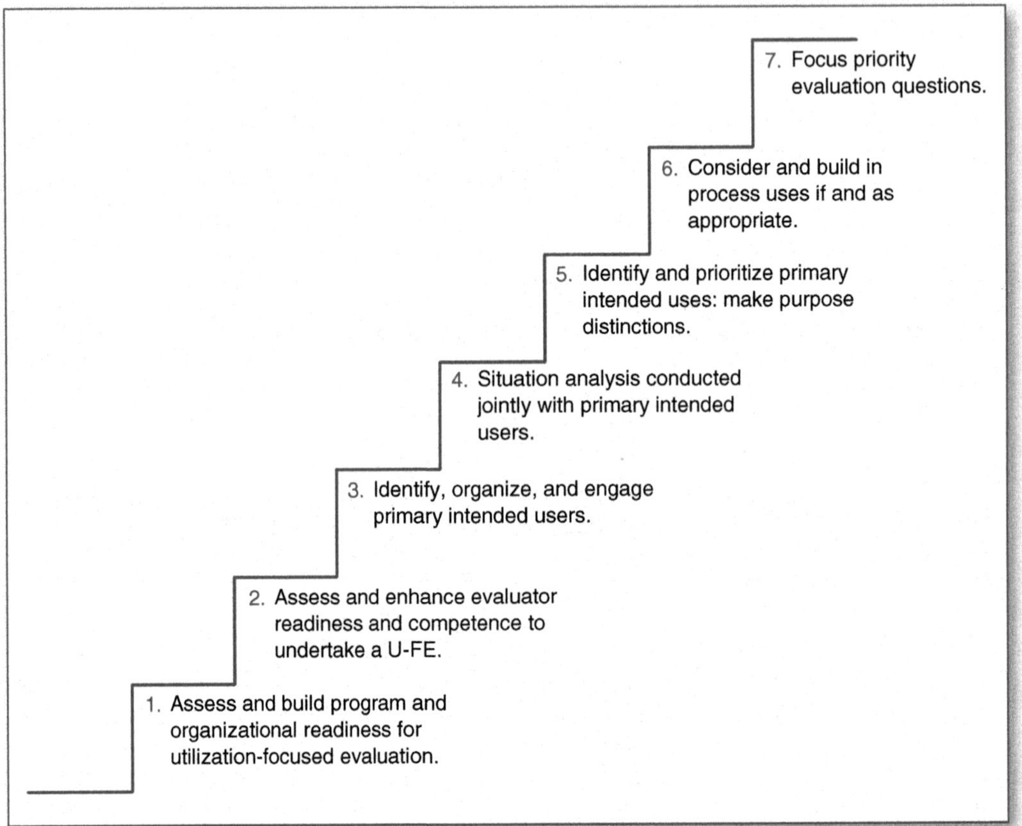

7. Focus priority evaluation questions.

6. Consider and build in process uses if and as appropriate.

5. Identify and prioritize primary intended uses: make purpose distinctions.

4. Situation analysis conducted jointly with primary intended users.

3. Identify, organize, and engage primary intended users.

2. Assess and enhance evaluator readiness and competence to undertake a U-FE.

1. Assess and build program and organizational readiness for utilization-focused evaluation.

Details about what is involved in each step are provided in the summary *U-FE Checklist* in the concluding chapter. (See pages 406–414.)

As we've seen in previous interludes between chapters, each new step in the checklist also becomes another element in the complex dynamic systems understanding that is emerging as we proceed through the steps. Step 7 focuses on prioritizing evaluation questions, but *every step involves asking questions and focusing on use.*

From the beginning, U-FE involves working to create a culture of inquiry and learning in which stakeholders are thinking about important questions they want to ask and how they would use the answers. One of the exercises offered in Step 1 to enhance readiness for evaluation involved generating potential evaluation questions. (See option 10 in Menu 1.1, Step 1.) A key issue in Step 2, assessing and enhancing evaluator readiness, is the evaluator's skill in facilitating question generation among stakeholders and negotiating priorities with sensitivity, including cultural competence, and political sophistication. The skills involved include listening to stakeholder concerns, issues, rants, rambles, and conflicts—hearing their bad questions (unanswerable, nonactionable, rhetorical, biased, philosophical)—and helping them turn those into answerable evaluation questions that will inform action. Step 3, identifying, organizing, and engaging primary intended users, involves determining *whose questions* will take priority. The corollary of the assertion that no evaluation can answer all potential questions is that no evaluation can answer everyone's questions. Some focusing process is needed to determine whose questions get answered. That involves moving from a large number of potential stakeholders to a smaller, identifiable number of primary intended users. Representing their diverse stakeholder constituencies and organized for decision making, they decide what questions take priority. In the chapter on Step 3, I described the exemplary evaluation of the Colorado Healthy Communities Initiative, an 8-year study that involved community-based health promotion projects in 29 communities across the state, conducted by Ross Connor (2005). The evaluation brought together key stakeholders from different communities at various times to prioritize evaluation questions. These people were called the "*primary question askers.*" I like that designation. It nurtures a culture of inquiry and learning and highlights the importance of framing evaluation as a question-asking enterprise.

Step 4 involves engaging with primary intended users to analyze the situation within which the evaluation will occur. This is done by asking a series of probing questions about the program and evaluation context (see Exhibit 4.1), which includes identifying factors that could affect use. Situation analysis sets the stage for Step 5, identifying the evaluation's priority purposes, and Step 6, considering and building in process uses, if appropriate. Indeed, one use of the evaluation process can be to enhance the capacity of those involved to think evaluatively, including deepening their skills at question-asking.

Thus, once again the steps of U-FE are interconnected and interdependent, as depicted in the complex dynamic graphic presented on the next page. Every step involves focusing and questioning, and the ongoing focusing process and answers that emerge at any point along the way interact with and inform the questions asked and answers that emerge in other steps.

Complex Interconnections and Adaptive Interactions Among U-FE Steps 1 Through 7

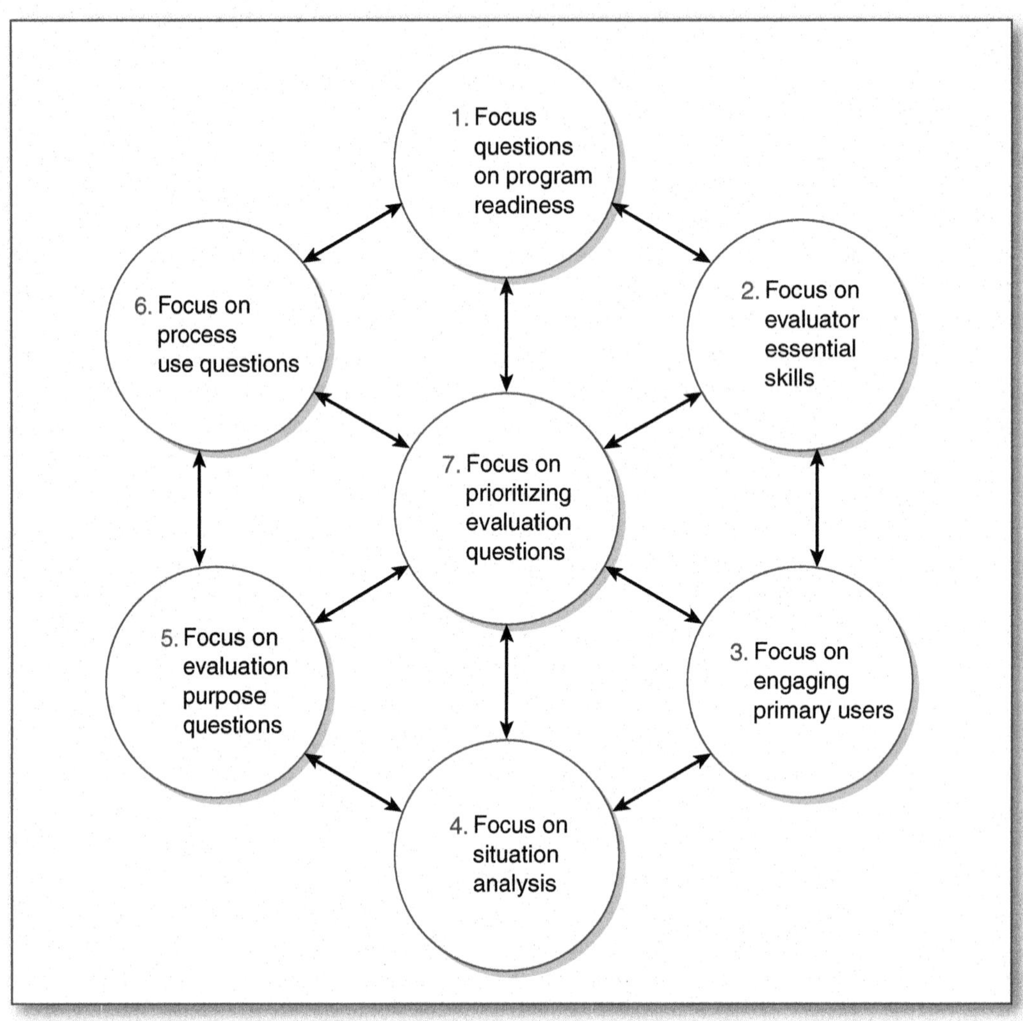

8

Check That Fundamental Areas for Evaluation Inquiry Are Being Adequately Addressed

Implementation, Outcomes, and Attribution Questions

Gordon Moore co-founded the technology and semiconductor giant Intel and originated Moore's law, which famously and accurately predicted that computer capacity would double every 2 years. For our purposes, his insight about the importance of fundamentals is more immediately relevant:

> The technology at the leading edge changes so rapidly that you have to keep current after you get out of school. I think probably the most important thing is having good fundamentals. (Moore, 2000, p. 1)

The same can be said of evaluation. At the core, the *Essentials of Utilization-Focused Evaluation* is about mastering the fundamentals of working with primary intended users to achieve primary intended uses. This requires facilitation and process fundamentals. It also requires knowledge of evaluation fundamentals. Every field of endeavor has fundamentals. Sports teams begin each new season by practicing fundamentals. Musicians practice basic rhythms and singers practice scales. Building designers can get quite creative but, to be practical and buildable, the designs must attend to fundamentals. So, too, evaluation.

Step 7 concerned prioritizing questions and offered a menu of both basic and creative options. This chapter places those diverse options within the context of traditional evaluation fundamentals: implementation analysis, goal attainment evaluation, and evaluating the connection between program implementation and outcomes (the attribution question). New developments in evaluation, like innovations in technology, emerge from and rest on a foundation of fundamentals. Knowing those evaluation fundamentals and engaging primary intended users around the classic fundamentals are essential. This chapter, then, reminds us to be sure that, in working with primary intended users, we've discussed the three classic evaluation questions:

1. The *implementation question:* What happened in the program?
2. The *outcomes question:* What resulted?
3. The *attribution question:* Can what resulted be attributed to what was implemented?

Evaluation Fundamentals: Three Classic Evaluation Questions

1. The *implementation question:* What happens in the program?
2. The *outcomes question:* What results from the program?
3. The *attribution question:* Can what results be attributed to what is implemented?

The *IT* Question

Answers to all three questions are necessary to answer the ***IT*** question: Does ***IT*** work?

The ***IT*** is the program model (what is implemented). "Does ***IT*** work" asks what outcomes result from and can be attributed to the model's implementation.

The processes of focusing priority questions (Step 7) and checking that fundamentals are being adequately addressed go on together. Step 8 could precede Step 7, beginning with fundamentals and then considering additional or complimentary possibilities and issues. Or one can begin with Step 7, explore what is most relevant, important, and actionable, then review whatever priority questions emerge through the lens of fundamentals (Step 8). In working with primary intended users, these two processes tend to go on simultaneously as the evaluation priorities come into focus. The primary reason for putting Step 7 before Step 8 in this sequence is to assure that traditional expectations about how to focus an evaluation (implementation and outcomes) do not cut off the exploration of other potential approaches to determining what will be most useful to primary intended users.

Step 7, especially Menu 7.1, invited consideration of the diverse ways evaluations can be focused, from the A's of accountability, accreditation, and appreciative inquiry to the R-models of realist evaluation, RealWorld evaluation, and responsive evaluation, and through the alphabet banquet of options to theory-driven or transformative evaluation. The *Encyclopedia of Evaluation* offers even more options, models, and approaches (Mathison, 2005). But the issues of implementation, outcomes, and attribution are mainstays. In the full book on *Utilization-Focused Evaluation* (Patton, 2008), each of these topics commanded a full chapter (Chapters 7, 9, and 10). This chapter presents the essence of these issues and puts them together in this one overarching step: *checking that fundamental areas for evaluation inquiry are being adequately addressed.* That's a lot to cover, so Step 8 is still a pretty giant step, which will take us into logic modeling and theory-of-change conceptualizations discussed in Step 9.

Implementation Evaluation: What Happened in the Program?

Implementation evaluation focuses on finding out if the program has all its parts, if the parts are functional, and if the program is operating as it's supposed to be operating. Most fundamentally, it means answering the question: What is the program? This involves finding out what actually happens in the program. What are its key characteristics? Who is participating? What does staff do? What do participants experience? What's being implemented as planned and what is not? Answering such questions is essential because implementation problems are a common cause of program failure.

A Beginning Point: Does the Program Exist?

A state legislature established a program to teach welfare recipients the basic rudiments of parenting and household management. The state welfare department was charged with conducting workshops and training caseworkers on how low-income people could better manage their meager resources and become better parents. A single major city was selected for pilot-testing the program, with a respected independent research institute contracted to evaluate the program. The evaluators interviewed a sample of welfare recipients before the program began, collecting data about parenting, household management, and budgetary practices. Eighteen months later, they interviewed the same welfare recipients again. The results showed no measurable change in parenting or household management behavior. The evaluators judged the program ineffective, a conclusion they reported to the state legislature and the newspapers. Following legislative debate and adverse publicity, the legislature terminated funding for the program—a dramatic case of using evaluation results to inform a major decision.

However, the evaluation as conducted shed no light on what went wrong because it focused entirely on measuring the attainment of intended program outcomes: changed parenting and household management behaviors of welfare recipients. As it turns out, there is a very good reason why the program didn't attain the desired outcomes. It was never implemented. When funds were allocated from the state to the city, the program became embroiled in the politics of urban welfare. Welfare rights organizations questioned the right of government to tell poor people how to spend their money or rear their children. These and other political battles meant that no workshops were held and no caseworkers were ever trained. In short, *the program was never implemented.* But it was evaluated! It was found to be ineffective—and was killed.

The Importance of Implementation Analysis: Distinguishing Theory Failure From Implementation Failure

It is important to know the extent to which a program attains intended outcomes and meets participant needs, questions we'll turn to shortly. But to answer those questions it is essential to know what occurred in the program that can reasonably be connected to outcomes. The classic primer *How to Assess Program Implementation* put it this way:

> To consider only questions of program outcomes may limit the usefulness of an evaluation. Suppose the data suggest emphatically that the program was a success. You can say, "It worked!" But unless you have taken care to describe the details of the program's operations, you may be unable to answer a question that logically follows such a judgment of success: "*What worked?*" If you cannot answer that, you will have wasted the effort measuring the outcomes of events that cannot be described and therefore remain a mystery. . . . Few evaluation reports pay enough attention to describing the processes of a program that helped participants achieve its outcomes. (King, Morris, & Fitz-Gibbon, 1987; emphasis in the original)

Not knowing enough about implementation limits the usefulness of findings about effective programs and contributes to confusion about why programs succeed or fail. At the most simple level, programs may fail for two fundamental reasons: (1) failure of implemented programs to attain desired outcomes, which is called *theory failure*; that is, the idea didn't work as hoped, versus (2) failure to actually implement the idea (or theory), which is *implementation failure,* and means the idea (program) was never really tested for effectiveness because it was not implemented adequately or sufficiently. For an evaluation to support decision making, it is critical to be able to distinguish theory failure (ideas that don't work) from implementation failure (ideas that haven't been appropriately tested).

- *Headline:* Major school reform fails to produce increases in student achievement. Theory failure (the reform didn't work) or implementation failure (the reform was never adequately implemented)?

- *Headline:* Hospital initiative fails to reduce in-hospital infections. Theory failure (the initiative didn't work) or implementation failure (the proposed changes were never adequately implemented)?
- *Headline:* Community policing innovation fails to reduce crime rates. Theory failure (the innovation didn't work) or implementation failure (the innovation was never adequately implemented)?
- *Headline:* HIV/AIDS campaign fails to increase condom use and reduce the rate of infection. Theory failure (the campaign didn't work) or implementation failure (the campaign was never adequately implemented)?

Working with stakeholders to distinguish theory failure from implementation failure can include assessing the *viability of implementation,* what Chen has called "viable validity" (Chen, 2010).

Focus on Utility: Information for Action and Decisions

Simply learning that outcomes are high or low doesn't tell decision makers much about what to do. They also need to understand the nature of the program. In the example that opened this chapter, legislators learned that targeted welfare parents showed no behavioral changes, so they terminated the program. The evaluators failed to include data on implementation that would have revealed the absence of any of the mandated activities that were supposed to bring about the desired changes. By basing their decision only on outcomes information, the legislators terminated a policy approach that had never actually been tried.

Terminating a policy inappropriately is only one possible error when outcomes data are used without data about implementation. Expanding a successful program inappropriately can also occur when decision makers lack information about the basis for the program's success. In one instance, a number of drug addiction treatment centers in a county were evaluated based on rates of re-addiction for treated patients. All had relatively mediocre success rates except one program that reported a 100% success rate over 2 years. The county board immediately voted to triple the budget of that program. Within a year, the re-addiction rates for that program had fallen to the same mediocre level as other centers. By enlarging the program, the county board had eliminated the key elements in the program's success—its small size and dedicated staff. It had been a six-patient halfway house with one primary counselor who ate, slept, and lived that program. He established such a close relationship with each addict that he knew exactly how to keep each one straight. When the program was enlarged, he became administrator of three houses and lost personal contact with the clients. The successful program became mediocre. A highly effective program, though small in scale, was lost because the county board acted without understanding the basis for the program's success.

Renowned global investor and philanthropist George Soros tells a similar story. Through a foundation he established in Moscow when the Cold War thawed, he funded a successful program aimed at transforming the education system. "I wanted to make it bigger, so I threw a lot of money at it—and in so doing, I destroyed it, effectively. It was too much money" (quoted by Buck 1995, pp. 76–77).

In new initiatives, implementation evaluation should precede outcomes evaluation. Consider the case of a statewide evaluation of early childhood interventions in Tennessee that began by asking stakeholders in state government what they wanted to know—an exercise in focusing the evaluation questions. The evaluators expected outcomes data to be the legislators' priority. However, interviews revealed that key policymakers and program managers "were more concerned about the allocation and distribution of resources than about the effectiveness of projects" (Bickman, 1985, p. 190). They wanted to know whether every needy child was being served. What services were being delivered to whom? State agencies could use this kind of implementation and service delivery information to "redistribute their resources to unserved areas and populations or encourage different types of services" (p. 191). They could also use descriptive information about programs to increase communications among service providers about what ideas were being tried and to assess gaps in services. Before "the more sophisticated (and expensive) questions about effectiveness" were asked, "policymakers wanted to know simpler descriptive information. . . . If the currently funded programs could not even be described, how could they be improved?" (pp. 190–191).

Ideal Plans Versus Actual Implementation

Why is implementation so difficult? And so frustrating? Part of the answer may lie with how programs are legislated and planned. Policymakers seldom seem to analyze the feasibility of implementing their ideas during decision making. The tasks of both implementing a program and evaluating it are made all the more difficult when the feasibility of implementation has not been thoughtfully considered in advance. As a result, either as part of evaluability assessment or in early interactions with primary intended users, the evaluator will often have to facilitate discussion of what the program should look like before it can be said to be fully implemented and operational. Criteria for evaluating implementation may have to be developed at the beginning of the evaluation when implementation plans are vague or benchmarks are absent.

Different stakeholders will often hold different views of what implementation should include. In the Food Stamps Program for poor people in the United States, there was a vociferous debate about whether program implementation should include active recruitment of needy people. Advocates for the poor argued that access depended on vigorous outreach. Antiwelfare interests argued that it was not part of the program design to actively recruit those who might be eligible and that to do so would increase the costs of the program and might even put it in jeopardy.

Given the reality that actual implementation will typically look different from original ideals, a primary evaluation challenge is to help identified decision makers determine how far from the ideal the program can deviate, and in what ways it can deviate, while still constituting the original idea (as opposed to the original ideal). In other words, a central evaluation question is: *How different can an actual program be from its ideal and still be said to have been implemented?* The answer must be clarified between primary intended users and evaluators as part of the process of specifying criteria for assessing implementation.

Adaptation Versus Fidelity

How closely must implementation of a program follow an original blueprint? This question takes on additional complexity when applied to expansion of a successful pilot program, or what is called "taking an innovation *to scale,*" in which an intervention is enlarged or disseminated to new communities. This gives rise to one of the central issues in implementation: *adaptation versus fidelity as a premier evaluation criterion of excellence.*

Consider the case of JUMP Math, an approach to teaching developed by mathematician John Mighton in 1998. Although originally conceived as an after-school supplement for inner-city students struggling with math, by 2003 JUMP programs ran in 12 Toronto inner-city elementary schools involving more than 1,600 students. It has evolved into a classroom curriculum with a complete package of materials intended to cover all elementary school grades. The program has been adopted in schools throughout North America and other regions of the world. With such widespread adoption, there will be variations in implementation. For teachers and students to realize the full benefits of the approach, those who are supporting dissemination of the program want *high-fidelity implementation.* This is true for any model that gets identified as a "best practice" or "evidence-based model."

To evaluate fidelity is to assess adherence to the core blueprint specifications of how a model program is supposed to be implemented. Models that aim at widespread dissemination strive for careful replication and the degree to which that replication is attained is a primary implementation evaluation question. It is a question made all the more important by the substantial evidence that it is very difficult to maintain fidelity of a widely disseminated program. Adoption of a model often becomes *adaptation* of the model. In such cases, how much adaptation is appropriate and what gets adapted are significant evaluation questions (Patton, 2011, Chapter 7).

Adaptation involves quite different evaluation questions than fidelity. When adaptation is expected as an innovation is disseminated, the evaluation questions focus on the nature, extent, reasons for, and consequences of adaptation. Adaptation occurs as original ideas and plans are changed in the face of what proves actually possible and how different sites respond to innovation in a local context. In a renowned large-scale study of innovation, the Rand Corporation, under contract to the U.S. Office of Education, studied 293 federal programs supporting educational change—one of the most comprehensive studies of educational innovation ever conducted. The study concluded that implementation "dominates the innovative process and its outcomes":

> In short, where implementation was successful, and where significant change in participant attitudes, skills, and behavior occurred, implementation was characterized by a process of mutual adaptation in which project goals and methods were modified to suit the needs and interests of the local staff and in which the staff changed to meet the requirements of the project. This finding was true even for highly technological and initially well-specified projects; unless adaptations were made in the original plans or technologies, implementation tended to be superficial or symbolic, and significant change in participants did not occur. (McLaughlin, 1976, p. 169)

The Change Agent Study found that the usual emphasis on fidelity in dissemination of models was inappropriate. McLaughlin concluded:

> An important lesson that can be derived from the Change Agent Study is that unless the developmental needs of the users are addressed, and unless projects are modified to suit the needs of the user and the institutional setting, the promise of new technologies is likely to be unfulfilled. (McLaughlin, 1976, p. 180)

The emphasis on the "user" in the Rand study brings us back to the importance of the personal factor and attention to primary intended users in evaluation of implementation processes. Formative, improvement-oriented evaluations can help users make the kinds of program adaptations to local conditions that Rand found so effective—*or* it can be used to maintain the fidelity of a model if it begins to depart from the prescribed blueprint. These are two fundamentally different purposes for and uses of formative evaluation. And they lead to two fundamentally different summative criteria: (1) successful adaptation of a model to local conditions *versus* (2) successful replication of a model that carefully follows prescribed processes. Utilization-focused criteria for evaluating implementation must be developed through interaction with primary intended users.

Variations and Options for Implementation Evaluation

Several alternative purposes of implementation evaluation can be considered based on different intended uses. Let's consider an evaluation of emergency health services at a hospital.

- Implementation evaluation for *accountability* would focus on the extent to which the program is complying with mandated specifications. In the emergency room this could involve a standard that all incoming patients with problems that are not life-threatening are examined by a qualified medical person within one half-hour. To what extent is that standard being met?
- Implementation evaluation for *program improvement* focuses on identifying a program's strengths and weaknesses so that problems can be solved and staff can build on what's working well while correcting deficiencies. In the emergency room example this could involve getting feedback from incoming patients and those who brought them to the emergency room about how they were treated.
- *Summative* implementation evaluation determines the core characteristics of a program to inform a decision about continuing, expanding, reducing, terminating, or disseminating the program model. There are competing models of how to run an emergency unit, for example, what tests are routinely administered for what conditions. A summative evaluation would make a judgment about the relative merit and worth of those competing models.
- *Developmental evaluation* would document ongoing processes of adaptation and innovation to increase the capacity to do rapid and accurate environmental sensing and provide quick feedback for development. For example, if an influx of recent immigrants started using emergency services, what adaptations would be needed?
- Implementation evaluation for *lessons learned* aims to extract practice wisdom from staff to inform future implementation endeavors. In the emergency room, this could involve experienced staff from several emergency units synthesizing what they've learned about how they managed triage during community-wide emergencies like Hurricane Katrina, a major fire, or a terrorist attack. Menu 8.1 presents different evaluation questions for these distinctive purposes.

MENU 8.1

Sample Implementation Questions for Different Evaluation Purposes

Accountability and Compliance Issues

1. How does the program as actually implemented compare to the original design?
2. What implementation benchmarks were established? To what extent have those benchmarks been met?
3. Were resources for full implementation available as needed?
4. Do program staff members have necessary competencies?
5. How do the characteristics of program participants compare to those of the intended target population for the program?

Formative Evaluation Questions

1. What is participant and staff feedback about program implementation processes: What's working well and not working so well? What do participants like and dislike?
2. What challenges and barriers have emerged as the program has been implemented? What "bugs" need to be worked out?
3. To what extent, if at all, are participants' actual needs different from what was planned for?
4. How well are staff functioning together?
5. What monitoring system has been established to assess implementation on an ongoing basis and how is it being used?

Developmental Evaluation Implementation Questions

1. How are changes in the program's environment being tracked so the program can adapt to emergent conditions?
2. For each new development, what progress markers provide feedback on how that development is working out?
3. When have incremental changes accumulated to the point of constituting an innovation in implementation?

Summative Implementation Questions

1. Has implementation proved feasible? What aspects or components have been fully implemented? What aspects of implementation have raised concerns about feasibility?
2. How stable and standardized has the implementation become both over time and, if applicable, across different sites?
3. To what extent is the program amenable to implementation elsewhere? What aspects of implementation were likely situational? What aspects are likely generalizable?
5. What are the start-up and continuing costs of implementation?

Lessons Learned Implementation Questions

1. What has been learned about implementation of this specific program that might inform similar efforts elsewhere?
2. What has been learned about implementation in general that would contribute to scholarly and policy research on implementation?

NOTE: For a larger menu of over 300 implementation evaluation questions, see King et al., 1987, pp. 129–141.

Different purposes render varying implementation evaluation questions. Cutting across these variations are options for focusing an implementation review. These options involve specific types of implementation evaluation.

1. Effort and input evaluation

Effort and input evaluations focus on documenting the quantity and quality of activity that takes place and the resources available for program activities. Effort evaluation moves up a step from asking if the program exists to asking how active the program is and at what level it is being or has been implemented. If relatively inactive, it is unlikely to be very effective; if inputs don't materialize in a timely way, the program will get off to a slow start.

Effort questions include: Have sufficient staff been hired with the proper qualifications? Are staff-client ratios at desired levels? How many clients with what characteristics are being served by the program? Are necessary materials available? Is needed technology in place and operational? An effort evaluation involves making *an inventory of program operations*. Such questions are especially important at initiation of a program when evaluation questions focus on getting services started. Later, questions concerning the appropriateness, quantity, and quality of services become more important. Continuing with the example of emergency hospital services, an effort and input evaluation would inventory whether staffing levels were adequate for patient loads, whether there are enough examination rooms with access to needed equipment, and how long waits are for getting initial care and then getting transferred to a regular hospital room, if needed.

2. Process evaluation

Process evaluation focuses on the internal dynamics and actual operations of a program in an attempt to understand its strengths and weaknesses. Process evaluations ask: What's happening and why? How do the parts of the program fit together? What do participants experience and how do they perceive the program? This approach takes its name from an emphasis on looking at *how* a product or outcome is produced rather than looking at the product itself; that is, it is an analysis of the processes whereby a program produces outcomes. A process evaluation of an emergency room would map what happens to a patient from the moment the emergency call is placed to the discharge of the patient. How are the emergency calls handled? What happens upon arrival at the emergency room? How does treatment unfold? How are discharges handled? What's the experience of family, friends, or coworkers accompanying the patient? How do patients experience and describe their treatment? What's the perspective of nurses? Of doctors? Of security personnel? Of administrators?

Process evaluations search for explanations of the successes, failures, and changes in a program. Under field conditions in the real world, people and unforeseen circumstances shape programs and modify initial plans in ways that are rarely trivial. The process evaluator sets out to understand and document the day-to-day reality of the setting or settings under study. This means unraveling what is actually happening in a program by searching for the major patterns and important nuances that give the program its character. A process evaluation requires sensitivity to both qualitative and quantitative changes in programs throughout their development; it means becoming intimately acquainted with the details of the program. Process evaluations not only look at formal activities and anticipated outcomes, but they also investigate informal patterns and unanticipated consequences in the full context of program implementation and development.

A process evaluation can provide useful feedback during the developmental phase of a program as well as later, in providing details for diffusion and dissemination of an effective program. The Office on Smoking and Health (2007) at the Centers for Disease Control and Prevention has published a process evaluation guidebook that includes a number of examples of how process evaluation has been useful in programs aimed at tobacco use prevention and control. They found again and again that to make sense of and learn from outcomes data (reduced smoking by target populations like high school students) they needed in-depth process evaluation.

3. Component evaluation

The component approach to implementation evaluation involves a formal assessment of the distinct parts of a program. Programs can be conceptualized as consisting of separate operational efforts that may be the focus of a self-contained implementation evaluation. For example, the Hazelden Foundation Chemical Dependency Program typically includes the following components: detoxification, intake, group treatment, lectures, individual counseling, family events, release, and outpatient services. While these components make up a comprehensive chemical dependency treatment program that can be and is evaluated on the outcome of continued sobriety over time, there are important questions about the operation of any particular component that can be the focus of evaluation, either for improvement or to decide if that component merits continuation. In addition, linkages between one or more components may be evaluated.

4. Treatment specification and intervention dosage

Treatment specification involves identifying and measuring precisely what it is about a program that is supposed to have an effect. It means conceptualizing the program as a carefully defined intervention or treatment—or at least finding out if there's enough consistency in implementation to permit such a conceptualization. This requires elucidation of the program's *theory:* what precise mechanisms are hypothesized to produce desired results. Twelve-step programs to treat alcoholism are based on a series of propositions about what happens at each step and how one step leads to the next. In technical terms, treatment specification means identifying independent variables (the intervention dimensions) that are expected to lead to outcomes (the dependent variables). Treatment specification reveals the causal assumptions undergirding program activity. Funnell and Rogers (2011) have produced an in-depth guide to developing an evaluation program theory, and we'll return to this issue later in this chapter when we consider the attribution question and look at program modeling options, as well as in Step 9 (the next chapter) when we look at modeling the program.

Measuring the degree to which the proposed treatment is actually implemented is critical to distinguishing theory failure from implementation failure. For example, in a study of whether worm medicine affected school attendance in an African community with high rates of worm infestation, implementation analysis found that children who received the worm medicine cut the pills into smaller portions and shared them with siblings and friends who did not receive the medicine, thus decreasing dosage to the point of being ineffective. Compliance with minimum dosage requirements was so poor as to undermine the treatment, an example of implementation failure. In any program, including educational and social programs, the dosage issue concerns how much of the treatment (the program) participants must experience to achieve desired outcomes. If a mother in a maternal education and nutrition program only attends half the time, did she experience enough of the intervention to expect the program to have had its intended impact? What about attending two-thirds of the sessions? Or one-third? These questions involve establishing a "dosage" level for minimum program effectiveness.

Thus, one approach to implementation evaluation is to attempt to identify and operationalize the program treatment, including establishing dosage criteria. This is sometimes referred to as getting inside and opening up the *black box* of the program to see what's inside: What is the treatment or intervention? What actually happens in the program? Evaluations that just do pre- and posttesting will lack information about what happened to participants *between* the pre- and posttest, including how much of the intended intervention they actually experienced.

Implementation Fundamentals Summary

This section has reviewed options in focusing all or part of an evaluation on implementation issues and questions. What is the program or intervention? When one says IT worked or IT didn't work, what was the IT? Implementation evaluation answers that question. Options for implementation evaluation include: (1) effort evaluation, (2 process evaluation, (3) component evaluation, and (4) treatment specification. Depending on the nature of the issues involved and the information needed, any one, two, or all four approaches might be employed. Indeed, over time, a comprehensive evaluation might include all four types of implementation evaluation. The implementation evaluation focus will depend on the purpose and intended uses of the evaluation. But the essential bottom-line point is that without information about actual program operations and causal mechanisms, decision makers are limited in interpreting outcomes and performance data as the basis for informed action. Let's turn now to the fundamentals of goals and outcomes.

Focusing on Program Goals and Participant Outcomes

Traditionally, evaluation has been synonymous with measuring goal attainment. The basic logic of goals-based evaluation involves, at a minimum, three points of comparison: (1) a starting point, or baseline; (2) a goal or target (the ideal or hoped-for result); and (3) the ending point, or actual result. The most classic evaluation question is: To what extent is the program attaining its goals? To evaluate goal attainment, goals have to be operationalized: made clear, specific and measureable. This original trinity of criteria has evolved into SMART goals with 5 evaluation criteria:

Specific

Measurable

Achievable

Relevant

Timebound

Generating SMART goals involves both skill (knowing how to do it) and commitment (a willingness to get SMART by program leadership). The evaluation literature is replete with complaints about goals that are fuzzy, vague, abstract, too general, impossible to find indicators for, and generally inadequate. An example: Improved quality of life. What are the dimensions of "quality of life"? What constitutes improvement? Thomas Jefferson's "pursuit of happiness" would not pass muster today as a SMART goal.

Add to the litany of problems multiple and conflicting goals, or that different stakeholders emphasize different goals. This has meant that evaluators are called on not only to evaluate goal attainment, but to facilitate goals clarification in order to evaluate whether intended outcomes are being achieved. Enter *evaluability assessment* (Smith, 2005; Wholey, 2005).

Evaluability Assessment and Goals Clarification

Evaluability assessment involves determining if the program is ready for evaluation, which usually includes meeting the criteria of having SMART goals. Evaluators have become heavily involved in goals clarification because, when we are invited in, we seldom find a statement of clear, specific, prioritized, and measurable goals. This can take novice evaluators by surprise if they think that their primary task will be formulating an evaluation design for already established goals. Even where goals exist, they are frequently unrealistic, having been exaggerated to secure funding—what are called *BHAG*s (big hairy audacious goals). One reason evaluability assessment has become an important pre-evaluation process is that, by helping programs get ready for evaluation, it acknowledges the frequent need for a period of time to work with program staff, administrators, funders, and participants on clarifying goals—making them realistic, meaningful, agreed on, and evaluable. Evaluability assessment can include interviews to determine how much consensus there is among various stakeholders about goals and to identify where differences lie. Based on this kind of contextual analysis, an evaluator can work with primary intended users to plan a strategy for goals clarification.

From a utilization-focused point of view, the challenge is to calculate how early interactions in the evaluation process will affect later use. Typically, it's not useful to ignore goals conflict, accept poorly formulated or unrealistic goals, or let the evaluator assume responsibility for writing clear, specific, and measurable goals. Primary intended users need to be involved in assessing how much effort to put into goals clarification and who should be involved in the process so that ownership of the goals remains with the program. It's critical that revised goals not become viewed as the evaluator's goals. They remain the program's goals—but now ready for evaluation.

Questions for Goals Clarification

Facilitating goals clarification doesn't mean just asking: What are the program's goals? The very formality of this question can intimidate staff. And, as noted earlier, goals are often exaggerated vision statements aimed at securing funding rather than focused outcome statements about what the program aims to accomplish. Thus, a different inquiry strategy may be needed to facilitate goals clarification. I've found program staff quite animated and responsive to the following kinds of questions:

- What are you trying to achieve with program participants?
- If you are successful, how will those who complete the program be different after the program than they were before?
- What kinds of changes do you want to see in program participants as a result of participation?
- When your program works as you want it to, how do those who complete the program *behave* differently? What do they say that is different from when they began? What would I see in them that would tell me they are different?

These are variations on the theme of clarifying expected outcomes. Program staff can often provide quite specific answers to these questions, answers that reveal their caring and involvement with the participant change process, yet when the same staff members are asked to specify their goals and objectives, they freeze. Or come up with abstract mutterings like, "To enhance the decision-making process about life decisions that affect a transition to income sustainability." Say what? Oh, you mean: *Get and keep a living wage job.* There are clear and specific measures for living wage jobs, at least in American communities (Glasmeier, 2010).

After querying staff about what results they hope to accomplish with program participants, I may then tell them that what they have been telling me constitutes their goals and objectives. This revelation can surprise them: "But we haven't said anything about what we would count." This, as clearly as anything, I take as evidence of how widespread the confusion is between the conceptualization of goals and their measurement. Help program staff and other intended users be realistic and concrete about goals and objectives, but don't make them hide what they are really trying to do because they're not sure how to write a formally acceptable (to evaluators) statement of goals and objectives, or because they don't know what measurement instruments might be available to get at some of the important things they are trying to do. Instead, *take them through a process that focuses on achieving outcomes and results rather than writing goals*. The difference, it turns out, can be huge.

Focusing on Outcomes and Results

In the minds of many program people, from board members to frontline staff and participants, goals are abstract statements of ideals meant to inspire, but never be achieved. Consider this poster on the office wall of a program I evaluated:

> *The greatest danger is not that we aim too high and miss, but that our goal is too low and we attain it.*

For this director, goals were something you put in proposals and plans, and hung on the wall, then went about your business.

Let me illustrate the difference between common program goals and a focus on participant outcomes with plans submitted by county units to a state human services agency. The plans required statements of outcomes. Each statement below promises something, but that something is not a change in participant functioning, status, or well-being. These statements reveal how people in social services often have been trained to think about program goals. My comments following each of the eight goals below are meant to illustrate how to help program leaders and other intended evaluation users reframe traditional goals to focus on participant outcomes.

Problematic Outcome Examples

1. To continue implementation of a case management system to maintain continued contact with clients before, during, and after treatment.

   Comment: Continued implementation of the system is the goal. And what is promised for the program client? "Continued contact."

2. To develop needed services for chronically chemically dependent clients.

   Comment: This statement focuses on program services rather than the client outcomes. My review of county plans revealed that most managers focus planning at the program delivery level, that is, the program's goals, rather than how participants' lives will improve.

3. To develop a responsive, comprehensive crisis intervention plan.

   Comment: A plan is the intended outcome. I found that many service providers confuse planning with getting something done. The characteristics of the plan—"responsive, comprehensive"—reveal nothing about results for intended beneficiaries.

4. Develop a supportive, family-centered empowering, capacity-building intervention system for families and children.

   Comment: This goal statement has lots of human services jargon, but, carefully examined, the statement doesn't commit to empowering any families or actually enhancing the capacity of anyone receiving services through the system.

5. County consumers will receive services which they value as appropriate to their needs and helpful in remediating their concerns.

   Comment: Consumer satisfaction can be an important outcome, but it's rarely sufficient by itself. Especially in tax-supported programs, taxpayers and policymakers want more than happy consumers of services. They want people to have jobs, be productive, stay sober, parent effectively, and so on. Consumer satisfaction needs to be connected to other desired outcomes.

6. Improve ability of adults with severe and persistent mental illness to obtain employment.

   Comment: This goal could be met even if clients remain in the program for years getting their ability to obtain employment enhanced—without ever getting a job.

7. Adults with serious and persistent mental illness will engage in a process to function effectively in the community.

   Comment: Engaging in the process is as much as this aims for, in contrast to those served actually functioning effectively in the community.

8. Adults in training and rehab will be involved in an average of 120 hours of community integration activities per quarter.

   Comment: Quantitative and specific, but the outcome stated goes only as far as being involved in activities, not actually being integrated into the community.

Facilitating Understanding of and a Focus on Outcomes

The point of reviewing these examples has been to show the kinds of goal statements an evaluator may encounter when beginning to work with a program. A utilization-focused evaluator can help intended users review plans and stated goals to see if they include an outcome focus. There's nothing wrong with program-level goals (e.g., improve access or quality) or system-level goals (e.g., reduce costs), but such goals ought to connect to outcomes for program participants. An evaluator can facilitate discussion of why, in the current political environment, one hears increased demand for *outcomes-based management and accountability*. Given that increased focus, there are helpful guides for working with outcomes in evaluation:

- *Making Measures Work for You: Outcomes and Evaluation,* a GrantCraft guide supported by the Ford Foundation (McGarvey, 2006)
- *Outcome Mapping* (Earl, Carden, & Smutylo, 2001; IDRC, 2010)

Some outcome guides are aimed at specific kinds of organizations, like the training manual of the National Network for Collaboration (2010), which focuses on clarifying and evaluating the goals of collaborations. Or there's the guide for *Getting to Outcomes with Developmental Assets: Ten Steps to Measuring Success in Youth Programs and Communities* (Fisher, Imm, Chinman, & Wandersman, 2006). Fink (2004) has written on the fundamentals of outcomes for health care evaluation. There are now specific outcome guides for virtually any programming area. Evaluators can use these to provide technical assistance in helping program planners, managers, and other potential evaluation users understand the difference between a participant outcomes approach and traditional program or system goals approaches. In particular, they often need assistance understanding the difference between service-focused goals versus participant-focused outcome goals. Exhibit 8.1 compares these two kinds of goals. Both can be useful, but they place emphasis in different places.

Utilization-Focused Outcomes Framework

Having discussed the importance of and challenges associated with clarifying program goals and outcomes, let me offer a *Utilization-Focused Outcomes Framework* that I use in working with primary intended users to facilitate designing an outcomes evaluation. This framework distinguishes six separate elements that need to be specified for focusing an evaluation on participant or client outcomes:

1. A specific participant or client target group
2. The desired outcome(s) for that target group
3. One or more indicators for each desired outcome
4. Performance targets
5. Details of data collection
6. How results will be used

EXHIBIT 8.1

Service-Focused Versus Outcome-Focused Goals: Examples From Parenting Programs

Service-focused goals	*Outcome-focused goals*
Provide coordinated case management services with public health to pregnant adolescents	Pregnant adolescents will give birth to healthy babies and care for the infants and themselves appropriately
Improve the quality of child protection intervention services	Children will be safe; they will not be abused or neglected
Develop a supportive, family-centered, capacity-building intervention system for families and children	Parents will adequately care and provide for their children
Provide assistance to parents to make employment-related child care decisions	Parents who wish to work will have adequate child care

I'll discuss each of these elements and offer illustrations from actual programs to show how they fit together.

1. **Identify specific participant target groups**

I'll use the generic term *participant* to include program participants, consumers of services, intended beneficiaries, students, and customers, as well as traditional program client groups. The appropriate language varies, but for every program, there is some group that is expected to benefit from and attain outcomes as a result of program participation. However, the target groups identified in enabling legislation or existing reporting systems typically are defined too broadly for meaningful outcomes measurement. Intended outcomes can vary substantially for subgroups within general eligible populations. The trick is to be as specific as necessary to conceptualize meaningful outcomes. Some illustrations may help clarify why this is so.

Consider a program aimed at supporting the elderly to continue living in their homes, with services ranging from "meals on wheels" to home nursing. Not all elderly people can or want to stay in their homes. Therefore, if the desired outcome is "continuing to live in their own home," it would be inappropriate to specify that outcome for all elderly people. A more appropriate target population, then, would be people over the age of 55 who want to and can remain safely in their homes. For this group, it is appropriate to aim to keep them in their homes. It is also clear that some kind of screening process will be necessary to identify this subpopulation of the elderly.

There are many ways of specifying subpopulation targets. Outcomes are often different for young, middle-aged, and elderly clients in the same general group (e.g., persons with serious and persistent mental illness). Outcomes for first-time offenders may be different from those for repeat offenders. The point is that categories of funding eligibility often include subgroups for which outcomes appropriately vary. It is important, then, to make sure an intended outcome is meaningful and appropriate for everyone in the identified target population.

2. Specify desired outcomes

The choice of language varies under different evaluation approaches. Some models refer to *expected outcomes* or *intended outcomes.* Others prefer the language of *client goals* or *client objectives.* What is important is not the phrase used but that there be a clear statement of the targeted change in circumstances, status, level of functioning, behavior, attitude, knowledge, or skills. Other outcome types include maintenance and prevention. Exhibit 8.2 provides examples of outcomes.

3. Select outcome indicators: Operationalizing

An indicator is just that, an indicator. It's not the same as the phenomenon of interest, but only an indicator of that phenomenon. A score on a reading test is an indicator for reading capability but should not be confused with a particular person's true capacity to

EXHIBIT 8.2

Outcome Examples

Type of change	*Illustration*
Change in circumstances	Children safely reunited with their families of origin from foster care
Change in status	Unemployed to employed
Change in behavior	Truants will regularly attend school
Change in functioning	Increased self-care; getting to work on time
Change in attitude	Greater self-respect
Change in knowledge	Understand the needs and capabilities of children at different ages

read. All kinds of things affect a test score on a given day. Thus, indicators are inevitably approximations. They are imperfect and vary in validity and reliability.

Figuring out how to measure a desire outcome is called *operationalizing* the outcome. The resources available for measurement will greatly affect the kinds of data that can be collected for indicators. For example, if the desired outcome for abused children is that there be no subsequent abuse or neglect, regular in-home visitations and observations, including interviews with the child, parent(s), and knowledgeable others, would be desirable, but such data collection is expensive. With constrained resources, one may have to rely on data collected routinely by government through mandated reporting: that is, official substantiated reports of abuse and neglect over time. Moreover, when using such routine data, privacy and confidentiality restrictions may limit the indicator to aggregate results quarter by quarter rather than one that tracks specific families over time.

As resources change, the indicator may change. Routine statistics may be used by an agency until a philanthropic foundation funds a focused evaluation to get better data for a specific period of time. In such a case, the indicator would change, but the desired outcome would not. This is the advantage of clearly distinguishing the desired outcome from its indicator. As the state of the art of measurement develops or resources change, indicators may improve without changing the desired outcome.

Time frames also affect indicators. The ultimate goal of a program for abused children would be to have them become healthy, well-functioning, and happy adults, but policymakers cannot wait 10 to 15 years to assess the outcomes of a program for abused children. Short-term indicators must be relied on, things like school attendance, school performance, physical health, and the psychological functioning of a child, as well as any re-determinations of abuse. These short-term indicators provide sufficient information to make judgments about the likely long-term results. It takes 30 years for a forest to grow, but you can assess the likelihood of ending up with a forest by evaluating how many saplings are still alive 1 year and 3 years after the trees are planted.

Another factor affecting indicator selection is the demands data collection will put on program staff and participants. Short-term interventions such as food shelves, recreational activities for people with developmental disabilities, drop-in centers, and one-time community events do not typically engage participants intensely enough to justify collection of much, if any, data. Many programs can barely collect data on end-of-program status, much less follow-up data 6 months after program participation.

In short, a variety of factors influence the selection of indicators, including the importance of the outcome claims being made, resources available for data collection, the state of the art of measurement of human functioning, the nature of decisions to be made with the results, and the willingness of staff and participants to engage in assessment. Some kind of indicator is necessary, however, to measure degree of outcome attainment. The key is to make sure that the indicator is a reasonable, useful, and meaningful measure of the intended participant outcome.

The framework offered here will generate outcome statements that are *clear, specific*, and *measurable,* but getting clarity and specificity is separated from selecting measures. The reason for separating the identification of a desired outcome from its measurement is to ensure the utility of both. This point is worth elaborating. The following is a classic goal statement:

> Student achievement test scores in reading will increase one grade level from the beginning of first grade to the beginning of second grade.

Such a statement mixes together and potentially confuses the (1) specification of a desired outcome with (2) its measurement and (3) the desired performance target. The desired outcome is increased student achievement. The indicator is the score on a norm-referenced standardized achievement test. The performance target is one year's academic gain on the test. These are three separate decisions that primary intended evaluation users need to discuss. For example, there are ways other than standardized tests for measuring achievement, like student portfolios or competency-based tests. The desired outcome should not be confused with its indicator. In the framework offered here, outcome statements are clearly separated from operational criteria for measuring them.

When I work with groups on goals clarification, I have them state intended outcomes without regard to measurement. Once they have stated as carefully and explicitly as they can what they want to accomplish, then it is time to figure out what indicators and data can be collected to monitor outcome attainment. They can then move back and forth between conceptual level statements and operational (measurement) specifications, attempting to get as much precision as possible in both.

To emphasize this point, let me overstate the trade-off. **I prefer to have less-than-ideal or rough measures of important goals rather than highly precise measures of goals that no one much cares about.** In too many cases, evaluators focus on the latter (meaningless but measurable goals) instead of on the former (meaningful goals with less-than-ideal measures). Of course, it is desirable to have as much precision as possible. By separating the process of goals clarification from the process of selecting indicators, it is possible for program staff to focus first on what they are really trying to accomplish and to state their goals and objectives as explicitly as possible without regard to measurement, and then to worry about how one would measure actual attainment of those goals and objectives.

This is also a good place to note that evaluating outcomes can include qualitative data like case studies and stories of how participants have changed (Patton, 2002). Later we'll consider qualitative evaluation in greater depth, but it's important to know that there are both quantitative and qualitative approaches to evaluating outcomes, including mixed methods combinations that integrate statistics and illuminating stories.

4. **Performance targets**

A performance target specifies the amount or level of outcome attainment that is expected, hoped for, or, in some kinds of performance contracting, required. What percentage of participants in employment training will have full-time jobs 6 months after graduation: 40%? 65%? 80%? What percentage of fathers failing to make child support payments will be meeting their full child support obligations within 6 months of intervention? 15%? 35%? 60%?

The best basis for establishing future performance targets is past performance. "Last year we had 65% success. Next year we aim for 70%." Lacking data on past performance, it may be advisable to wait until baseline data have been gathered before specifying a performance target. Arbitrarily setting performance targets without some empirical baseline may create artificial expectations that turn out unrealistically high or embarrassingly low. One way to avoid arbitrariness is to seek norms for reasonable levels of attainment from other, comparable programs, or review the evaluation literature for parallels.

As indicators are collected and examined over time, from quarter to quarter, and year to year, it becomes more meaningful and useful to set performance targets. The relationship between resources and outcomes can also be more precisely correlated longitudinally, with trend data, all of which increases the incremental and long-term value of an outcomes management approach. The challenge is to make performance targets meaningful.

5. Details of data collection: The evaluation design

The details of data collection are a distinct part of the framework; they must be attended to, but they shouldn't clutter the focused outcome statement. Unfortunately, I've found that people can get caught up in the details of refining methods and lose sight of the outcome. The details typically get worked out after the other parts of the framework have been conceptualized. Details include answering the following kinds of questions:

- What existing data will be used and how will they be accessed? Who will collect new indicators data?
- Who will have oversight and management responsibility for data collection?
- How often will indicators data be collected? How often reported?
- Will data be gathered on all program participants or only a sample? If a sample, how selected?
- How will findings be reported? To whom? In what format? When? How often?

These pragmatic questions put flesh on the bones of the outcomes framework. They are not simply technical issues, however. How these questions get answered will ultimately determine the credibility and utility of the entire approach. Primary intended users need to be involved in making decisions about these issues to ensure that they feel ownership of and responsibility for all aspects of the evaluation.

6. How results will be used

The final element in the framework is to make sure that the data collected on the outcomes identified will be useful. One way to do this is to engage intended users in a simulation exercise in which the evaluator fabricates some potential results and intended users practice interpreting and using those results. The evaluation facilitator asks: "If the results came out of this way, what would you do? If the findings came out this other way, what would that tell you, and what actions would you take? Given what you want the evaluation to accomplish, have we focused on the right outcomes and useful indicators?" (In Step 12 I will discuss this simulation approach in greater depth.) At every stage of a utilization-focused evaluation, the evaluator facilitator pushes intended users to think seriously about the implications of design and measurement decisions for use.

Interconnections Among the Distinct Parts of the Framework

The utilization-focused outcomes framework, as just reviewed, consists of six parts: (1) a specific participant target group, (2) a desired outcome for that group, (3) one or more outcome indicators, (4) a performance target (if appropriate and desired), (5) details of data collection, and (6) specification of how findings will be used. While these are listed in the order in which an evaluator typically facilitates the work with intended users, the conceptualization process is not linear. Groups often go back and forth in iterative fashion; for example, starting with a preferred indicator then jumping back to consider how that indicator would work for a specific target population, then jumping ahead to consider how results would be used, then going back to set a performance target. Thus, a target group may not become really clear until the desired outcome is specified or an indicator designated. Sometimes formulating the details of data collection will give rise to new indicators, and those indicators force a rethinking of how the desired outcome is stated. The point is to end up with all elements specified, consistent with each other, and mutually reinforcing. That doesn't necessarily mean marching through the framework lockstep, but it does mean eventually determining all six elements. Exhibit 8.3 provides an example of all the elements specified for a parenting program aimed at high school–age mothers.

Staying Focused on Primary Intended Users

A central issue in implementing an outcomes evaluation approach is who will be involved in the process of developing the outcomes and making them evaluable. When the purpose is ongoing management by outcomes, the program's executives and staff must buy into the process. Who else is involved is a matter of political judgment. For accountability-focused evaluators, funders and accountability authorities would typically approve the outcomes and indicators. Some processes include advisory groups from the community. Collaboration between funders and service providers in determining outcomes is critical where contracts for services are involved. Those involved will feel the most ownership of the resulting system.

Where there is the time and inclination, I prefer to have key program people work on their own outcomes framework, including identifying indicators and uses of monitoring data, so that those involved in delivering the program feel ownership and understand what commitments have been made. This can be part of the training function served by

EXHIBIT 8.3

Example of a Fully Specified Utilization-Focused Outcomes Framework

Target subgroup	Teenage mothers at Central High School
Desired outcome	Appropriate parenting knowledge and practices
Outcome indicator	Score on Parent Practice Inventory (knowledge and behavior measures)
Data collection	Pre- and posttest, beginning and end of program; 6-month follow-up; district evaluation office will administer and analyze results
Performance target	75% of entering participants will complete the program and attain a passing score on both the knowledge and behavior scales
Use	The evaluation advisory task force will review the results (principal, two teachers, two participating students, one agency representative, one community representative, an associate superintendent, one school board member, and the district evaluator). The task force will decide if the program should be continued at Central High School and expanded to other district high schools. A recommendation will be forwarded to the superintendent and school board.

evaluators, increasing the likelihood that staff will internalize the evaluative thinking embedded in a utilization-focused outcomes framework. On the other hand, for individualized, participatory, and empowerment approaches to programming, having program participants engaged in determining their own individual and group outcomes can be part of the intervention, an example of process use, in which involvement by program participants in focusing on outcomes, including how to measure outcomes attainment and set performance targets, deepens their commitment to work on attaining those outcomes.

With the utilization-focused outcomes framework as background, here are 10 principles for working with intended users to identify meaningful and useful goals.

10 Principles for Meaningful and Useful Goals

1. **Identify outcomes that matter to those who do the work.** Outcomes and performance measures often look and feel like academic exercises to those involved. They think they're involved in a paperwork process to please some funder. But a meaningful outcomes statement articulates fundamental values. It should remind practitioners why they get up

in the morning and go to work: to protect children, feed the hungry, fight disease, reduce the ravages of poverty, and house the homeless. It should be inspirational. As the great management guru Peter Drucker (2000) said when asked about the bottom line for not-for-profit organizations: "The end results are people with changed lives." Outcomes should specify how lives will be changed.

2. **Distinguish between outcomes and activities.** Outcomes describe desired impacts of the program on participants: Students will read with understanding. Participants will stop smoking. Activity goals describe *how* outcome goals will be achieved: Students will read 2 hours a day. Participants will openly discuss their dependence on cigarettes. People in the program will be treated with respect.

Outcome goals should clearly state how people will be different as a result of a program. Program staff may write goals describing intended activities thinking that they have stated desired outcomes. An agricultural extension agent told me his goal was "to get 50 farmers to participate in a farm tour." But what, I asked, did he want to result from the farm tour? After some dialogue, it became clear that the desired outcome was this: "Farmers will adopt improved milking practices in their own farm operations, and thus have more income."

3. **Specificity matters. More specific outcomes are more powerful.** Some goal statements are amazingly adept at saying nothing. I worked with a school board whose overall goal was "Students will learn." There is no way *not* to attain this goal. It is the nature of the species that young people learn. Fortunately, they can learn in spite of the schools. The issues are *what* and *how much* they will learn from schooling.

Another favorite is "increasing awareness." It's fairly difficult to put people through 2 weeks of training on some topic (e.g., chemical dependency) and *not* increase awareness. Under these conditions, the goal of "increasing awareness of chemical dependency issues" is hardly worth aiming at. Further dialogue revealed that the program staff wanted to change knowledge, attitudes, and behaviors. Specific outcomes identify what knowledge, what attitudes, and what behaviors.

4. **Each goal should contain only one outcome.** There is a tendency in writing goal statements to overload the content. "Our program will help parents with employment, nutrition, health, and parenting needs so that their children do well in school and reach their full potential, and families are integrated into neighborhoods feeling safe and connected, and being productive." Now there's a goal written by committee with a little bit for everyone. Ten different possible outcomes are implied for three different target populations in that statement. For evaluation purposes, they must be separated.

5. **Outcome statements should be understandable.** Goals should communicate a clear sense of direction. Avoid difficult grammatical constructions and complex interdependent clauses. Goal statements should also avoid internal program or professional jargon. The general public should be able to make sense of goals. Consider these two versions of goal statements for what amount to the *same* outcome:

(a) To maximize the capabilities of professional staff and use taxpayer resources wisely while engaging in therapeutic interventions and case management processes so that children's development capacities are unencumbered by adverse environmental circumstances or experiences.

(b) Children will be safe from abuse and neglect.

6. **Formal goals statements should focus on the most important program outcomes.** Writing goals should not be a marathon exercise in seeing how long a document one can produce. As human beings, our attention span is too short to focus on long lists of goals and objectives. Limit them to outcomes that matter and for which the program intends to be held accountable.

7. **State intended outcomes separately from how they are to be attained.** An agricultural extension program posited this goal: "Farmers will increase yields through the education efforts of extension including farm tours, bulletins, and related activities." Everything after the word *yields* describes how the goal is to be attained. Keep the statement clear and crisp—focused on the intended outcome.

8. **Separate goals from indicators and performance targets.** Advocates of *management by objectives* and *behavioral objectives* often place more emphasis on measurement than on establishing a clear sense of direction. *Desired outcome:* All children will be immunized against polio. Indicator: Health records when children enter school show that they received 4 doses of IPV: a dose at 2 months; at 4 months; at 6 to 18 months; and a booster dose at 4 to 6 years. When vision, mission, goals, indicators, and performance targets are all run together in a single sentence, the whole may be less than the sum of its parts, even when the whole is 100%. Consider this goal from a youth program: "We strive hard for every participant to achieve their goals and dreams by nurturing their self-esteem as they grow up. It is our goal that 85% will feel motivated or good about themselves and 15% will not." It seems likely that they can at least achieve the last target in their goal statement.

9. **Thou shalt not covet thy neighbor's goals and objectives.** Goals and objectives don't travel very well. They often involve matters of nuance. It is worth taking the time for primary stakeholders to construct their own goals so that they reflect their own values, expectations, and intentions in their own language. Buy-in happens through engagement.

10. Help all involved keep their eyes on the prize. Use outcome statements to stay focused on achieving results. Goals clarification should be an invigorating process of prioritizing what those involved care about and hope to accomplish (see item No. 1 above). Goals should not become a club for assaulting staff but a tool for helping staff focus and realize their ideals. Too often outcomes are written into proposals and reports, then forgotten. Make monitoring outcomes attainment part of staff meetings. Find out if it's true that what gets measured gets done. Orient new staff members to the program's outcome commitments. Staff should share intended outcomes with participants so that everyone knows what's expected and envisioned. Report outcomes in newsletters and other program communications. Revisit outcomes at annual retreats. An informative and revealing exercise can be to conduct an outcomes communications audit: Where in the life and work of the program are priority outcomes shared and used?

Using These Guidelines

These are guidelines, not rigid rules. There are exceptions to all of these guidelines. For example, contrary to the ninth principle, one option in working with groups is to have them review the goals of other programs, both as a way of helping stakeholders clarify their own goals and to get ideas about format and content. From this beginning point, those in a particular situation can fine-tune others' goals to fit their values and context.

Prioritizing Outcomes for Evaluation: Importance Versus Utility

Let me elaborate the distinction between writing goals for the sake of writing goals and writing them to use as tools in narrowing the focus of an evaluation. In utilization-focused evaluation, goals are prioritized in a manner quite different from that usually prescribed. The classic criterion for prioritizing goals is ranking or rating in terms of *importance*. The reason seems commonsensical: Evaluations ought to focus on important goals. But, from a utilization-focused perspective, what appears to be most sensible may not be most useful.

The most important goal may not be the one that decision makers and intended users most need information about. In utilization-focused evaluation, goals are also prioritized on the basis of what information is most needed and likely to be most useful, given the evaluation's purpose. For example, a final end-of-project summative evaluation would likely evaluate goals in order of overall importance, but a formative (improvement-oriented) evaluation might focus on a goal of secondary importance because it is an area being neglected or proving particularly troublesome. An accountability-driven evaluation might focus on an outcome over which the program has substantial control (feeding hungry children) versus a more important long-term outcome over which the program has more limited control (children are healthy).

In my experience, the most frequent reasons for differences in importance and usefulness rankings is variation in the degree to which decision makers already have what they consider good information about performance on the most important goal and the overall purpose of the evaluation (formative versus summative versus developmental versus knowledge-generating). At the program level, staff members may be so involved in trying to achieve their most important goal that they are relatively well informed about performance on that goal. Performance on less important goals may involve less certainty for staff; information about performance in that goal area is therefore more useful for improvement because it tells staff members something they do not already know. On the other hand, for summative evaluations aimed at funders, they will typically want to know about attainment of the most important goals.

What I hope is emerging through these examples is an image of the evaluator as an active-reactive-interactive-adaptive problem solver. The evaluator actively solicits information about program contingencies, organizational dynamics, environmental uncertainties, and decision makers' goals in order to focus the evaluation on questions of real interest and utility to primary intended users at a particular stage in the life of the program and for a specific evaluation purpose.

Turbulent Environments and Changing Goals

The clarity, specificity, and stability of goals are contingent on the degree of stability or turbulence in a program's environment. Evaluators, having traditionally defined their task as measuring goal attainment, have been slow to incorporate this understanding by adapting what we do to different conditions. Uncertainty includes things like funding instability, changes in governmental rules and regulations, mobility and transience of clients and suppliers, technological innovation, political conflicts, and economic or social turbulence. The degree of uncertainty facing an organization directly affects **the degree to which goals and strategies for attaining goals can be made concrete and stable.** The less certain the environment, the less stable and concrete will be the organization's goals. Effective organizations in turbulent environments adapt their goals to changing demands and conditions (Patton, 2011). For example, a program that originally focused on general health education goals had to change its priority to focus on preventing the spread of HIV/AIDS when that epidemic overwhelmed all other health education concerns. Thus, utilization-focused evaluators need to facilitate goals clarification processes and outcomes specification in ways that are sensitive to the larger context and include the possibility that changed conditions will lead to emergent outcomes and a new evaluation focus. This is especially true where the purpose of the evaluation is developmental: that is, where the program is exploring and innovating. In such cases it is inappropriate to force conceptualization of SMART goals. Such specificity, imposed prematurely, can interfere with and short-circuit the processes of exploration, innovation, and adaptation.

Alternatives to Goals-Based Evaluation

One can conduct useful evaluations without ever seeing an objective.

Nick Smith (1980, p. 39)

Dealing with goals and outcomes is fundamental. Dealing with goals and outcomes includes *knowing when not to make goals the focus of the evaluation.* That's why Step 7 included a variety of ways of focusing an evaluation that did not make evaluating goal attainment the centerpiece of the evaluation. As just noted, highly innovative and exploratory programs may benefit from a period of open-ended goals exploration and innovation. Moreover, too much attention to measurable goals can distort a program's priorities. Lee J. Cronbach and Associates (1980) at the Stanford Evaluation Consortium, in their classic treatise on reforming evaluation, warned:

> It is unwise for evaluation to focus on whether a project has "attained its goals." Goals are a necessary part of political rhetoric, but all social programs, even supposedly targeted ones, have broad aims. Legislators who have sophisticated reasons for keeping goal statements lofty and nebulous unblushingly ask program administrators to state explicit goals. Unfortunately, whatever the evaluator decides to measure tends to become a primary goal of program operators. (p. 5)

In other words, what gets measured gets done. An example is when teachers focus on whether students can pass a reading test rather than on whether they learn to read. The result can be students who pass mandated competency tests but are still functionally illiterate. There are, then, two sides to the goals sword: (1) a powerful focusing purpose (what gets measured gets done) and (2) a potentially distorting consequence (doing only what can be quantitatively measured, which is dependent on the state of the art of measurement and limited by the complexities of the real world).

Goal-Free Evaluation

Philosopher-evaluator Michael Scriven, a strong critic of goals-based evaluation, has offered an alternative: *goal-free evaluation.* Goal-free evaluation involves gathering data on a broad array of *actual effects* and evaluating the importance of these effects in meeting demonstrated needs. The evaluator makes a deliberate attempt to avoid all rhetoric related to program goals. No discussion about goals is held with staff and no program brochures or proposals are read; only the program's actual outcomes and measurable effects are studied, and these are judged on the extent to which they meet *demonstrated participant needs.*

Scriven (1972b) offered four reasons for doing goal-free/needs-based evaluation:

1. To avoid the risk of narrowly studying stated program objectives and thereby missing important unanticipated outcomes;
2. To remove the negative connotations attached to the discovery of unanticipated effects, because "the whole language of 'side-effect' or 'secondary effect' or even 'unanticipated effect' tended to be a put-down of what might well be the crucial achievement, especially in terms of new priorities" (pp. 1–2);
3. To eliminate the perceptual biases and tunnel vision introduced into an evaluation by knowledge of goals; and
4. To maintain evaluator objectivity and independence through goal-free conditions.

In Scriven's own words:

> It seemed to me, in short, that consideration and evaluation of goals was an unnecessary but also a possibly contaminating step. . . . The less the external evaluator hears about the goals of the project, the less tunnel vision will develop, the more attention will be paid to *looking* for *actual* effects (rather than checking on *alleged* effects). (1972b, p. 2; emphasis in original)

Scriven distrusts the grandiose goals of most projects. Such great and grandiose proposals "assume that a gallant try at Everest will be perceived more favorably than successful mounting of molehills. That may or may not be so, but it's an unnecessary noise source for the evaluator" (p. 3). He sees no reason to get caught up in distinguishing alleged goals from real goals: "Why should the evaluator get into the messy job of trying to disentangle that knot?" He would also avoid resolving stakeholder conflicts over goals: "Why try to decide which goal should supervene?" Since almost all projects either fall short of their goals or overachieve them, why waste time rating the goals, which usually aren't what is really achieved? Moreover, goal-free evaluation is unaffected by—and hence does not legislate against—the shifting of goals midway in a project, an approach congruent with the flexibility and adaptability of developmental evaluation.

It is important to note that Scriven's goal-free proposal assumes both internal and external evaluators. Thus, part of the reason the external evaluators can ignore program staff and local project goals is because the internal evaluator attends to outcomes evaluation.

> Planning and production require goals, and formulating them in testable terms is absolutely necessary for the manager as well as the internal evaluator who keeps the manager informed. That has nothing to do with the question of whether the external evaluator needs or should be given any account of the project's goals. (Scriven, 1972b, p. 4)

In later reflections, Scriven (1991, p. 181) proposed "hybrid forms" in which one part of a comprehensive evaluation includes a goal-free evaluator working parallel to a goals-based evaluator. For our purposes, Scriven's critique of goals-based evaluation is useful in affirming why evaluators need more than one way of focusing an evaluation.

The challenge nicely illustrated by the goal-free approach is that different types of evaluation serve different purposes. That goal-free evaluation is controversial, and even shocking to many when they hear about it for the first time, reinforces the point that dealing with goals is fundamental in evaluation. And I emphasize again, this includes knowing about alternatives to goals-based, outcomes evaluation. I often tell primary intended users about goal-free evaluation as a way of opening their minds to thinking outside the box, the box being a narrow expectation that evaluation is always and only about measuring goal attainment.

The utilization-focused evaluation issue is what information is needed by primary intended uses, not whether goals are clear, specific, and measurable. Evaluators have a responsibility in their active-reactive-interactive-adaptive interactions with intended users to explore and explain options with intended users in order to decide jointly what will be most useful in the particular circumstances at hand.

The Attribution Question: The Fundamentals of Evaluating the Connection Between Implementation and Outcomes

This chapter on Step 8 is focused on checking that fundamental areas for evaluation inquiry are being adequately addressed in the evaluation. The three fundamentals are implementation evaluation, outcomes evaluation, and the connection between implementation and outcomes—the attribution question: To what extent can the outcomes of the program be attributed to the program? The final part of this chapter examines that connection, the third of the three fundamentals.

Evaluability Assessment and Program Theory

Earlier I noted that turning vague, fuzzy, and immeasurable goals into SMART goals was often undertaken as part of an *evaluability assessment.* Once that was done, the next issue was how the program intended to accomplish those goals. The notion was basically this: Before undertaking an evaluation the program should be clearly conceptualized as some identifiable set of activities that are expected to lead to some identifiable outcomes. The linkage between those activities and outcomes should be both logical and testable. "Evaluability assessment is a systematic process for describing the structure of a program and for

While working on his degree and dreaming of becoming an evaluator, Ernie did odd jobs to pay for tuition.

"It's just a preliminary finding, but it seems we might have an intervention/context misalignment."

analyzing the plausibility and feasibility of achieving objectives; their suitability for in-depth evaluation; and their acceptance to program managers, policymakers, and program operators" (M. F. Smith 2005, p. 136).

One primary outcome of an evaluability assessment, then, is conceptualization of a program's model or theory. This means specifying the underlying logic (cause and effect relationships) of the program, including what resources and activities are expected to produce what results. An evaluability assessment is also expected to gather various stakeholders' perspectives on the program theory and assess their interest in evaluation. Also assessed are the program's capacity to undertake an evaluation and its readiness for rigorous evaluation (e.g., whether the program's theory is sufficiently well conceptualized and measures of outcomes adequately validated to permit a meaningful summative evaluation). In essence, readiness for summative evaluation means readiness to take on *the attribution question:* Can the observed and measured program outcomes be attributed to the program's inputs, activities, and processes (implementation)? Program theory specifies the attribution model, specifying what interventions and change mechanism are expected (hypothesized) to produce what outcomes—and why. Program staff are more likely to talk about testing *the program model* rather than program theory, but the issue is the same. Does the model produce the desired results?

Evaluation as an Up-Front Activity

As evaluators became involved in working with program people to more clearly specify the program's model (or theory), it became increasingly clear that evaluation was an *up-front activity* not just a back-end activity. That is, traditional planning models laid out some series of steps in which planning comes first, then implementation of the program, and then evaluation, making evaluation a back-end, last-thing-done task. But to get a program plan or design that could actually be evaluated meant involving evaluators—and evaluative thinking—from the beginning.

Evaluative thinking, then, becomes part of the program design process including, especially, conceptualizing the program's theory of change (model). Engaging in this work is an example of *process use,* discussed in Step 6, in which the evaluation has an impact on the program quite apart from producing findings about program effectiveness. (The next chapter discusses theory of change work in depth.) The very process of conceptualizing the program's intervention model or theory of change can have an impact on how the program is implemented, understood, talked about, and improved.

This has huge implications for evaluators. It means that evaluators have to be (1) astute at conceptualizing program and policy theories of change, or attribution models, and (2) skilled at working with program people, policymakers, and funders to facilitate their articulation of their implicit theories of change. Given the importance of these tasks, it matters a great deal what theory of change frameworks the evaluator can offer. Step 9, the next chapter, involves checking out what kind of theory of change or model development is appropriate. This topic is big enough to deserve its own step. For now, we'll complete discussion of Step 8 with a simple framework for examining the relationship between implementation and outcomes.

Beginning by Connecting Implementation Elements With Specific Outcomes

In programs with multiple elements and several intended outcomes, which is typical, it can be useful to begin taking on the challenge of linking implementation to outcomes by engaging staff in an exercise that concretely and specifically links specific activities to specific outcomes by specifying measures for each. Exhibit 8.4 offers a matrix to guide this exercise.

EXHIBIT 8.4

Simple Format for Connecting Goals With Implementation Plans and Measurement

Goals: Expected outcomes	*Indicators: Outcome measures*	*How outcomes will be attained (implementation mechanisms)*	*Data on implementation progress: Benchmarks*
1.			
2.			
3.			
4.			

Once completed, the matrix can be used to focus the evaluation and decide what information would be most useful for program improvement and decision making.

Causality and Attribution Questions

Attribution questions are fundamental. They are also difficult to answer. There are both conceptual challenges and methodological challenges. Establishing causality becomes more complicated over longer periods of time, when there are multiple interventions occurring at the same time, influences are interdependent because of feedback loops, or the dynamics of the system in which the program operates mean that all kinds of interconnected elements are changing at the same time. I'll review the conceptual challenges of evaluating attribution models in the next chapter and the methodological challenges in the chapters on Steps 10 through 14. At this point, we'll conclude discussion of Step 8 with the admonition to find out from primary intended users how important the attribution question is and whether they believe establishing the causal relationship between program activities and outcomes is a priority *at this point in the life of the program and at this stage of the evaluation.* Early in the life of a program, implementation issues and formative evaluation may be primary. Sometimes the evaluation mandate and resources only allow for outcomes evaluation without adding the challenging question of the extent to which observed attributing outcomes can be confidently attributed to the intervention.

Unless one knows that a program is operating according to design, there may be little reason to expect it to produce the desired outcomes. Furthermore, until the program is implemented and a "treatment" is believed to be in operation, there is little reason to evaluate outcomes. Once both implementation and outcomes have been evaluated, the connection between them, the attribution question, becomes a greater priority.

Causality can be a central issue in making judgments about a program's merit, worth, or significance. The classic causal question, in all its simple brilliance, is: Did the program produce the desired and intended results? Or, to what extent can the observed outcomes be attributed to the program's intervention? Answering these questions will require a model of how the program works. Considering creating such a model is the next step—and next chapter.

Conclusion: Staying Focused on the Fundamentals of Being Useful

Step 8 involves checking that fundamental areas for evaluation inquiry are being adequately addressed, which means considering implementation, outcomes, and attribution questions. The complex systems interlude and graphic that follow this chapter will depict the dynamic, interactive, and interdependent relationship between Step 7, prioritizing evaluation questions, and Step 8. Together, Steps 7 and 8 address evaluation basics. Sometimes, however, what primary users consider fundamental and basic is different from the evaluator's expectations. Consider this cautionary tale.

> *Former Ambassador to China, The Honorable Winston Lord, was once driving in the Chinese countryside with his wife. They stopped at an ancient Buddhist temple, where the senior monk greeted them enthusiastically. "Would you do this temple a great honor and favor for our future visitors, to guide and instruct them? Would you write something for us in English?"*
>
> *Ambassador Lord felt quite flattered because he knew that, traditionally, only emperors and great poets were invited to write for the temple. The monk returned shortly carrying two wooden plaques and said: "To guide and instruct future English visitors, would you write on this plaque the word 'Ladies' and on this plaque the word 'Gentlemen'?"*
>
> *May the contributions of evaluators be as useful.*

> Details about what is involved in each step are provided in the summary *U-FE Checklist* in the concluding chapter. See pages 414–415 for the checklist items for Step 8 discussed in this chapter.

PRACTICE EXERCISES

1. Find an evaluation report. (An Internet search will turn up evaluation reports in any area of interest.) Locate the section of the report that describes the program. Use Menu 8.1 to identify different implementation evaluation questions that this evaluation might have undertaken. Show that you can differentiate different kinds of implementation evaluation questions for different purposes using this program. What approaches to implementation evaluation did the evaluation report you are reviewing actually take?
2. Find three different program websites online. Examine each program's stated goals and objectives. Use the "10 Principles for Meaningful and Useful Goals" in this chapter to review, compare, and critique those goals and objectives statements.
3. Select a program that you might evaluate. Identify specifically the three fundamental evaluation questions reviewed in this chapter as they would be framed for this program.
   a. What are examples of possible priority implementation evaluation questions?
   b. What are examples of possible priority outcome evaluation questions?
   c. What are examples of possible priority attribution questions?

   Discuss how and why you would sequence these questions in an evaluation over time.

INTERLUDE, STEPS 1 THROUGH 8. COMPLEX DYNAMIC SYSTEMS INTERCONNECTIONS:

Attending to Fundamental Interconnections

In writing this book, I struggled with how to sequence Steps 7 and 8. Step 7 discusses focusing evaluation questions. Step 8 focuses on fundamental questions related to implementation, outcomes, and attribution. Step 8 could precede Step 7, beginning with fundamentals and then considering additional or complimentary possibilities and issues. Or one can begin with Step 7, exploring what is most relevant, important, and actionable, then reviewing whatever priority questions emerge through the lens of fundamentals (Step 8). I considered putting everything in Steps 7 and 8 into one large chapter, but that proved unwieldy and made such a giant step that it felt like climbing a huge wall. The whole point of steps is to create a manageable sequence. So, should focusing priority questions precede or follow checking on fundamentals? An argument can be made either way. Indeed, the two are so interlinked that, in reality, they occur together. Once again we face the challenge of presenting utilization-focused evaluation as a series of steps while also communicating the interactive, iterative, interdependent, and nonlinear dynamics of working with intended users. I eventually decided to present Step 7 before Step 8. Step 7 offers lots of possibilities, so it is generative and open. Step 8 converges those many options around evaluation fundamentals. The complex systems dynamic graphic depicts the interconnections, adaptive interactions, and interdependencies among the U-FE steps.

Complex Interconnections, Adaptive Interactions and Interdependence of U-FE Steps 7 and 8, in Relation to Steps 1–6

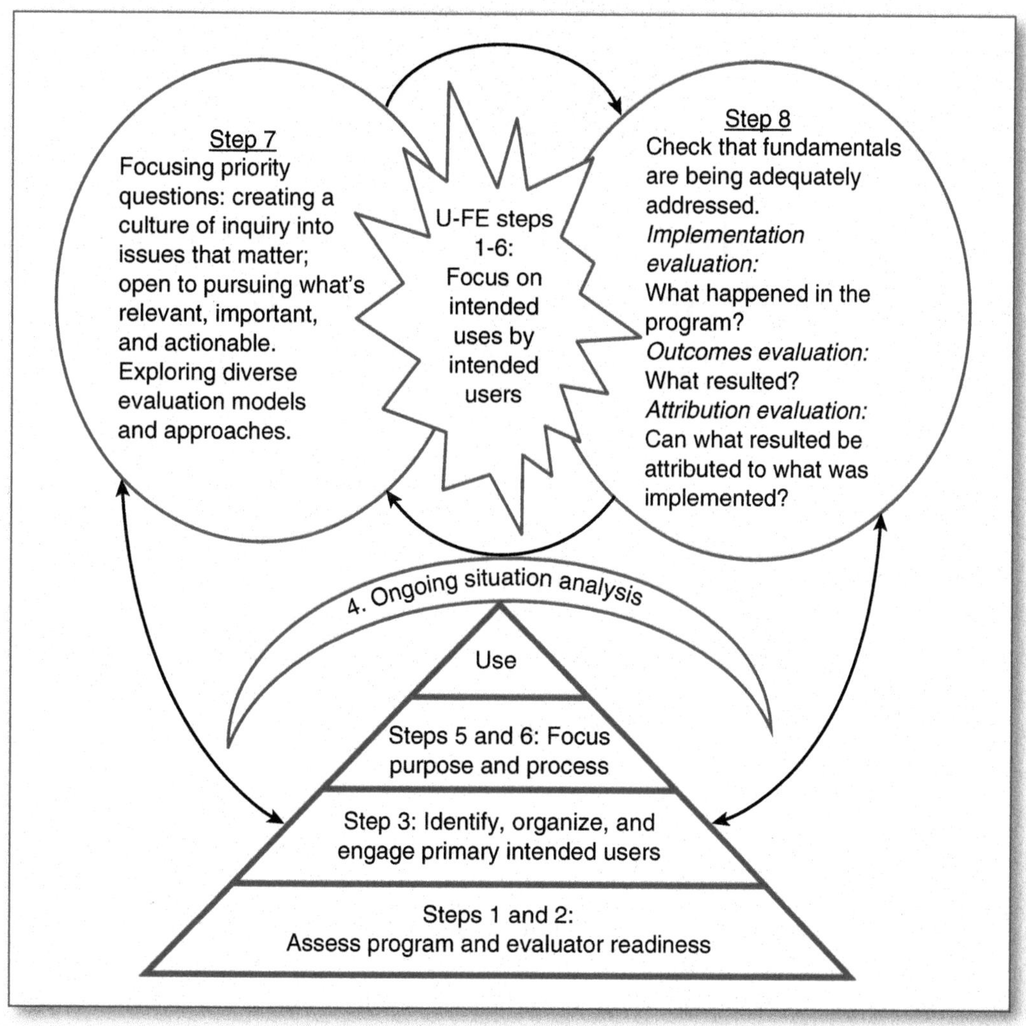

9

Determine What Intervention Model or Theory of Change Is Being Evaluated

There is nothing so practical as a good theory.

Kurt Lewin (1890–1947),
pioneer of social and applied psychology

He who loves practice without theory is like the sailor who boards ship without a rudder and compass and never knows where he may cast.

Leonardo da Vinci (1452–1519),
Italian Renaissance artist and inventor

These famous and widely repeated quotations take us into the realm of evaluating program models and testing their underlying theories of change. Sometimes theories of change are immediately testable, as when King Canute, the 11th-century sovereign who simultaneously reigned over Denmark, Norway, and England, stood at the seashore and ordered the tide to stop rolling in and out. His order had no effect. He repeated the order, shouting at the top of his lungs for the rolling tides to cease. Again, no effect. According to the legend, he conducted this experiment, not with the expectation that it would succeed, but to demonstrate to the hyperbolic flatterers who surrounded him, ever assuring him that his every command would always be obeyed, that he knew the limits of royal power. The natural inclination to flatter those in power, however, has proved as persistent as the tides. Social science tests theories of human behavior, like flattery. Natural science tests theories of nature, like the ebb and flow of tides. Evaluators test theories of change in the realm of interventions, like how to change behavior.

In the opening chapter I offered DARE (Drug Abuse Resistance Education) as an example of an intervention model that has been widely evaluated and found to be ineffective. The intervention involved a 17-week drug education program targeted at middle school children in which police officers went into schools to teach the dangers of drug use and alcohol abuse. The theory was that knowledge presented by a credible and authoritative source (police officers) would lead to attitude and behavior change (resisting illicit drugs). The program model was based on the underlying theory. Evaluations of DARE tested both the model and the theory on which it was based. The model has been shown not to work and the theory to be overly simplistic. Knowledge alone, it turns out, is rarely sufficient to bring about lasting behavior change.

How to bring about lasting change is a central issue of our times. *Evaluation is fundamentally about increasing the effectiveness of change efforts.* Programs and projects of all kinds try to make the world a better place. Health programs aim to make people healthier and prevent disease. School programs strive to increase student learning. Employment training programs try to help the unemployed get jobs. Homelessness initiatives work to get people off the streets and into safe housing. Chemical dependency programs help people using alcohol and drugs. Community development programs plan initiatives to increase prosperity among those in poverty. Juvenile diversion programs try to keep kids out of jail and put them on a path to becoming productive adults. There are hundreds of thousands of programs like these all over the world trying to help people deal with the full variety of societal problems and challenges.

How those engaged in change propose to change things is their intervention strategy. The results they hope to achieve are the intended outcomes and impacts of the proposed intervention. Putting together the intervention strategy with the intended outcomes constitutes a change model. The previous chapter ended with the fundamental question: To what extent can the outcomes of the program be attributed to the program? This chapter takes that question a step further by clarifying the intervention model being evaluated as well as articulating and testing the underlying theory on which a model is based. As we explore these issues, we will find that the very process of conceptualizing the program's intervention model or theory of change can have an impact on how the program is developed, implemented, understood, talked about, improved, and, ultimately, evaluated.

The Logic of Program Interventions and Attribution

Let's start with a simple example of an employment training program.

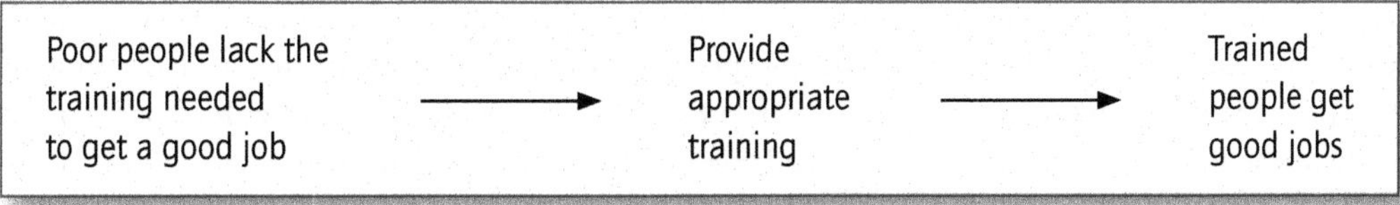

This is a simple (and common) program model. It hypothesizes that if inadequately or untrained people get appropriate training, then they will get good jobs. It focuses on a single problem: lack of training. It provides a focused intervention: job training. It has a straightforward, measurable outcome: a good job. That's a starting place—and it's the starting place for many policymakers and program designers who want to help poor people get better jobs. Then we start asking deeper questions and surfacing assumptions. Does "training" mean just skill training (how to do keyboarding and data entry), or does it also include "soft skills" (how to get along in the workplace)? What is "appropriate" training? What is a "good" job? At this stage, these aren't measurement questions. We're not asking how we would measure whether or not a person got a good job. We're asking conceptual and values-based questions: Will the kind of training provided lead to the kind of job desired? Is it enough to give the person keyboarding skills? What if the person is a recent immigrant and speaks English poorly? Does the program intervention need to include language training? What if the trainee uses drugs? Does the program need to include drug screening or treatment? What if the poor person is a single mother with young children? Does the program intervention need to include child care? How will the poor person get to training? Will the program intervention have to include transportation support to be effective? Is it enough to provide training, or will there need to be job placement services? And what about the workplace? If the poor person being training is African American and the job opportunities are in companies with mostly White employees, will some kind of support be needed in the workplace to create an environment in which this newly trained person can succeed? As the questioning proceeds, the simple intervention above may morph into a much more complicated program intervention. The questions we've just raised are aimed at identifying the critical assumptions and underlying theory on which the intervention model is based. Clarifying models, questioning assumptions, and articulating testable theories of change have become part of the work of evaluation. Utilization-focused evaluation makes sure that these clarifying and questioning processes are not just academic and intellectual exercises, but aimed at increasing the utility of the evaluation for primary intended users.

The Logic Model Option in Evaluation

A logic model is a way of depicting the program intervention by specifying inputs, activities, outputs, outcomes, and impacts in a sequential series. Inputs are resources like funding, qualified staff, participants ready to engage in the program, a place to hold the program, and basic materials to conduct the program. These inputs, at an adequate level, are necessary precursors to the program's activities. Participating in program activities and processes logically precede outputs, like completing the program or getting a certificate of achievement. Outputs lead to outcomes, discussed in Step 8, the previous chapter. Individual participant outcomes, like a better job or improved health, lead to longer-tem impacts, like a more prosperous or healthy community. Exhibit 9.1 displays the elements of a classic logic model.

EXHIBIT 9.1

Basic Logic Model

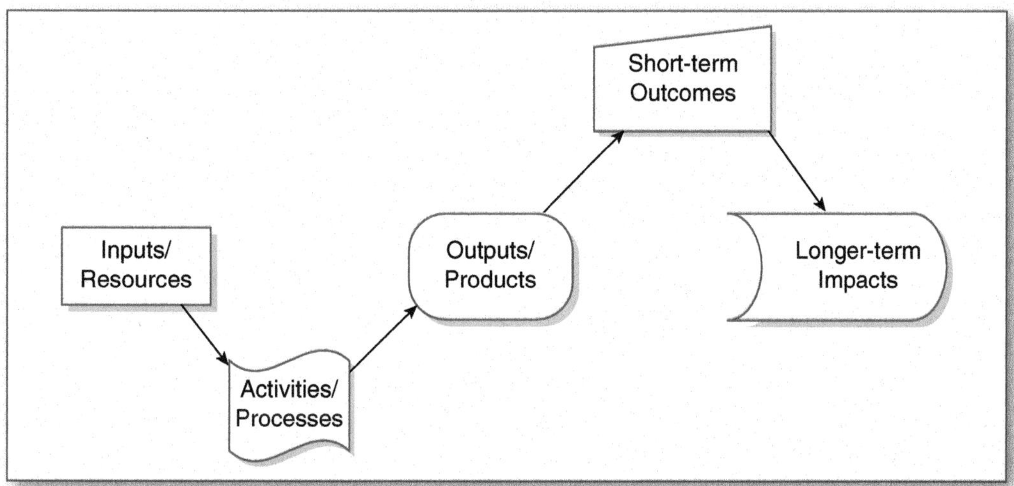

Logic Modeling Resources

Centers for Disease Control and Prevention (2010)

Duignan (2010)

Funnell & Rogers (2011)

Kellogg Foundation (2005)

University of Wisconsin Cooperative Extension (2010)

Constructing a Chain of Objectives

Causation. The relation between mosquitoes and mosquito bites.

Michael Scriven (1991, p. 77)

Another option for conceptualizing an intervention is to construct a means-ends hierarchy.

This can provide a comprehensive description of the program's model. Instead of the logic model language of inputs, outputs, and outcomes, you work with program staff to build a *chain of objectives* by trichotomizing objectives into immediate, intermediate, and ultimate outcomes. The linkages between these levels make up a continuous series of outcomes wherein immediate objectives (focused on implementation) logically precede intermediate goals (short-term outcomes) and therefore must be accomplished before higher-level goals (long-term outcomes or impacts). Any given objective in the chain is the outcome of the successful attainment of the preceding objective and, in turn, is a precondition to attainment of the next higher objective.

> Immediate goals refer to the results of the specific act with which one is momentarily concerned, such as the formation of an obesity club; the intermediate goals push ahead toward the accomplishment of the specific act, such as the actual reduction in weight of club members; the ultimate goal then examines the effect of achieving the intermediate goal upon the health status of the members, such as reduction in the incidence of heart disease. (Suchman, 1967, pp. 51–52)

Any particular paired linkage in the chain of objectives displays an action and reaction: a hypothesized cause and effect. As one constructs a hierarchical/sequential model, it becomes clear that there is only a relative distinction between ends and means. Any end or goal anywhere on the chain can be seen as a means to another goal, so it is possible in an evaluation to enter the hierarchy of means and ends at any point in the chain. In utilization-focused evaluation, the decision about where to enter the means-ends hierarchy for a particular evaluation is made on the basis of what information would be most useful to the primary intended evaluation users. In other words, a formative evaluation might focus on the connection between inputs and activities (an implementation evaluation) and not devote resources to measuring outcomes higher up in the hierarchy until implementation was ensured. Elucidating the entire hierarchy does not incur an obligation to evaluate every linkage in the hierarchy. The means-ends chain of objectives hierarchy displays a series of choices for more focused evaluations while also establishing a context for such narrow efforts. Evaluation pioneer Edward Suchman, in his classic evaluation text (1967), used the example of a health education campaign to show how a means-ends hierarchy can be stated in terms of a series of measures or evaluation findings. Exhibit 9.2, which shows that hierarchy, is still illuminative and informative more than four decades after his original conceptualization of it.

Logic Models Versus Theories of Change: What Are We Talking About?

Let's pause for a moment to consider the language problem. Many different terms are used to describe how program activities lead to program outcomes. I've already discussed theories of change, logic models, means-ends hierarchies, and outcome chains. Some of the language emphasizes elucidating the logic of what the program does, so we have logic models, logical frameworks, and intervention logic. Some focus on theory: program theory, theory-based

EXHIBIT 9.2

Chain of Measureable Outcomes for a Public Health Education Campaign

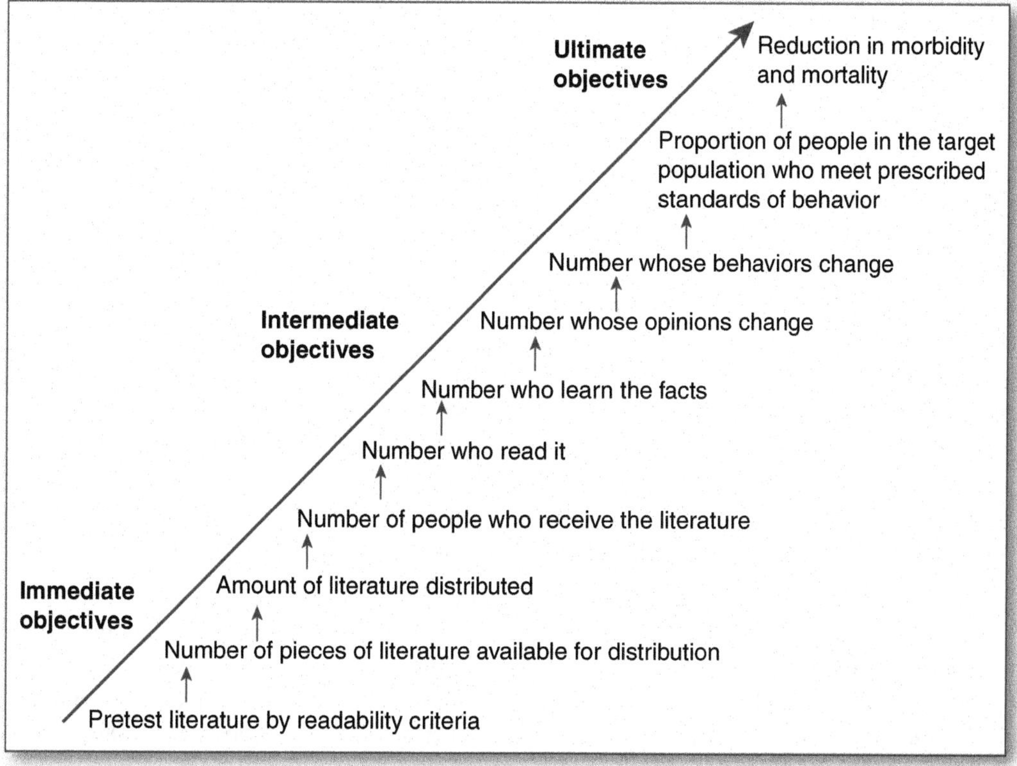

Adapted from Suchman, 1967, p. 55.

evaluation, theory-driven evaluation, theory of change, theory of action, and intervention theory. Some approaches emphasize linkages: chain of objectives, outcomes mapping, and impact pathway analysis. Three important distinctions are embedded in these different terms.

1. *Logic modeling versus theory of change.* Does the model simply describe a logical sequence or does it also provide *an explanation* of why that sequence operates as it does? Specifying the causal mechanisms transforms a logic model into a theory of change.

A logic model only has to be logical and sequential. The logic of a logic model is partially temporal: It is impossible for an effect or outcome to precede its cause. A logic model expresses a sequence in the sense that one thing leads to another. You crawl before you walk before you run is a descriptive logic model. Crawling precedes walking which precedes running. It becomes a theory of change when you explicitly add the change mechanism. You crawl and crawling develops the gross-motor skills and body control capabilities that make it possible to walk; you walk and walking develops the balance, further gross-motor skills, and body control needed to run. *Adding the causal mechanism moves the model from program logic to program theory.*

2. A second critical distinction involves the source of the model. The terms *program logic* or *program theory* imply that what is being depicted is what people who run the program believe is going on. It is the theory articulated by the program staff, administrators, and funders. In contrast, *theory-driven evaluation* or *theory-based evaluation* typically refers to the program as a test of some larger social science theory. Staff in a faith-based initiative may explain a program by saying it puts participants in touch with their inherent spiritual nature; this would be the program's theory. A social science researcher might look at the same program through the lens of a sociological theory that explains how cohesive groups function to create shared beliefs and norms that determine behavior; that approach would be theory-driven. *Theory of change* can be a hybrid of both program theory and social science theory, and often is, as the idea of theory-based evaluation has evolved over the years (Funnell & Rogers, 2011) and come to include both "small theories" that are program specific and the larger theories of which a specific program theory is but one manifestation.

3. A third distinction concerns the *unit of analysis*—or we might say the *unit of logic,* or the *boundaries of the theory of change.* In elucidating a program model, the term "program" is sometimes a discrete local effort, like a local employment training program. That local program has its own logic model and/or program theory that constitutes a specific intervention. But in large organizations like international development agencies or philanthropic foundations, a program can refer to a collection of interventions made up of several projects and grants. For example, The Atlantic Philanthropies, an international philanthropic foundation, has a reconciliation and human rights strategic focus that consists of three program areas each with several distinct projects, grants, and intervention strategies, some of which fit together into a cluster. The cluster has its own theory of change distinct from but based on the logic models of individual grants. In such settings, one has to be careful to specify the unit of analysis for the theory of change. The language of intervention logic or intervention theory avoids confusion about what the word "program" means by focusing on a specific intervention which might be one strategy within an umbrella program (that has several interventions) or a strategy that cuts across a number of programs (where the overall intervention is a comprehensive, multifaceted, integrated, and omnibus development strategy).

Program Theory and Logic Model Babel

Confusion reigns in the language describing how program activities lead to program outcomes:

* logic model * logical framework * program logic * program model * intervention logic * intervention model * chain of objectives * outcomes map * impact pathway analysis * program theory * theory-based evaluation * theory-driven evaluation * theory of change * theory of action * intervention theory *

Which term is best? That best designation is the one that makes the most sense to primary intended users—the term they resonate to and has meaning within their context given the intended uses of the evaluation.

Evaluative Thinking: Comparing Rhetoric With Reality

We're discussing options for working with intended users to conceptualize the intervention model that will be evaluated. Whatever language is used, evaluating whether the program produces desired outcomes will involve comparing what the program model (or theory) is hypothesized to accomplish with what it actually accomplishes. That is a fundamental evaluation comparison. A related, but different, comparison is whether the model actually being used is the same as the model that is espoused. For example, a chemical dependency treatment model may depict the steps a person must go through to achieve sobriety. But close observation and interactions with staff and participants reveal that the real model is one of managing alcohol use not total abstinence. The actual model in practice, managed appropriate use, is quite different from the officially espoused model, total abstinence. This same discrepancy occurs in sex education programs. The official program model may be abstinence before marriage, but the actual model is careful, intentional, and thoughtful sexual activity among unmarried young people. This kind of ideal versus actual comparison involves implementation analysis discussed in Step 8. Let's look at the ideal-actual comparison more closely.

Espoused Versus Actual Program Theories

Comparing the rhetoric about the program theory to what the program actually does involves distinguishing "espoused theory" (what practitioners say they are attempting to do) from "theory-in-use" (what their behavior reveals about what actually guides what they do). The major thrust of evaluating rhetoric versus reality is helping practitioners examine, reflect on, and deal with the discrepancies between their espoused theory and their theory-in-use. Organizational sociologist Chris Argyris (1980), in his seminal research on "espoused theory" versus "theory-in-use," found that congruence between theory-in-use and espoused theory increases effectiveness.

In this conundrum of dissonance between stated belief and actual practice lies a golden opportunity for reality testing: *the heart of evaluation*. Sociologist W. I. Thomas posited in what has become known as *Thomas' Theorem* that what is perceived as real is real in its consequences. Espoused theories are what practitioners perceive to be real. Those espoused theories, often implicit and only espoused when asked for and coached into the open, have real consequences for what practitioners do. Elucidating the theory of change held by primary users can help them be more deliberative about what they do and more willing to put their beliefs and assumptions to an empirical test through evaluation. Evaluation challenges decision makers, program staff, funders, and other users to engage in reality testing: that is, to test whether what they believe to be true (their espoused theory of change) is what actually occurs (theory-in-use).

Process Use and Theory of Change

Assisting primary intended users to conceptualize the program's theory of change (model) can have an impact on the program before any evaluative data are gathered about whether the program's theory works. This is an example of the *process use* of evaluation (as opposed to findings use). The very process of conceptualizing the program's theory of change can affect how the program is implemented, understood, talked about, and improved.

Facilitating a Theory of Change Model

Facilitating the program theory articulation process involves working with those who are knowledgeable about the program to construct a flow chart of what happens from the time a person enters a program to the time he or she leaves. How are people recruited or selected into the program? What's their baseline situation when they enter? How are they oriented to the program once they enter? What are the early activities they engage in? How much are they expected to participate? What are they supposed to be doing, learning, acquiring, or changing during those early activities? During later activities? What's the sequence or stages of participants' experiences? What happens as the program approaches the end? What changes should have occurred in participants by the time they reach the end of the program? What mechanisms explain why these changes take place? To what extent are these changes expected to be sustained? What additional outcomes are expected to occur after leaving the program (for example, keeping a job or staying off of drugs)?

Exhibit 9.3 offers four criteria from Carol Weiss (2000) for deciding whether to make a theory of change the focus of an evaluation:

1. To what extent do people involved in and funding a program believe they are following a model as the basis for their work?
2. To what extent is the program's theory plausible given what actually occurs in the program?
3. What is the state of knowledge about the theory that would suggest whether it is worth testing?
4. How important is the theory of change to what the program does?

EXHIBIT 9.3

Criteria for Selecting a Program Theory to Test: Expert Advice From Distinguished Evaluation Pioneer and Expert, Carol Weiss

- The first criterion is the beliefs of the people associated with the program, primarily the designers and developers who planned the program, the administrators who manage it, and the practitioners who carry it out on a daily basis. Also important may be the beliefs of the sponsors whose money funds the program and the clients who receive the services of the program. What do these groups assume are the pathways to good outcomes?
- A second criterion is plausibility. . . . Can the program actually do the things the theory assumes, and will the clients be likely to respond in the expected fashion?
- A third criterion is lack of knowledge in the program field. This allows the evaluation to contribute knowledge to the field.
- A final criterion for choosing which theories to examine in a theory-based evaluation is the centrality of the theory to the program. Some theories are so essential to the operation of the program that no matter what else happens, the program's success hinges on the viability of this particular theory.

Carol Weiss (2000, pp. 38–41)

Getting at Causal Mechanisms and Assumptions

The purpose of thoroughly delineating a program's theory of change is to assist practitioners in making explicit their assumptions about the linkages between inputs, activities, immediate outputs, intermediate outcomes, and ultimate goals. For example, many education programs are built on the validity assumptions that (1) new information leads to attitude change and (2) attitude change affects behavior.

But does new knowledge change attitudes? Do changed attitudes lead to changed behaviors? Or more directly, does knowledge lead to behavioral change? These questions, based on the classic assumptions embedded in educational interventions of all kinds, are testable. Evaluation can examine whether these presumed and hypothesized linkages actually occur among participants in real programs. Carol Weiss has commented on the widespread nature of these assumptions:

> Many programs seem to assume that providing information to program participants will lead to a change in their knowledge, and increased knowledge will lead to positive change in behavior. This theory is the basis for a wide range of programs, including those that aim to reduce the use of drugs, prevent unwanted pregnancies, improve patients' adherence to medical regimens, and so forth. Program people assume that if you tell participants about the evil effects of illegal drugs, the difficult long-term consequences of unwed pregnancies, and the benefits of complying with physician orders, they will become more conscious of consequences, think more carefully before embarking on dangerous courses of action, and eventually behave in more socially acceptable ways.
>
> The theory seems commonsensical. Social scientists—and many program people—know that *it is too simplistic.* Much research and evaluation has cast doubt on its universal applicability. . . . So much effort is expended in providing information in an attempt to change behavior that careful investigation of this theory is warranted. (Weiss, 2000, pp. 40–41; emphasis added)

Knowing this, when an evaluator encounters a program theory that posits that information will produce knowledge change, and knowledge change will produce behavior change, it is appropriate to bring to the attention of those involved the substantial evidence **that this model generally doesn't work.** In being active-reactive-interactive-adaptive when working with primary intended users, the evaluator can and should bring social science and evaluation knowledge to the attention of those with whom they're working.

Consider this example. The World Bank provided major funding for a program in Bangladesh aimed at improving maternal and child health and nutrition. The theory of change was the classic one we are reviewing here: Information leads to knowledge change, knowledge change leads to practice change. It didn't work. Women in extreme poverty did not have the resources to follow the desired behaviors, even if they were inclined to do so (in other words, they could not afford the recommended foods). Moreover, they live in a social system where what they eat is heavily influenced, even determined, by their mothers-in-law and husbands. The World Bank commissioned an impact evaluation of the project which documented this substantial "knowledge-practice gap" and found that the program was ineffective in closing the gap.

> All forms of knowledge transmitted by the project suffer from a knowledge-practice gap, so attention needs to be paid to both the resource constraints that create this gap and transmitting knowledge to other key actors: mothers-in-law and husbands. (World Bank, 2005, p. 43)

The larger question is: Why are those designing interventions aimed at women in extreme poverty still operating on a theory of change that has been discredited time and time again? I want to use this example to introduce the critical role evaluators play in helping surface and then test a program's causal assumptions.

Identifying Critical Assumptions

Validity assumptions are the presumed causal mechanisms that connect steps in a logic model turning it into a theory of change. The proposition that gaining knowledge will lead to behavior change is undergirded by a validity assumption: namely, that the reason people aren't behaving in the desired manner is because they lack knowledge about what to do. Poor women in Bangladesh don't eat the right foods when they are pregnant because they don't know enough about proper nutrition. Teach them about proper nutrition and they will eat the right foods. It turned out that they gained the knowledge but didn't change their behavior. The validity assumption proved false, or at least insufficient. Knowledge of nutrition may be *a necessary but not sufficient condition* for proper eating.

As validity assumptions are articulated in a means-ends hierarchy, the evaluator can work with intended users to focus the evaluation on those critical linkages where information is most needed at that particular point in the life of the program. It is seldom possible or useful to test all the validity assumptions or evaluate all the means-ends linkages in a program's theory of action. The focus should be on testing the validity of critical assumptions. In a utilization-focused evaluation, the evaluator works with the primary intended users to identify the critical validity assumptions where reduction of uncertainty about causal linkages could make the most difference.

While the evaluators can and should bring their own knowledge of social science to bear in interactions with primary intended users, the evaluator's beliefs about critical assumptions is ultimately less important than what staff and decision makers believe. An evaluator can often have greater impact by helping program staff and decision makers empirically test their own causal hypotheses than by telling them such causal hypotheses are nonsense. This means working with them where they are. So, despite my conviction that knowledge change alone seldom produces behavior change, I still find myself helping young program staff rediscover that lesson for themselves. Not only does the wheel have to be re-created from time to time, its efficacy has to be restudied and reevaluated. The evaluator's *certain belief* that square wheels are less efficacious than round ones may have little impact on those who believe that square wheels are effective. The evaluator's task is to delineate the belief in the square wheel, share other research on square wheels when available, and if they remain committed to a square wheel design, assist the true believers in designing an evaluation that will permit them to *test for themselves* how well it works.

I hasten to add that this does not mean that the evaluator is passive. In the active-reactive-interactive-adaptive process of negotiating the evaluation's focus and design, the evaluation facilitator can suggest alternative assumptions and theories to test, but first priority goes to evaluation of validity assumptions held by primary intended users.

Filling in the Conceptual Gaps and Testing the Reasonableness of Program Theories

Helping stakeholders examine conceptual gaps in their theory of change is another task in building program theory and making it evaluatable. In critiquing a famous prison reform experiment, Rutman (1977) argued that the idea of using prison guards as counselors to inmates ought never have been evaluated because, on the face of it, *the idea is nonsense.* Why would anyone ever believe that prison guards could also be inmate counselors? But clearly, whether they should have or not, some people did believe that the program would work. Without reaching an evaluation conclusion prior to gathering data, the evaluator can begin by filling in the conceptual gaps in this program theory so that critical validity assumptions can be identified and examined. For example, is some kind of screening and selection part of the design so that the refined theory is that only certain kinds of guards with certain characteristics and in certain roles can serve as counselors to particular kinds of inmates? And what kind of training program for guards is planned? In what ways are guards supposed to be changed during such training? How will changed guard behavior be monitored and rewarded? The first critical assumptions to be evaluated may be whether prison guards can be recruited and trained to exhibit desired counselor attitudes and behaviors. Whether prison guards can learn and practice human relations skills can be evaluated without ever implementing a full-blown program.

Filling in the gaps in the program's theory of change goes to the heart of the implementation question: What series of activities must take place before there is reason even to hope that the desired outcomes will result? I once reviewed a logic model for an after-school program that would provide crafts, arts, and sports activities for middle school students once a week for 2 hours for one semester—a total of 30 contact hours. The expected outcome was "increased self-esteem." On the face of it, is this a reasonable outcome? What are the causal mechanisms that link 30 hours of after-school group activities to increased self-esteem?

Or consider a "dress for success" program that provided appropriate dress clothes for poor people to wear to job interviews. The program's stated outcome was the rather modest goal that the appearance of job applicants would make a positive impression. In order to justify funding the program, the funder wanted the program to change the outcome to getting a job. Now the clothes might help in that regard, but it would at best be a minor factor. The "dress for success" program appropriately resisted being evaluated on whether those to whom they provided clothes got a job.

The logic of a chain of objectives is that if activities and objectives lower in the means-ends hierarchy will not be achieved or cannot be implemented, then evaluation of ultimate outcomes is problematic.

> There are only two ways one can move up the scale of objectives in an evaluation: (a) by proving the intervening assumptions through research, that is, changing an assumption to a fact, or (b) by assuming their validity without full research proof. When the former is possible, we can then interpret our success in meeting a lower-level objective as automatic progress toward a higher one. (Suchman, 1967, p. 57)

The Research-Evaluation Connection

Research that supports a theory of change can affect how an evaluation is conceptualized. For example, research shows that children immunized against polio do not get polio. The causal connection between the immunization and immunity against polio has been established *by research.* Therefore, the evaluation can stop at determining that children have been immunized and confidently calculate how many cases of polio have been prevented based on epidemiological research. The evaluation design does not have to include follow-up to determine whether immunized children get polio. That question has been settled by research.

One important reason for testing critical validity assumptions is that some findings are counterintuitive. The Bangladesh maternal and child nutrition program provides an excellent example of the interface between research and evaluation. The program theory posited that proper nutrition for women during pregnancy would reduce the incidence of low birth weight babies. It seems commonsensical that the proper focus for maternal health would be on nutrition *during the pregnancy.* The evaluation findings questioned this assumption and added to the interpretation results from research showing that the pregnant women's *pre-pregnancy weight* was more predictive of babies' birth weight than weight gain during pregnancy. The evaluation concluded:

> Supplementary feeding for pregnant women appears to be a flawed approach on two grounds: (1) the pregnancy weight gain achieved is mostly too small to have a noticeable impact on birth weight; and (2) it is pre-pregnancy weight that evidence suggests to be the most important determinant of birth weight. . . . The fact that it is pre-pregnancy weight that matters suggests that a different approach altogether ought perhaps be considered, such as school feeding programs or targeting adolescent females in poorer areas. (World Bank, 2005, p. 43)

However, this evaluation finding appears to come with its own assumption: namely, that there are not sufficient resources to provide needed food and nutritional supplements to impoverished women *both before and during pregnancy.* By framing the evaluation conclusion as a choice between providing nutrition before pregnancy *or* during pregnancy, the evaluator has limited the policy and programming options. This illustrates how evaluators' own theories of change and assumptions come into play and need to be made explicit—and questioned.

Using the Theory of Change to Focus the Evaluation

Once an espoused theory of change is delineated, the issue of evaluation focus remains. This involves more than mechanically evaluating lower-order validity assumptions and then moving up the hierarchy. Not all linkages in the hierarchy are amenable to testing. Different causal linkages require different resources for evaluation, and data-gathering strategies vary for different objectives. In a summative evaluation, the focus will be on outcomes attainment and causal attribution. For formative evaluation, the most important factor is determining what information would be most useful at a particular point in time. This means identifying those targets of opportunity where additional information could make a difference to the direction of incremental, problem-oriented, program decision making. Having information about and answers to those select questions can make a difference in what is done in the program. So, having conceptualized the logic model or theory of change, the evaluator asks: On which linkages should we focus the evaluation? For example, in a model that posits that knowledge changes attitudes, and attitudinal change leads to behavior change, a formative evaluation might focus on whether participants are acquiring knowledge and changing attitudes. If that linkage doesn't work, there's no need to design a follow-up evaluation focused on behavior change. On the other hand, a summative evaluation would surely include follow-up data on both behavior change and whether those changes have been sustained over some subsequent time period.

Cautions Against Theory of Change Work

Eminent evaluation theorist Michael Scriven (1991) warns evaluators against thinking that logic modeling and theory testing are central to the work of evaluation. He wants evaluators to stay focused on the job of judging a program's merit or worth. He also cautions that considerable time and expense can be involved in doing a good job of developing and testing a program theory. Because program theory development is really program development work rather than evaluation work, he would prefer to separate the cost of such work from the evaluation budget and scope of work.

As always, the decision about whether and how much to focus the evaluation on testing the program's theory is driven by the question of utility: Will helping primary intended users elucidate and test their theory of change lead to program improvements and better decisions? And as Scriven advises, ask the cost-benefit question: Will program theory work yield sufficient benefits to justify the likely added costs involved in such work?

As advocates of theory-driven evaluation assert, a better understood program theory can be the key that unlocks the door to effective action. But how much to engage stakeholders and intended users in articulating their theories of change is a matter for negotiation. Helping practitioners test their espoused theories and discover real theories-in-use can be a powerful learning experience, both individually and organizationally. The delineation of assumed causal relationships in a chain of hierarchical objectives can be a useful exercise in the process of focusing an evaluation. It is not appropriate to construct a detailed program theory for every evaluation situation, but it is important to consider the option. Therefore, one of the fundamental skills of a utilization-focused evaluation facilitator is being able to help intended users construct a means-ends hierarchy, specify validity assumptions, link means to ends, and lay out the temporal sequence of a hierarchy of objectives.

But that's not all. In the last decade the options for conceptualizing and mapping program theories have expanded and now include bringing systems perspectives into evaluation. Let's look at what it means to bring systems thinking and complexity concepts to bear in evaluating theories of change.

Systems Theory and Evaluation

> We contend that the primary challenge in research-practice integration is a failure to frame the effort from a systems perspective. Systems thinking includes a philosophical approach to science and evaluation that provides a way to handle complexity, link local and global, account for dynamic changes in the system or program, recognize the natural evolution of the program, and help identify leverage points. (Jennifer Brown Urban & William Trochim, 2010, p. 539)

> All models are wrong, but some are useful. (George Box, quoted by Berk, 2007, p. 204)

Let's look at how modeling a program using systems thinking changes a program theory. We'll use as an example a program for pregnant teenagers that I've found helpful to illustrate systems mapping as a theory of change approach (Patton, 2008, pp. 361–365). The purpose of the program is to teach pregnant teenagers how to take care of themselves so that they have healthy babies. The teenager learns proper prenatal nutrition and self-care (increased knowledge), which increases the teenager's commitment to taking care of herself and her baby (attitude change), which leads to changed behavior (no smoking, drinking, or drug use; eating properly; and attending the prenatal clinic regularly). This is a linear model because *a* leads to *b* leads to *c*, and so forth, as in classic educational logic models: program participation leads to knowledge change which leads to attitude change which leads to behavior change which produces the desired outcome (a healthy baby). This is a linear cause-effect sequence as depicted in Exhibit 9.4. This is the traditional, widespread approach to logic modeling.

Now, let's ask some systems questions. What various influences actually affect a pregnant teenager's attitudes and behaviors? The narrowly focused, linear model in Exhibit 9.4 focuses entirely on the program's effects and ignores the rest of the teenager's world. When we ask about that world, we are inquiring into the multitude of relationships and connections that may influence what the pregnant teenager does. We know, for example, that teenagers are heavily influenced by their peer group. The linear, narrowly focused logic model, targets the individual teenager. A systems perspective that considered the influence of a pregnant teenager's peer group might ask how to influence the knowledge, attitudes, and behaviors of the entire peer group. This would involve changing the subsystem (the peer group) of which the individual pregnant teenager is a part. Likewise, the system's web of potential influences invites us to ask about the relative influence of the teenager's parents and other family members, the pregnant teenager's boyfriend (the child's father), or teachers

EXHIBIT 9.4

Linear Program Logic Model for Teenage Pregnancy Program

Program reaches out to pregnant teens

↘

Pregnant teens enter and attend the program (participation)

↘

Teens learn prenatal nutrition and self-care (increased knowledge)

↘

Teens develop commitment to take care of themselves and their babies (attitude change)

↘

Teens adopt healthy behaviors: no smoking, no drinking, attend prenatal clinic, eat properly (behavior change)

↙

Teens have healthy babies (desired outcome)

and other adults, as well as the relationship to the staff of the prenatal program. In effect, this systems perspective reminds us that the behavior of the pregnant teenager and the health of her baby will be affected by a number of relationships and not just participation in the prenatal program. In working with such a model with program staff, the conceptual elaboration of the theory of change includes specifying which direction arrows run (one way or both ways, showing mutual influence), which influences are strong (heavy solid lines) versus weak (dotted lines), and which influences are more dominant (larger circles versus smaller circles). Exhibit 9.5 is a rough sketch of such possible system connections and influences.

Exhibit 9.6 presents yet another systems perspective depicting possible institutional influences affecting pregnant teenagers' attitudes and behaviors. The narrowly focused,

EXHIBIT 9.5

Systems Map Showing Possible Influences on the Behavior of a Pregnant Teenager

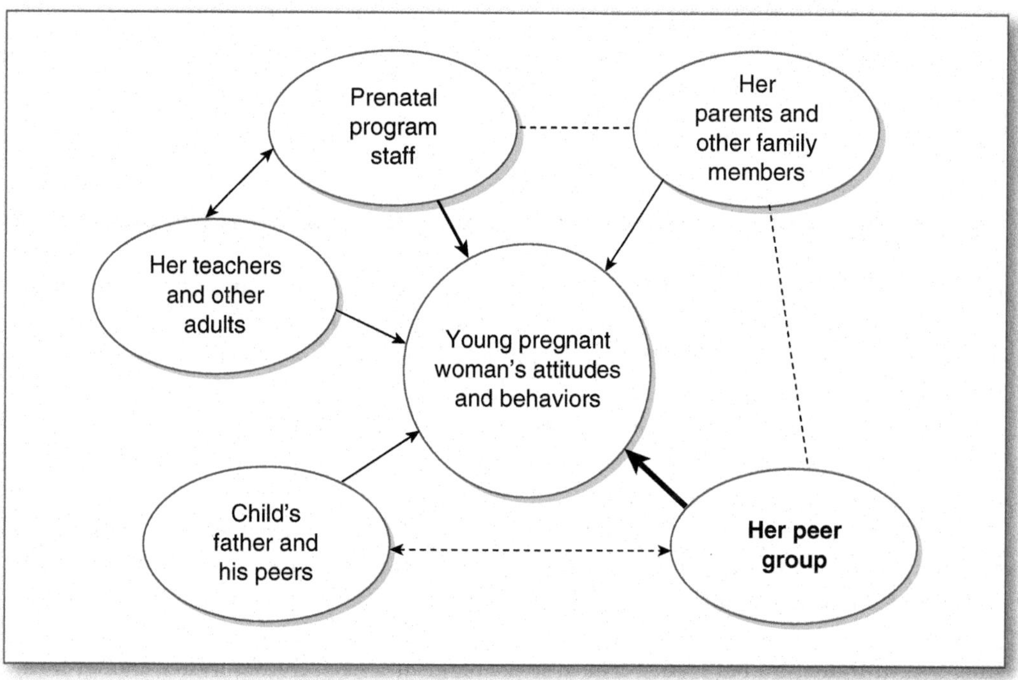

EXHIBIT 9.6

Program Systems Web Showing Possible Institutional Influences Affecting Pregnant Teenagers' Attitudes and Behavior

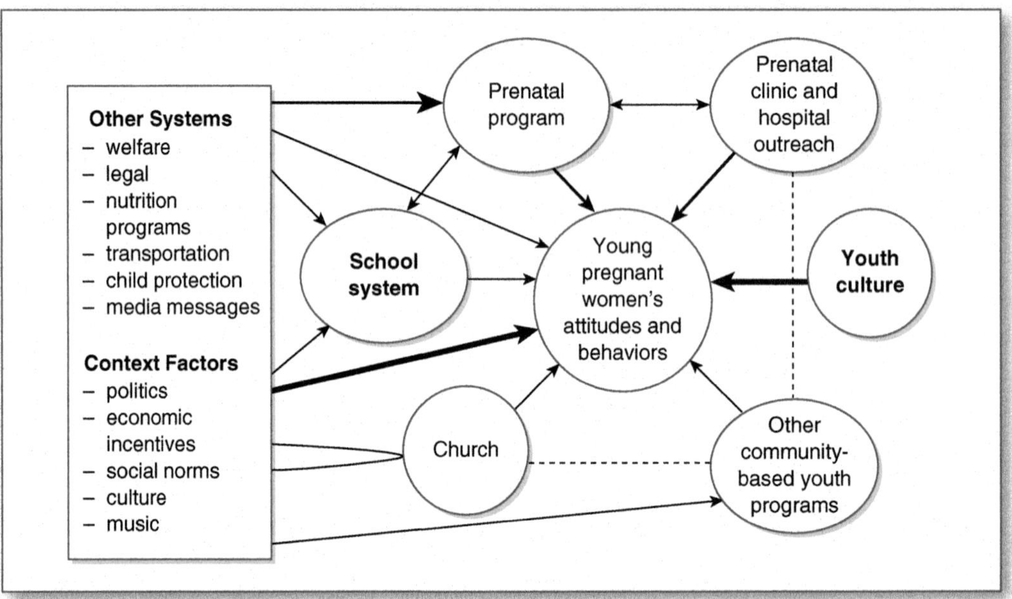

linear logic model in Exhibit 9.4 treats the program's impact in isolation from other institutional and societal factors. In contrast, the systems web in Exhibit 9.6 shows the prenatal program as one potentially strong influence on pregnant teenagers but also takes into account the important influences of the youth culture, the school system, other community-based youth programs, the local clinic and hospital, and possibly the local church. Moreover, during her pregnancy the teenager may be affected by other systems: the welfare system (eligibility for financial support and food stamps), the legal system (laws governing the degree to which the teenager can make independent decisions or live on her own), nutrition programs that might collaborate with the prenatal program, the transportation system (which affects how the teenager gets to clinic visits and the program), and the pervasive influences of the media (television, movies, music) that affects teenager attitudes and behaviors. The systems diagram in Exhibit 9.6 also includes larger contextual factors like the political environment; economic incentives that can affect a teenagers' ability to live independently, get child care, continue to attend school, or get a job; and social norms and larger cultural influences that affect how society responds to a teenager's pregnancy.

Constructing such a systems map with a prenatal program may lead the program to consider a more collaborative effort in which various institutional partners come together to work toward the desired outcome of a healthy pregnant teenager who delivers a healthy baby. The system diagrams suggest that the prenatal program by itself, focusing only on the teenager and only on its own delivery of knowledge to the teenager, is less likely to achieve the desired outcome than a model which takes into account the influences of other people in the teenager's system (the teenager's world) and collaborates with other institutions that can have an effect upon the attainment of desired outcomes. For additional examples of such systems maps for evaluation, see *Systems Thinking and Complexity Concepts for Developmental Evaluation* (Patton, 2011, chap. 5).

Systems Framework Premises

Looking at a program from a systems perspective is one way to deepen our understanding of the program and its outcomes. A systems framework is built on some fundamental relationships premises. We'll examine those premises using the program for pregnant teenagers to illustrate each one.

1. *The whole is greater than the sum of the parts.* If you look at Exhibit 9.5, you see interconnected parts—the pregnant teenager, her peer group, her family, her boyfriend, teachers and other adults who interact with her, and program staff. This *whole web of relationships* will be a unique constellation of interactions for each pregnant teenager. The *whole* may include consistent or contradictory messages about the teenager and her pregnancy. Moreover, that web of relationships isn't just built around her pregnancy. Messages about school, family, life, work, and love are all part of the mix. The system's picture reminds us that the teenager's life consists of a number of relationships and issues that extend well beyond her experience in the prenatal program. The program is but *one influence in her whole life.* Linear program theories tend to be conceptualized as if the program is the only thing going on in the participant's life. Looking at a program as but one part of a participant's whole life is what Saville Kushner has described as "personalizing evaluation."

> I will be arguing for evaluators approaching programs through the experience of individuals rather than through the rhetoric of program sponsors and managers. I want to emphasize what we can learn about programs from Lucy and Ann. . . . So my arguments will robustly assert the need to address "the person" in the program. (Kushner, 2000, pp. 9–10)

Exhibit 9.5 is an abstract conceptualization of a set of relationships. If we put Lucy in the circle depicting the pregnant teenager, and capture her story as a case study, we get a more holistic understanding of Lucy's life and where the program fits in Lucy's life. We then do the same thing for Ann. Each of those stories is its own whole, and the combination of stories of teenagers in the program gives us a sense of the program whole. But that program whole cannot be reduced to the individual stories (the parts) any more than Lucy's life can be reduced to the set of relationships in Exhibit 9.5. The whole is greater than the sum of its parts. Moreover, Exhibit 9.6 reminds us that the program cannot be understood as a free-standing, isolated entity. The program as a whole includes relationships with other entities—schools, community organizations, churches—and larger societal influences. A systems framework invites us to understand the program in relation to other programs and as part of a larger web of institutions.

2. *Parts are interdependent such that a change in one part has implications for all parts and their interrelationships.* Imagine that when Lucy becomes pregnant and enters the prenatal program, she has a close relationship with her boyfriend (the child's father) and her family, is doing well in school, and is active in church. The stress of the pregnancy leads Lucy and her boyfriend to break up. Things become tense in her family as everyone wants to give her advice. Her school attendance becomes irregular and she stops going to church. Without her boyfriend and with increased family tension, a small number of female peers become increasing central to Lucy's life. What we begin to understand is that Lucy's *system of relationships* existed before she became pregnant. Her pregnancy affects all of her relationships and those changes in relationships affect each other, ebbing and flowing. The pregnancy can't really be said to "cause" these changes. What happens between Lucy and her boyfriend when she becomes pregnant is a function of their whole relationship and their relationships with others. The program is part of that mix—but only a part. And how Lucy experiences the program will be affected by the other relationships in her life.

3. *The focus is on interconnected relationships.* The change in perspective that comes with systems thinking focuses our attention on how the web of relationships functions together rather than as a linear chain of causes and effects. It is different to ask how things are connected than to ask does *a* cause *b*. It's not that one inquiry is right and the other is wrong. The point is that different questions and different frameworks provide different insights. Consider the example of your reading this book. We can ask: To what extent does reading this book increase your knowledge of evaluation? That's a fairly straightforward linear evaluation question. Now we ask: How does reading this book *relate to* the other things going on in your life? That's a simple systems question. Each question has value, but the answers tell us very different things.

4. *Systems are made up of subsystems and function within larger systems.* Exhibit 9.5 shows a pregnant teenager's relationships with other people. Exhibit 9.6 shows the program's relationships with other institutions and how these, in combination, influence the

teenager's attitudes and behavior. The "subsystems" are the various circles in these two exhibits. Theses subsystems—family, school, church, community, peer group—function within larger systems like society, the legal system, the welfare system, culture, and the economy. How subsystems function within larger systems and how larger systems connect to and are influenced by subsystems can be part of a systems inquiry into understanding a program and its effects. Both the content and processes of a prenatal program for pregnant teenagers will be affected by larger societal norms. That's why programs in rural Mississippi, inner city Chicago, East Los Angeles, southern France, northern Brazil, and Burkina Faso would be different—*even if they supposedly were based on the same model.* The societal and cultural contexts would inevitably affect how the programs functioned.

5. *Systems boundaries are necessary and inevitably arbitrary.* Systems are social constructions (as are linear models). Systems maps are devices we construct to make sense of things. It is common in hiking to remind people in the wilderness that "the map is not the territory." The map is an abstract guide. Look around at the territory. What to include in a systems diagram and where to draw the boundaries are matters of utility. Including too much makes the system overwhelming. Including too little risks missing important elements that affect program processes and outcomes. Given the purpose of evaluation—to inform judgment and action—the solution is to be practical. If we are mapping the relationships that affect a teenager's health during her pregnancy (Exhibit 9.6), we ask: What are the primary relationships that will affect what the teenager does? List those and map them in relationship to each other. Don't try to include every single relationship (a distant cousin in another city with whom she seldom interacts), but include all that are important—including that distant cousin if she is a teenager who has recently been through a pregnancy, which might be represented by a circle designating "other teenagers who have been or are pregnant who this teenager knows." The systems map of a program is a guide, a way to ask questions and understand the dynamics of what occurs. The systems map is not, however, the program.

Systems Framework Premises

A systems framework is built on some fundamental relationships premises.

1. The whole is greater than the sum of the parts.
2. Parts are interdependent such that a change in one part has implications for all parts and their inter-relationships.
3. Systems are made up of subsystems and function within larger systems.
4. The focus is on interconnected relationships among parts, and between parts and the whole.
5. Systems boundaries are necessary and inevitably arbitrary.

The Increasing Importance of Systems Thinking in Evaluation

> The core aspects of systems thinking are gaining a bigger picture (going up a level of abstraction) and appreciating other people's perspectives on an issue or situation. An individual's ability to grasp a bigger picture or a different perspective is not usually constrained by lack of information. The critical constraints are usually in the way that the individual thinks and the assumptions that they make—both of which are usually unknown to that individual.
>
> *Jake Chapman (2004, p. 14)*
> *System Failure: Why Governments Must Learn to Think Differently*

The preceding has provided only a brief introduction to the possibilities for incorporating systems perspectives in evaluation. Part of the challenge of incorporating systems thinking in evaluation is that there are so many different systems meanings, models, approaches, and methods, including system dynamics, soft systems methodology, cultural-historical activity theory, and critical systemic thinking, each of which has specific implications for evaluation (Williams, 2005; Williams & Hummelbrunner, 2011). But a literature on systems thinking and evaluation has emerged that offers distinct and important alternative ways of conceptualizing theories of change when working with primary intended users to focus an evaluation (Fujita, 2010; Funnell & Rogers, 2011; Morell, 2010; Williams & Iman, 2006). *Developmental evaluation* (Patton, 2011), in particular, is an approach that makes systems thinking fundamental and essential to working with social innovators as the primary intended users of evaluation.

Evaluating Systems Reform

Systems thinking is pushing evaluators to conceptualize what we do in new ways and offers new frameworks for use in working with primary intended users to think about what they do and how they do it. This is especially the case where the targeted unit of change is, itself, *a system*. Thus, while much program evaluation has traditionally focused on the outcomes of programs aimed at individuals—students, farmers, chemically dependent people, parents, children, professionals—some initiatives target systems for reform and change. Policy initiatives can be aimed at reforming systems: the health care system, the educational system, the judicial system, the farming system, *et cetera*. While systems thinking is an option in looking at program outcomes for individuals, it is essential for evaluating system reform initiatives. And that provides a segue to one particularly challenging systems evaluation problem: how to evaluate emergent processes in complex nonlinear systems.

Evaluation in Complex Adaptive Systems

A *Complex Adaptive System* is a dynamic network of many interacting parts, continuously acting and reacting. The results of these interactions are dynamic, emergent, uncertain, and unpredictable. Examples are weather systems, stock markets, ecosystems, and anthills. One of the characteristics of complex adaptive systems is that small effects can have large consequences as expressed by the butterfly effect metaphor which suggests that a butterfly flapping its wings today in China may lead to a typhoon forming in the Pacific Ocean months later. This is represented in our everyday experience by the story of a chance, brief encounter that changes your life, or a phrase offered at an opportune moment that turns you in a new direction and alters forever your path.

Complexity science is being used to understand phenomena in the biological world, policy analysis, ecosystems, economic systems, and in organizations. *But what does this have to do with evaluation?* The answer lies in situational responsiveness and problem definition, which affect how we conceptualize and design evaluations.

Three Kinds of Problems: Simple, Complicated, Complex

To pursue greatness is to pursue Maybe.

John Bare, vice president,
The Arthur M. Blank Family Foundation
Atlanta, Georgia

The challenge of evaluating innovations offers a context for distinguishing different kinds of program and evaluation situations. In studying social innovations with two Canadian scholars, we became focused on the uncertainty and unpredictability of the innovative process, even looking back from a mountaintop of success, which is why we called the book we did on what we learned *Getting to Maybe* (Westley, Zimmerman, & Patton, 2006). Evaluating social innovations is a complex problem, as opposed to evaluating simple and complicated problems. A *simple* problem is how to bake a cake following a recipe. A recipe has clear cause and effect relationships and can be mastered through repetition and developing basic skills. There is a chance to standardize the process and to write the recipe with sufficient detail that even someone who has never baked has a high probability of success. Best practices for programs are like recipes in that they provide clear and high-fidelity directions since the processes that have worked to produce desired outcomes in the past are highly likely to work again in the future. Assembly lines in factories have a "recipe" quality as do standardized school curricula. Part of the attraction of the 12-Step Program of Alcoholics Anonymous is its simple formulation.

A *complicated* problem is more like sending a rocket to the moon. Expertise is needed. Specialists are required, and coordination of the experts is another area of expertise itself. Formulae and the latest scientific evidence are used to predict the trajectory and path of the rocket. Calculations are required to ensure sufficient fuel based on current conditions. If all of the "homework" is completed, and if the coordination and communication systems are sophisticated enough to access the expertise, there is a high degree of certainty of the outcome. It is *complicated,* with many separate parts that need coordination, but it can be controlled by knowledgeable leaders and there is a high degree of predictability about the outcomes. Cause and effect relationships are still very clear, although not as straightforward as with simple problems. Coordinating large-scale programs with many local sites throughout a country or region is a complicated problem.

Parenting is *complex.* Unlike the recipe and rocket examples, there are no clear books or rules to follow to guarantee success. Clearly there are many experts in parenting and many expert books available to parents. But none can be treated like a cookbook for a cake, or a set of formulae to send a rocket to the moon. In the case of the cake and the rocket, for the most part, we were intervening with inanimate objects. The flour does not suddenly decide to change its mind, and gravity can be counted on to be consistent too. On the other hand, children, as we all know, have minds of their own. Hence our interventions are always in relationship with them. There are very few stand-alone parenting tasks. Almost always, the parents and child interact to create outcomes. *Any highly individualized program has elements of complexity.* The outcomes will vary for different participants based on their differing needs, experiences, situations, and desires.

Simple formulations invite linear logic models that link inputs to activities to outputs to outcomes like a formula or recipe. Complicated situations invite system diagrams and maps that depict the relationships among the parts. Complex problems and situations are especially appropriate for *developmental evaluation* in which the evaluation design is flexible, emergent, and dynamic, mirroring the emergent, dynamic, and uncertain nature of the intervention or innovation being evaluated.

- Simple interventions are defined by high agreement and high causal certainty; immunization to prevent disease is an example.
- Socially complicated situations are defined by fairly high predictability of outcomes, but great values conflict among stakeholders; abortion is an example.
- Technically complicated situations are defined by high agreement among stakeholders but low causal certainty; everyone wants children to learn to read but there are ferocious disagreements about which reading approach produces the best results.
- Complex situations are characterized by high values conflict and high uncertainty; what to do about global warming is an example of complexity.

Let me now explain and illustrate the evaluation implications of these different ways of understanding a program or intervention.

An Evaluation Example Illustrating Simple, Complicated, and Complex Designs

Consider a nationwide leadership development program that aims to infuse energy and vitality into a moribund nonprofit sector (a judgment based on funder assessment). The intensive 18-month program includes:

(1) *Skill development* (e.g., communications training, conflict resolution, needs assessment, strategic planning, appreciative inquiry methods) and knowledge acquisition (e.g., introduction to various theories of change, systems thinking, complexity science);

(2) *An organizational change project* in participants' own organizations; and

(3) *Networking* with other participants around nonprofit sector issues of common interest and concern.

Skill development and knowledge acquisition can be modeled and evaluated with a linear framework. The desired outcomes are specifiable, concrete, and measurable, and the outcomes are connected directly to the curriculum and training in a short, observable time frame. Participants demonstrate their skills and knowledge by writing papers, carrying out assignments, and doing team projects. A linear logic model can appropriately capture and depict the hypothesized connections between inputs, activities, outputs, and outcomes as a framework for evaluation.

The second program component—carrying out organizational change projects in their own organizations—is congruent with relationship-focused systems modeling and systems change evaluation. The operations, culture, and constellation of units within each participant's organization constitute a baseline organizational system at the time each participant enters the leadership development program. Each organization functions within some context and environment. As part of the leadership development experience, participants undertake some self-selected change effort, for example, board development, strategic planning, staff development, reorganization, or evaluation, among many possibilities. These are efforts aimed at increasing the effectiveness of the participating organizations and can be modeled and evaluated as systems change initiatives. Evaluative case studies would capture the changed relationships within the organizations, both changed relationships among internal elements (e.g., between board and staff, or between technology support units and line management units) as well as changed relationships with organizations in the environment (e.g., collaborations, new or changed partnerships, new suppliers, changed community or funder relationships). The focus on changed relationships, linkages, and connections makes systems change evaluation an especially appropriate framework for this aspect of the program.

The third overall thrust of the program involves supporting self-organizing networks among participants to infuse new energies and synergies into the nonprofit sector. This constitutes a vision rather than a measurable goal. It's not at all clear what may emerge from such networking (no clear causal model) and the value of such networking is hard to measure. Indeed, there's no particular plan to support such networking other than bringing these leaders together and have them interact for intense periods of time. Beyond the networking, it's both impossible to predetermine what might occur as a result of the infusion of new leadership into the nonprofit sector and it would be politically inappropriate for the philanthropic funder to make such a determination because it would be controversial. Indeed, part of the intervention is support for the nonprofit and voluntary sector leaders to engage in dialogue around what actions and initiatives would revitalize the sector. The outcomes in this case will be entirely emergent. The evaluation would involve real-time monitoring of emergent initiatives watching for what the self-organizing networking yields. Indeed, in a real case where this form of emergent evaluation was actually undertaken, the results turned up conferences organized, regional institutes established, lobbying efforts coordinated, collaborations created, new partnerships, and shared development of materials. *None of these efforts were*

EXHIBIT 9.7

Characteristics of Complex Adaptive Systems

Nonlinearity. Small actions can stimulate large reactions. Improbable, unpredictable, and unexpected events can have substantial impacts.

Emergence. Patterns emerge from self-organization among interacting agents. Each agent or element pursues its own path but as paths intersect and the elements interact, patterns of interaction emerge and the whole of the interactions becomes greater than the separate parts.

Dynamic. Interactions within, between, and among subsystems and parts within systems are volatile, turbulent, cascading rapidly, and changing.

Adaptive. Interacting elements and agents respond and adapt to each other so that what emerges and evolves is a function of ongoing adaptation both among interacting elements and the responsive relationships interacting agents have with their environment.

Uncertainty. Under conditions of complexity, processes and outcomes are unpredictable, uncontrollable, and unknowable in advance. *Getting to Maybe* (Westley, Zimmerman, & Patton, 2006) captures the sense that interventions under conditions of complexity take place in a *Maybe World.*

Co-evolutionary. As interacting and adaptive agents self-organize, ongoing connections emerge that become *co-evolutionary* as the agents evolve together (co-evolve) within and as part of the whole system, over time.

Developmental evaluation applies these complexity concepts to evaluation to enhance innovation and use (Patton, 2011).

predictable in advance. They *emerged* from the process and were captured through developmental evaluation: specifically, periodically e-mailing participants to inquire about how they were working with others and, when something turned up, interviewing them about the details. For more examples of evaluations under conditions of complexity, and the application of complexity concepts to enhance innovation and use, see Patton (2011).

Matching the Evaluation Framework to the Nature of the Intervention

The principle illustrated by the preceding leadership development program is that the modeling framework and evaluation approach should be congruent with the nature of a program intervention. Understanding an intervention as simple, complicated, or complex can significantly affect how an evaluation is conducted. When the intervention is readily understood as fitting traditional linear logic modeling, then the evaluation would document the program's inputs, processes, outputs, outcomes, and impacts including viable and documentable linkages connecting the elements of the model. This is the traditional and dominant approach to program theory modeling and evaluation. In most cases, the outcomes for a linear logic model will be changes at the individual level among intended beneficiaries, for example, changes in attitudes, knowledge, behavior, and status (well-being, health, employment, etc.). In other words, the unit of analysis for the evaluation is typically individuals and individual-level change.

Systems mapping offers an approach for evaluating systems change efforts. In many cases the object of an intervention is a change in a system: for example, developing an organization (an organizational system change effort) or creating collaborative relationships among organizations, or connecting organizations and communities in some new ways. The unit of analysis is the system, and the focus is on changed relationships and interconnections, which are the defining elements of how the system functions. For example, philanthropic funders or government grants often seek to create genuinely collaborative relationships among organizations operating independently of each other (often referred to at the baseline as operating in "silos" or "elevator shafts"). An evaluation looking at the effectiveness and results of such a systems change initiative would map changes in relationships. Network analysis and mapping are powerful tools for capturing and depicting such dynamic and evolving system relationships (or absence of same when the change process fails to work).

Developmental evaluation is especially appropriate for situations with a high degree of uncertainty and unpredictability where an innovator or funder wants to "put things in motion and see what happens." Using the example of the leadership development program, infusing a hundred highly trained and supported national leaders into the nonprofit sector fits these parameters. All kinds of things can happen; many unexpected results may emerge (and did in the actual initiative on which this example is based). Some form of real-time, open-ended tracking is needed to capture what emerges. This is especially appropriate for venture capital and highly entrepreneurial, seed money efforts where the strategy is to infuse people and resources to shake up a system, increase the rate and intensity of interactions among system elements and actors, and see what happens. As things start to happen, additional resources can be infused to support further development. The very act of capturing what emerges and feeding information back into the evolving system makes this form of developmental evaluation part of the intervention (a form of process use). In such developmental evaluation there is not and cannot be a classic separation between the measurement process and what is being observed. The observations affect the emergent self-organizing by injecting new information into the dynamic and emergent system. For example, following up with the trained leaders to find out who they are networking with and what is emerging can stimulate them to network. Even the unit of analysis can change in emergent, developmental evaluation as the evaluator tracks whatever emerges; that is, the very definition of units of analysis is emergent as the evaluator follows the complex nonlinear dynamics of the connections and linkages among those exchanging information and engaged in some forms of self-organized collective action.

Complexity concepts are catching on. Under "relationship status" Facebook just added "dynamical" as an option.

Attention to complex adaptive systems provides a framework for understanding such common evaluation issues as unintended consequences, irreproducible effects, lack of program fidelity in implementation, multiple paths to the same outcomes, "slippery" program requirements, and difficulty in specifying treatments (Morell, 2010). Glenda Eoyang (2006) has described how a complexity-based approach to evaluation was used in a large social services department with 3,000 employees at the county level to help integrate services and functions. The evaluation elucidated emergent "networks of meaning," supported new approaches to alignment in looking at how different units connected to each other, and tracked the evolution of language about what was happening, which shaped emergent meanings. Eoyang and Berkas (1998) have examined and generalized the particular contributions that the lens of complex adaptive systems can bring to evaluation. They concluded:

> The system-wide behaviors of a Complex Adaptive System (CAS) emerge over time. For this reason, the evaluation system should focus on developmental and emergent patterns of behavior that:
>
> - Match the developmental stage of the system. . . . Consider the dynamical pattern that the system exhibits over time to design an evaluation program to capture the "differences that make a difference."
> - Track patterns and pattern changes over time, rather than focusing exclusively on behaviors of specific individuals or groups. While it may be unreasonable to expect a particular path of development or a predetermined outcome from a CAS, emergent patterns of behavior can be expected outcomes. An effective evaluation system must be able to capture and report on these evolving patterns. (Eoyang & Berkas, 1998)

Theory Informing Practice, Practice Informing Theory

The notion of cause and effect can lose all meaning in highly dynamic and complex adaptive systems characterized by nonlinear patterns of interaction, where small actions can connect with other smaller and larger forces and factors that wander hither and yon, but then suddenly emerge, like a hurricane, as major change at some unpredicted and unpredictable tipping point. Evaluation methods, designs, and tools for measuring predetermined outcomes and attributing causes for simple interventions that can be depicted as linear logic models are of little use in tracking the effects of interventions in complex adaptive systems. Indeed, the imposition of such linear designs and simple measures can do harm by trying to control and thereby stifling the very innovative process being tracked. Different kinds of theories of change, then, demand different evaluation approaches, thus the importance of developmental evaluation for use in complex adaptive systems. The challenge is to match the evaluation approach to the nature of the situation, the theory of change at work, and the information needs of primary intended users.

In all this, it is important to interpret results about causal linkages with prudence and care. In that regard, consider the wisdom of this Buddhist story adapted for evaluation:

> Two evaluators were discussing a project. One said: "The project results occurred because of the intervention." The other said: "No, the project results occurred because of the natural cycles of change." Another evaluator happened to be passing by. He told them: "Not the intervention, not natural cycles of change; it is you who are changing." (Russon & Russon, 2010, p. 129)

Details about what is involved in each step are provided in the summary *U-FE Checklist* in the concluding chapter. See pages 415–416 for the checklist items for Step 9 discussed in this chapter.

PRACTICE EXERCISES

1. The Centers for Disease Control and Prevention (2010) has pulled together Internet resources on logic models:

   http://www.cdc.gov/eval/resources.htm#logic model. From this list of resources, select and review three different guides to constructing logic models. How are they alike? How are they different?

2. Take a linear logic model aimed at producing specific outcomes for individuals and reconceptualize the logic model as a systems map. See Exhibits 9.4 and 9.5 in this chapter as an example for a teenage pregnancy prenatal program. For an example of a program aimed at police officers with sleep disorders, see Patton (2011, pp. 118–119). You can even do this exercise for yourself using the reading of this book as the focus. Create a linear logic model of your experience and outcomes reading this book. Then create a systems map of the people who have and/or will affect the outcomes you retain from reading this book. Comment on the different perspectives involved in these alternative depictions.

3. Use the distinctions between simple, complicated, and complex presented in this chapter to identify these elements of a major initiative. The example in this chapter is of a leadership development initiative with simple, complicated, and complex aspects. Using an initiative you know as an example, what elements are simple? What elements are complicated? What elements are complex? Discuss the evaluation implications of these distinctions. Note: (a) a simple program element can be depicted as a linear model; (b) a complicated intervention requires understanding and changing system relationships; and (c) a complex situation is portrayed as emergent and uncertain. In essence, this exercise involves looking at an intervention through these three different lenses. Compare and contrast what each illuminates and makes possible—and the evaluation implications of each perspective.

INTERLUDE, STEPS 1 THROUGH 9. COMPLEX DYNAMIC SYSTEMS INTERCONNECTIONS

Considering Model and Theory Formulation Issues Through the U-FE Process

The steps in the checklist are necessarily linear and sequential. But to depict utilization-focused evaluation as a complex adaptive system, each new step in the checklist also becomes another element in the complex systems understanding that runs through and interconnects the steps of the checklist. Step 9 focuses on clarifying the program intervention to make it evaluable, but every step involves asking questions about the intervention. For example, this can take the form of developing a logic model in Step 1 as part of enhancing program readiness for evaluation. Indeed, evaluability assessment at the beginning of an evaluation consultation often includes logic model development.

A key issue in Step 2, assessing and enhancing evaluator readiness, is the evaluator's skill in facilitating logic modeling or theory of change work. Step 3, identifying, organizing, and engaging primary intended users, can include consideration of particular stakeholders' interest in model and program theory clarification and testing. Indeed, every U-FE step can be affected by how well conceptualized the intervention is. Thus, an ongoing question through the U-FE process is whether model or theory testing will be useful. And if so, how?

The complex dynamic graphic on the next page attempts to depict the ways in which logic model and theory of change questions are potentially embedded in and a part of all the U-FE steps.

Complex Interconnections and Adaptive Interactions Around Model and Theory Work Throughout U-FE Steps 1 Through 9

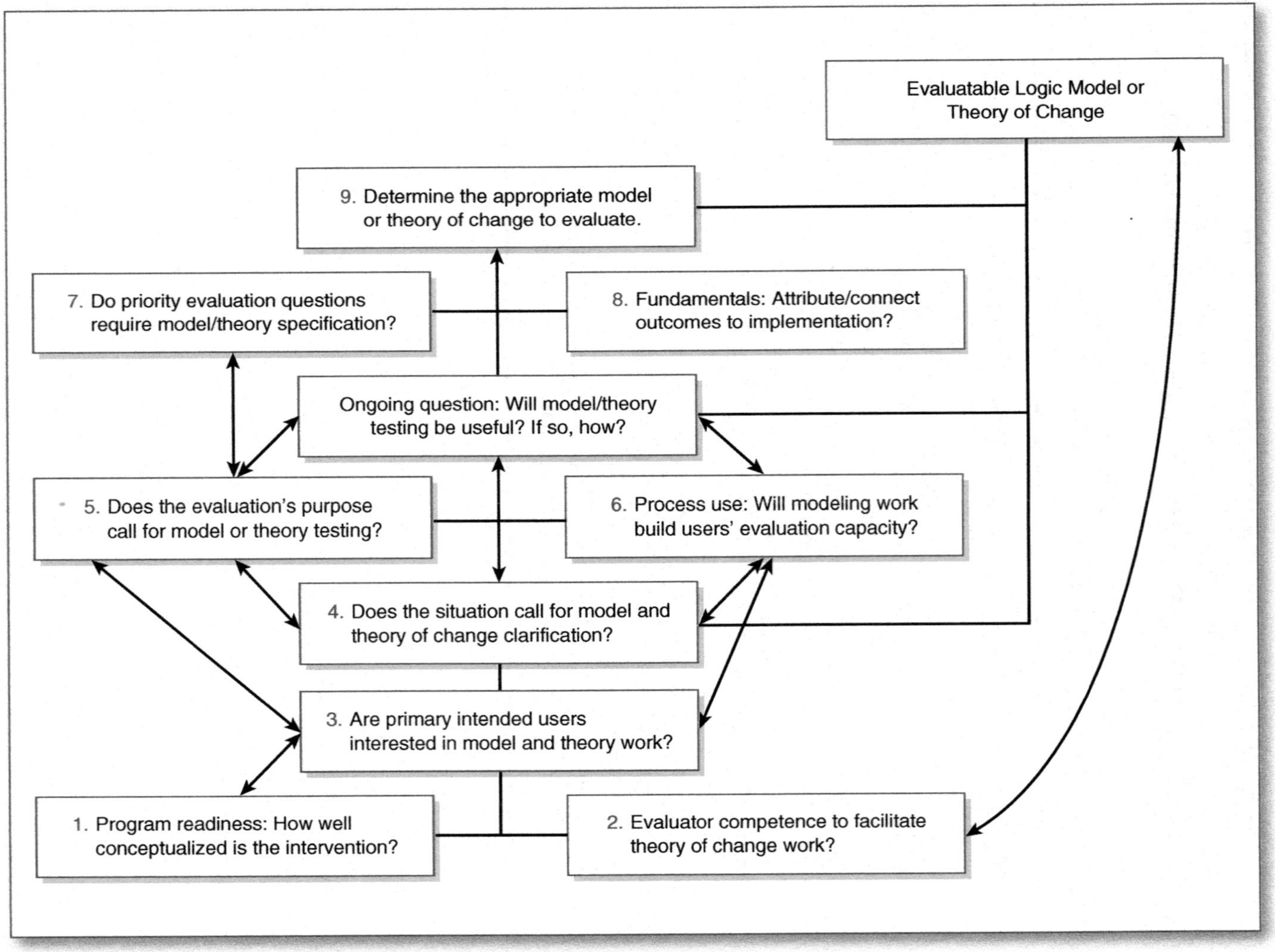

Evaluatable Logic Model or Theory of Change

9. Determine the appropriate model or theory of change to evaluate.

7. Do priority evaluation questions require model/theory specification?

8. Fundamentals: Attribute/connect outcomes to implementation?

Ongoing question: Will model/theory testing be useful? If so, how?

5. Does the evaluation's purpose call for model or theory testing?

6. Process use: Will modeling work build users' evaluation capacity?

4. Does the situation call for model and theory of change clarification?

3. Are primary intended users interested in model and theory work?

1. Program readiness: How well conceptualized is the intervention?

2. Evaluator competence to facilitate theory of change work?

10

Negotiate Appropriate Methods to Generate Credible Findings That Support Intended Use by Intended Users

The scientific method, so far as it is a method, is nothing more than doing one's damnedest with one's mind, no holds barred.

Harvard Physicist Percy W. Bridgman, Winner,
Nobel Prize, 1946 for discoveries in high-pressure physics
(quoted by Waller, 2004, p. 106)

Methods decisions, like decisions about focus and priority issues, are guided and informed by our evaluation goal: *intended use by intended users*. Attaining this goal is enhanced by having intended users actively involving in methods decisions. This turns out to be a controversial approach, evidence about its desirability and effectiveness notwithstanding. Let me explain.

For the most part, evaluation professionals have come to accept that use can be enhanced by actively involving intended users in decisions about the evaluation's purpose, scope, and focus to ensure relevance and buy-in. In other words, they can accept playing a consultative and collaborative role during the conceptual phase of the evaluation. Where my colleagues often part company with me is in the role to be played by intended users in making measurement and design decisions. "The evaluator is nothing," they argue, "if not an expert in methods and statistics. Clearly social scientists ought to be left with full responsibility for operationalizing program goals and determining data collection procedures." *Utilization-focused evaluation takes a different path.*

Beyond Technical Expertise

The common perception of methods decisions among nonresearchers is that such decisions are primarily technical in nature. Sample size, for example, is determined by a mathematical formula. The evaluation methodologist enters the values of certain variables, makes calculations, and out pops the right sample size to achieve the desired level of statistical robustness, significance, power, validity, reliability, generalizability, and so on—all technical terms that dazzle, impress, and intimidate practitioners and nonresearchers. Evaluation researchers have a vested interest in maintaining this technical image of scientific expertise, for it gives us prestige, inspires respect, and, not incidentally, it leads nonresearchers to defer to us, essentially giving us the power to make crucial methods decisions and then interpret the meaning of the resulting data. It is not in our interest, from the perspective of maintaining prestige and power, to reveal to intended users that methods decisions are far from purely technical. But, contrary to public perception, evaluators know that methods decisions are never purely technical. *Never.* Ways of measuring complex phenomena involve simplifications that are inherently somewhat arbitrary, always constrained by limited resources and time, inevitably involve competing and conflicting priorities, and rest on a foundation of values preferences that are typically resolved by pragmatic considerations, disciplinary biases, and measurement traditions.

The reason to debunk the myth that methods and measurement decisions are primarily technical is to enhance use. For we know that use is enhanced when practitioners, decision makers, and other users fully understand the strengths and weaknesses of evaluation data, and that such understanding is increased by being involved in making methods decisions. We know that use is enhanced when intended users participate in making sure that, when trade-offs are considered, as they inevitably are because of limited resources and time, the path chosen is informed by relevance. We know that use is enhanced when users buy into the design and find it credible and valid within the scope of its intended purposes as determined by them. And we know that when evaluation findings are presented, the substance is less likely to be undercut by debates about methods if users have been involved in those debates prior to data collection.

As in all other aspects of the evaluation, then, the utilization-focused evaluator advises intended users about options; points out the consequences of various choices; offers creative possibilities; engages with users actively, reactively, interactively, and adaptively to consider alternatives; and facilitates their involvement in methods decisions through a process of negotiation. At the stage of choosing methods, the evaluator engages as a technical adviser, consultant, teacher, and advocate for quality. The evaluator has a clear stake in the quality of the evaluation because, if nothing else, the evaluator's reputation is at stake in every evaluation. And the primary intended users have a stake in assuring a credible evaluation that meets their information needs. Together, then, the evaluator and primary intended users negotiate the design, select methods, and make measurement decisions.

Exhibit 10.1 summarizes issues to anticipate when involving primary intended users in methods decisions. In the pages that follow, I'll elaborate on these rationales, explore the implications of this approach, and provide examples.

EXHIBIT 10.1

Issues to Anticipate When Involving Primary Intended Users in Methods Decisions

1. **Connect utility with data quality and methods credibility.** Intended use affects methods choices, and methods choices affect what useful data will result from an evaluation. Intended users can and should understand and judge the utility of various design options and kinds of data.

2. **Negotiate trade-offs.** Limited time and resources necessitate trade-offs: more of this, less of that. Primary users have a significant stake in such decisions since findings are affected. No design can do everything. Those who will use the findings should be part of trade-off considerations.

3. **Deal with practical considerations that affect data collection.** Methods decisions are never purely technical. Practical considerations constrain technical alternatives. Everything from how to classify program participants to how to aggregate data has utility implications that deserve users' consideration. Intended users can help anticipate and resolve potential data collection problems, including especially access to needed data.

4. **Identify design strengths and weaknesses.** No design is perfect. Intended users need to know the strengths and weaknesses of an evaluation to exercise informed judgment.

5. **Make explicit criteria for judging methodological quality.** Different users (and evaluators) may have different criteria for judging methodological quality. These should be made explicit and negotiated during methods discussions.

6. **Establish what data are credible.** Credibility of the evidence and the perceived validity of the overall evaluation are key factors affecting use. These are matters of subjective user judgment that should inform methods decisions.

7. **Be transparent about methodological debates.** Evaluators and researchers debate the relative merits of various methods and measures, like quantitative versus qualitative data, and mixed methods combinations. Intended users should know that methods choices can be controversial.

8. **Increase users' capacity and support their learning.** Intended users learn about and become more knowledgeable and sophisticated about methods and using data by being involved in methods decisions. This benefits both the current and future evaluations.

9. **Surface methods debates before data collection.** Methods debates should take place before data collection, as much as possible, so that findings are not undercut by bringing up concerns that should have been addressed during design. Methods debates among intended users after findings are reported distract from using evaluation results.

10. **Evaluator's stake is made clear.** The evaluator has a clear stake in the quality of the evaluation because, if nothing else, the evaluator's reputation is at stake in every evaluation. And the primary intended users have a stake in assuring a evaluation that meets their information needs. Together, then, the evaluator and primary intended users negotiate the design, select methods, and make measurement decisions—and in so doing the evaluator's stake is made clear to intended users.

Examples of Methods and Measurement Decisions That Benefit From Intended User Involvement

Important Program Performance Rates

Performance rates are indicators like program completion rates, drop-out rates, levels of participation, and degrees of outcomes attainment. Consider the drop-out rate. In most programs the drop-out rate is an important indicator of how participants are reacting to a program. But when has someone dropped out? After they miss three sessions? Five sessions? Ten sessions? Who decides? Drop-out rates typically turn out to involve some arbitrary cutoff. For example, school districts vary widely in how they define, count, and report dropouts, as do chemical dependency, adult literacy, parent education, and all kinds of other programs. These variations exist because there is no universal right answer for when someone has dropped out of a program.

It seems simple. Participants have dropped out when they stop coming. So a parent misses three consecutive parent education sessions. The program decides that missing three consecutive sessions means they've dropped out. There are only 30 sessions, so missing three means missing 10% of the program. Then the parent returns for the next session after missing three in a row. Does the program allow re-entry? Did the parent drop out and re-enter, or is this treated as continuation? Does missing three sessions trigger a staff intervention to encourage potential dropouts to re-engage? Or if someone stops coming, are they left alone? What is the data system for monitoring attendance? Are potential dropouts noted in real time (when they've missed the third session) or only tabulated at the end of the program? These are just a few of things that have to be determined and understood to calculate *and interpret* a drop-out rate.

No less vague and difficult are concepts like *in the program* and *finished the program.* Many programs lack clear beginning and ending points. For example, a job training program aimed at chronically unemployed minority men has a month-long assessment process, including testing for drug use and observing a potential participant's persistence in staying with the process. During this time, the participant, with staff support and coaching, develops a plan. The participant is on probation until he completes enough of the program to show seriousness and commitment, but the program is highly individualized so different people are involved in the early assessment and probation processes over very different time periods. There is no clear criterion for when a person has begun probation or completed probation and officially *entered* the program. These processes, in aggregate, will determine key drop-out, completion, and acceptance rates. Making sure that such categories are meaningful and valid, so that the numbers are credible and useful, involves far more than statistics. Careful thought must be given, with primary intended users, to how the numbers and reported rates will be calculated and used, including whether they can be used for comparisons with similar programs.

Nor are these kinds of categorical decisions only a problem when measuring human behavior. The Minnesota Department of Transportation has categorized road projects as *preservation, replacement,* and *new or expansion.* How these categories are used to allocate funding to regions throughout the state has enormous implications. Consider the Lake Street Bridge that connects Minneapolis and Saint Paul. Old and in danger of being condemned, the bridge was torn down and a new one built. The old bridge had only two lanes and no decorative flourishes. The new bridge has four lanes and attractive design features. Should this project be categorized as replacement or expansion? In a time of economic optimism and expanding resources, such as the 1960s, new and expansion projects were favored. In a time of downsizing and reduced resources, like the 2000s, replacement projects were more politically viable. In 2009 and 2010, such projects became part of the federal economic stimulus package and had as much to do with creating jobs and stimulating the economy as upgrading infrastructure. Perhaps, you might argue, the Lake Street Bridge illustrates the need for a new category: part replacement/part expansion/part job creation. But no replacements are pure replacements when new materials are used and updated codes are followed. And few expansions are done without replacing something. How much mix, then, would have to occur for a project to fall into the new, combined part replacement/part expansion category? A doctoral degree in research and statistics provides no more guidance in answering this question than thoughtful consideration of how the data will be used, grounded in common sense and pragmatism—a decision that should be made by intended users with intended uses in mind. Such inherently arbitrary measurement decisions determine what data will emerge in findings.

Methods and Measurement Options

Mail questionnaires, telephone interviews, or personal face-to-face interviews? Individual interviews or focus groups? Even-numbered or odd-numbered scales on survey items? Opinion, knowledge, and/or behavioral questions? All closed questions or some open-ended? If some open-ended, how many? Norm-referenced or criterion-referenced tests? Develop our own instruments or adopt measures already available? Experimental design, quasi-experimental design, or case studies? Participant observation or spectator observation? A few in-depth observations or many shorter observations? Single or multiple observers? Standardized or individualized protocols? Fixed or emergent design? Follow up after 2 weeks, 3 months, 6 months, or a year? Follow up everyone or a sample? What kind of sample: simple random, stratified, and/or purposeful? What size sample? Should interviewers have the same characteristics as program participants: Gender? Age? Race? What comparisons to make: Past performance? Intended goals? Hoped-for goals? Other programs? A utilization-focused evaluator works with primary intended users to consider the strengths and weaknesses of major design and measurement possibilities.

Christie (2007) found that decision makers could distinguish among the merits and uses of different kinds of designs. Using a set of scenarios derived from actual evaluation studies, she conducted a simulation to examine what decision makers reported as evaluation design preferences and likely influences. Each scenario described a setting where results from one of three types of evaluation designs would be available: large-scale study data, case study data, or anecdotal accounts. The simulation then specified a particular decision that needed to be made. Decision makers were asked to indicate which type of design would influence their decision making. Results from 131 participants indicated that participants were influenced by all types of information, yet large-scale and case study data were more influential relative to anecdotal accounts, certain types of evaluation data were more influential among certain groups of decision makers, and choosing to use one type of evaluation data over the other two depended on the independent influence of other types of evaluation data on the decision maker, as well as prior beliefs about program efficacy. In essence, these decision makers had varying design preferences and were quite capable of distinguishing the credibility and utility of various types of evaluation studies—or measurement options. Let me illustrate with a common issue that arises in survey design.

The Odd-Even Question

Should response scales be even-numbered (e.g., 4 or 6 response choices) or odd-numbered (e.g., 3 or 5 choices)? It doesn't seem like such a big deal actually, but I've seen evaluators

"The main thing I can tell you about the evaluation design is that it fits our budget, is intended to get us from where we are to where we want to be, and it fits in a 5'X8' utility trailer."

on both sides of the question go at each other with the vehemence of Marxists versus capitalists, osteopaths versus chiropractors, or cat lovers versus dog lovers. What's all the ruckus about? It's about the value and validity of a midpoint on questionnaire items. In conducting workshops on evaluation, one of the most common questions I get is: "Should we give people a midpoint?"

An even-numbered scale has no midpoint.

The workshop should be expanded from 1 day to 2 days.

Strongly Agree	Agree	Disagree	Strongly Disagree

An odd-numbered scale has a midpoint.

The workshop should be expanded from 1 day to 2 days.				
Strongly Agree	Agree	No Opinion	Disagree	Strongly Disagree

Even-numbered scales force respondents to lean in one direction or the other (although a few will circle the two middle responses creating their own midpoint if not provided one on the survey). Even-numbered scales allow the respondent to hedge, to be undecided, or, in less kind terms, to cop out of making a decision one way or the other, or yet again, to be genuinely in the middle.

One thing about surveys is clear: If given a midpoint, many respondents will use it. If not given a midpoint, most respondents will answer leaning one way or the other (though some ornery respondents will create their own midpoint).

Which one is best? Should respondents be given a midpoint? Having carefully considered the arguments on both sides of the issue, having analyzed large number of questionnaires with both kinds of items, and having meditated on the problem at great length, I find that I'm forced to come down firmly and unwaveringly right smack in the middle. *It depends.* Sometimes odd-numbered scales are best and sometimes even-numbered scales are best. How to decide?

The issue is really not technical, statistical, or methodological. The issue is one of utility. What do intended users want to find out? Will the findings be more useful if respondents are forced to lean in one direction or the other? Or is it more useful to find out how many people are undecided, or "don't know." The evaluator helps the primary intended users determine the value and implications of offering a midpoint. Do they believe that "down deep inside" everyone really leans one way or the other on the issue, or do they believe that some people are genuinely in the middle on the issue and they want to know how many have no opinion?

Not only can nonresearchers make this choice, but they often enjoy doing so; engaging them in thinking about such alternatives and their implications teaches evaluative thinking.

Assuring Methodological Quality and Excellence

One of the myths believed by nonresearchers is that researchers have agreed among themselves about what constitutes methodological quality and excellence. This belief can make practitioners and other nonacademic stakeholders understandably reluctant to engage in methods discussions. In fact, researchers disagree with each other vehemently about what constitutes good research and, with a little training and help, I find that nonresearchers can grasp the basic issues involved and make informed choices.

To increase the confidence of nonresearchers that they can and should contribute to methods discussions—for example, to consider the merits of telephone interviews versus face-to-face interviews or mail questionnaires—I'll often share the perspective of journal editors. Eva Baker, director of the UCLA Center for the Study of Evaluation and former editor of *Educational Evaluation and Policy Analysis (EEPA),* established a strong system of peer review for *EEPA,* requiring three independent reviewers for every article. Eva has told me that in several years as editor, **she never published an article on which all three reviewers agreed the article was good!** I edited the peer-reviewed *Journal of Extension* for 3 years and had the same experience. Robert Donmoyer (1996), features editor of *Educational Researcher,* reported that "peer reviewers' recommendations often conflict and their advice is frequently contradictory. . . . There is little consensus about what research and scholarship are and what research reporting and scholarly discourse should look like" (p. 19).

This kind of inside look at the world of research, like an inside look at how the Supreme Court makes decisions, can be shocking to people who think that there surely must be consensus regarding what constitutes "good" research or good jurisprudence. The real picture is more chaotic and warlike, dominated by competing perspectives, ideological arguments, and value preferences, not just rules and formulas. Perspectives and value commitments imply stakes, which leads to stakeholders, which leads to involving stakeholders to represent their stakes, even in methods decisions, or should we say, *especially* in methods decisions, since those decisions determine what findings will be available for interpretation and use.

The fact that researchers disagree about criteria for judging quality will not surprise those inside science who understand that a major thrust of methodological training in graduate school is learning how to pick apart and attack any study. There are no perfect studies. And there cannot be, for there is no agreement on what constitutes perfection.

This has important implications for methods decisions in evaluation. The consensus that has emerged within evaluation, as articulated by the Metaevaluation Checklist (Stufflebeam 1999b), the Joint Committee on Standards for Educational Evaluation (2010) and the American Evaluation Association's Guiding Principles (Shadish, Newman, Scheirer, & Wye, 1995) is that evaluations are to be judged on the basis of appropriateness, utility, practicality, accuracy, propriety, credibility, and relevance. These criteria are necessarily situational and context bound. One cannot judge the adequacy of methods used in a specific evaluation without knowing the purpose of the evaluation, the intended uses of the findings, the resources available, and the trade-offs negotiated. Judgments about validity and reliability, for example, are necessarily and appropriately relative rather than absolute in that the rigor and quality of an evaluation's design and measurement depend on the purpose and *intended use* of the evaluation. The Accuracy Standards of the Joint Committee on Standards (2010) make it clear that validity and reliability of an evaluation depend on the intended purposes and uses of the evaluation:

> Valid Information Evaluation information should serve the intended purposes and support valid interpretations. (A2)
>
> Reliable Information Evaluation procedures should yield sufficiently dependable and consistent information for the intended uses. (A3)

A Framework for Methods Decisions

For nonresearchers, being expected to participate in design decisions can be intimidating. I try to make the process manageable and understandable by using poet Rudyard Kipling's basic questions as a design framework.

I keep six honest serving men

They taught me all I knew:

Their names are What and Why and When

And How and Where and Who.

Rudyard Kipling (1865–1936)
The Elephant's Child

A Framework for Methods Decisions

What? What do we want to find out?

Why? Why do we want to find that out?

When? When do we need the information?

How? How can we get the information we need?

Where? Where should we gather information?

Who? Who is the information for and from whom should we collect the information we need?

These questions guide the primary focus in making evaluation measurement and methods decisions—getting the best-possible data to adequately answer primary users' evaluation questions given available resources and time. The emphasis is on *appropriateness and credibility*—measures, samples, and comparisons that are appropriate and credible to address key evaluation issues.

No Perfect Designs:
The Art of Making Methods Decisions

Lee J. Cronbach (1982), an evaluation pioneer and author of several major books on measurement and evaluation, directed the Stanford Evaluation Consortium and was president of the American Educational Research Association, the American Psychological Association, and the Psychometric Society. He observed that designing an evaluation is as much art as science: "Developing an evaluation is an exercise of the dramatic imagination" (p. 239).

This perspective can help nonresearchers feel that they have something important to contribute. It can also, hopefully, open the evaluator to hearing their contributions and facilitating their "dramatic imaginations." The art of evaluation involves creating a design that is appropriate for a specific situation and particular action or policy-making context. In art there is no single, ideal standard. Beauty is in the eye of the beholder, and the evaluation beholders include decision makers, policymakers, program managers, practitioners, participants, and the general public. Thus, any given design is necessarily an interplay of resources, possibilities, creativity, and personal judgments by the people involved. As Cronbach concluded,

> There is no single best plan for an evaluation, not even for an inquiry into a particular program, at a particular time, with a particular budget. (p. 231)

Utilization-Focused Methods Principles

This is not a detailed methods book. Rather, I am offering basic utilization-focused principles for and guidance about involving primary intended users in methods decisions.

Having, hopefully, established the value of involving primary intended users in methods decisions, let me conclude with some overall principles of engagement.

1. *Connect methods, credibility, and use*

Methods and measurement choices affect the credibility of findings. That's basic. And credibility affects use. Throughout methods negotiations with primary intended users, stay aware of and help intended users stay attentive to these fundamental connections between methods, credibility and use.

Quality methods ⟶ credible findings ⟶ greater utility

2. *Attend to the evaluation's overall validity*

The government ministries are very keen on amassing statistics. They collect them, raise them to the nth power, take the cube root, and prepare wonderful diagrams. But you must never forget that every one of these figures comes in the first place from the village watchman, who just puts down what he damn well pleases.

—Sir Josiah Stamp, 1911,
English economist (1880–1941)

House (1980, p. 249) has suggested that validity means "worthiness of being recognized": For the typical evaluation this means being "true, credible, and right" (p. 250). Different approaches to evaluation establish validity in different ways. House applies the notion of validity to *the entire evaluation,* not just the data. An *evaluation* is perceived as valid in a global sense that includes the overall approach used, the competence and stance of the evaluator, the nature of the process, the rigor of the design, how systematically data are gathered, and the way in which results are reported. Both the evaluation *and* the evaluator must be perceived as trustworthy for the evaluation to have high validity.

3. *Pay special attention to face validity*

Face validity concerns the extent to which an instrument *looks* as if it measures what it is intended to measure. An instrument has face validity if stakeholders can look at the items and understand what is being measured. From a utilization-focused perspective, it is perfectly reasonable for decision makers to want to understand and believe in data they are expected to use. Face validity, however, is generally held in low regard by measurement experts. Predictive validity, concurrent validity, construct validity—these technical approaches are much preferred by psychometricians. Here are three examples of how face validity affects use.

- The board of directors of a major industrial firm commissioned an evaluation of a campaign to increase worker morale. The sociologist hired to do the evaluation used a standardized worker morale instrument. The board dismissed the findings, which were negative, because they didn't think the instrument's items were relevant to their company. They had not been asked to review the instrument before it was used.
- The marketing director for a major retail merchandising company presented the chief executive officer (CEO) with results from a representative sample of a major metropolitan area to forecast consumer behavior. The sample size had been determined by a university statistician, but the CEO rejected the findings—and recommendations in the report—because he didn't trust the sample size. He had not been asked in advance what sample size he would have found credible.

- An elected government official rejected results from a citizen satisfaction survey because the survey had even-numbered rather than odd-numbered items. He believed that "in a democracy people have the right to be undecided." He had not seen the instrument before it was administered.

4. *Be explicit about trade-offs*

Designing an evaluation often involves trade-offs since no design can do everything. Those who will use the findings should be part of trade-off considerations. An example is the trade-off between breadth versus depth. Getting more data usually takes longer and costs more, but getting less data usually reduces confidence in the findings. Studying a narrow question or very specific problem in great depth may produce clear results but leave other important issues and problems unexamined. On the other hand, gathering information on a large variety of issues and problems may leave the evaluation unfocused and result in knowing a little about a lot of things, but not knowing a lot about anything.

During methods deliberations, some boundaries must be set on data collection. Should all parts of the program be studied or only certain parts? Should all participants be studied or only some subset of clients? Should the evaluator aim at describing all program processes and outcomes or only certain priority areas?

In my experience, determining priorities is challenging. Once a group of primary stakeholders gets turned on to learning from evaluative information, they want to know everything. The evaluator's role is to help them move from a rather extensive list of potential questions to a much shorter list of realistic questions and finally to a focused list of essential and necessary questions. This process moves from divergence to convergence, from generating many possibilities (divergence) to focusing on a few worthwhile priorities (convergence).

This applies to framing overall evaluation questions as well as to narrowing items in a particular instrument, such as a survey or interview. Many questions are interesting, but *which are crucial?* These end up being choices not between good and bad, but among alternatives, all of which have merit.

In the real world of trade-offs and negotiations, the evaluator too often determines what is evaluated according to his or her own expertise or preference in what to measure, rather than by deciding first what intended users determine is worth evaluating and then doing the best he or she can with methods. Methods are employed in the service of relevance and use, not as their master. Exhibit 10.2 contrasts three pragmatic versus ideal design trade-offs.

5. *Understand and deal with both truth and utility concerns*

Stakeholders want accurate information; they apply "truth tests" (Weiss & Bucuvalas, 1980) in deciding how seriously to pay attention to an evaluation. They also want useful and relevant information. The ideal, then, is both truth and utility. But these may be in conflict and choices have to be made about which to emphasize more. A simple example of

EXHIBIT 10.2

Pragmatic Design Principles

Principles offer directional guidelines. They are not recipes, laws, or concrete, absolute prescriptions. Principles help in dealing with trade-offs in the less-than-perfect real world of evaluation design. Below are three ideals contrasted with three pragmatic options when the ideals cannot be achieved because of real-world constraints. These can be used to generate discussion and get people thinking about which way to lean when faced with tough choices.

Evaluation ideal	*Pragmatic principle*
1. Get the best-possible data on time to affect decisions	1. Less-than-perfect data available in time to affect decisions are better than more-perfect data available *after* decisions have been taken.
2. "Hard" data on important questions	2. Softer data on important questions are better than harder data on less important questions (whatever "softer" and "harder" may mean in a particular context).
3. More and better data	3. Given the potential for data overload, less can be more so that users can focus. A little data are better than no data to get people dealing with data, focusing on their uses, relevance, and limitations.

such a choice is time. The time lines for evaluation are often ridiculously short. A decision maker may need whatever information can be obtained in 3 months, even though researchers insist that a year is necessary to get data of reasonably quality and accuracy. This involves a trade-off between truth and utility. Highly accurate data in a year will be useless to this decision maker. Utility demands getting the best data possible in 3 months.

Decision makers regularly face the need to take action with imperfect information. They prefer more accurate information to less accurate information, but they also prefer some information to no information. The effects of methodological quality on use must be understood in the full context of a study, its political environment, the degree of uncertainty with which the decision maker is faced, and thus his or her relative need for any and all clarifying information. If information is scarce, then new, timely information, even of less-than-ideal quality, may be somewhat helpful.

The scope and importance of an evaluation greatly affect the emphasis that will be placed on technical quality. Eleanor Chelimsky, former president of the American Evaluation Association and founding director of the Program Evaluation and Methodology Division of the U.S. Government Accountability Office, has insisted that technical quality is paramount in policy evaluations to Congress. The technical quality of national policy research matters, not only in the short term, when findings first come out, but over the long term as policy battles unfold and evaluators are called on to explain and defend important findings (Chelimsky, 2007).

On the other hand, debates about technical quality are likely to be less rancorous in local efforts to improve programs at the street level, where the policy rubber hits the day-to-day programming road. Technical quality (truth tests) may get less attention than researchers desire because many stakeholders are not very sophisticated about methods. Yet, they know (almost intuitively) that the methods and measures used in any study are open to question and attack, a point emphasized earlier, given that experts often disagree among themselves. As a result, experienced decision makers often apply less rigorous standards than academics and, as long as they find the evaluation effort credible and serious, they're more interested in discussing the substance of findings than in debating methods. Credibility involves more than technical quality, as important as technical quality is. Credibility, and therefore utility, are affected by balance, transparency, and open discussion of both strengths and weaknesses. *The perception of impartiality is at least as important as methodological rigor in highly political environments.*

In utilization-focused evaluation, attention to technical quality is tied to and balanced by concern for relevance and timeliness. As no study is ever methodologically perfect, it is important for primary stakeholders to know firsthand what imperfections exist—and to be included in deciding which imperfections they are willing to live with in making the inevitable leaps from limited data to decision and action.

6. *Watch for and point out threats to data quality*

Evaluators have an obligation to think about, anticipate, and provide guidance about how threats to data quality will affect interpreting and using results. However, it is impossible to anticipate all potential threats to data quality. Even when faced with the reality of particular circumstances and specific evaluation problems, it is impossible to know in advance precisely how a creative design or measurement approach will affect results. For example, having program staff conduct client interviews in an outcomes evaluation could (1) seriously reduce the validity and reliability of the data, (2) substantially increase the validity and reliability of the data, or (3) have no measurable effect on data quality. The nature and degree of effect would depend on staff relationships with clients, how staff members were assigned to clients for interviewing, the kinds of questions being asked, the training of the staff interviewers, attitudes of clients toward the program, and so on. Program staff might make better or worse interviewers than external evaluation researchers, depending on these and other factors.

Evaluators and primary intended users must grapple with these kinds of data quality questions for all designs. No automatic rules apply. There is no substitute for thoughtful analysis based on the specific circumstances and information needs of a particular evaluation, both initially and as the evaluation unfolds.

7. *Watch for and point out threats to utility*

Whereas traditional evaluation methods texts focus primarily on threats to validity, this chapter has focused primarily on threats to utility. Exhibit 10.3 summarizes common threats to utility. We now have substantial evidence that paying attention to and working to counter these threats to utility will lead to evaluations that are worth using—and are actually used.

8. *Be adaptive and responsive to the dynamics of measurement and design decisions*

Research quality and relevance are not set in stone once an evaluation proposal has been accepted. Changing conditions in the midst of an evaluation may necessitate revising methods and adapting the design. In the first year of a 3-year evaluation of an affordable housing initiative that involved case studies on six American Indian reservations, a tribal election led to a new leader who withdrew his reservation from the study. A decision had to be made about whether to add a replacement site or change the sample to five case studies.

EXHIBIT 10.3

Threats to Utility

- Failure to focus on intended use by intended users
- Failure to design the evaluation to fit the context and situation
- Inadequate involvement of primary intended users in making methods decisions
- Focusing on unimportant issues—low relevance
- Inappropriate methods and measures given stakeholders questions and information needs
- Poor stakeholder understanding of the evaluation generally and findings specifically
- Low user belief and trust in the evaluation process and findings
- Low face validity
- Unbalanced data collection and reporting
- Perceptions that the evaluation is unfair or that the evaluator is biased or less than impartial
- Low evaluator credibility
- Political naïveté
- Failure to keep stakeholders adequately informed and involved along the way as design alterations are necessary

Actively involving intended users in making methods decisions about these issues means more than a one-point-in-time acquiescence to a research design.

In every one of the 20 federal health studies we investigated, significant methods revisions and redesigns had to be done after data collection began. While little attention has been devoted in the evaluation literature to the phenomenon of slippage between the original design and methods as actually implemented, the problem is similar to that of program implementation where original specifications typically differ greatly from what finally gets delivered by a program (see Step 8 on implementation evaluation). Thus, making decisions about methods is a continuous process that involves checking out changes with intended users as they are made. While it is impractical to have evaluator-stakeholder discussions about every minor change in methods, utilization-focused evaluators prefer to err in the direction of consultative rather than unilateral decision making, when there is a choice.

- The design of the evaluation of an advocacy campaign's policy influence had to be changed once the evaluation got underway because the planned points of data collection didn't match up well with the ebb and flow of the actual campaign. Key actors also changed over the course of the year, so the key informant interview sample had to be adjusted accordingly.
- A standardized pretest/posttest design had to be abandoned when the program made major changes in focus as a result of formative feedback from participants. The end-of-program instrument had to be revised to reflect these changes. Many of the pretest items had become irrelevant.
- A national evaluation that included case studies of local sites had to be redesigned when several of the local sites in the sample were terminated unexpectedly due to funding cuts.

9. *Anticipate criticism without becoming defensive*

Given that quality and excellence are situational, and that different researchers, evaluators, and stakeholders emphasize varying and diverse criteria for what constitutes credible evidence, it is futile to attempt to design studies that are immune from methodological criticism. There simply is no such immunity. Intended users who participate in making methods decisions should be prepared to be criticized regardless of what choices they make. Especially futile is the desire, often articulated by nonresearchers, to conduct an evaluation that will be accepted by and respected within the academic community. As we demonstrated above in discussing peer review research, the academic community does not speak with one voice. Any particular academics whose blessings are especially important for evaluation use should be invited to participate in the evaluation design task force and become, explicitly, intended users. Making no pretense of pleasing the entire scientific community (an impossibility), utilization-focused evaluation strives to attain the more modest and attainable goal of pleasing primary intended users. This does not mean that utilization-focused evaluations are less rigorous. It means the criteria for judging rigor must be articulated for each evaluation.

10. *Develop skills in facilitating methods decisions*

Graduate schools teach aspiring researchers how to make methods decisions. They don't typically teach how to facilitate methods decisions among nonresearchers. This takes us back to Step 2: Assessing and enhancing evaluator readiness to engage in utilization-focused evaluation. Facilitation skills include knowing when to open up discussion and when to close it off, listening for differing degrees of affect around alternative criteria of quality, offering limited but significant and meaningful options for engagement, and keeping the discussion focused on issues related to use. Practice doesn't make perfect, but it does make you better.

Designing Evaluations Worth Using: Reflections on the State of the Art

This chapter on Step 10 has described the challenges evaluators face in working with intended users to design evaluations worth using. My consulting brings me into contact with hundreds of evaluation colleagues and users. I know from direct observation that many evaluators are meeting these challenges with great skill, dedication, competence, and effectiveness. Much important and creative work is being done by evaluators in all kinds of difficult and demanding situations as they fulfill their commitment to do the most and best they can with the resources available, the short deadlines they face, and the intense political pressures they feel. They share a belief that doing something is better than doing nothing, so long as one is realistic and honest in assessing and presenting the limitations of what is done.

This last caveat is important. I have not attempted to delineate all possible threats to validity, reliability, and utility. This is not a design and measurement text. My purpose has been to stimulate thinking about how attention to intended use for intended users affects all aspects of evaluation practice, including methods decisions. Pragmatism undergirds the utilitarian emphasis of utilization-focused evaluation. In designing evaluations, it is worth keeping in mind World War II General George S. Patton's Law: *A good plan today is better than a perfect plan tomorrow.*

Then there is Halcolm's evaluation corollary to Patton's law: *Perfect designs aren't.*

> Details about what is involved in each step are provided in the summary *U-FE Checklist* in the concluding chapter. See pages 416–417 for the checklist items for Step 10 discussed in this chapter.

PRACTICE EXERCISES

1. The chapter opens by asserting that involving primary intended users in making methods decisions is controversial and resisted by many evaluators. What is the controversy? What is the basis for the resistance? Present the essence of the argument against involving nonresearchers in methods decisions. Then present the essence of the argument in favor of involvement. Finally, present your own philosophy and preference on this issue.

2. Using Rudyard Kipling's poem, present the primary design features of an evaluation for an actual program. Describe the program and then describe the evaluation specifying *What, Why, When, How, Where, Who.*

   I keep six honest serving men

   They taught me all I knew:

   Their names are What and Why and When

   And How and Where and Who.

3. Select an evaluation design or measurement issue (e.g., odd or even responses in surveys) and write a script for how you would present and explain the primary options available to nonresearchers who are primary intended users for the evaluation. Include in your explanation the likely consequences for credibility and utility of the results. Another example would be telephone interviews versus face-to-face interviews. Select your own example and present the options in lay terms.

INTERLUDE, STEPS 1 THROUGH 10. COMPLEX DYNAMIC SYSTEMS INTERCONNECTIONS

Attending to Methods and Design Decisions Throughout the U-FE Process

Once again we face the challenge of presenting utilization-focused evaluation as a series of steps while also communicating the interactive, iterative, interdependent, and nonlinear dynamics of working with intended users. Step 10 has discussed negotiating appropriate methods to generate credible findings that support intended use by intended users. Methods, design, and measurement decisions can and do arise at any and every step throughout the U-FE process. The complex graphic on the next page attempts to depict the ways in which methods issues arise along the way and intersect with other steps.

Complex Interconnections and Adaptive Interactions Around Methods, Design, and Measurement Issues and Options Throughout U-FE Steps 1 Through 10

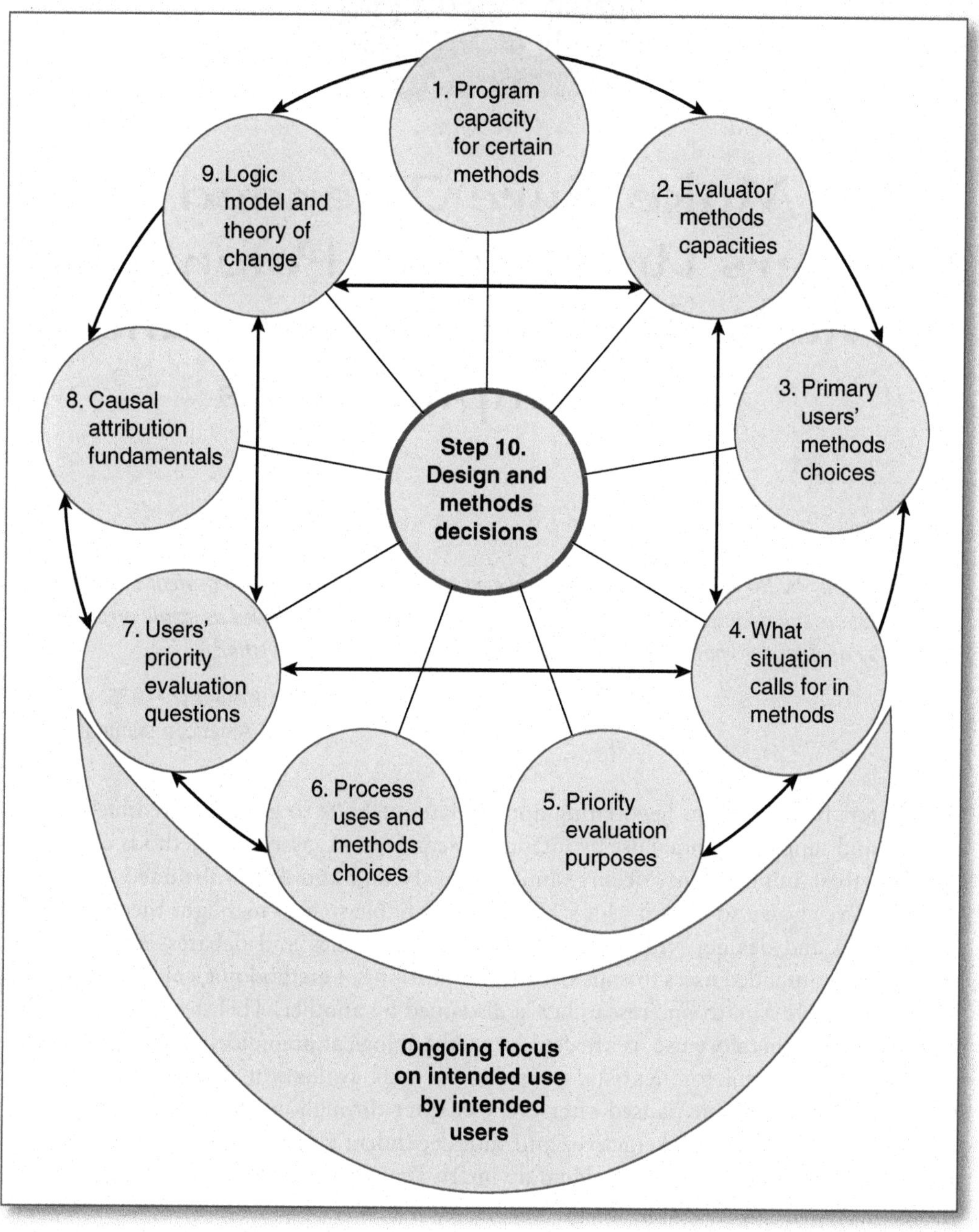

11

Make Sure Intended Users Understand Potential Methods Controversies and Their Implications

It is not only by the questions we have answered that progress may be measured, but also by those we are still asking. The passionate controversies of one era are viewed as sterile preoccupations by another, for knowledge alters what we seek as well as what we find.

Freda Schaffer Adler (1975, p. 31),
American criminologist

Step 10 focused on negotiating appropriate methods to generate credible findings and support intended use by intended users. Step 11, assessing methods controversies and their implications, occurs simultaneously and could be subsumed as part of Step 10. I've chosen to treat it as a separate, identifiable step to highlight the importance of knowing and dealing with methodological controversies and debates—and working with primary intended users to consider the implications of methodological disagreements. What is credible data to one researcher is disdained by another. This step highlights how credibility, and therefore use, is affected by methodological prejudices and paradigms.

While it is helpful for heuristic purposes to treat evaluation design decisions as a sequence of steps, I have paused after every chapter throughout this book to emphasize and depict the dynamic, interactive, and interdependent relationships among the steps. Exhibit 11.1 shows the complex dynamic interactions between Steps 10 and 11, adding

Step 9 to the mix, determining what intervention model or theory of change is being evaluated. This graphic explicitly connects the theory of change conceptualization with methods debates and decisions.

EXHIBIT 11.1

Complex Dynamic Interactions Among Steps 9, 10, and 11

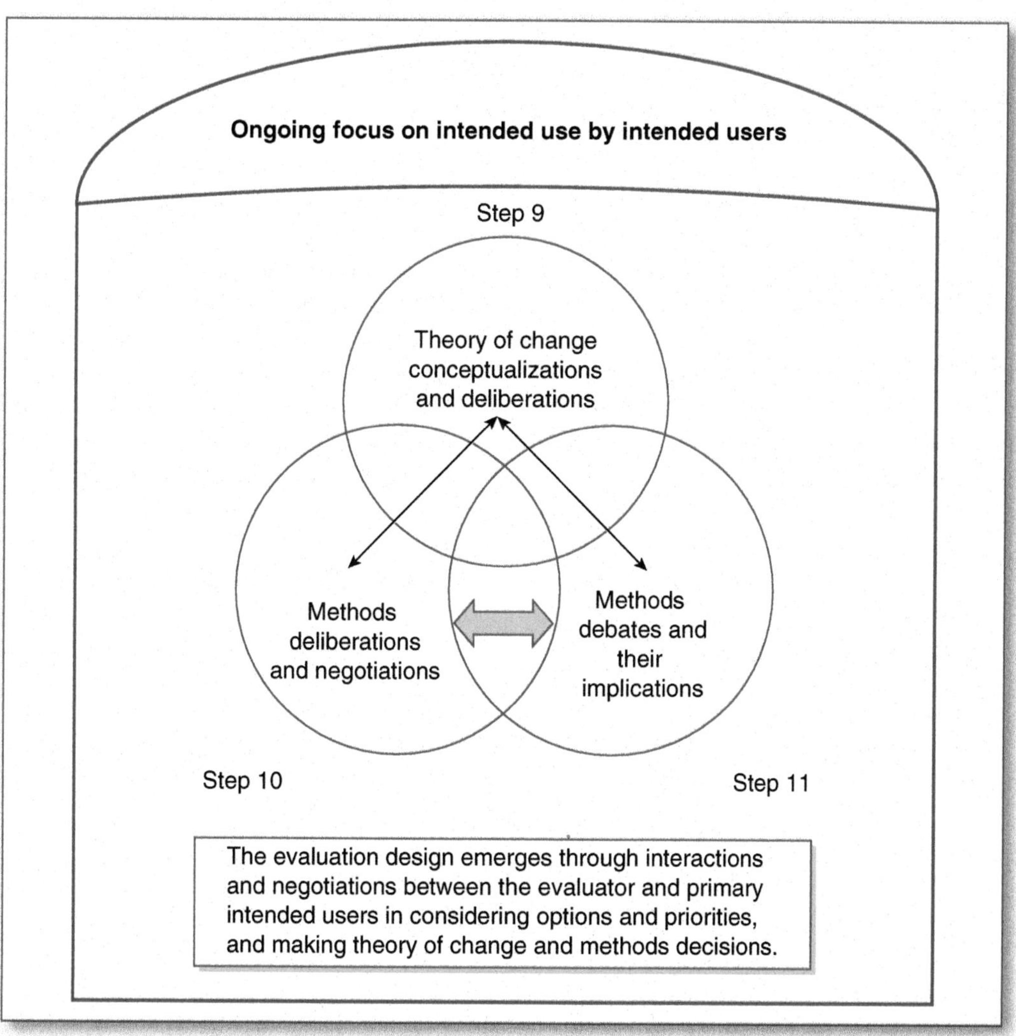

The landscape of evaluation involves navigating the landmine field of methodological debates and ideology so that the evaluation doesn't get blown up at the end through some naive belief that methods are judged only by their appropriateness to answer key questions. They are also judged by whether they adhere to certain methodological orthodoxies. Forewarned is forearmed. Step 11 is the forewarning—to evaluators and primary intended users.

Methodology, Ideology, and Paradigms

> Ideology is to research what Marx suggested the economic factor was to politics and what Freud took sex to be for psychology. (Scriven, 1972a, p. 94)

The scientific myth is that methods are just that—methods—systematic ways of going about inquiring into the empirical nature of the world that produce objective findings. Ideology, in contrast, involves ideas and beliefs. What's the connection between methods and ideology? Ideology filters our inquiries into and experiences of the world and influences our interpretation of what empirical findings mean. Ideology encompasses worldview, our philosophical orientation, and is grounded in, often hidden in, paradigm assumptions.

A paradigm is a worldview built on implicit assumptions, accepted definitions, comfortable habits, values defended as truths, and beliefs projected as reality. As such, paradigms are deeply embedded in the socialization of adherents and practitioners: Paradigms tell us what is important, legitimate, and reasonable. Paradigms are also normative, telling the practitioner what to do without the necessity of long existential or epistemological consideration. In his influential classic, *The Structure of Scientific Revolutions,* Thomas Kuhn (1970) explained how paradigms work.

> Scientists work from models acquired through education and subsequent exposure to the literature, often without quite knowing or needing to know what characteristics have given these models the status of community paradigms. . . . That scientists do not usually ask or debate what makes a particular problem or solution legitimate tempts us to suppose that, at least intuitively, they know the answer. But it may only indicate that neither the question nor the answer is felt to be relevant to their research. Paradigms may be prior to, more binding, and more complete than any set of rules for research that could be unequivocally abstracted from them. (p. 46)

Two scientists may look at the same thing, but because of different theoretical perspectives, assumptions, or ideology-based methodologies, they may literally not see the same thing. Indeed, Kuhn asserted:

> Something like a paradigm is prerequisite to perception itself. When a man sees depends both upon what he looks at and also upon what his previous visual-conceptual experience has taught him to see. (p. 113)

The existence of methodological ideologies and paradigms has profound implications for methods decisions. *What constitutes rigorous methods or quality evidence can be and is debated intensely.* We won't go into all the epistemological and ontological issues that undergird those debates. Instead, I want to focus on the practical implications for working with primary intended users in making methods decisions. Stakeholders need to know that researchers are divided about what constitutes rigorous evidence. Methods debates have spilled over from the academy into the public policy domain. These debates can and often do arise in considering methods options at every level, from the local community program to large multinational evaluations. Contention about methods often surfaces without those involved even knowing that the competing premises of the debate are mired in deeply held ideological paradigms. Indeed, those advocating for particular standards of rigor often deny that their views are based on fundamental and problematic paradigm assumptions. But that's the nature of paradigms.

Whether called theoretical disputes, paradigm wars, philosophical worldviews, epistemological differences, or just methods debates, the point is that people disagree about what constitutes credible evidence. George Julnes and Debra Rog (2007) edited an important volume of *New Directions for Program Evaluation* aimed at "building the evidence base for method choice" that inform federal policies on evaluation methodology. They introduced the volume by observing:

> Almost since inception, the field of evaluation has experienced recurring conflict over the value of various available approaches to methodology. Whether viewed as crises or moderate disagreements more political than foundational, one can identify turning points where the prevailing view of methodology was challenged. . . . There has been no shortage of serious efforts to reconcile opposing views on proper approaches to evaluation . . ., but reconciliation, in whatever form achieved, is rarely final. . . . We should note that in our view, the way forward is not to *resolve* the controversy; there are real disagreements that are unlikely to go away. Rather, we hope to clarify the issues to yield a more productive dialogue. (Julnes & Rog, 2007, pp. 1–2)

In that spirit, I shall briefly review six methods and design debates that persist. My purpose is to illuminate the choices and trade-offs that arise in making methods decisions. Let me be clear that the paradigm that informs my own preferences in these debates is pragmatism and, as the reader will certainly have figured out by now, I have a strong values preference for meaningful and appropriate evaluation use. Stated as succinctly as I can, my position is this: As a utilization-focused evaluator, I advocate methodological eclecticism and adapting evaluation methods to the nature of the evaluation question and the information needs of primary intended users. *Methodological appropriateness is the utilization-focused gold standard.*

In practice this means that if evaluators are to involve intended users in methods decisions, evaluators and intended users need to understand paradigm-based methods debates and evaluators need to be able to facilitate choices that are appropriate to a particular evaluation's purpose. This means educating primary stakeholders about the legitimate options available, the strengths and weaknesses of various approaches, the potential advantages and costs of using multiple and mixed methods, and the controversies that surround such choices.

The interrelated debates we'll briefly review are:

- Quantitative versus qualitative data
- The Gold Standard Debate (experimental versus nonexperimental designs)
- Randomization versus naturally occurring and purpose sampling approaches
- Internal versus external validity as a design priority
- Generalizations versus context-sensitive extrapolations
- Pragmatism versus methodological purity

What Constitutes Rigor and High-Quality Evidence?

Quants and Quals

Who are *quants?* They're numbers people who, in rabid mode, believe that if you can't measure something, it doesn't exist. They live by Galileo's admonition: "Measure what is measurable, and make measurable what is not so." Their mantra is: "What gets measured gets done." And *quals*? They quote management expert W. Edwards Deming: "The most important things cannot be measured." *Quals* find meaning in words and stories, and are ever ready to recite Albert Einstein's observation that "Everything that can be counted does not necessarily count; everything that counts cannot necessarily be counted." Relatively speaking, of course.

Quants demand "hard" data: statistics, equations, charts, and formulae. *Quals,* in contrast, are "softies," enamored with narratives and case studies. *Quants* love experimental designs and believe that the only way to prove that an intervention caused an outcome is with a randomized control trial. *Quants* are control freaks, say the *quals*; simplistic, even simple-minded, in their naive belief that the world can be reduced to independent and dependent variables. The *qual's* world is complex, dynamic, interdependent, textured, nuanced, unpredictable, and understood through stories, and more stories, and still more stories. *Quals* connect the causal dots through the unfolding patterns that emerge within and across these many stories and case studies.

Quants aspire to operationalize key predictor variables and generalize across time and space—the holy grail of truth: if *x,* then *y,* and the more of *x,* the more of *y. Quals* distrust generalizations and are most comfortable immersed in the details of a specific time and place, understanding a story in the richness of context and the fullness of thick description. For *quals,* patterns they extrapolate from cross-case analyses are possible principles to think about in new situations but are not the generalized, formulaic prescriptions that quants admire and aspire to. *Quants* produce *best practices* that assert: Do this because it's been proven to work in rigorous studies. *Quals* produce themes and suggest: Think about this and what it might mean in your own context and situation.

Quantitative and Qualitative Data: Different Perspectives on the World

Quantitative measures strive for precision by focusing on things that can be counted. Quantitative data come from questionnaires, tests, standardized observation instruments, information systems, official indicators, and program records. Gathering numerical data requires conceptualizing categories that can be treated as ordinal or interval data and subjected to statistical analysis. The experiences of people in programs and the important variables that describe program outcomes are fit into these standardized categories to which numerical values are attached. The following opinion item is a common example:

How would you rate the quality of course instruction?

1. Excellent   2. Good   3. Fair   4. Poor

In contrast, the evaluator using a qualitative approach seeks to capture what a program experience means to participants *in their own words*, through interviews or open-ended questionnaire items, and in day-to-day program settings, through observation. An open-ended course evaluation question would ask:

In your own words, how would you describe the quality of the instruction in this course?

Exhibit 11.2 contrasts other examples of quantitative and qualitative questions.

Qualitative data consist of words and narratives: quotations from open-ended questionnaires; detailed descriptions of situations, events, people, interactions, and observed behaviors; interview responses from people about their experiences, attitudes, beliefs, and thoughts; and excerpts or entire passages from documents, correspondence, records, and case histories. The data are collected as open-ended narrative without predetermined, standardized categories such as the response choices that make up typical questionnaires or tests. The evaluation findings are presented as case studies and analysis of patterns across cases (Patton 2002; Stake, 2005).

Numbers are parsimonious and precise; words provide individualized meanings and nuance. Each way of turning the complexities of the world into data has strengths and weaknesses. Qualitative data capture personal meaning and portray the diversity of ways people express themselves; quantitative data facilitate comparisons because all program participants respond to the same questions on standardized scales within predetermined response categories. Standardized tests and surveys measure the reactions of many

EXHIBIT 11.2

Quantitative Versus Qualitative Questions: Examples From Evaluation Questionnaires

Standardized, quantitative items	*Qualitative, open-ended items*
A. The program's goals were clearly communicated to us? 1. Strongly agree 2. Agree 3. Disagree 4. Strongly disagree	A. From your perspective, and in your own words, what are the primary goals of this program?
B. How relevant was this training to your job? 1. Very relevant 2. Somewhat relevant 3. A little relevant 4. Not at all relevant	B. How, if at all, does this training relate to your job? *Please be as specific as possible.*
C. How much did you learn from this program? *I learned . . .* 1. A great deal 2. A fair amount 3. A little bit 4. Nothing at all	C. What are the most important things you learned from your participation in this program?

respondents in a way that statistical aggregation and analysis are relatively straightforward, following established rules and procedures. By contrast, qualitative methods typically produce a wealth of detailed data about a much smaller number of people and cases; finding patterns and themes in the diverse narratives can be painstaking, time-consuming, and uncertain. But qualitative data in program evaluation are aimed at letting people in programs express their reactions in their own terms rather than impose upon them a preconceived set of limited response categories.

So what is there to debate about quantitative versus qualitative when each can contribute in important ways to our understanding of a program? And why not just use both approaches, what is called a *mixed-methods design?* Mixed methods are often used, but one kind of data is often valued over the other. The debate about the relative merits of qualitative versus qualitative data stems from underlying assumptions and deeply held values. "If you can't measure it, if you can't quantify it, it doesn't exist," is a refrain many program staff have heard from evaluators insisting on "clear, specific, and measurable goals." Statistics, because they are concrete and precise, seem more factual—and "getting the facts right" is at the heart of good evaluation. "What gets measured gets done," the mantra of management by objectives and performance measurement, communicates that only what can be quantified is important. Statistical presentations tend to have more credibility, to seem more like "science," whereas qualitative narratives tend to be associated with "mere" journalism. A certain assertiveness, even machismo, often accompanies the demand that outcomes be quantified: hard data connote virility; soft data are flaccid. (Sexual innuendo works in science no less than in advertising, or so it would seem.) But qualitative advocates have their own favorite quotations, among them the famous assertion of 19th-century British Prime Minister Benjamin Disraeli: "There are three kinds of lies: lies, damned lies, and statistics." Disraeli also observed that, "As a general rule the most successful man in life is the man who has the best information." The quantitative-qualitative debate is about what constitutes the "best information."

Kuhn (1970), a philosopher and historian of science, observed that the values scientists hold "most deeply" concern predictions: "quantitative predictions are preferable to qualitative ones" (pp. 184–185). It's a short distance from a preference for quantitative data to the virtual exclusion of other types of data. For example, the federal *What Works Clearinghouse* only uses quantitative findings and ignores qualitative data, even in mixed-methods studies (at least as of this writing).

Valuing quantitative measures to the exclusion of other data limits not only what one can find out but also what one is even willing to ask. It is appropriate and easy to count the words a child spells correctly, but what about that same child's ability to use those words in a meaningful way? It is appropriate to measure a student's reading level, but what does reading *mean* to that student? Different kinds of problems require different types of data. If we only want to know the frequency of interactions between children of different races in desegregated schools, then statistics are appropriate. However, if we want to understand the *meanings of interracial interactions*, open-ended, in-depth interviewing will be more appropriate.

The problem in education has been defined as raising test scores and reducing disparities in scores. A particular way of measuring learning has come to define the very nature of the problem. Asking a broader question leads to different kinds of evaluation data: What are ways in which children can demonstrate what they have learned? The answer can include test scores, to be sure, but can also include examining the work children do in the classroom, their performance on teacher-made tests, portfolios of students' work, examples of their homework, and their performance on integrated projects where they use what they know. If the educational problem and corresponding evaluation question is defined at the outset as how to increase test scores, then the curriculum becomes based on that intended outcome (teach to the tests because what gets measured gets done) and the definition of learning becomes entirely quantitative and standardized. Those who value qualitative evaluation data tend to emphasize individualized learning, diverse ways of capturing what students know, and placing what children can do in the context of what opportunities they have to demonstrate what they know. Thus, the methods debate in educational evaluations is integrally interconnected to competing educational paradigms about how children learn and what is important to learn.

The quantitative-qualitative debate is sometimes framed as "hard data" versus "soft data." But the issue is not hard versus soft, but relevant and appropriate versus irrelevant and inappropriate. Participants in the Stanford Evaluation Consortium (Cronbach and Associates, 1980) observed that "merit lies not in form of inquiry but in relevance of information" (p. 7). My experience with stakeholders suggests that they would rather have "soft data" about an important question than "hard data" about an issue of less relevance. Obviously, the ideal is hard data about important questions, *whatever hard data may mean in a particular context.*

The evaluation standards give equal weight to both quantitative and qualitative data, emphasizing that analysis in each case should be *appropriate.* (See Exhibit 11.3.) One approach to strengthening data collection is to use mixed methods, including both quantitative and qualitative data.

EXHIBIT 11.3

Evaluation Standards for Quantitative and Qualitative Data

The original Joint Committee (1994) evaluation standards gave equal attention, weight, and credence to qualitative and quantitative data.

- A8 Analysis of Quantitative Information–Quantitative information in an evaluation should be appropriately and systematically analyzed so that evaluation questions are effectively answered.
- A9 Analysis of Qualitative Information–Qualitative information in an evaluation should be appropriately and systematically analyzed so that evaluation questions are effectively answered.

The revised standards (Joint Committee, 2010) do not distinguish quantitative and qualitative data, but treat the issue of methodological appropriateness more generally:

A6 Sound Designs and Analyses Evaluations should employ technically adequate designs and analyses that are appropriate for the evaluation purposes.

Mixed-Methods Designs: Combining Qualitative and Quantitative Data

An example of mixed methods is a college exam that asks both multiple-choice questions and open-ended essay questions. In evaluations, the equivalent means collecting data with both fixed-choice surveys and statistical indicators of outcomes as well as conducting open-ended interviews and case studies. Evaluators should be able to use a variety of tools if they are to be sophisticated and flexible in matching research methods to the nuances of particular evaluation questions and the idiosyncrasies of specific decision-maker needs. In *Qualitative Research and Evaluation Methods* (Patton, 2002), I have elaborated the conditions under which qualitative methods are particularly appropriate in evaluation research: for example, when program outcomes are highly individualized so case studies are essential to capture variations in outcomes. Sometimes quantitative methods alone are most appropriate as in counting how many graduates of an employment program get and keep jobs. But in many cases, *both qualitative and quantitative methods should be used together* and there are no logical reasons why both kinds of data cannot be used together.

All mixed-methods designs combine qualitative and quantitative data in some way. Some mixed designs are primarily quantitative, with qualitative data as supplementary; others are primarily qualitative with quantitative data as ancillary, as when using ethnography in conjunction with statistical data in a mixed-methods strategy. More fully integrated mixed-methods designs give equal status to quantitative and qualitative data. In whatever combinations multiple methods are used, the contributions of each kind of data should be fairly assessed. In many cases, this means that evaluators working in teams will need to work hard to overcome their tendency to dismiss certain kinds of data without first considering seriously and fairly the merits of those data.

The Gold Standard Debate: Experimental Versus Nonexperimental Designs

Do opposites attract? Indeed, they do. They attract debate, derision, and dialectical differentiation—otherwise known as **the paradigms war.** In evaluation this takes the form of a vociferous debate about the relative merits of experimental versus nonexperimental methods. The bone of contention is whether randomized controlled experiments are *the gold standard* for impact evaluations. This debate has moved from academic conferences to the public policy arena and arises worldwide in arguments about impact evaluation of aid initiatives in developing countries. Thus, this debate often affects interactions with primary intended users about what kind of evaluation design is most appropriate and credible.

The debate has taken different forms over time, including periods of intense rancor as well as times of rapprochement. The validity of experimental methods and quantitative measurement, appropriately used, has never been in doubt. By the 1990s, qualitative methods, appropriately used, had ascended to a level of comfortable respectability, at least as an

"It's a tricky new step called the Evaluation kual-kuant kan-kan. The lead shifts back and forth with the change in beat."

adjunct to quantitative methods in mixed-methods evaluations. A consensus has emerged in the profession that evaluators need to know and use a variety of methods in order to be responsive to the nuances of particular evaluation questions and the idiosyncrasies of specific stakeholder needs. Still, the question of what constitutes *the methodological gold standard* remains hotly contested. There is some contradiction in the assertion that (1) methods should be selected that are *appropriate* for a specific evaluation purpose and question, and that where possible, using multiple methods—both quantitative and qualitative—can be valuable, *but* (2) one question is more important than others (the causal attribution question) and one method (randomized control trials) is superior to all other methods in answering that question. This is what is known colloquially as talking out of both sides of your mouth. Thus, we have a problem. The ideal of evaluators being situationally responsive, methodologically flexible, and sophisticated in using a variety of methods runs headlong into the assertion that experiments are *the* gold standard and all other methods are, by comparison, inferior. These conflicting criteria—situational appropriateness and methodological diversity versus an experimental gold standard—play out amidst the realities of limited evaluation resources, political considerations of expediency, and the narrowness of disciplinary training available to most evaluators—training that imbues them with methodological prejudices. Nor is the debate just among evaluation methodologists. Evaluation practitioners are deeply affected, as are users of evaluation—policymakers, program staff, managers, and funders. All can become mired in the debate about whether statistical results from experiments ("hard" data) are more scientific and valid than quasi-experiments and qualitative case studies ("softer" data). Who wants to conduct (or fund) a second-rate evaluation if there is an agreed-on gold standard? What really are the strengths and weaknesses of various methods, including experiments (which, it turns out, also have weaknesses)? What does it mean to match the method to the question?

As noted earlier, and worth repeating, if evaluators are to involve intended users in methods decisions, evaluators and intended users need to understand the paradigms debate and evaluators need to be able to facilitate choices that are appropriate to a particular evaluation's purpose. This means educating primary stakeholders about the legitimate options available, the potential advantages of multiple methods, and the strengths and weaknesses of various approaches. I advocate methodological eclecticism and adapting evaluation methods to the nature of the evaluation question and the information needs of primary intended users. I reiterate: From my perspective, *methodological appropriateness is the utilization-focused gold standard.*

The danger of the gold standard accolade assigned to experimental designs means that funders and evaluators begin by asking "How can we do an experimental design" rather than asking "Given the evaluation situation and the information needed, what is the appropriate evaluation design?" The prestige of the method determines the evaluation question and design rather than considerations of utility, feasibility, propriety, accuracy, and accountability.

The Gold Standard Debate

While it's not so hard to combine numbers with narratives to create mixed-methods evaluations, it is not so easy to combine experimental designs with naturalistic inquiry designs. The rigor and validity of experiments depend on controlling, standardizing, and precisely measuring the intervention and its effects. Naturalistic inquiry designs eschew control and observe the program as it unfolds naturally including the emergent and diverse effects on participants.

Evaluation researchers who advocate experimental designs as the gold standard emphasize the power of randomized experiments to enhance rigor, assure well-controlled interventions, reduce threats to internal validity, generate precise estimates of program effects, and statistical power—which in combination increase confidence in attributing an outcome to an intervention. Naturalistic inquiry, in contrast, involves observing ongoing programs as they unfold without attempting to control or manipulate the setting, situation, people, or data. Naturalistic inquiry evaluations look at programs within and in relation to their naturally occurring context. Instead of random assignment, for example, which controls who gets the treatment (program), naturalistic inquiry looks at how staff select participants or how they self-select into a program.

Debate about whether experimental designs constitute the methodological gold standard revolves, in part, around what level and kind of evidence is needed to determine that an intervention is effective. Consider the challenge of eradicating intestinal worms in children, a widespread problem in developing countries. Suppose we want to evaluate an intervention in which school-age children with diarrhea are given worm medicine to increase their school attendance and performance. In order to attribute the intervention to the desired outcome, advocates of randomized controlled trials would insist on an evaluation design in which students suffering from diarrhea are randomly divided into a treatment group (those who receive worm medicine) and a control group (those who do not receive the medicine). The school attendance and test performance of the two groups would then be compared. If, after a month on the medicine, those receiving the intervention show higher attendance and school performance at a statistically significant level compared to the control group (the counterfactual), then the increased outcomes can be attributed to the intervention (the worm medicine).

Advocates of naturalistic inquiry question the value of the control group in this case. Suppose that students, parents, teachers, and local health professionals are interviewed about the reasons students miss school and perform poorly on tests. Independently, each of these groups assert that diarrhea is a major cause of the poor school attendance and performance. Gathering data separately from different informant groups (students, parents, teachers, health professionals) is called *triangulation,* a way of checking the consistency of findings from different data sources. Following the baseline interviews, students are given a regimen of worm medicine. Those taking the medicine show increased school attendance and performance, and in follow-up interviews, the students, parents, teachers, and health professionals independently affirm their belief that the changes can be attributed to taking the worm medicine and being relieved of the symptoms of diarrhea. Is this credible, convincing evidence?

Those who find such a design sufficient argue that the results are both reasonable and empirical, and that the high cost of adding a control group is not needed to establish causality. Nor, they would assert, is it ethical to withhold medicine from students with diarrhea when relieving their symptoms has merit in and of itself. The advocates of randomized controlled trials (RCTs) respond that without the control group, other unknown factors may have intervened to affect the outcomes and that *only the existence of a counterfactual* (control group) will establish with certainty the impact of the intervention.

As this example illustrates, those evaluators and methodologists on opposite sides of this debate have different worldviews about what constitutes sufficient evidence for attribution and action in the real world. This is not simply an academic debate. Millions of dollars of evaluation funds are at stake, and the results of these evaluations around the world will affect billions of dollars of international development assistance.

In a utilization-focused decision-making and negotiating process, alternative design scenarios can be presented to primary intended users to help them determine what level of evidence is needed and appropriate given the purposes of and intended audiences for the evaluation. For example, an RCT design compares doing something (a program or "treatment") with not doing something (control). But doing nothing, the control condition, may not be a viable policy option. A comparison design that examines delivering a program in different ways and comparing results may be of greater policy relevance. An RCT answers one and only one question: Did this one particular approach produce this one particular outcome in this one particular situation compared to a control group? That question tends to be of much less policy relevance and interest than the question: What are the costs, benefits, and effects of delivering the intervention in different ways? Remember, at the root of paradigm debates are different formulations of the problem, different evaluation questions, and different beliefs about what level of evidence is needed to take action.

One final critique of randomized controlled designs is that they fail to account for and be responsive to nonlinear dynamics in complex adaptive systems (Patton, 2011, pp. 288–289). Experiments depend on control and standardization of treatment interventions, but real-world complexities and uncertainties (Morell, 2010) can make such controls artificial. Innovations in evaluation methods for dealing with complexity include agent-based modeling based on simulations and network theory. A model can be tested and its effects evaluated through "computational implementation of a real system in which enough relationships are maintained to reflect a reasonable degree of real world behavior, but which strip out enough detail to allow the observation of relationships" (Morell, Hilscher, Magura, & Ford, 2010, p. 33). Simulations are created that involve running a model over time to study model dynamics. Such simulations are already being used in epidemiology and to study economic behaviors (Feldman, 2010). As these techniques are more widely applied to evaluation inquiries, the methods available to evaluators to deal with complexity will correspondingly expand. Thus, an important issue in working with primary intended users is whether they conceive of the challenge as evaluating a fixed and standardized intervention that will be widely replicated if found effective, making an RCT an appropriate design, or whether they conceive of the situation as complex and dynamic, which will require an intervention approach that is adaptive and developmental, and which invites a more developmental approach to evaluation to deal with complexity (Patton, 2011).

Experimental designs can be appropriate where the program is conceived of as a simple intervention that yields discrete, identifiable outcomes through a process of bounded and linear cause-effect relationships, as discussed in Step 9 on theories of change. Experimental designs make the causal attribution question primary: Can the observed outcomes be directly attributed to the program? Under conditions of complexity, with multiple interdependent variables interacting (often in the form of simultaneous program interventions overlapping and collaborating), traditional attribution analysis gives way to context-sensitive *contribution analysis* (Mayne, 2008; Patton, 2008, pp. 494–496; Patton, 2011, p. 244).

These design choices are also greatly affected by the stage of program development and the primary purpose of the evaluation. Formative and developmental evaluations focus, respectively, on improving and developing a program. Summative evaluation aims to render an overall judgment of merit or worth. Accountability-focused evaluations report on the extent to which what was supposed to occur in a program was actually implemented and attained the targeted outcomes. Experimental designs, if appropriate and feasible, are most likely to be conducted for summative evaluation. This means it would be inappropriate to impose an experimental design on a new or innovative intervention before it has undergone a period of formative evaluation. The 2009 conference of the Australasian Evaluation Society in Canberra featured a presentation by a rabid RCT fundamentalist who opened his presentation by asserting unequivocally: "The purpose of evaluation is to estimate the effect of a program relative to a counterfactual and the RCT is the Gold Standard method for doing so." Former American Evaluation Association president and distinguished evaluation methodologist William Trochim, who shared the stage for the session, responded that the gentleman appeared to be suffering from a severe case of "premature experimentation." Here we see that how one defines evaluation will affect design preferences.

Methodological Appropriateness:
The Utilization-Focused Evaluation Gold Standard

Methodological appropriateness means matching the evaluation design to the evaluation situation taking into account the priority questions and intended uses of primary intended users, the costs and benefits of alternative designs, the decisions that are to be made, the level of evidence necessary to support those decisions, ethical considerations, and utility. No design should be lauded as a gold standard without regard to context and situation. To do so is to create incentives to do randomized control experiments regardless of their appropriateness or meaningfulness.

A variety of design options can be considered for summative evaluation beyond RCTs including quasi-experimental designs, theory-driven evaluation designs, in-depth case studies that focus on empirically and logically examining the relationship between what was done and what resulted, and "realistic evaluation" (Pawson, 2002a, 2002b; Pawson & Tilley, 1997, 2005) which changes the summative question from "Did the program work?" to "What worked for whom in what ways with what results?" Giving serious consideration to these and other design options is increased if the gold standard is *methodological appropriateness and relevance.*

Now, let's turn to another controversial evaluation design issue: the relative merits of randomization.

Randomization

Many evaluators won't even recognize that randomization is controversial and that there are credible alternatives to randomization. Randomization is considered essential for generalizing from samples to populations in surveys and for ruling out selection effects in experimental designs. The problem is that people often don't come into or participate in programs as random individuals. Humans are social animals so program participants often enter programs with friends or, if entering alone, quickly find others to associate with; these subgroups can have unique program experiences that affect evaluation conclusions about an intervention and its effects. Knowing about and tracking the experiences and outcomes of subgroups competes with a purely randomized approach to measurement that treats the unit of analysis as the autonomous individual. Moreover, the people attracted to a program under natural and normal operating conditions are unlikely to have the same characteristics (for example, motivation, needs, interest, baseline knowledge) as people randomly assigned in an experiment, creating what is known as "randomization bias" (Heckman & Smith, 1995; Deaton, 2010).

Strong advocates for randomization have been labeled "randomistas." Martin Ravallion, the highly experienced director of the World Bank's research department, has asked: "Should the randomistas rule?" His answer: "No." Why?

> The very idea of randomized assignment is antithetical to most development programs, which typically aim to reach certain types of people or places. Governments will (hopefully) be able to do better in reaching poor people than would a random assignment. Randomization is also better suited to relatively simple projects, with easily identified "participants" and "non-participants." (Ravallion, 2009, p. 2)

There is also the practical question of using results from randomized experiments. One of the field-level development workers I met at a World Bank conference on evaluation told me of the difficulties she experienced in administering a microfinance program (small loans to people in poverty) because of the design rigidities of the experimental design. She was having trouble understanding and explaining the value of randomization beyond its status among academic researchers. She asked, "Can you imagine an agency, government, or bank running a microfinance program based on randomization? What of any practical significance do you learn from randomization? We have limited resources," she went on. "We have to make selections. Even if randomization was more fair and equitable, giving loans randomly to applicants is not a viable political option. Indeed, the critical questions about microfinance are about how people become eligible, how they are selected to receive a loan, and how the decision is made about how much to give them. *Administering loans randomly is just not a viable policy option,"* she emphasized, shaking her head in frustration.

The randomization process, she felt, made the evaluation results less useful because the design was rigid and artificial. This, she had concluded, was a primary reason why no major businesses conduct such randomized controlled trials for their services. They do, however, engage in thorough and rigorous evaluation. Banks try out pilot programs before going to scale. They seek customer feedback. They observe carefully what customers respond to and how they behave. They compare one delivery approach with another, with real customers in the real world, and they adjust their services accordingly. Likewise, Microsoft does not introduce and study new software through RCTs. They have a large group of pilot testers (as many as 750,000 worldwide) who provide real-time feedback from real-world uses of their software. One would think that if RCTs were so valuable in determining the effectiveness of services, this field worker speculated, businesses would use them routinely to boost profits. In point of fact, businesses engage in continuous improvement evaluation based on feedback and observing the reactions and behaviors of real customers as well as soliciting feedback from noncustomers. RCTs are more often an academic laboratory-like enterprise for research, not a real-world evaluation exercise to figure out how things work under real-world conditions. Or so goes the critique—and the debate.

The implication is that evaluators need to understand when randomization is appropriate, and alternatives to randomization, like studying naturally occurring groups in programs, purposeful sampling of information-rich cases (Patton, 2002, pp. 230–246), success case sampling (Brinkerhoff, 2003, 2005), or positive deviance sampling to identify best practices (Positive Deviance Initiative, 2009). As Ravallion concludes: "The important task of investigating what works and what does not in the fight against poverty cannot be monopolized by one method" (p. 5).

The U.S. federal Government Accountability Office (GAO) independently investigated the relative value of experimental designs. In a report titled *A Variety of Rigorous Methods Can Help Identify Effective Interventions,* the investigation concluded:

> The program evaluation literature generally agrees that well-conducted randomized experiments are best suited for assessing effectiveness when multiple causal influences create uncertainty about what caused results. However, they are often difficult, and sometimes impossible, to carry out.

An evaluation must be able to control exposure to the intervention and ensure that treatment and control groups' experiences remain separate and distinct throughout the study.

Several rigorous alternatives to randomized experiments are considered appropriate for other situations: quasi-experimental comparison group studies, statistical analyses of observational data, and—in some circumstances—in-depth case studies. The credibility of their estimates of program effects relies on how well the studies' designs rule out competing causal explanations. Collecting additional data and targeting comparisons can help rule out other explanations.

GAO concludes that

- Requiring evidence from randomized studies as sole proof of effectiveness will likely exclude many potentially effective and worthwhile practices;
- Reliable assessments of evaluation results require research expertise but can be improved with detailed protocols and training;
- Deciding to adopt an intervention involves other considerations in addition to effectiveness, such as cost and suitability to the local community; and
- Improved evaluation quality would also help identify effective interventions (GAO, 2009, Summary).

Internal Versus External Validity as a Design Priority

Another issue of contention that can arise in designing an evaluation is the relative emphasis to be placed on internal versus external validity. Trade-offs between internal and external validity have become a matter of debate in evaluation since Campbell and Stanley (1963), in their influential design classic, asserted that "internal validity is the sine qua non" (p. 175). Internal validity in its narrowest sense refers to certainty about cause and effect. Did *x* cause *y*? Did the program intervention cause the observed outcomes? In a broader sense, it refers to the "trust-worthiness of an inference" (Cronbach, 1982, p. 106). External validity, on the other hand, refers to the degree of confidence one has in generalizing findings beyond the specific situation studied or evaluated.

Internal validity is increased by exercising rigorous control over a limited set of carefully defined variables. However, such rigorous controls create artificialities that limit generalizability. The highly controlled situation is less likely to be relevant to a greater variety of more naturally occurring, less controlled situations. In the narrowest sense, this is the problem of going from the laboratory into the real world. By contrast, increasing variability and sampling a greater range of experiences or situations typically reduce control and precision, thereby reducing internal validity. The ideal is high internal validity and high external validity. In reality, there are typically trade-offs involved in the relative emphasis placed on one or the other.

Cronbach's (1982) discussion of these issues for evaluation is quite comprehensive and insightful, and still relevant today. He emphasized that "both external validity and internal validity are matters of degree and external validity does not depend directly on internal validity" (p. 170). Being able to apply findings to future decisions and new settings is often more important than establishing rigorous causal relations under rigid experimental conditions. He introduced the idea of *extrapolation* rather than generalization. Extrapolation involves logically and creatively thinking about what specific findings mean for other situations, rather than the statistical process of generalizing from a sample to a larger population. He advocated that findings be interpreted in light of stakeholders' and evaluators' experiences and knowledge, and then applied or extrapolated using all available insights, including understanding about quite different situations. This focuses interpretation away from trying to determine truth in some absolute sense (a goal of basic research) to a concern with conclusions that are reasonable, justifiable, plausible, warranted, and useful.

The contrasting perspectives of Campbell and Stanley (emphasis on internal validity) and Cronbach (emphasis on external validity) have elucidated the trade-offs between designs that give first priority to certainty about casual inference versus those that better support extrapolations to new settings. In working with primary stakeholders to design evaluations that are credible, the evaluator will need to consider the degree to which internal and external validity are of concern, and to emphasize each in accordance with stakeholder priorities. Choices are necessitated by the fact that no single design is likely to attain internal and external validity in equal degrees. With that caveat in mind, let's look more closely at generalizations across time and space, the traditional scientific ideal, versus more contextually sensitive extrapolations.

Generalizations Versus Context-Sensitive Extrapolations

When the evaluation is aimed at generalization, some form of random probabilistic sampling is the design of choice. A needs assessment, for example, aimed at determining how many residents in a county have some particular problem would be strongest if based on a random sample of county residents.

Case studies, on the other hand, become particularly useful when intended users need to understand a problem, situation, or program in great depth, and they can identify cases rich in needed information—"rich" in the sense that a great deal can be learned from a few exemplars of the phenomenon of interest. For example, much can be learned about how to improve a program by studying dropouts or successes *within the context* of a particular program. Case studies are context-specific.

But what about generalizations? Cronbach (1975), in his classic work on the issue, observed that generalizations decay over time; that is, they have a half-life much like radioactive materials. Guba and Lincoln (1981), in their pioneering work—*Effective Evaluation: Improving the Usefulness and Evaluation Results Through Responsive and Naturalistic*

Approaches—were particularly critical of the dependence on generalizations in quantitative methods because, they asked, "What can a generalization be except an assertion that is context free? . . . [Yet] *it is virtually impossible to imagine any human behavior that is not heavily mediated by the context in which it occurs*" (p. 62; emphasis in original).

Cronbach and colleagues in the Stanford Evaluation Consortium (Cronbach & Associates, 1980) offered a middle ground in the paradigms debate with regard to the problem of generalizability and the relevance of evaluations. They criticized experimental designs that were so focused on controlling cause and effect that the results were largely irrelevant beyond the experimental situation. On the other hand, they were equally concerned that entirely idiosyncratic case studies yield little of use beyond the case study setting. They suggested, instead, that designs balance depth and breadth, realism and control, so as to permit reasonable *extrapolation* (pp. 231–235).

Unlike the usual meaning of the term *generalization,* an *extrapolation* connotes that one has gone beyond the narrow confines of the data to think about other applications of the findings. Extrapolations are modest speculations on the likely applicability of findings to other situations under similar, but not identical, conditions. Extrapolations are logical, thoughtful, and problem-oriented rather than purely empirical, statistical, and probabilistic. Evaluation users often expect evaluators to thoughtfully extrapolate from their findings in the sense of pointing out lessons learned and potential applications to future efforts.

Instead of one massive experiment or quasi-experiment (the "horse race" model of evaluation, said Cronbach), he favored an eclectic, broad-based, open methodological approach to evaluation—a fleet of smaller studies, each pursuing an important case or component of the policy or program under study. Cronbach encouraged evaluators to design evaluations to understand in some depth the nature of each context and the quality of the intervention in that context. Over time, then, with many such studies, the policy-shaping community could learn in some depth about the social problem and how best to address it. In addition, Cronbach encouraged evaluators to involve members of the setting in the evaluation study and to provide feedback throughout the course of the study (for program improvement purposes) rather than just at the end (Mathison, 2005, p. 95). Cronbach's advice about the value of multiple studies has taken on even greater importance with the recent findings that experimental findings are often difficult to replicate over time, even in biology and the natural sciences, and much more so in the social sciences (Lehrer, 2010b).

Designs that combine probabilistic and purposeful case study sampling (mixed-methods designs) have the advantage of extrapolations supported by quantitative and qualitative data. Larger samples of statistically meaningful data can address questions of incidence and prevalence (generalizations to a known population), while case studies add depth and detail to make interpretations more meaningful and grounded.

Pragmatism Versus Methodological Purity

Consider this situation. An evaluator is working with a group of educators, some of whom are "progressive, open education" adherents and some of whom are "back-to-basics" fundamentalists. The progressive education group wants to frame the evaluation of a particular program within a qualitative/naturalistic framework. The basic-skills people want a rigorous, quantitative/experimental approach. Should the evaluator facilitate a choice that frames the evaluation within either one or the other paradigm? Must an either/or choice be made about the kind of data to be collected? Are the views of each group so incompatible that each must have its own evaluation?

I've been in precisely this situation a number of times. I do not try to resolve their paradigms debate but, rather, to inform their dialogue. I try to establish an environment of tolerance and respect for different, competing viewpoints, and then focus the discussion on the actual information that is needed by each group: Test scores? Interviews? Observations? The design and measures must be negotiated. Multiple methods and multiple measures will give each group some of what they want. The naturalistic paradigm educators will want to be sure that test scores are interpreted within a larger context of classroom activities, observations, and outcomes. The quantitative paradigm educators will likely use interview and observational data as background to explain and justify test score interpretations. My experience suggests that both groups can agree on an evaluation design that includes multiple types of data and that each group will ultimately pay attention to and use "the other group's data." In short, a particular group of people can arrive at agreement on an evaluation design that includes both qualitative and quantitative data without resolving ultimate paradigmatic issues. Such agreement is not likely, however, if the evaluator begins with the premise that the paradigms are incompatible and that the evaluation must be conducted within the framework of either one or the other. By focusing on and negotiating data collection alternatives in an atmosphere of respect and tolerance, the participants can come together around a commitment to an empirical perspective; that is, bringing data to bear on important program issues. As long as the empirical commitment is there, the other differences can be negotiated in most instances.

Strong Evaluations

Strong evaluations employ methods of analysis that are appropriate to the question; support the answer with evidence; document the assumptions, procedures, and modes of analysis; and rule out the competing evidence. Strong studies pose questions clearly, address them appropriately, and draw inferences commensurate with the power of the design and the availability, validity, and reliability of the data. Strength should not be equated with complexity. Nor should strength be equated with the degree of statistical manipulation of data. Neither infatuation with complexity nor statistical incantation makes an evaluation stronger.

> The strength of an evaluation is not defined by a particular method. Longitudinal, experimental, quasi-experimental, before-and-after, and case study evaluations can be either strong or weak. . . . That is, the strength of an evaluation has to be judged within the context of the question, the time and cost constraints, the design, the technical adequacy of the data collection and analysis, and the presentation of the findings. A strong study is technically adequate and useful—in short, it is high in quality.
>
> From *Designing Evaluations*,
> Government Accountability Office (1991, pp. 15–16)

Debating paradigms with one's primary intended users, and taking sides in that debate, is different from debating one's colleagues about the nature of reality. I doubt that evaluators will ever reach consensus on fundamental paradigm differences. The evaluation profession is diverse, which is one of its strengths. But methodological paradigms debate can go on among evaluators without paralyzing the practice of practical evaluators who are trying to work responsively with primary stakeholders to get answers to relevant empirical questions. The belief that evaluators must be true to only one paradigm in any given situation underestimates the human capacity for handling ambiguity and duality, shifting flexibly between perspectives. In short, I'm suggesting that evaluators would do better to worry about understanding and being sensitive to the worldviews and evaluation needs of their clients than to maintain allegiance to or work within only one paradigm perspective.

Beyond Paradigm Orthodoxies: A Paradigm of Choices

One implication of this perspective—that quality and excellence are situational—is that it is futile to attempt to design studies that are immune from methodological criticism. There simply is no such immunity, a point made previously in discussing Step 10 on selecting methods. Intended users who participate in making methods decisions should be prepared to be criticized regardless of what choices they make. Alerting them to the methodological debates within the research and evaluation communities, and explaining that there are strong arguments on all sides of the debate, will hopefully free them to do what makes most sense in the situation at hand.

The paradigms debates elucidate the variety of choices available in evaluation. It is premature to characterize the practice of evaluation as completely flexible and focused on methodological appropriateness rather than disciplinary orthodoxy, but it is fair to say that the goals have shifted dramatically in that direction. The debate over which paradigm was the right path to truth has been replaced, at the level of methods, by *a paradigm of choices.*

Utilization-focused evaluation offers such a paradigm of choices. Today's evaluator must be sophisticated about matching research methods to the nuances of particular evaluation questions and the idiosyncrasies of specific decision-maker needs. The evaluator must have a large repertoire of research methods and techniques available to use on a variety of problems.

In essence, the utilization-focused evaluator works with intended users to include any and all data that will help shed light on evaluation questions, given constraints of resources and time. Such an evaluator is committed to research designs that are relevant, rigorous, understandable, and able to produce useful results that are valid, reliable, and credible. The pragmatic *paradigm of choices* recognizes that different methods are appropriate for different situations and purposes.

Details about what is involved in each step are provided in the summary *U-FE Checklist* in the concluding chapter. See pages 417–418 for the checklist items for Step 11 discussed in this chapter.

PRACTICE EXERCISES

1. What is your opinion about the methodological gold standard issue? Should there be a methodological gold standard? If so, what—and why? If not, why not? What is illuminating and what is distorting about the "gold standard" metaphor applied to evaluation methods? Develop a script to explain the debate issue to a nonresearcher.

2. Assess your own methodological strengths and weaknesses. What methods are you most knowledgeable about and comfortable with? Why? In what evaluation methods do you lack training and expertise? Discuss how your competences and training affect your capability to match methods to the nature of the evaluation questions. To what extent can you be methodologically flexible and eclectic? Do a capacity assessment. For assistance, see "A Professional Development Unit for Reflecting on Program Evaluation Competencies" (Ghere, King, Stevahn, & Minnema, 2006).

INTERLUDE, STEPS 1 THROUGH 11. COMPLEX DYNAMIC SYSTEMS INTERCONNECTIONS

Making Methods Choices That Are Appropriate

These chapter interludes aim to communicate the interactive, iterative, interdependent, and nonlinear dynamics of working with intended users. Step 10 discussed negotiating appropriate methods to generate credible findings that support intended use by intended users. Step 11 focused on making sure that intended users understand potential methods controversies and their implications. But methods choices and controversies can and do arise at any and every step throughout the U-FE process. The complex dynamic systems graphic on the next page reiterates the ways in which methods issues arise along the way and intersect with other steps. This graphic incorporates Exhibit 11.1 that opened the discussion of Step 11 showing the interconnections among Steps 9, 10, and 11 (see p. 285).

U-FE Complex Adaptive Systems Graphic: Interactions Among Steps 1 Through 11

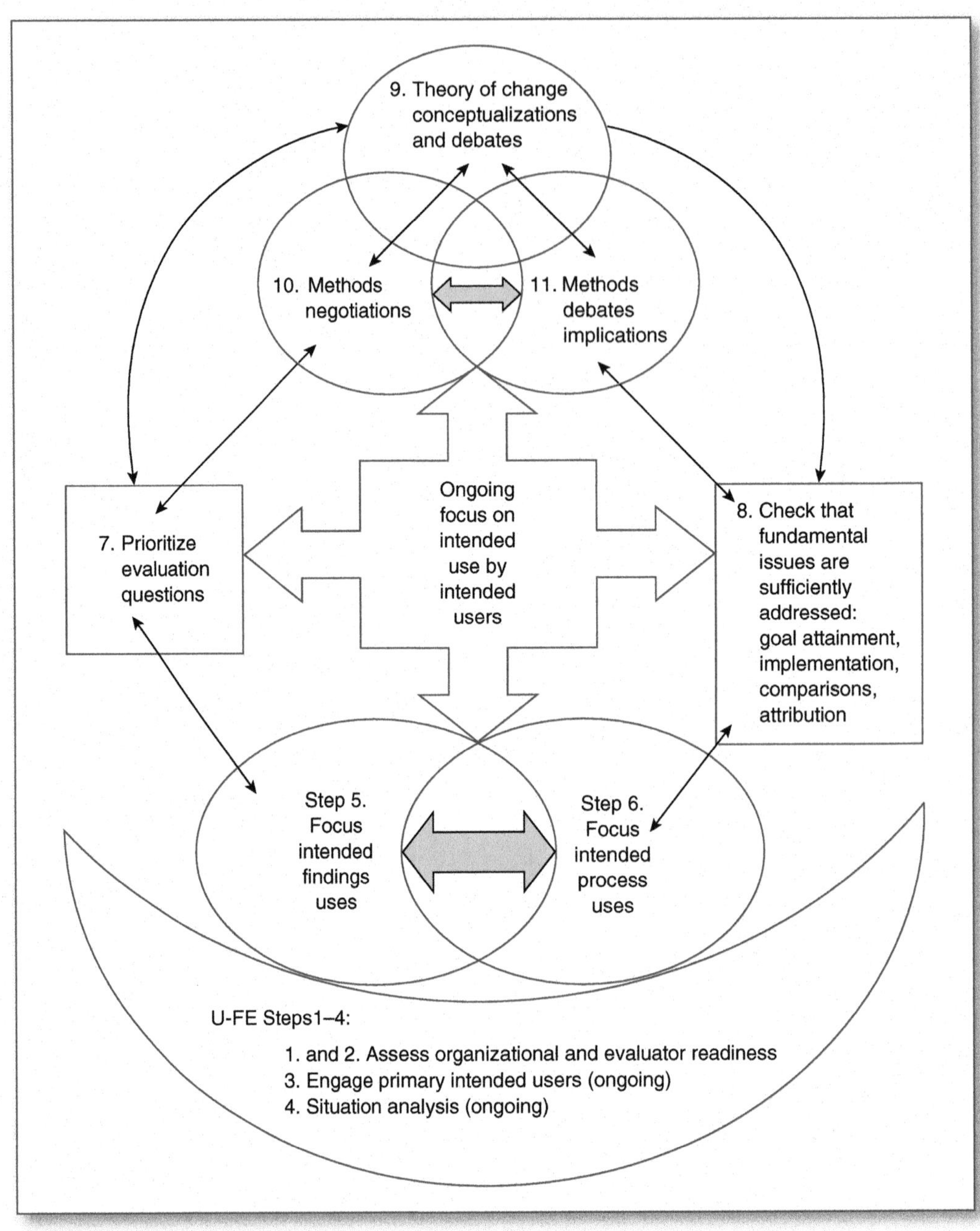

12

Simulate Use of Findings

Evaluation's Equivalent of a Dress Rehearsal

The purpose and intended uses of the evaluation have been established with primary intended users. Priority evaluation questions have been identified. Design, measurement, and data collection decisions have been made. Time to gather data? Not quite yet. First, do a final check to make sure that the data to be collected will really answer priority questions and support action. How? Well, one way is to do a utilization-focused dress rehearsal: Engage intended users in a simulation exercise in which the evaluator fabricates some potential results and intended users practice interpreting and using those results. The evaluation facilitator asks, "If the results came out this way, what would you do? If the findings came out this other way, what would that tell you, and what actions would you take? Given what you want the evaluation to accomplish, have we focused on the right outcomes and most useful indicators?"

Athletes, performing artists, astronauts, and entertainers spend hundreds of hours practicing for events that take only a few hours. Firefighters do fire drills. Actors do dress rehearsals. Is it too much to ask intended users to spend a couple of hours practicing to get mentally and analytically ready for the climax of an evaluation? Here's how it works.

Simulated Data Interpretation Scenarios

The stage can be set for analysis, interpretation, and use *before* data are ever collected. Once instruments have been designed—but before data collection—conduct a simulated use session. This involves fabricating possible results and interpreting the action implications of the made-up data. The evaluator prepares some possible "positive" and "negative" findings on the most important issues. For example, suppose primary users have chosen the job placement rate as the priority outcome variable for a vocational training program. The evaluator might construct data showing a placement rate of 40% for Black participants and 75% for White participants. The evaluator facilitates analysis by asking such questions as the following: "What do these results mean? What actions would you take based on these results? How would you use these data?"

Such a discussion accomplishes four things:

1. The simulated analysis is a check on the design to make sure that all the relevant data for interpretation and use are going to be collected. (Remember this session occurs before actually gathering data.) All too often, at the analysis stage, *after* data collection, evaluators and stakeholders realize that they forgot to ask an important question.

2. The simulated use session trains and prepares stakeholders for the real analysis later. They learn how to interpret data and apply results by practicing doing so.

3. Working through a use scenario prior to data collection helps set realistic expectations about what the results will look like. Strengths and limitations of the design emerge. Methodological and measurement issues can be further clarified and discussed. This helps prepare users for the necessity of interpreting findings in relation to possible actions and likely ambiguities.

4. Use scenarios help build the commitment to use—or reveal the lack of such commitment.

When intended users are unable to deal with how they would use findings prior to data collection, a warning flag goes up that they may be unable, or unwilling, to use findings after data collection. The commitment to use can be cultivated by helping intended users think realistically and concretely about how findings might be applied before data collection gets under way. This relatively safe, even fun, exercise of analyzing simulated data can help strengthen the resolve to use before being confronted with real findings and decisions. This can help overcome resistance to evaluation and remove any remaining barriers to implementing the evaluation data collection.

Quantitative data are fairly easy to fabricate once instruments have been developed. With qualitative data, it's necessary to construct imagined quotations and case examples. This extra work can pay large dividends as decision makers develop a utilization-focused mindset based on an actual experience struggling with data.

An Ancient Example

I often set up the dress rehearsal with fabricated data by taking primary intended users through an ancient evaluation example found in the Old Testament of the Bible.

The example isn't aimed at any religious message, I explain. Instead it shows how the issue of using data to improve programs and inform decisions goes back a long way.

The book of Daniel tells the story of what happened when Nebuchadnezzar, king of Babylon, conquered Jerusalem. He instructed Ashpenaz, the master of his eunuchs, to identify intelligent young children of Israel from respected families who could be trained as civil servants. Throughout history it has been a common practice of conquering nations to establish colonial governments administered by selectively trained and supervised indigenous people. Among those selected by Ashpenaz for service to Nebuchadnezzar were Daniel, Hananiah, Mishael, and Azariah. But when they arrived at the king's palace to begin their training, Daniel and his friends refused to eat the king's meat or drink his wine. They asked to be allowed to eat a vegetarian diet and drink only water. Ashpenaz, the program director, resisted this request, fearing that such a diet would be unhealthy and the king would think he was not feeding the trainees appropriately. Indeed, the stakes were high for Ashpenaz, who responded to Daniel's request by saying: "I fear my lord the king, who hath appointed your meat and your drink. What if he sees you looking worse than the others in the program. *Then shall ye make me endanger my head to the king.*"

Daniel wanted to assure Ashpenaz that the diet was healthy and they would not appear sickly if allowed to eat a vegetarian diet, so he proposed an experiment. He asked that he and his friends be allowed to eat the vegetarian diet while others in the program who preferred the meat and wine eat the king's food and see what happens. Daniel agreed that if they started to look unhealthy, they would eat the king's food, but Ashpenaz had to agree that if they appeared healthy at the end of the 10-day experiment, they would be allowed to continue their vegetarian and water diet.

As it turned out, the four vegetarians eating their kosher diet—Daniel, Hananiah, Mishael, and Azariah—not only didn't become sickly looking, "their countenances appeared fairer and fatter in flesh than all the children which did eat the king's meat." So, they were allowed to maintain their vegetarian diet, completed the program after 3 years, passed Nebuchadnezzar's test, and entered into the king's service. In essence, this is an example of a formative evaluation in which a group of program participants asked for a modification in the program, the modification was tried out, and, when the evidence showed it worked, the program was adapted accordingly. Indeed, one of the most common uses of formative evaluation is to adapt a program to the special needs of some subgroup because one size doesn't fit all.

So what does this have to do with a data use simulation?

In the story, all four participants in the vegetarian experimental group came out looking better. That makes the decision to allow them to continue their preferred diet easy. Likewise, if all four had looked worse, it would be clear that they would have to eat the king's diet. But what action should Ashpenaz take if two look better and two look worse? Or if one looks better, two look the same, and one looks worse? Or if three look the same but one looks worse? Discussing these scenarios prepares primary intended users for the possibility of having to deal with different kinds of results, including mixed or ambiguous findings. It's a simple warm-up exercise before doing the real simulation. And the simulation with fabricated data is a warm-up dress rehearsal before being faced with taking action on real findings.

"Based on the simulated evaluation findings, who thinks we should ask the donor for more money?"

Standards of Desirability

A simulated use session also offers a prime opportunity to think about and formalize criteria for making judgments—again, *before data collection.* With quantitative data this can be done quite precisely by establishing standards of desirability. I like to have users set at least three levels of attainment:

1. Results level at which the program is considered *highly effective,*
2. Results level at which the program is considered *adequate,* and
3. Results level at which the program is considered *inadequate.*

Such standards can be established for implementation targets (e.g., program participation and completion rates) as well as outcomes (like getting and retaining a job). Suppose you are collecting satisfaction data on a workshop. At what level of satisfaction is the workshop a success? At what level is it merely adequate? At what level of participant satisfaction (or dissatisfaction) is the workshop to be judged ineffective? It's better to establish these kinds of standards of desirability in a calm and deliberative manner *before* actual results are presented.

This exercise may also reveal that satisfaction data alone are an inadequate indicator of effectiveness, an important discovery while there's still time to measure additional outcomes. Let me elaborate.

Suppose the following performance target has been set: *75% of workshop participants will be satisfied.* This doesn't tell us what constitutes an outstanding accomplishment; it doesn't distinguish adequacy from excellence. Nor does it make it clear whether 65% satisfaction is inadequate or merely "lower than we hoped for but acceptable." In a dress rehearsal that targeted a 75% satisfaction rate, I fabricated data that showed only a 73% satisfaction rate. Did that mean the workshop was a failure? The workshop evaluation committee discussed this fabricated finding and decided that just having a single overall measure of satisfaction was not very useful. They wanted to know the characteristics of the people who were satisfied and dissatisfied (e.g., novices versus old-timers), and what were they satisfied or dissatisfied about (which would require an open-ended question). The data interpretation dress rehearsal led to a final revision of the evaluation form before data collection.

Sometimes objectives and performance targets have been established in a proposal or plan a long time before the program is under way or well before an actual evaluation has been designed. Reviewing objectives and targets, and establishing precise standards of desirability just before data collection, increases the likelihood that judgment criteria will be up to date, realistic, meaningful, and *actionable.*

During the early conceptual stage of an evaluation, questions of use are fairly general and responses may be vague. The evaluator asks, "What would you do if you had an answer to your evaluation question? How would you use evaluation findings?" These general questions help focus the evaluation, but once the context has been delineated, the priority questions focused, and methods selected, the evaluator can pose much more specific use questions based on what results might actually look like.

For example, if recidivism in a community corrections program is 55%, is that high or low? Does it mean the program was effective or ineffective? The program had some impact, but what level of impact is desirable? What level spells trouble? Thinking about how to interpret data in advance of getting actual results goes a long way in building the capacity of primary intended users to interpret real findings.

The key point is that if intended users are unwilling or unable to set expectancy levels *before data collection,* there is no reason to believe they can do so afterward. In addition, going through this process ahead of time alerts participants to any additional data they will need to make sense of and act on the results. Many of the most serious conflicts in evaluation are rooted in the failure to clearly specify standards of desirability ahead of data collection. This can lead both to collection of the wrong data and to intense disagreement about criteria for judging effectiveness. Without explicit criteria, data can be interpreted to mean almost anything about a program—or to mean nothing at all.

Preparing for Use

Another way of setting the stage for analysis and use is having stakeholders speculate about results prior to seeing the real data. This can be done prior to data collection or after data collection but prior to actual presentation of findings. Stakeholders are given an analysis table with all the appropriate categories but no actual data (a dummy table). They then fill in the missing data with their guesses of what the results will be. This kind of speculation prepares users for how the results will be formatted and increases interest by building a sense of anticipation. I've even had stakeholders establish a betting pool on the results. Each person puts in a dollar, and the person closest to the actual results on the major outcome wins the pot. That creates interest! And the winner must be present at the unveiling of the findings to win. Strange how attendance at the presentation of findings is increased under these conditions!

A second and more important function of having stakeholders write down their guesses is to provide a concrete basis for determining the extent to which actual results come close to expectations. Program staff members, for example, sometimes argue that they don't need formal evaluations because they know their clients, students, or program participants so well that evaluation findings would just confirm what they already know. I've found that when staff members commit their guesses to paper ahead of seeing actual results, the subsequent comparison often calls into question just how well some staff members know what is happening in the program. At least with written guesses on paper, program staff and other stakeholders can't just say, "That's what I expected." A baseline (in the form of their guesses) exists to document how much something new has been learned.

You can combine establishing standards of desirability and speculating on results. Give stakeholders a page with two columns. The first column asks them to specify what outcomes they consider desirable, and the second column asks them to guess what results they believe will be obtained. Having specified a standard of desirability and guessed at actual results, users have a greater stake in and a framework for looking at the actual findings. When real results are presented, the evaluator facilitates a discussion on the implications of the data that fall below, at, or above the desired response, and why the actual findings were different from or the same as what they guessed. In facilitating this exercise, the outcomes data presented must be highly focused and limited to major issues. In my experience, animated interactions among users follow as they fully engage and interpret the results. I find that, given sufficient time and encouragement, stakeholders with virtually no methods or statistics training can readily identify the strengths, weaknesses, and implications of the findings. The trick is to move people from passive reception—from audience status—to active involvement and participation.

Preparing for Interpretation: Making Comparisons

In the second quarter (April–June) of 2010, the Dow Jones Industrial Average dropped 9.97%, or some 1,082 points. Reports in the financial news tried a variety of comparisons to place this decline in perspective:

- The worst slide for the April–June quarter since 2002.
- Just 2 percentage points worse than the average for all 17 quarterly losses over the past 10 years.
- One of just five second-quarter losses over the past two decades.
- The first quarterly loss after four rising quarters that showed gains of 4.82% to 15.82%.
- One of only eight quarterly losses versus 12 quarterly gains in five years.
- Only the sixth-worst quarterly loss in 10 years.

All of these comparisons are accurate. Each provides a different perspective. Which ones are more or less useful depends on the situation of the investor. Those who have been investing for 10 years or more may value 10-year comparisons, or even data for two decades. Others may think that 5 years is the more illuminative time line. Some will prefer 1 year at a time. Still others will eschew quarterly results altogether and prefer monthly data or annual data. There is no right comparison. Offering intended users examples of different comparison possibilities before data are collected, analyzed, and presented helps them decide what comparisons will be most useful—and practice thinking comparatively.

Cost-Benefit Analysis Scenario

An interesting and illuminative scenario of decision options for cost-effectiveness analysis is presented in Exhibit 12.1. This table compares the costs and benefits of two programs,

EXHIBIT 12.1

Simulated Comparison of Cost-Benefit Comparisons of Two Program Options, A Versus B

	Program A lower cost than program B	*Program A higher cost than program B*
Program A higher benefit (better outcomes) than program B	*Cell 1* Program A has better outcomes and lower costs: easy decision to decide in favor of program A over B.	*Cell 2* Program A has higher benefits and higher costs. Decision question: Is the greater benefit worth the greater cost?
Program A lower benefit (worse outcomes) than program B	*Cell 3* Program A has lower outcomes and lower costs. Decision issue: Is absolute cost a more important criterion than cost-benefit level?	*Cell 4* Program A has worse outcomes and costs more: easy decision to reject program A in favor of B.

A versus B. When one program has both lower costs and higher benefits (better outcomes) as in cell 1, the decision is easy: favor that program. Likewise, when one program has higher costs and worse outcomes as in cell 4, reject that program. Those are the easy decisions and, in my experience, the rarer results. The tougher decision is what to do when one program has both higher costs and better outcomes as in cell 2. Is the greater benefit worth the greater cost? On the other hand, what's the appropriate decision when a program has lower costs and lower outcomes? Many decision makers are more interested in lower costs, even if that means lower outcomes, because, it turns out, cost trumps cost-benefit. Discussing these options and comparisons ahead of time makes it clear that interpretation and judgment will be needed to take action on findings.

Risk Assessment

As long as we're talking about cost-benefit analysis, let's acknowledge that designing an evaluation involves some kind of informal cost-benefit analysis in which potential benefits, for example, using results to improve the program, are considered in relationship to costs, which include financial resources, evaluator and staff time, and opportunity costs. (What else could have been done with the money spent on evaluation?)

Introducing the notion of risk into evaluation design and intended users' decisions is a way of acknowledging that things seldom turn out exactly the way they are planned. We have many adages to remind us that human endeavors inherently involve risks: "Even the best laid plans . . . ," "Many a slip between cup and lip." And the bumper sticker: "Stuff Happens" (or a more emphatic version that replaces "stuff" with a certain nonacademic 4-letter word).

Explicitly introducing risk into conversations and negotiations between evaluators and primary intended users begins by asking the following kinds of questions:

1. What can go wrong in this evaluation?
2. What is the likelihood that certain things will go wrong?
3. What are the consequences and how bad would they be?

The intent of such front-end risk assessment is *not* to deepen the illusion that one can anticipate and thereby prevent all difficulties. Rather, it is to lay the foundation for contingency thinking as a basis for evaluator–user negotiations and revisions as the evaluation unfolds. Risk analysis should push evaluators and intended users to be prepared for contingencies. Contingency thinking and planning acknowledges the reality that every design will run into execution problems. What distinguishes one evaluation from another is not the absence of problems but the preparation for and ability to solve them. Examining what can go wrong should include thoughtful consideration of what can really be accomplished with available resources. Risk is traditionally defined as the probability of an occurrence multiplied by the severity of the consequences associated with the hazard. Risk analysis requires evaluators and stakeholders to become explicit about different scenarios and how they might behave in each. This can help mentally prepare intended users to be ready to engage around whatever emerges. Examples of common scenarios include:

- Not getting access to promised data because of confidentiality concerns or finding out that the data supposedly available was never actually collected, or is in such bad condition as to be unusable
- Problems getting access to key informants or program participants in a timely manner because of scheduling problems or program administrative difficulties that interfere with access and data collection
- Sudden crisis in a program when a key staff person leaves, or funding is lost, or a critical incident occurs (for example, accidental death of a participant or staff member)
- Partners in a collaborative initiative refusing to participate in an evaluation despite initial promises to do so because of fear about what will be discovered and reported

Bottom line: *Expect the unexpected. Be prepared for contingencies.* And prepare primary intended users to be ready to adapt the evaluation design in the face of what actually unfolds during fieldwork and data collection. As former heavyweight boxing champion Mike Tyson observed: "Every boxer has a plan . . . until he gets hit." STUFF HAPPENS.

Virtuous and Vicious Utilization Circles

When actions lead to reactions that create still further reactions, a reinforcing systems dynamic is at work in which initial effects interact in what amounts to spiraling ripple effects. A positive spiral is called a virtuous system because it accelerates action in the desired direction. For example, in economics a tax cut for small companies leads to more investment which leads to higher productivity, which leads to higher profits and business expansion, which leads to new jobs, which leads to a healthier economy, which leads to higher tax revenues in the end. In contrast, a downward spiral is a vicious circle in which things get worse and worse: low-income people get hurt or sick, miss work, lose their job, can't pay their rent, get evicted, end up homeless and living on the streets, which makes it harder to get a new job. A virtuous cycle has favorable results and a vicious cycle has deleterious results. These cycles will continue in the direction of their momentum until some external factor intrudes and stops the cycle.

Evaluation use is subject to both vicious and virtuous spirals. A virtuous utilization circle is set in motion when primary intended users become interested and engaged in an evaluation; they communicate to others, like program staff and participants, that the evaluation is genuine and meaningful; staff and participants cooperate with the evaluation; relevant, high-quality data are generated through cooperation; high-quality data increase the credibility of the evaluation, which enhances use; primary intended users feel good about having participated in the evaluation, see and report to others that it was useful, which creates a positive and receptive environment for future evaluations.

A vicious evaluation circle emerges where primary intended users distrust the evaluation process, bad-mouth the evaluation to others creating resistance from staff and program participants, which undermines cooperation with the evaluation, which leads to poor data and weak findings, which undermines the credibility of the findings and makes the evaluation useless, which confirms and reinforces the intended users' negative suspicions and skepticism about evaluation.

Situation analysis and scenario planning can include creating scenarios with primary intended users about how virtuous use circles can be created and vicious evaluation circles avoided. Exhibit 12.2 depicts a virtuous utilization system dynamic. Exhibit 12.3 depicts a vicious utilization system dynamic. Evaluation risk assessment and stakeholder contingency planning can

EXHIBIT 12.2

A Virtuous Utilization Circle

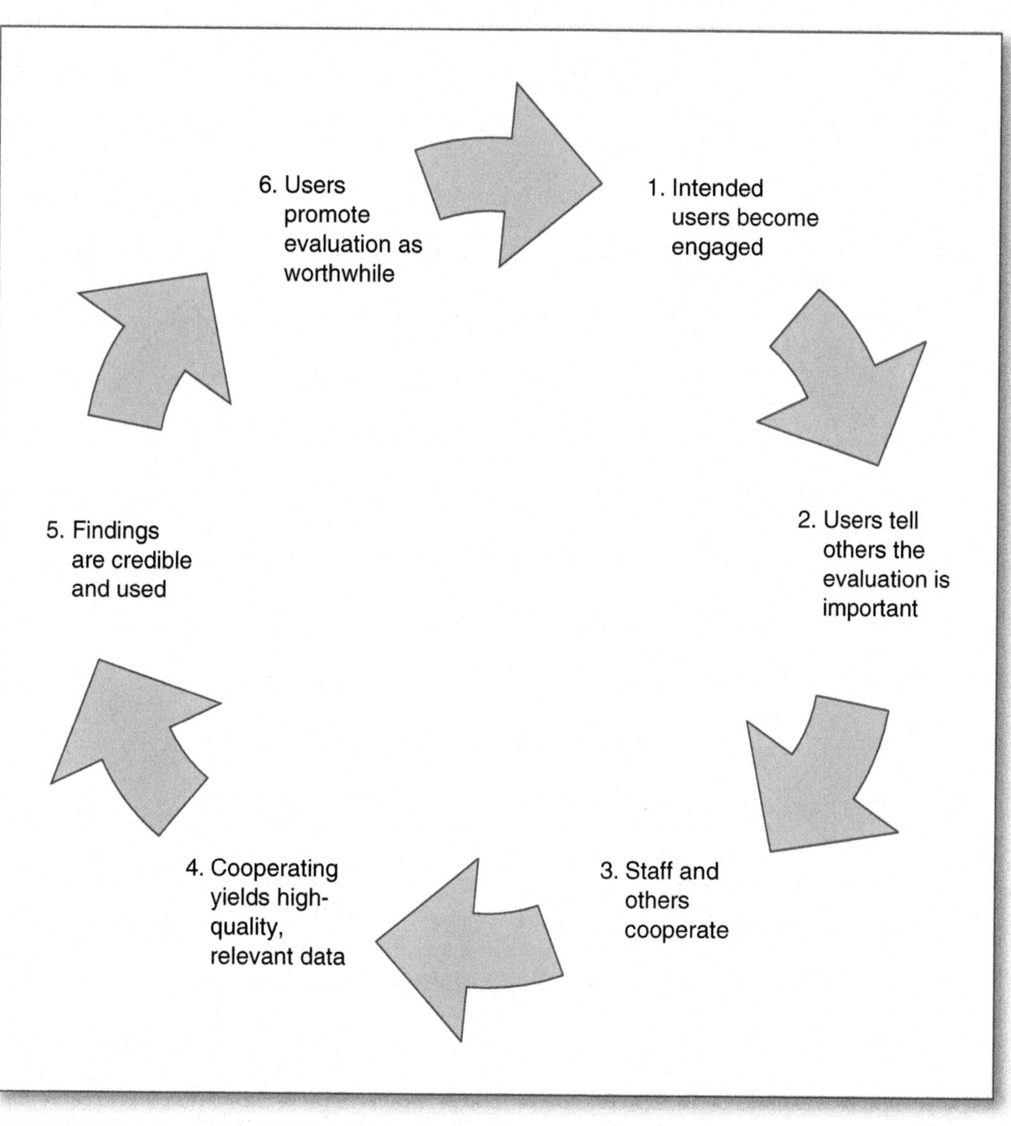

EXHIBIT 12.3

Vicious Circle Undermining Evaluation Use

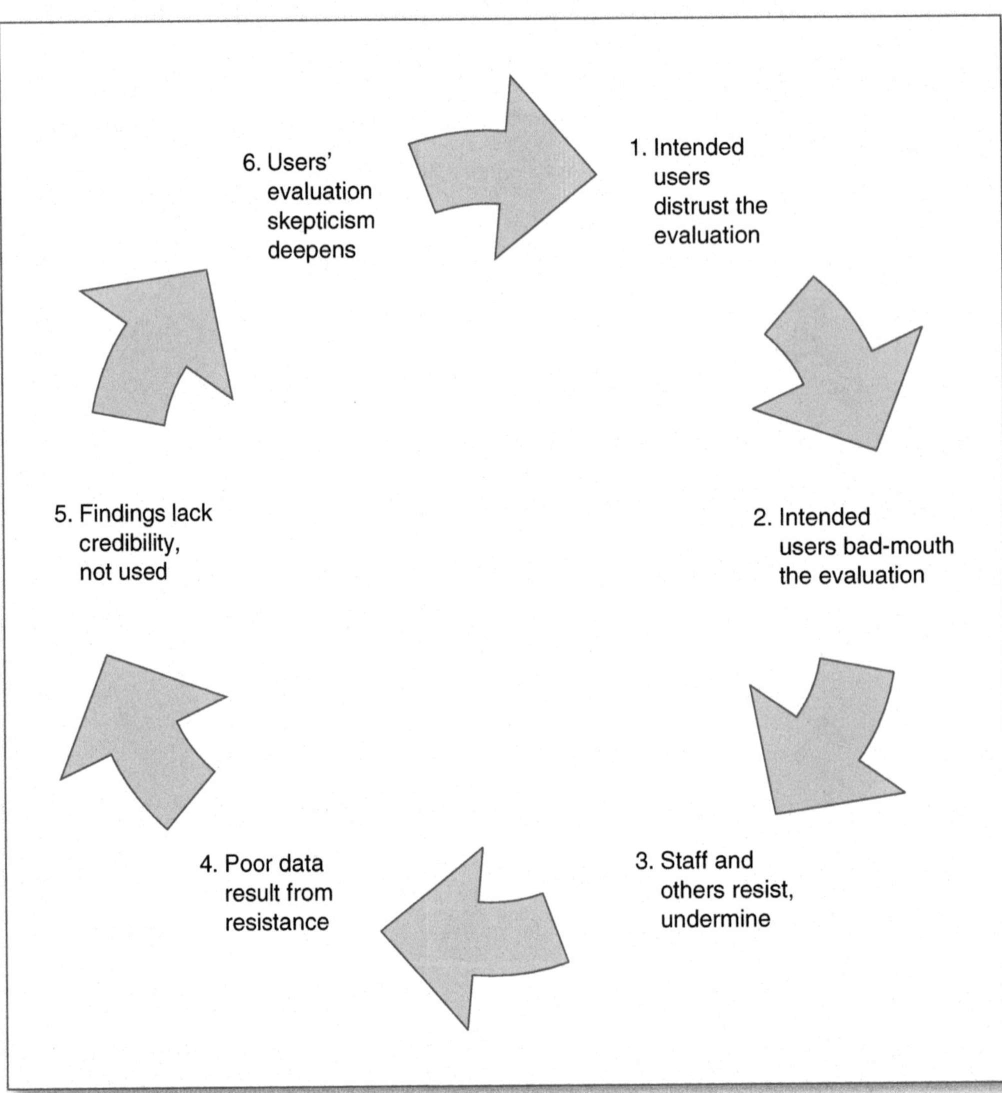

include what can occur within the specific context in which the evaluation will be conducted that would lead to a virtuous or vicious circle—and what would be early indicators of each.

Using Scenarios to Study Stakeholder Engagement and Evaluation Use

This chapter has advocated creating and using scenarios with primary intended users as a final form of engagement before data collection. These scenarios provide a final check that the right data will be collected to address priority issues and help train intended users for interpreting results when the findings have been generated. What does research show about the capacity of nonresearchers to participate in and learn from such scenario exercises?

Christina Christie (2007), a distinguished UCLA evaluation researcher, found that decision makers could distinguish among the merits and uses of different kinds of designs. Using a set of scenarios derived from actual evaluation studies, she conducted a simulation to examine what decision makers reported as evaluation design preferences and likely influences. I reported her findings in an earlier chapter, but they're worth reiterating here. Each scenario described a setting where results from one of three types of evaluation designs would be available: large-scale study data, case study data, or anecdotal accounts. The simulation then specified a particular decision that needed to be made. Decision makers were asked to indicate which type of design would influence their decision making. Results from 131 participants indicated that these decision makers had varying design preferences and were quite capable of distinguishing the credibility and utility of various types of evaluation studies or measurement options. Engaging concrete scenarios and considering trade-offs helped decision makers explicitly express their data preferences and interpretive frameworks.

The Ultimate Question

Step 12, simulating use, is the penultimate step before data collection. This next-to-last step before finalizing the evaluation design, methods, and measures sets up the ultimate question before data collection: *Given expected costs and intended uses, is the evaluation worth doing?* The simulation offers a *dress rehearsal* opportunity, a chance to practice use. Are the primary intended users committed to moving forward? Is the evaluation worth doing? I like to formalize this decision with primary intended users as the final step before data collection.

Details about what is involved in each step are provided in the summary *U-FE Checklist* in the concluding chapter. See page 418 for the checklist items for Step 12 discussed in this chapter.

PRACTICE EXERCISES

1. Using evaluation data or an indicator of any kind, fabricate alternative findings and identify the facilitation questions you would ask for a simulation with primary intended users.
2. Select a metaphor for an evaluation simulation (for example fire drill, dress rehearsal, or something relevant to your world) and discuss the advantages and disadvantages of that metaphor applied to introducing an evaluation simulation to primary intended users.
3. Comedian Mitch Hedberg (1968–2005) did a stand-up routine based on the following scenario:

> I bought a doughnut and they gave me a receipt for the doughnut. I don't need a receipt for the doughnut. I give you money and you give me the doughnut, end of transaction. We don't need to bring ink and paper into this. *I can't imagine a scenario that I would have to prove that I bought a doughnut.* When, perhaps some skeptical friend questions my purchase, I can say, "Don't even act like I didn't get that doughnut, I've got the documentation right here. It's in my file at home, filed under 'D.'"

Questions: Under what scenarios would a customer want such a receipt? What purposes beyond a customer's needs does a receipt serve? How would you use this example with primary intended users? To illustrate what?

13

Gather Data With Ongoing Attention to Use

If there is a 50–50 chance that something can go wrong, then 9 times out of 10 it will.

Paul Harvey,
American radio broadcaster

The previous chapter included a risk assessment of what *might* go wrong during data collection. Now, during data collection is when you find out what *will* go wrong—and what will go as planned. You've identified and engaged primary intended users. You've worked with them to be clear about the evaluation's purpose, prioritizing relevant questions and selecting appropriate methods. You've facilitated a practice session using fabricated findings to deepen the commitment to use and enhance their capacity to move from data to decision and action. Now comes the work of implementing the evaluation plan and gathering data. A marathoner trains for months to get ready for a big race, but the race still has to be run. An acting troupe rehearses for weeks to get ready for live performances with a real audience, then opening night arrives at last. Politicians campaign for months to get elected, then they still have to govern. Utilization-focused evaluators work diligently to engage primary intended users to design a relevant and meaningful evaluation, but the data still have to be collected. This chapter looks at how to gather data with ongoing attention to use. We'll consider four issues that are particularly likely to affect use: (1) effective management of the data collection process, (2) implementing any agreed-on participatory approaches to data collection that build capacity and support process use, (3) keeping primary intended users informed about how things are going, and (4) providing early feedback by reporting emergent and interim findings.

Effective Management of the Data Collection Process

> *Management is, above all, a practice where art, science, and craft meet.*
>
> *Henry Mintzberg,*
> management scholar and consultant

Step 2 focused on assessing evaluator readiness. In that chapter I reviewed essential competencies for evaluators (Ghere, King, Stevahn, & Minnema, 2006), among which is *project management*—the nuts and bolts of managing an evaluation from beginning to end. But managing data collection is especially important, for, as much as anything, this can determine whether the evaluation findings have integrity and credibility and are delivered in a timely manner. Some brilliant methodologists are lousy managers, and vice versa. Exhibit 13.1 identifies some critical checklist factors that affect competent evaluation management.

Six issues are especially critical in project management:

1. Managing funds to deliver what has been promised within budget
2. Managing time to deliver findings in time to be useful and actually used
3. Managing people, especially members of the evaluation team, so that everyone does his or her job well
4. Managing data collection so that the data have integrity and credibility
5. Managing relationships with people who provide data (program participants, program staff, administrators, program information systems personnel) so that they feel treated with respect, cooperate with the evaluation, and form and communicate a positive impression of how the evaluation is conducted
6. Managing the unexpected so that difficulties get dealt with early before they become a crisis that seriously damages the evaluation. Something will go wrong. Unexpected challenges will emerge. Stay close enough to the action to spot these problems sooner rather than later—and take action accordingly.

The basic message is that it's not enough to have an excellent, well-conceived, and agreed-on evaluation plan. That plan has to be implemented. Just as failures in program implementation often undermine good program ideas, failures in evaluation execution can undermine a well-conceived, utilization-focused evaluation design. "Execution Trumps

EXHIBIT 13.1

Critical Evaluation Management Checklist Factors

- ❑ Delivery schedule: What is the schedule of evaluation services and products?
- ❑ Access to data: What existing data may the evaluators use, and what new data may they obtain?
- ❑ Responsibility and authority: Have the system personnel and evaluators agreed on what persons and groups have both the responsibility and authority to perform the various evaluation tasks?
- ❑ Budget: What is the structure of the budget? Is it sufficient but reasonable, and how will it be monitored?
- ❑ Allocation of resources: Have the resources for the evaluation been appropriately distributed across data collection, analysis, and reporting, placing the most effort on the most important information requirements?
- ❑ Finances: What is the schedule of payments for the evaluation, and who will provide the funds?
- ❑ Data gathering: How will the data-gathering plan be implemented, and who will gather the data?
- ❑ Data storage and retrieval: What format, procedures, and facilities will be used to store and retrieve the data?
- ❑ Attention to trade-offs: How will the evaluation address trade-offs between comprehensiveness and selectivity in collecting, organizing, analyzing, interpreting, and reporting information?
- ❑ Work management: What oversight and control will be administered to assure that evaluators devote time and effort, as well as their reputations, to the evaluation?
- ❑ Facilities: What space, equipment, and materials will be available to support the evaluation?
- ❑ Data-gathering schedule: What instruments will be administered, to what groups, according to what schedule?
- ❑ Maintaining focus: Are there sufficient safeguards to prevent gathering extraneous information?
- ❑ Reporting schedule: What reports will be provided, to what audiences, according to what schedule?
- ❑ Realistic expectations: Have appropriate steps been taken to help stakeholders develop realistic expectations considering available financial, time, and personnel resources?

SOURCE: Based on *Evaluation Plans and Operations Checklist* (Stufflebeam, 1999a). For the full checklist: http://www.wmich.edu/evalctr/wp-content/uploads/2010/05/plans_operations1.pdf

Strategy, Every Time" was the title of a speech given to the philanthropic Evaluation Roundtable by Dr. Steven Schroeder (2002), former president of the Robert Wood Johnson Foundation as he recounted his efforts to eradicate tobacco use in the United States. Implementing good ideas had proved more difficult than generating good ideas, he recounted.

For many years, the importance of strategic planning and strategy development received primary emphasis in the business world, but recent books have emphasized the importance of execution, as in these best-selling titles:

Execution: The Discipline of Getting Things Done (Bossidy & Charan, 2002)

Execution Premium: Linking Strategy to Operations for Competitive Advantage (Kaplan & Norton, 2008)

Execution Revolution: Solving the One Business Problem That Makes Solving All Other Problems Easier (Harpst, 2008)

The general principle, then, is to manage evaluation data collection thoughtfully and diligently to ensure high-quality findings. The specific utilization-focused principle is to manage the process and solve inevitable problems with an eye to how such problem solving affects use. For example, adapting the design to the realities of fieldwork can change what primary intended users expect the findings to include. There may be problems getting access to certain records or key people. Scheduling problems and delays in administering questionnaires may arise. There may be missing data or even lost data. In all of these cases, decisions will have to be made to adapt the evaluation plan to what actually happens in the field. I hasten to add that such adaptations are par for the course. In 40 years I can't remember any evaluation plan that has unfolded exactly as planned. The point is to monitor how things are unfolding, get on top of problems early—and *keep primary intended users informed of what's happening,* what adjustments are being made, and why.

Managing Participatory Approaches to Data Collection

Managing data collection controlled by an evaluator or research team is one thing. Managing participatory approaches to data collection is a whole other ball game, a completely different kettle of fish, a horse of a different color, a . . .—pick any metaphor that says to you, this is a different matter entirely. Because it is.

Step 6 discussed process use as an evaluation option. Process use involves conducting the evaluation so as to build evaluation capacity among those involved, support active engagement at every stage of the process, including data collection and analysis, and help people learn about evaluation by doing evaluation. When participatory approaches to data collection are involved, managing the process extends beyond focusing on high-quality data collection to facilitating the active involvement of nonresearchers in data collection to support high-quality learning. Here are some examples.

- Participants in a leadership development program do round-robin interviews with each other as part of data collection. Bill interviews Sue, who interviews Abdul, who interviews Kaiya, who interviews Danielle, who interviews Jose, and so forth, back to Bill. The evaluator works with the participants to construct the interview, offers some interview training, creates a protocol for writing case studies based on the interviews, and monitors and supports the process, but actual data collection and writing the case studies is done by the program participants.

- Program staff in an adult education program for recent immigrants engages in monthly reflective practice sessions in which they report mini-case examples of their experiences with participants. The evaluator is a coach and co-facilitator of the reflective practice process, but participants take primary responsibility for choosing focused topics for reflection, capturing the stories, and identifying key themes. (For details on reflective practice as a participatory evaluation process, see Patton, 2011, pp. 265–275.)
- Young people in a youth engagement program help design a questionnaire to assess needs in their community. They go door-to-door in pairs to administer the questionnaire to residents. The evaluator helps with questionnaire design and trains the young people in how to collect the data. This gives them a direct experience with data collection, reduces the costs of getting data, and deepens their sense of ownership of the findings. (For examples of youth participatory evaluation see Campbell-Patton & Patton, 2010; Flores, 2003, 2007; McCabe & Horsley, 2008; Sherrod, Torney-Purta, & Flanagan, 2010.)
- Villagers in Bogui on the Ouagadougou-Niamey road 10 kilometers east of Fada'Gourma in Burkina Faso keep track of children sick with diarrhea using match sticks. Half of the villagers are using water from a new well while the other half use water as they have done traditionally from a nearby pond. The villagers participate in monitoring differences in illnesses and deciding if any measured differences are significant. This is an example of *participatory learning for responsive development evaluation* (Salmen & Kane, 2006).
- Farmers in India participate in data collection in an agricultural development initiative by keeping *seasonal calendars* (Bamberger, Rugh, & Mabry, 2006, pp. 100, 102). On a monthly basis farmers track and report on indicators like rainfall, what was planted, any chemicals used, what was harvested, labor used, water sources, market prices for agricultural products, and any diseases experienced in crops. A chart is drawn on paper or on the ground marking the months. Participants are then asked to place stones or seeds to indicate the months with, for example, the highest incidence of food shortages, sales of crops, and insect damage in storage. With facilitated discussion led by the evaluator, farmers learn to analyze patterns that affect productivity and use the information with agricultural extension staff to plan future improvements in the development initiative.
- Welfare recipients in a welfare-to-work program keep journals of critical incidents they experience in their job searches. Their journal entries are shared in program support sessions and also provide evaluation data about their experiences and the results of their job searches. The evaluators provide training in journaling and provide encouragement and support to participants to maintain the journals. The evaluators also help facilitate conversations about patterns across the diverse journal entries as part of the participatory evaluation learning experience.

As these examples hopefully make clear, the management and facilitation tasks involved in participatory approaches to data collection are significantly different from those in which evaluators and researchers collect all the data. Australian action researcher Yoland Wadsworth is one of the world's most experienced authorities on participatory research and evaluation processes. She pioneered participatory evaluation circles of inquiry among residents and staff in a psychiatric hospital in an effort that extended over several years. The mammoth nature of the work involved is merely hinted at in the characteristics of the participatory model that she developed and implemented with the program staff and consumers of mental health services. These elements included:

1. A quality assurance/quality improvement framework that all agreed to use.
2. Two-way staff–consumer communication and dialogue about what was happening in the mental health facility instead of just one-way consumer feedback.
3. Using numerous methods, in many sites, with many elements of resourcing, involving many staff, across the whole organizational network and bureaucracy instead of just producing a satisfaction survey.
4. Using *multiple* consumer feedback and communication methods: for example, exit interviews as patients left and case study narratives of service usage.
5. Doing data collection with consumer and staff participation in three kinds of sites: decision-making sites, consumer-only sites, and staff–consumer dialogue sites.
6. Including data collection and dialogue at the "hardest' spots" (the acute unit and other high-risk situations) instead of focusing only on the "easier" community-based areas.
7. Providing support resources infrastructure (personal peer supports: e.g., pair teaming), check-ins and check-outs, incident debriefing, mentoring, networking, and discretionary funds for additional flexible and responsive ad hoc costs for data collection and engagement (Wadsworth, 2010, pp. 211–212).

The overall participatory effort was aimed at systemic, holistic culture change toward regular staff–consumer collaboration around seeking and acting together on evaluative feedback. Given the comprehensive nature of both the change process and multiple data collection dimensions, effective project management was critical to maintain momentum, demonstrate utility, and keep it all from becoming overwhelming to all involved.

Undergirding this kind of participatory data collection is an astute and realistic assessment of what participants can handle. Engage participants too little and the effort may reek of tokenism. Involve them too much and the data collection can overwhelm them or interfere with program participation. Finding the appropriate and useful level of participation in data collection, and then managing that participation effectively and efficiently, are the central challenges of participatory evaluation approaches. Done well, participatory evaluation enhances use, deepens learning, and builds organizational capacity for ongoing evaluation. Done poorly, it can annoy all involved. As writer Paul Dickson (2010, p. 1) has advised:

> Never try to teach a pig to sing;
> it wastes your time and it annoys the pig.

"The sound effects, choreography and costumes were spectacular! I can't wait for the final de-briefing."

Keeping Primary Intended Users Informed About How Things Are Going

Research studies on useful evaluations turn up this finding again and again: *Avoid surprises.*

- The Treasury Board of Canada (2002) reviewed 15 major Canadian evaluations identifying "drivers of effective evaluations" that "were felt, by both the evaluation staff and the program staff, to have contributed significantly to making the evaluations useful and worthwhile." One of their recommendations: *Ensure that there are no last-minute surprises.*
- The World Bank (2004) synthesized lessons from influential evaluations that improved performance and impacts of development programs. One lesson was: *Keep key stakeholders informed*

of the progress of the evaluation. "There should be no surprises when evaluation findings are presented" (p. 22). Related lessons included that "key results must often be communicated informally before the final report is completed," "findings must be delivered in time to affect decisions," "a successful evaluation must adapt to the context within which it will be used," and "the evaluator must understand when and how the findings can most effectively be used" (p. 22).

- The longer the evaluation, the more important it is to work to keep key stakeholders engaged. The 2009 Outstanding Evaluation Award from the American Evaluation Association went to a 10-year experimental abstinence education evaluation. The evaluation included a technical workgroup of key stakeholders. Ongoing attention to stakeholder relations was deemed of critical importance to the evaluation's credibility and use, both because of the length of the evaluation and its controversial subject matter. The evaluators concluded that "making sure that you constantly engage them is important. . . . We gave them briefings and we gave them preliminary results. When we released the report, we used quotations from some of them" (Brandon, Smith, Trenholm, & Devaney, 2010, p. 526).

In our study of the use of federal health evaluations (Patton, 2008), we asked about how surprises affected use. We found that minor surprises on peripheral questions created only minor problems, but major surprises on central questions were unwelcome. One decision maker we interviewed made the point that a "good" evaluation process should build in feedback mechanisms to primary users.

> Evaluation isn't a birthday party, so people aren't looking for surprises. If you're coming up with data that are different than the conventional wisdom, a good evaluation effort, I would suggest, would get those ideas floated during the evaluation process so that when the final report comes out, they aren't a surprise. Now, you could come up with findings contrary to the conventional wisdom, but you ought to be sharing those ideas with the people being evaluated during the evaluation process and working on acceptance. If you present a surprise, it will tend to get rejected. See, we don't want surprises. We don't like surprises around here.

So, what kinds of things do key stakeholders need to be informed about during data collection? Exhibit 13.2 provides 10 examples. The trick is to keep them sufficiently informed to maintain interest and engagement without making the updates a burden.

Providing Feedback and Reporting Interim Findings

It is worth distinguishing feedback from interim findings. Feedback, in this context, is what you tell people from whom you're gathering data and program staff at the end of a site visit. Feedback can be as specific and timely as telling someone you're interviewing that their responses are helpful. Interviewees value such acknowledgement and feedback. They have no way of knowing if their responses are relevant and useful unless they are given feedback during the interview. This doesn't bias their subsequent responses. It makes them more

EXHIBIT 13.2

Ten Examples of Updates to Intended Users During Data Collection

1. Did you get access to important data? Evaluators seeking access to management information system data, government statistics, or program records often encounter unanticipated obstacles. Primary intended users should be informed of both successes and obstacles, and may be able to help with the latter.

2. How is the response rate unfolding? For example, surveys often involve an initial request with two follow-up requests aimed at increasing the response rate. The response rate will be key to the credibility of findings.

3. How is the time line for data collection working out? Evaluation designs typically include schedules for data collection. Delays in data collection can affect time lines and use. Let intended users know about delays sooner rather than later.

4. How are key informants responding to interviews? Key informants are typically knowledgeable and influential people whose opinions matter. In seeking their perspective on key evaluation issues, they will form a perspective about the evaluation itself. Interviewers can usually tell whether key informants are interested, helpful, resistant, suspicious, apathetic, or engaged—or all of these things during a long interview. On large projects with multiple interviewers, I follow up by e-mail with key informants to get their reactions to the interview process. If I'm the interviewer, I give them the e-mail address of the chair of the primary user evaluation task force or group and invite them to share reactions to the interview. This opportunity to play a quality control and feedback role keeps primary intended users engaged—and adds a meaningful layer of direct utility as they play this role.

5. How are focus groups unfolding? Focus groups can involve lots of logistics. Not everyone shows up. Some come late and others leave early. Incentives are often provided that create reactions. Unexpected discussions can occur when focus group participants come together. Key evaluation stakeholders appreciate getting tidbits about how focus groups are working.

6. How is the random assignment of target groups to experimental and control conditions working out? If a randomized control trial is the design of choice, smooth implementation is critical to the credibility of findings. Random assignment can be tough to implement. Once completed, the first test is whether the treatment and control groups are equivalent on important background variables. Share that information with primary intended users. It gives an early heads-up about how the design is unfolding.

7. What's the level of "experimental mortality"? Experimental mortality is the friendly term for losing people during an experiment. There are usually some people who drop out of program interventions as well as the control or comparison group. The issue for credibility is what proportion drop out and how they are distributed between treatment and comparison groups. Even in nonexperimental designs that use pre- and posttests, some people who complete

the pretest fail to complete the posttest. The "mortality" rate among respondents is an early indicator of the quality of the findings.

8. What's going as planned during data collection? Sometimes evaluators only communicate with intended users when there are problems and delays. Don't just communicate bad news. Hopefully—HOPEFULLY!—some things will actually unfold as planned. Successful implementation of the evaluation plan is not just success for the evaluator. It's also success for the primary intended users who were involved in developing the plan.
9. What early findings are emerging? Interim findings must clearly be labeled as interim and preliminary—and not appropriate for wider dissemination. But intended users typically welcome early results on key questions as they emerge. Be sure to follow up quickly as those preliminary findings are confirmed or revised.
10. When will findings be ready for discussion and sharing? Keep critical dates for engagement with the intended users before them. Key stakeholders are typically busy, juggling lots of commitments. Alerting them sufficiently in advance of a critical meeting or conference call about findings will help ensure their involvement in interpreting findings. This prepares them to be involved in supporting and facilitating use.

---

likely to be thoughtful in subsequent responses. Skilled interviewing involves offering appropriate and respectful feedback during the interview (Patton, 2002, chap. 7).

Site Visit Feedback

Feedback to program staff at the end of site visit, at completion of a set of interviews, or after program observations is another matter altogether. Evaluation induces anxiety. When program staff members know that participants are being interviewed or see an evaluator observing them, they are understandably anxious. Some evaluators believe that their independence and objectivity require maintaining distance. They do their site visits and tell program staff that they'll get a copy of the evaluation report when it is done. I consider such behavior disrespectful and insensitive, and it is easily experienced as arrogant. In contrast, aware of process use opportunities, a utilization-focused evaluator wants to create positive regard for evaluation, including among those who provide data and those who may feel they are the object of the evaluation (program staff and leadership). Thus, three kinds of feedback are appropriate, respectful and even useful.

1. Offer a reminder about the purpose of and time lines for the evaluation, with special emphasis on where the site visit just completed fits into the overall data collection of the evaluation; this information will have been communicated in setting up the site visit or interviews, but should be reiterated on site.

2. Explain the data collection details: sampling approach, questions being asked, design being used, and nature of the analysis to be done. Explain these features without jargon. Program participants and staff are not researchers. They won't readily know about how data are collected and analyzed. Be prepared to provide a straightforward explanation. For example, instead of just saying, "We interviewed a random probability sample" and watching eyes glaze over, say:

> We chose the participants we interviewed randomly, like drawing the names out of a hat, so we didn't pick people to interview for any special reason. We wanted to get a balanced picture from a variety of participants, so that's why we chose people randomly. Does that make sense? I'd be happy to answer questions about how we chose who to interview. We're using the same process in all the program sites where we're interviewing people.

3. Provide some specific feedback about the emergent findings, if possible and appropriate. This can be a chance to clarify something observed as well as provide a sense of what the data revealed. For example, after observing an employment program for 3 days and interviewing 20 participants, I met with the program director and senior staff to debrief the site visit. I reported:

> Participants were quite responsive during the interviews and seemed to appreciate the opportunity to tell their stories. Many expressed appreciation that this program exists and that the staff is supportive. They generally reported that they are learning new skills and hopeful about getting jobs, but are anxious about what kind of on-the-job follow-up help they will get from the program, if any. What is your relationship with participants after they graduate? Many of them seem unsure about this.

In this debriefing, I'm both providing a general sense of the findings and using the debrief to clarify an ambiguous issue that arose during the interviews.

Reporting Interim Findings to Primary Intended Users

Feedback to and debriefs with program staff are part of the process of data collection and help them understand the evaluation's purpose and focus as well as providing immediate information about what the evaluation is uncovering. Reporting interim findings to primary intended users has a different purpose: keeping them engaged and preparing for interpretation and use of the eventual findings. Collaborating with primary users means that evaluators should not wait until they have a highly polished final report to share some findings. Evaluators who prefer to work diligently in the solitude of their offices until they can spring a final report on a waiting world may find that the world has passed them by.

Different kinds of interim reports match different evaluation purposes and questions. Formative reporting will focus on potential areas of improvement and is most useful as part of a process of thinking about a program rather than as a one-time information dump. In the more formal environment of a major summative evaluation, the final report will involve high stakes so primary intended users will want early alerts about the likely implication of findings for a program's future. Accountability-focused evaluation will typically focus on whether implementation and outcome targets are being met and whether resources have been allocated and used appropriately. Here again, early alerts about potential problems and advance reports on the direction of findings will be appreciated by intended users. In contrast, developmental evaluation is designed for ongoing, timely feedback, and may not even produce a final report. Thus, interim reporting depends on the evaluation's purpose, time lines, and stakes. That said, the overall themes are keeping intended users interested and engaged—and avoiding surprises. Surprise attacks may make for good war strategy, but in evaluation, the surprise attack does little to add credence to a study. Here are three tips for interim reporting.

1. Emphasize in headlines the *interim* and *confidential* nature of the findings. Let intended users know that you're giving them an early look at some emerging results, but such findings are not ready to be shared widely and are far from definitive.

2. Keep interim reporting limited to one to three findings on important issues. Interim reports should be short and focused, no more than bullet points.

3. The longer the data collection period, the more important it is to find ways to keep intended users updated. Some evaluations are completed in 3 to 6 months; one interim report would suffice. In contrast, the abstinence education evaluation discussed earlier took 10 years to complete. Interim reports on how data collection was proceeding and baseline indicators would gradually yield, over time, to interim reports on overall results.

Gather Data With Ongoing Attention to Use

The basic message of this chapter is that strategizing about use continues throughout data collection. I've offered a few suggestions, examples, and ideas for ongoing engagement with primary intended users during data collection, but these are meant to be illuminative rather than definitive or exhaustive. Each evaluation is different. The overall principle is to analyze your situation and develop ways of maintaining momentum toward use. This includes (1) effective management of the data collection process to enhance the evaluation's credibility, (2) effectively implementing any agreed-on participatory approaches to data collection that build capacity and support process use, (3) keeping primary intended users informed about how things are going so as to maintain interest and engagement, and (4) providing timely feedback and reporting emergent and interim findings.

Parting Shot

One final point: Be attentive to turnover among primary intended users. The longer data collection takes, the more likely it becomes that one or more intended users may move on to other things. When turnover occurs, don't delay connecting with any replacement intended user or key stakeholder. Bring them up to date. Get their buy-in. Connect them with the continuing intended users. Make this a priority. The primary intended users are the pathway to use.

Checklist details about what is involved in each step are provided in the summary *U-FE Checklist* in the concluding chapter. See pages 418–420 for the checklist items for Step 13 discussed in this chapter.

PRACTICE EXERCISES

1. Assess your project management skills. What are you good at? What are your management weaknesses? Make a plan to build on your strengths and improve in areas of weakness. Remember: Research design and data collection skills are not enough. Effective, timely project management can make or break an evaluation.

2. Create a classic evaluation scenario in which you are conducting a 3-year evaluation with 1 ½ years of formative evaluation followed by 1 ½ years of summative evaluation. Describe the program and primary intended users. Generate an interim feedback and reporting plan for both the formative and summative evaluation. Discuss and explain the similarities and differences.

3. Describe an evaluation in which you're doing in-depth interviews with participants in a program. Identify several major open-ended interview questions you would ask. Now, write out a script for how you provide appropriate feedback to the interviewee during the interview. Give three examples of what you consider appropriate feedback. Also give three examples of what you would consider inappropriate feedback, comments that might bias the interview, make the interviewee uncomfortable, or otherwise impede the quality of the data collection process.

14

Organize and Present the Data for Interpretation and Use by Primary Intended Users

Analysis, Interpretation, Judgment, and Recommendations

When it comes to evidence, what is believable to one analyst is incredible to another. Evidence may be hard or soft, conflicting or incontrovertible, it may be unpersuasive or convincing, exculpatory or damning, but with whatever qualifier it is presented, the noun evidence is neutral: it means "a means of determining whether an assertion is truthful or an allegation is a fact."

William Safire,
political linguist and New York Times *columnist (2006, p. 18)*

A Framework for Engaging Findings

What? What are the findings? What do the data say?

So what? What do the findings mean? Making interpretations and judgments

Now what? Action implications and recommendations

Four distinct processes are involved in making sense out of evaluation findings:

(1) *Analysis* involves organizing raw data into an understandable form that reveals basic patterns and constitutes the evaluation's empirical findings, thereby answering the *what?* question.

(2) *Interpretation* involves determining the significance of and explanations for the findings; this is part one of the *so what?* question.

(3) *Judgment* brings values to bear to determine merit, worth, and significance, including the extent to which the results are positive or negative; this is part two of the *so what?* question.

(4) *Recommendations* involve determining the action implications of the findings. This means answering the *so what?* question.

Primary intended users should be actively involved in all four of these processes so that they fully understand and buy into the findings and their implications. Facilitating these processes involves helping intended users understand these four fundamental distinctions. Exhibit 14.1 summarizes this framework. We'll now consider each of these processes in greater depth.

EXHIBIT 14.1

A Utilization-Focused Framework for Engaging Findings

Four distinct processes are involved in helping primary intended users make sense out of evaluation findings. This involves answering the basic questions: What? So what? Now what?

1. *What was found?* Present basic findings. This involves description and analysis, essentially organizing raw data, both quantitative and qualitative, into a form that reveals basic patterns so that primary intended users can understand the findings and make sense of the evaluation evidence generated by the data.
2. *So what does it mean?* This involves making *interpretations.* The evaluator facilitates interpreting the findings with primary intended users. Help them ask: What do the results mean? What's the significance of the findings? Why did the findings turn out this way? What are possible explanations of the results? Interpretations *go beyond the data* to add context, determine meaning, and tease out substantive significance.

3. Add *judgments* about what the findings mean: *So what?* (part 2). Values are added to analysis and interpretations to make judgments. Judging merit, worth, and significance means determining the extent to which results are positive or negative. What is good or bad, desirable or undesirable, in the findings? To what extent have standards of desirability been met?

4. *Recommendations: Now what?* The final step (if agreed to be undertaken) adds action to analysis, interpretation, and judgment. What should be done? What are the action implications of the findings? Only recommendations that follow from and are grounded in the data ought to be formulated.

* * * * *

The graphic below depicts the interrelationships among these four dimensions of evaluation sense-making. The three fundamental questions—What? So what? Now what?—are connected to the four evaluation processes of (1) organizing basic findings, (2) making interpretations, (3) rendering judgments, and (4) generating recommendations.

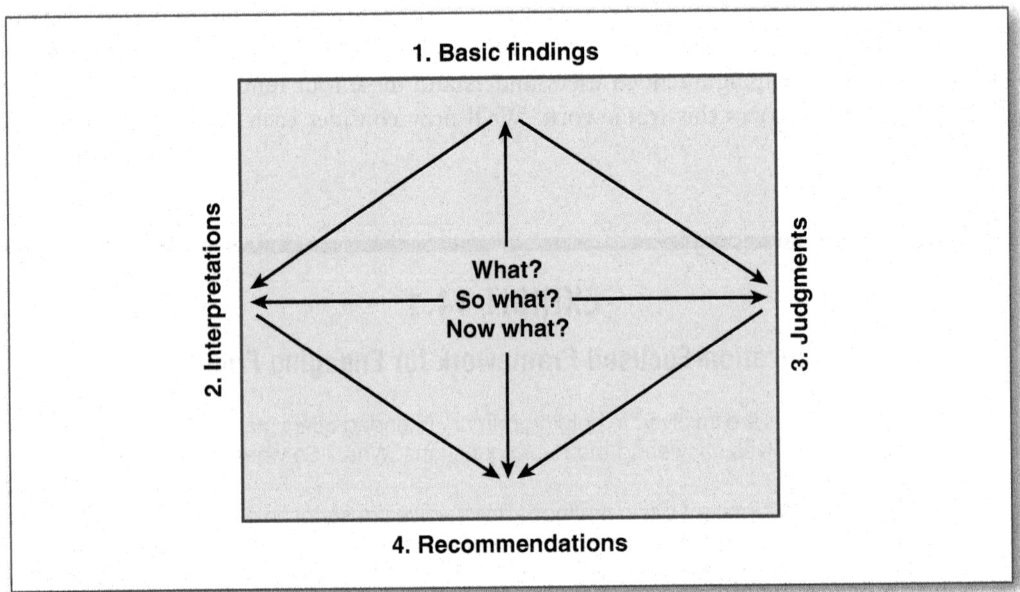

Arranging Data for Ease of Interpretation: Focusing the Analysis

Unless one is a genius, it is best to aim at being intelligible.

Sir Anthony Hope (1863–1933)

The first analytical task in evaluation is assembling and organizing the evidence to answer priority evaluation questions. Once presented, evidence can then be interpreted and a judgment rendered. In working with primary intended users, aim for the simplest presentation that will handle the facts. Evaluators may need and use sophisticated statistical techniques to enhance analytic power or uncover nuances in data, but understandable presentations are needed to give decision makers who are not researchers access to evaluation findings. Certainly, an evaluator can use sophisticated techniques to confirm the strength and meaningfulness of discovered patterns, but the next step is to think creatively about how to organize those findings into a straightforward and understandable format. This means, for example, that the results of a regression analysis might be reduced to nothing more complex than a chi-square table or a set of descriptive statistics (percentages and means). This need not distort the presentation. Quite the contrary, it will usually focus and highlight the most important findings while allowing the evaluator to explain in a footnote or appendix the more sophisticated techniques that were used to confirm the findings.

Our presentations must be like the skilled acrobat who makes the most dazzling moves look easy, the audience being unaware of the long hours of practice and the sophisticated calculations involved in what appear to be simple movements. Likewise, skilled evaluators craft and polish their presentations so that those participating will quickly understand the results, unaware of the long hours of arduous work involved in sifting through the data, organizing it, arranging it, testing relationships, taking the data apart, and creatively putting it back together to arrive at that moment of public unveiling. Here are seven tips for organizing and presenting findings.

1. **Answer the primary evaluation questions.** This would seem like a no-brainer, especially since Step 7 is focusing the priority evaluation questions with primary intended users. But some evaluators seem to get distracted and fail to keep the priority questions as the focus of analysis.

2. **Keep it simple.** This is also known as the KISS principle: *Keep it simple, stupid.* But evaluators being sensitive, diplomatic, and smart, we'll stick to KIS. Simplicity as a virtue means that we are rewarded not for how much we complicate the analysis or impress with our expertise, but for how much we enlighten. It means that we make users feel they can master what is before them, rather than intimidating them with our own knowledge and sophistication. It means distinguishing the complexity of analysis from the clarity of presentation and using the former to inform and guide the latter. Simplicity as a virtue is not simple. It often involves more work and creativity to simplify than blithely rest contented with a presentation of complicated statistics as they originally emerged from analysis.

Providing descriptive statistics in a report means more than simply reproducing the results in raw form. Data need to be arranged, ordered, and organized in some reasonable format that permits decision makers to detect patterns. Consider the three presentations of data shown in Exhibit 14.2. Each presents data from the same survey items, but the focus and degree of complexity are different in each case.

The first presentation reports items in the order in which they appeared on the survey with percentages for every category of response. It is difficult to detect patterns with 40 numbers to examine, so primary intended users will be overwhelmed by the first presentation. The second presentation simplifies the results by dividing the scale at the midpoint and reducing the four categories to two. Sometimes, such an analysis would be very

EXHIBIT 14.2

Three Presentations of the Same Data

Presentation 1: Raw results presented in the same order as items appeared in the survey.

Expressed Needs of 478 Physically Disabled People	*Great Need for This*	*Much Need*	*Some Need*	*Little Need*
Transportation	35%	36%	13%	16%
Housing	33	38	19	10
Educational opportunities	42	28	9	21
Medical care	26	45	25	4
Employment opportunities	58	13	6	23
Public understanding	47	22	15	16
Architectural changes	33	38	10	19
Direct financial aid	40	31	12	17
Changes in insurance regulations	29	39	16	16
Social opportunities	11	58	17	14

Presentation 2: Results combined into two categories. No priorities emerge.		
	Great or much need	*Some or little need*
Transportation	71%	29%
Housing	71	29
Educational opportunities	70	30
Medical care	71	29
Employment opportunities	71	29
Public understanding	69	31
Architectural changes in buildings	71	29
Direct financial assistance	71	29
Changes in insurance regulations	68	32
Social opportunities	69	31

Presentation 3: Utilization-focused results arranged in rank order by "Great Need" to highlight priorities.	
Rank order	*Great need for this*
Employment opportunities	58%
Public understanding	47
Educational opportunities	42
Direct financial assistance	40
Transportation	35
Housing	33
Architectural changes in buildings	33
Changes in insurance regulations	29
Medical care	26
Social opportunities	11

revealing, but, in this case, no priorities emerge. Since *determining priorities was the purpose of the survey,* decision makers would conclude from the second presentation that the survey had not been useful.

The third presentation arranges the data so that decision makers can immediately see respondents' priorities. Support for employment programs now ranks first as a great need (58%) in contrast to social programs (11%), rated lowest in priority. Users can go down the list and decide where to draw the line on priorities, perhaps after "direct financial assistance" (40%). Failure to arrange the data as displayed in the third presentation places decision makers at an analytical disadvantage. Presentation three is utilization-focused because it facilitates quick understanding of and engagement with the results for their intended purpose: setting priorities for programs supporting people with disabilities.

This same principle applies to qualitative data. A single synthesis case study that captures and communicates major findings will focus the attention of intended users. The more detailed case studies on which the synthesis is based should be available as evidence for the validity of the synthesis, but for purposes of making sense of qualitative data, a summary of major themes and a synthesis case example will make the findings manageable.

3. **Provide balance.** The counterpoint to valuing simplicity is that evaluation findings are seldom really simple. In striving for simplicity, be careful to avoid simplemindedness. This happens most often when results are boiled down, in the name of simplicity, to some single number—a single percentage, a single cost-benefit ratio, a single proportion of the variance explained, or a significance test level. Balance and fairness should not be sacrificed to achieve simplicity. Multiple perspectives and conflicting findings have to be represented through several different numbers, all of them presented in an understandable fashion. Much advertising is based on the deception of picking the one number that puts a product in the best light, for example, gas mileage instead of price. Politicians often pick the statistic that favors their predetermined position.

An example comes from a study of Internal Revenue Service (IRS) audits conducted by the U.S. Government Accountability Office. The cover page of the report carried the sensational headline that IRS audits in five selected districts missed $1 million in errors in four months. The IRS response pointed out that those same audits had uncovered over $26 million in errors that led to adjustments in tax. Thus, the $1 million represented only about 4% of the total amount of money involved. Moreover, the IRS disputed the GAO's $1 million error figure because the GAO included all potential audit items whereas the IRS ignored differences of $100 or less, which are routinely ignored as not worth pursuing. Finally, the $1 million error involves cases of two types: instances in which additional tax would be due to the IRS and instances in which a refund would be due the taxpayer from the IRS. In point of fact, the $1 million in errors would have resulted in virtually no additional revenue to the government had all the errors been detected and corrected.

The gross simplification of the evaluation findings and the headlining of the $1 million error represent considerable distortion of the full picture. *Simplicity at the expense of accuracy is no virtue; complexity in the service of accuracy is no vice.* The point is to present complex matters in ways that achieve both clarity and balance.

4. **Be clear about definitions.** Confusion or uncertainty about what was actually measured can lead to misinterpretations. In workshops on data analysis I give the participants statistics on farmers, families, and juvenile offender recidivism. In small groups the participants interpret the data. Almost invariably they jump right into analysis without asking how farmer was defined, how family was defined, or what recidivism actually meant in the data at hand. A simple term like "farmer" turns out to be enormously variable in meaning. When does the weekend gardener become a farmer, and when does the large commercial farm become an "agribusiness"? A whole division of the Census Bureau wrestles with these definitional challenges.

Defining "family" is quite complex. There was a time, not so long ago, when Americans may have shared a common definition of family. Now there is real question about who has to be together under what arrangement before they constitute a family. Single-parent families, foster families, same-sex civil unions or marriages, and extended families are just a few of the possible complications. Before interpreting any statistics on families, it would be critical to know how family was defined.

Measuring recidivism is common in evaluation, but the term offers a variety of definitions and measures. Recidivism may mean (1) a new arrest, (2) a new appearance in court, (3) a new conviction, (4) a new sentence, (5) or actually committing a new crime regardless of whether the offender is apprehended. The statistics will vary considerably depending on which definition of recidivism is used.

A magazine cartoon I like shows a group of researchers studying cartoon violence. As they watch a television cartoon, one asks: "When the coyote bounces after falling off the cliff, does the second time he hits the ground count as a second incidence of violence?" Of such decisions are statistics made. But widespread skepticism about statistics ("lies and damn lies") is all the more reason for evaluators to exercise care in making sure that data are useful, accurate, and understandable. Clear definitions provide the foundation for utility, accuracy, and understandability.

5. **Make comparisons carefully and appropriately.**

> *Noncomparative evaluations are comparatively useless.*
>
> *Michael Scriven (1993, p. 58)*

Virtually all evaluative analysis ends up in some way being comparative. Numbers presented in isolation, without a frame of reference or basis of comparison, seldom make much sense. A recidivism rate of 40% is a relatively meaningless statistic. Is that high or low? Does that represent improvement or deterioration? An error of $1 million in tax audits is a meaningless number. Some basis of comparison or standard of judgment is needed in order to interpret such statistics. The challenge lies in selecting the appropriate basis of comparison. In the earlier example of the IRS audit, the GAO evaluators believed the appropriate comparison was an error of zero dollars—absolute perfection in auditing. The IRS considered such a standard unrealistic and suggested, instead, comparing errors against the total amount of corrections made in all audits.

Skepticism can undermine evaluation when the basis for the comparison appears arbitrary or unfair. Working with users to select appropriate comparisons involves considering a number of options. Menu 14.1 presents 10 possibilities for making comparisons. Evaluators should work with stakeholders to decide which comparisons are appropriate and relevant to give a full and balanced view of what results are being achieved.

MENU 14.1

Menu of Program Comparisons

The outcomes of a program can be compared to

1. The outcomes of selected "similar" programs
2. The outcomes of the same program the previous year (or any other trend period, e.g, quarterly reports)
3. The outcomes of a representative or random sample of programs in the field
4. The outcomes of special programs of interest, for example, those known to be exemplary models (a purposeful sample comparison, Patton, 2002, pp. 230–234)
5. The stated goals of the program
6. Participants' goals for themselves
7. External standards of desirability as developed by the profession
8. Standards of minimum acceptability: for example, basic licensing or accreditation standards
9. Ideals of program performance
10. Guesses made by staff or other decision makers about what the outcomes would be

Combinations of these comparisons are also possible and usually desirable.

Consider the new jogger or running enthusiast. At the beginning, runners are likely to use as a basis for comparison their previously sedentary lifestyle. By that standard, the initial half-mile run appears pretty good. Then the runner discovers that there are a lot of other people running, many of them covering 3, 5, or 10 miles a week. Compared to seasoned joggers, the runner's half-mile doesn't look so good. On days when new runners want to feel particularly good, they may compare themselves to all the people who don't run at all. On days when they need some incentive to push harder, they may compare themselves to people who run twice as far as they do. Some adopt medical standards for basic conditioning, something on the order of 30 minutes of sustained and intense exercise a least three times a week. Some measure their progress in miles, others in minutes or hours. Some compare themselves to friends; others get involved in official competitions and races. All these comparisons are valid, but each yields a different conclusion because the basis of comparison is different in each case, as is the purpose of each comparison.

In politics it is said that conservatives compare the present to the past and see all the things that have been lost, while liberals compare the present to what could be in the future and see all the things yet to be attained. Each basis of comparison provides a different perspective. Fascination with comparisons undergirds sports, politics, advertising, management, and certainly, evaluation.

6. **Decide what is significant: Identify and focus on important and rigorous claims.** The level of evidence needed in an evaluation involves determining just what level of certainty is required to make findings useful. One way of meeting this challenge is to engage with primary stakeholders, especially program funders, administrators, and staff, about *making claims.* I ask: "Having reviewed the data, what can you claim about the program?" I then ask them to list possible claims; for example, (1) participants like the program, (2) participants get jobs as a result of the program, (3) the drop-out rate is low, (4) changes in participants last over the long term, (5) the program is cost-effective, and (6) the program does not work well with people of color, as examples. Having generated a list of possible claims, I then have them sort the claims into the categories (or cells) shown in Exhibit 14.3. This matrix distinguishes claims by their importance and rigor. Important claims speak to major issues of societal concern. Participants getting and keeping jobs as a result of a training program is a more important claim than that they're satisfied. Rigor concerns the amount and quality of evidence to support claims. The program might have very strong evidence of participant satisfaction, but very weak follow-up data about job retention. The most powerful, useful, and credible claims are those of major importance that have strong empirical support.

This claims framework can also be useful in the design phase to help intended users focus on gathering rigorous data about important issues so that, at the end, the evaluation will be able to report important and strong claims.

EXHIBIT 14.3

Important and Rigorous Claims

		Importance of claims	
		Major	*Minor*
Rigor of claims	Strong	*	
	Weak		

*GOAL: *Strong claims of major importance.*

The most powerful, useful, and credible claims are those that are of major importance and have strong empirical support.

Characteristics of Claims of *Major Importance*

- Involve making a difference, having an impact, or achieving desirable outcomes
- Deals with a problem of great societal concern
- Affects large numbers of people
- Provides a sustainable solution (claim deals with something that lasts over time)
- Saves money
- Saves time: that is, accomplished something in less time than is usually the case (an efficiency claim)
- Enhances quality
- Claims to be "new" or innovative
- Shows that something can actually be done about a problem: that is, claims the problem is malleable
- Involves a model or approach that could be used by others (meaning the model or approach is clearly specified and adaptable to other situations)

Characteristics of *Strong Claims*

- Valid, believable evidence to support the claim
- Follow-up data over time (longer periods of follow-up provide stronger evidence than shorter periods, and any follow-up is stronger than just end-of-program results)
- The claim is about a clear intervention (model or approach) with solid implementation documentation
- The claim is about clearly specified outcomes and impacts:

  Behavior outcomes are stronger than opinions, feelings, and knowledge

- The evidence for claims includes comparisons:
  —*To program goals*
  —*Over time (pretest, posttest, follow-up)*
  —*With other groups*
  —*With general trends or norms*
- The evidence for claims includes replications:
  —*Done at more than one site*
  —*More than one staff person attained outcomes*
  —*Different cohort groups of participants attained comparable outcomes over time*
  —*Different programs attained comparable results using comparable approaches*
- Claims are based on more than one kind of evidence or data (i.e., triangulation of data):
  —*Quantitative and qualitative data*
  —*Multiple sources (e.g., kids, parents, teachers, and staff corroborate results)*
- There are clear, logical, and/or empirical linkages between the intervention and the claimed outcomes
- The evaluators are independent of the staff (or where internal evaluation data are used, an independent, credible person reviews the results and certifies the results)
- Claims are based on systematic data collection over time
- Claims can be triangulated with and are supported by findings from research and other evaluations

CAVEAT: Importance and rigor are not absolute criteria. Different stakeholders, decision makers, and claims makers will have different definitions of what is important and rigorous. What staff deem to be of major importance may not be so to outside observers. What is deemed important and rigorous changes over time and across contexts. Making public claims is a political action. Importance and rigor are, to some extent, politically defined and dependent on the values of specific stakeholders.

One way to strengthen claims is to connect the evaluation's findings to results from other evaluations and triangulate with research findings. Former AEA President Bill Trochim calls the connection between research and evaluation the Golden Spike (Urban & Trochim, 2009).

7. **Distinguish facts from opinion.**

Everyone is entitled to his own opinion, but not his own facts.

Daniel Patrick Moynihan (1927–2003)
United States senator and distinguished social scientist

Moynihan's observation says it all, which takes us to opinions and interpretations.

"So you're anxious about conflicting positive and negative data. I'm afraid you're suffering from Bipolar Findings Disorder, a common evaluator affliction. It's caused by thinking people are rational and that the world makes sense. I can help."

Summary Principles of Analysis

Before turning to interpretations, let's review the seven principles of solid analysis just presented.

1. Answer the priority evaluation questions.
2. Keep the presentation as simple as the data will allow.
3. Be balanced in presenting alternative perspectives and conflicting data.
4. Be clear about definitions of key concepts.
5. Make comparisons carefully and appropriately.
6. Identify and focus on important and rigorous claims.
7. Distinguish facts from opinion.

Interpretations

We have been discussing how to analyze and organize data so that primary intended users can engage the evaluation findings. We turn now from describing the basic findings—answering the *What?* question—to interpretation—the *So what?* question. *Interpretation involves deciding what the findings mean.* How significant are the findings? What explains the results? Even when those receiving evaluation findings agree on the facts and findings, they can disagree vociferously about what the findings *mean.*

The Importance of Interpretive Frameworks

Management scholars Kathleen Sutcliffe and Klaus Weber (2003) examined the performance of business organizations in relation to the amount and accuracy of information used by senior executives as well as the "interpretive frameworks" they used to make sense of information. They concluded that *the way senior executives interpret their business environment is more important for performance than the accuracy of data they have about their environment.* That is, they concluded that there was less value in spending a lot of money increasing the marginal accuracy of data available to senior executives compared to the value of enhancing *their capacity to interpret* whatever data they have. Executives were more limited by a lack of capacity to make sense of data than by inadequate or inaccurate data. In essence, they found that interpretive capacity, or "mind-sets," distinguish high performance more than data quality and accuracy.

Enhancing the quality and accuracy of our evaluation data through better methods and measures will add little value unless those using the data have the capacity to think evaluatively, think critically, and be able to appropriately interpret findings to reach reasonable and supportable conclusions.

In resisting the temptation to bear alone the burden of interpretation, the utilization-focused evaluator views the interpretive process as a training opportunity through which users can become more sophisticated about data-based decision making. Researchers have internalized the differences between analysis and interpretation, but that distinction will need reinforcement for nonresearchers. In working with stakeholders to understand interpretation, four themes deserve special attention.

1. **Numbers and qualitative data must be interpreted to have meaning.** Numbers are neither bad nor good, they're just numbers. Interpretation means thinking about what the data mean and how they ought to be applied. No magic formulas, not even those for

statistical significance, can infuse meaning into data. Only thinking humans can do that. Interpretation is a human process, not a computer process. Statisticians have no corner on the ability to think and reason. The best guideline may be Einstein's dictum that "the important thing is to keep on questioning."

2. Data are imperfect indicators or representations of what the world is like. Just as a map is not the territory it describes, the statistical tables describing a program are not the program. That's why they have to be interpreted.

3. Statistics and qualitative data contain errors. Research offers probabilities, not absolutes. The switch from absolute assertions (things either are or are not) to probabilistic thinking (things are more or less likely) is fundamental to empirical reasoning and careful interpretations.

4. Look for intraocular significance. Fred Mosteller, an esteemed statistician, cautioned against overreliance on statistically significant differences. He was more interested in "interocular differences, *the differences that hit us between the eyes*" (quoted in Scriven, 1993, p. 71).

Different stakeholders will bring varying perspectives to the evaluation. Those perspectives will affect their interpretations. The first task is get agreement on the basic findings—the "facts." Once there is understanding of the findings, the evaluator facilitates interpretation by having participants consider possible interpretations. Then follows the work of seeking convergence—aiming to reach consensus, if possible, on the most reasonable and useful interpretations supported by the data. Where different perspectives prevail, those varying interpretations should be reported and their implications explored. Judgments (discussed later) follow analysis and interpretations.

An Example of a Utilization-Focused Data-Based Deliberation With Stakeholders

In an evaluation of foster group homes for juvenile offenders, we collected data from natural parents, foster parents, juveniles, and community corrections staff. The primary intended users, the Community Corrections Advisory Board, agreed to a findings review process that involved a large number of stakeholders from both the field and policy levels. We had worked closely with the board in problem identification, research design, and instrumentation. Once the data were collected, we employed a variety of statistical techniques, including alpha factor analysis and stepwise forward regression analysis. We then reduced these findings to a few pages in a simplified form and readable format for use at a half-day meeting that included some 40 of the most powerful elected and appointed officials in the county as well as another 160 field professionals and foster parents.

A major purpose of the evaluation was to describe and conceptualize effective foster group homes for juvenile delinquents so that future selection of homes and training of foster parents could be improved. The evaluation was also intended to provide guidance about how to achieve better matches between juvenile offenders and foster parents. We presented findings on how recidivism, runaway rates, and juvenile attitudes varied by different kinds of group home environments. We had measured variations in foster home environments with a 56-item instrument. Factor analysis of these items uncovered a single major factor that explained 54% of the variance in recidivism. *The critical task in data interpretation was to label that factor in such a way that its relationship to dependent variables would represent something meaningful to primary intended users.* We focused the half-day work session on this issue.

The session began with a brief description of the evaluation's methods, then the results were distributed. In randomly assigned groups of four, these diverse stakeholders were asked to look at the factor analysis items and *label the factor or theme represented by those items in their own words.* After the groups reported their distinct labels, discussion followed. Consensus emerged around distinguishing *supportive and caring environments* from *authoritarian and nonsupportive foster home environments.*

The groups then studied tables showing the relationships between this treatment environment factor and program outcome variables (runaway and recidivism rates). The relationships were not only statistically significant but intraocularly so. Juveniles who reported experiencing more supportive foster home environments had markedly lower recidivism rates, lower runaway rates, and more positive attitudes. Having established the direction of the data, we discussed the limitations of the findings, methodological weaknesses, and the impossibility of making firm causal inferences. Key decision makers were already well aware of these problems. Then, given those constraints, the group was asked for recommendations. The basic thrust of the discussion concerned ways to increase the supportive experiences of juvenile offenders. The people carrying on that discussion were the people who fund, set policy for, operate, and control juvenile offender programs. The final written evaluation report included the recommendations that emerged from that meeting as well as our own independent conclusions and recommendations as evaluators. But, the final written report took another 4 weeks to prepare and print; the use process was already well under way as the meeting ended (both *findings use* and *process use*).

Four main points are illustrated by this example. First, nonresearchers can understand and interpret data when presented with clear, readable, and focused statistical tables. Second, as experienced data analysts know, the only way to really understand a data set is to spend some time getting inside it; busy decision makers are unwilling and unable to spend days at such a task, but a couple of hours of structured time spent in facilitated analysis and interpretation can pay off in greater understanding of and commitment to using results. Third, evaluators can learn a great deal from stakeholders' interpretations of data if they are open and listen to what people knowledgeable about the program have to say. Just as decision makers do not spend as much time in data analysis as do evaluators, so evaluators do not spend as much time in program analysis, operations, and planning as do decision makers. Each can learn from the other in the overall effort to make sense out of the data and provide future direction for the program. Fourth, the transition from analysis to action is facilitated by having key actors involved in analysis. Use does not then depend on having to wait for a written report.

Making Causal Inferences

> *No discussion of evaluation nuts and bolts is complete without some mention of the* causation *issue. . . . [C]ausation is both one of the most difficult and one of the most important issues in evaluation.*
>
> *E. Jane Davidson,* Evaluation Methodology Basics (2005, p. 67)

> *Because almost every evaluation involves some claim about causation—for example, that the program being evaluated had certain outcomes—this issue is of crucial importance in evaluation.*
>
> *Michael Scriven,* Causation (2005, p. 43)

Step 8 discussed attribution questions in designing an evaluation. Step 9 discussed conceptualizing the program's theory of change as partly a challenge of mapping causal hypotheses. Step 11 discussed making sure intended users understand potential methods controversies and their implications, especially the debate about whether experimental designs with randomized control groups as counterfactuals is the gold standard for establishing causality. Attribution and causality as prominent themes in question formulation and evaluation design highlight why these are also prominent themes when interpreting findings. The extent to which an intervention can be said to have caused observed outcomes is one of the crucial interpretation issues in evaluation.

A central question is: *Given the evaluation's purpose and intended use, what level of evidence is needed?* What degree of certainty is needed by primary intended users to use the evaluation findings? I discussed this earlier in considering the claims that are made in an evaluation's findings and making sure that major claims are supported by rigorous evidence.

An example from the chapter on Step 11 is worth reconsidering here. Suppose decision makers need to determine whether to give worm medicine to school-age children with diarrhea to increase their school attendance and performance. First, some context: 600 million people have hookworms. In Congo, one study found that 82% of children have worms making 70% anemic and affecting school attendance. Worms, elephantiasis, and trachoma kill 500,000 people annually; ordinary worms kill 130,000 people a year, through anemia and intestinal obstruction. Citing these statistics, advocates argue: "The cheapest way to increase school attendance in poor countries isn't to build more schools, but to deworm children. Yet almost no government aid goes to deworming. In Africa, you can deworm a child for 50 cents" (Kristof, 2007, p. A19). So, what kind of evaluation evidence is needed to take action? Does one need a randomized controlled experiment to establish the linkage between deworming and school attendance—and the cost benefit of spending 50 cents per child per year? Or, if students, parents, teachers, and health professionals all affirm in interviews that diarrhea is a major cause of the poor school attendance and performance, and we follow up with those given a regimen of worm medicine, can we infer causation at a reasonable enough level to recommend action? If those taking the medicine show increased school attendance and performance, and in follow-up interviews the students, parents, teachers, and health professionals independently affirm their belief that the changes can be attributed to taking the worm medicine and being relieved of the symptoms of diarrhea, is this credible, convincing evidence? *Primary intended users ultimately must answer these questions with discussion and implications facilitated by the evaluator.*

Direct inquiry into the relationship between worm medicine and school attendance, without an experimental design, involves tracing the causal chain and looking for *reasonable evidence* of linkages along the causal chain. This is how coroners determine cause of death, how arson investigators determine the cause of a fire, and how accident investigators determine the cause of an airplane crash. Epidemiologists follow backward the chain of events and contacts to establish the source of a disease or explain the outbreak of an epidemic. In all these cases, those carrying out the investigation examine the evidence and determine *the most probable cause.* Often they apply the principle of Occam's razor in choosing among alternative explanations:

> *All things being equal, the simplest solution tends to be the best one.*

Occam's Razor: Valuing Straightforward Explanations

In the 14th century, an English logician, William of Ockham, postulated the principle that the explanation of any phenomenon should make as few assumptions as possible–eliminating or "shaving off" unnecessary complications. The simplest explanation *compatible with the data* is most valued. This principle, sometimes called the "law of parsimony," is popularly known as **Occam's razor:**

> *All things being equal, the simplest solution tends to be the best one.*

Occam's razor is a heuristic guide to interpretation that emphasizes economy, parsimony, and simplicity–useful attributes for evaluators to aspire to in working with primary intended users.

Michael Scriven has called a related form of causal tracing the *modus operandi method*. This language comes from detective work in which a criminal's MO (*modus operandi* or method of operating) is established as a *signature trace* that connects the same criminal to different crimes. "The modus operandi method works best for evaluands that have highly distinctive patterns of effects" (Davidson, 2005, p. 75). I evaluated an employment training program aimed at chronically unemployed, poorly educated men of color. Prior to the program they blamed society for their problems and expressed overt anger. After the program, which included an intense empowerment component, they described themselves as taking control of their lives, abandoning anger, no longer indulging in a "victim mentality," and taking responsibility for their actions and the consequences of those actions. This language was the "signature" of the program. When graduates who had attained jobs attributed their success to being "empowered" and continued to express themselves in this way a year after leaving the program, it seemed reasonable to attribute this change in outlook to the program. Connecting the dots along the causal chain means looking at the participants' baseline attitudes and behaviors, looking at what they experienced in the program, and examining their subsequent attitudes, behaviors, and job status. The connections in this case were direct and reasonable.

Direct observation and logic are a powerful source of attribution. We don't need a randomized controlled trial to understand why parachutes work as they do (see sidebar).

A study in the *British Medical Journal* by Smith and Pell (2003) concluded:

No randomized control trials of parachute use have been undertaken.

As with many interventions intended to prevent ill health, the effectiveness of parachutes has not been subjected to rigorous evaluation by using randomized controlled trials. Advocates of evidence-based medicine have criticized the adoption of interventions evaluated by using only observational data. We think that everyone might benefit if the most radical protagonists of evidence-based medicine organized and participated in a double blind, randomized, placebo-controlled, crossover trial of the parachute.

SO

Only two options exist. The first is that we accept that, under exceptional circumstances, common sense might be applied when considering the potential risks and benefits of intervention.

OR

Those who criticize interventions that lack an evidence base will not hesitate to demonstrate their commitment by volunteering for a double-blind, randomized, placebo-controlled, crossover trial.

Engineers design machines, bridges, and buildings based on meeting specific criteria about what works. You don't need a counterfactual to determine if a bridge will get people across a river—or if using solar cookers in Africa reduces wood use (and deforestation). The evidence is direct and observable.

Contribution Analysis

In working with primary intended users, it can be quite useful to distinguish between attribution analysis and contribution analysis. John Mayne (2008, 2011) distinguishes attribution questions from contribution questions as follows:

Traditional causality questions (attribution)

- Has the program caused the outcome?
- To what extent has the program caused the outcome?
- How much of the outcome is caused by the program?

Contribution questions

- Has the program made a difference? That is, has the program made an important contribution to the observed result? Has the program influenced the observed result?
- How much of a difference has the program made? How much of a contribution?

Contribution analysis is especially appropriate where there are multiple projects and partners working toward the same outcomes, and where the ultimate impacts occur over long time periods influenced by several cumulative outputs and outcomes over time. Exhibit 14.4 elaborates *contribution analysis.*

A utilization-focused evaluator can support and facilitate primary intended users, including program staff and substantive experts, interpreting the data in search of explanations. Since the question of "Why did these results occur?" will inevitably arise, the evaluator can help primary intended users anticipate what level of evidence they will need to credibly answer that question to their own satisfaction, including understanding the challenges of establishing causality, and what expertise will be needed to generate explanations if so doing is deemed important.

Rendering Judgment

The four-part framework of this chapter on elucidating the meanings of evaluation findings consists of (1) analyzing and organizing the data so that primary intended users can

EXHIBIT 14.4

Contribution Analysis

Contribution analysis (Mayne, 2008, 2011) examines a causal hypothesis (theory of change) against logic and evidence to examine what factors could explain evaluation findings. The result of a contribution analysis is not definitive proof that the program has made an important contribution, but rather evidence and argumentation from which it is reasonable to draw conclusions about the degree and importance of the contribution, within some level of confidence. The aim is to get *plausible association* based on a preponderance of evidence, as in the judicial tradition. The question is whether a reasonable person would agree from the evidence and argument that the program has made an important contribution to the observed result. In utilization-focused evaluation, the "reasonable" persons making this assessment are the primary intended users.

A contribution analysis produces a *contribution story* that presents the evidence and other influences on program outcomes. A major part of that story may tell about behavioral changes that intended beneficiaries have made as a result of the intervention.

Attributes of a credible contribution story

A credible statement of contribution would entail:

- A well-articulated context of the program, discussing other influencing factors
- A plausible theory of change (no obvious flaws) which is not disproven
- A description of implemented activities and resulting outputs of the program
- A description of the observed results
- The results of contribution analysis
    - The evidence in support of the assumptions behind the key links in the theory of change
    - Discussion of the roles of the other influencing factors
- A discussion of the quality of the evidence provided, noting weaknesses

understand and engage the findings, (2) facilitating interpretation, (3) rendering judgment, and (4) generating recommendations. Having covered the first two, we arrive at the third, *the essence of the evaluative function.* At the center of the word *evaluation* is "valu[e]." Rendering a judgment involves applying values to the data and interpretation of the findings. Data are data. Findings alone do not determine whether a result is good or bad. Values and standards are needed for that determination. Data may show that gender equity or racial integration has increased as a result of a project intervention. Whether that increase is "good" or "enough to demonstrate merit or worth" depends on what values inform that judgment. Those who support gender equity or racial integration will render a judgment of *good.* Those who oppose gender equity or racial integration will judge increases as *bad.* Regardless, the findings remain the findings. It is the judgment that varies depending on the values brought to bear.

Who makes this judgment? One perspective is that the evaluator must independently render judgment (Scriven, 1980, 1993). Others have argued that the evaluator's job can be limited to supplying the data and that the stakeholders alone make the final judgment (e.g., Stake, 1996). Utilization-focused evaluation treats these opposing views as options to be negotiated with primary users. The evaluator's job can include offering interpretations, making judgments, and generating recommendations if, as is typical, that is what the evaluation users want. Even so, in order to facilitate direct engagement and increase users' ownership, prior to offering *my* interpretations, judgments, and recommendations, I first give decision makers and intended users an opportunity to arrive at their own conclusions unencumbered by my perspective, but facilitated by me. That puts me in the role of *evaluation facilitator*—facilitating others' interpretation, judgments, and recommendations. In doing so, I find that I have to keep returning, sensitively and diplomatically, to the distinctions among analysis, interpretation, judgment, and recommendations.

Having facilitated the engagement of primary intended users, I can also render my own interpretations and judgments, either separately or as part of our interactive process. At that point I am playing the role of *evaluator.* In the active-reactive-interactive-adaptive role of a utilization-focused evaluation, I can move back and forth between the roles of evaluation facilitator and independent evaluator. In so doing I am alternating between the tasks of facilitating others' judgments and rendering my own. Some are skeptical that these dual roles of evaluation facilitator and independent judge can be played without confusion about roles or contamination of independence. Poorly executed, those are real dangers. But I find that primary intended users easily understand and value both roles.

I liken this process to that of skilled teachers who engage in both asking students questions (facilitating their critical thinking) and, alternatively, direct instruction (giving them answers and telling them what they need to know).

In facilitating judgments, I typically begin by offering three caveats:

- The quality of your judgment depends on the quality of the findings and thinking that informs it, thus the hand-in-glove link between findings and judgment.
- Don't condemn the judgment of another because it differs from your own. You may both be wrong.
- Forget "judge not that ye be not judged." The evaluator's mantra: Judge often and well so that you get better at it.

Practice Judging

Forget "judge not that ye be not judged."
The evaluator's mantra: Judge often and well so that you get better at it.

Halcolm

Recommendations

Student: What is the major source of problems in the world?

Sage: Solutions

Student: How can one recognize a problem in advance?

Sage: Look for a recommendation about to be implemented.

Student: What does this mean?

Sage: Evaluators who make recommendations are assuring future work for evaluators.

Halcolm

Recommendations are often the most visible part of an evaluation report. Well-written, carefully derived recommendations and conclusions can be the magnet that pulls all the other elements of an evaluation together into a meaningful whole. Done poorly, recommendations can become a lightning rod for attack, discrediting what was otherwise a professional job because of hurried and sloppy work on last-minute recommendations. I suspect that one of the most common reasons evaluators get into trouble when writing recommendations is that they haven't allowed enough time to really think through the possibilities and discuss them with people who have a stake in the evaluation. I've known cases in which, after working months on a project, the evaluators generated recommendations just hours before a final report was due, under enormous time pressure.

Useful and Practical Recommendations: 10 Guidelines

Recommendations, when they are included in a report, draw readers' attention like bees to a flower's nectar. Many report readers will turn to recommendations before anything else. Some never read beyond the recommendations. Given their importance, then, let me offer 10 guidelines for evaluation recommendations.

1. **Whether to include recommendations should be negotiated and clarified with stakeholders and evaluation funders as part of the design.** Not all evaluation reports include recommendations. What kinds of recommendations to include in a report, if any, are a matter for negotiation. For example, are recommendations expected about program improvements? About future funding? About program expansion? About sustainability? Asking questions about what recommendations are expected can clarify the focus and purpose of an evaluation *before data collection.*

2. **Recommendations should clearly follow from and be supported by the evaluation findings.** The processes of analysis, interpretation, and judgment should lead logically to recommendations.

3. **Distinguish different kinds of recommendations.** Recommendations that deal directly with central questions or issues should be highlighted and separated from recommendations about secondary or minor issues. Distinctions should be made between summative and formative recommendations. It may be helpful to distinguish recommendations that can be implemented immediately from those that might be implemented within 6 months to a year and those aimed at the long-term development of the program. In still other cases, it may be appropriate to orient recommendations toward certain groups of people: one set of recommendations for funders and policymakers; others for program administrators; still others for program staff or participants.

Another way of differentiating recommendations is to distinguish those that are strongly supported from those that are less so. Strong support may mean the findings directly lead to the recommendations or that the evaluation task force had strong agreement about the recommendation; other recommendations may be less directly supported by the data or there may be dissension among members of the task force. In similar fashion, it is important to distinguish between recommendations that involve a firm belief that some action should be taken and recommendations that are meant merely to stimulate discussion or suggestions that might become part of an agenda for future consideration and action.

The basic point here is that long, indiscriminate lists of recommendations at the end of an evaluation report diffuse the focus and diminish the power of central recommendations. By making explicit the different amounts of emphasis that the evaluator intends to place on different recommendations, and by organizing recommendations so as to differentiate among different kinds of recommendations, the evaluator increases the usefulness of the recommendations as well as the likelihood of the implementation of at least some of them.

4. **Some decision makers prefer to receive multiple options rather than recommendations that advocate only one course of action.** This approach may begin with a full slate of possible recommendations: Terminate the program, reduce funding for the program, maintain program funding at its current level, increase program funding slightly, and

increase program funding substantially. The evaluator then lists pros and cons for each of these recommendations, showing which findings, assumptions, interpretations, and judgments support each option.

5. **Discuss the costs, benefits, and challenges of implementing recommendations.** When making major recommendations that involve substantial changes in program operations or policies, evaluators should study, specify, and include in their reports some consideration of the benefits and costs of making the suggested changes, including the costs and risks of not making them.

6. **Focus on actions within the control of intended users and those they can influence.** Decision makers become frustrated when recommendations suggest actions over which they have no control. For example, a school desegregation study that focuses virtually all its recommendations on needed changes in housing patterns is not very useful to school officials, even though they may agree that housing changes are needed. Is the implication of such a recommendation that the schools can do nothing? Is the implication that anything the school does will be limited in impact to the extent that housing patterns remain unchanged? Or, again, are there major changes a school could make to further the aims of desegregation, but the evaluator got sidetracked on the issue of housing patterns and never got back to concrete recommendations for the school? Of course, the best way to end up with recommendations that focus on actionable variables is to make sure that, in conceptualizing the evaluation, the focus was on manipulability of the problem.

7. **Exercise political sensitivity in writing recommendations.** Ask yourself these questions: If I were in their place with their responsibilities, their political liabilities, and their personal perspectives, how would I react to this recommendation stated in this way? What arguments would I raise to counter the recommendations? Work with stakeholders to analyze the political implications of recommendations. This doesn't mean recommendations should be weak but, rather, that evaluators should be astute. Controversy may or may not serve the cause of getting findings used. But, at the very least, controversies should be anticipated and acknowledged.

8. **Be thoughtful and deliberate in wording evaluations.** Important recommendations can be lost in vague and obtuse language. Powerful recommendations can be diluted by an overly meek style, while particularly sensitive recommendations may be dismissed by an overly assertive style. Avoid words that confuse or distract from the central message. Here are examples.

> *Obtuse and meek recommendation*: Consider whether current staffing competencies meet program needs and professional standards in light of changing knowledge and skill expectations.
>
> *Straightforward recommendation*: Increase the amount and quality of staff development to meet accreditation standards.

9. **Allow time to do a good job on recommendations.** Plan time to develop recommendations collaboratively with stakeholders and time to pilot-test recommendations for clarity, understandability, practicality, utility, and meaningfulness.

10. **Develop strategies for getting recommendations taken seriously.** Simply listing recommendations at the end of a report may mean they get token attention. Think about how to facilitate serious consideration of recommendations. Help decision makers make decisions on recommendations, including facilitating a working session that includes clear assignment of responsibility for follow-up action and time lines for implementation.

Involving Intended Users in Generating Recommendations

As with everything else, utilization-focused evaluation actively involves primary intended users in the process of generating recommendations based on their knowledge of the situation and their shared expertise. Utilization-focused recommendations are not the evaluator's alone; they result from a collaborative process that seeks and incorporates the expertise of primary intended users.

Putting It All Together: Findings, Interpretation, Judgment, and Recommendations

This chapter has reviewed and discussed the four elements in a comprehensive framework for engaging evaluation results: basic findings, interpretation, judgment, and recommendations. A useful report brings these elements together in a coherent manner and relates them together so that analysis informs interpretations; analysis and interpretations, together, are the basis for judgments; and analysis, interpretations, and judgments lead to and are the explicit basis for recommendations. Exhibit 14.5 shows the outline for an evaluation summary that brings together and reports in sequence the data analysis findings, interpretations, judgments, and recommendation options for an employment training program targeted at high school dropouts.

While the distinction between description (what?) and prescription (so what and now what?) is fundamental in research and evaluation, it is important to note that description and prescription are ultimately intricately interconnected. As the Thomas theorem in social science asserts: What is perceived as real is real in its consequences. Distinguished *New York Times* journalist David Brooks (2010) puts the case more directly:

> Description is prescription. If you can get people to see the world [in a particular way] . . . , you have unwittingly framed every subsequent choice. (p. A37)

EXHIBIT 14.5

Putting It All Together: Basic Findings, Interpretation, Judgment, and Reporting

Evaluation of employment training program for high school dropouts

This shows the outline for an evaluation summary that brings together and reports in sequence the data analysis findings, interpretations, judgments, and recommendation options.

Findings from data analysis:

—All participants admitted to the program met the selection criteria of being high school dropouts who were chronically unemployed
—47% dropped out during the first 6 months this year (45 of 95) compared to a 57% drop-out rate in the same period the previous year.
—The drop-out rate for comparable programs that target a similar population is above 50%
—Of those who completed the program in the past year (35), 86% got a job and kept it for a year, making at least $12 an hour with benefits. The goal was 70%.

Interpretation: The program is serving its target population and exceeding its goal with those who complete the program. The drop-out rate is in line with other programs. The program attained these results at a time when the economy is sluggish and unemployment is somewhat higher than the historical average for this season. No one has solved the drop-out problem. This is a tough target population and difficult problem. The problem remains significant. The program has learned important lessons about how to retain and graduate participants (lessons reported separately).

Judgment: These are positive results. This is a fairly good program addressing an important societal issue. There is room for improvement, and the program shows promise for improvement based on results to date and lessons learned.

Recommendation options:

1. Renew funding at the current level for 2 more years to give the program more time to prove itself.
2. Increase funding to expand the program by 50% to test the program's capacity to increase its impact and go to scale.

Preparing for Use

As discussed in Step 12 on practice simulations, one dramatic way of setting the stage for analysis and use is having stakeholders speculate about results prior to seeing the real data. This can be done prior to data collection or after data collection but prior to actual presentation of findings. Stakeholders are given an analysis table with all the appropriate categories but no actual data (a dummy table). They then fill in the missing data with their guesses of what the results will be.

This kind of speculation prepares users for how the results will be formatted and increases interest by building a sense of anticipation.

A second and more important function of having stakeholders write down their guesses is to provide a concrete basis for determining the extent to which actual results come close to expectations. Program staff members, for example, sometimes argue that they don't need formal evaluations because they know their clients, students, or program participants so well that evaluation findings would just confirm what they already know. I've found that when staff members commit their guesses to paper in advance of seeing actual results, the subsequent comparison often calls into question just how well some staff knows what is happening in the program. At least with written guesses on paper, program staff and other stakeholders can't just say, "That's what I expected." A database (in the form of their guesses) exists to determine and document how much new has been learned.

You can combine establishing standards of desirability (see Step 12) and speculating on results. Give stakeholders a page with two columns. The first column asks them to specify what outcomes they consider desirable and the second column asks them to guess what results they believe actually will be attained. Having specified a standard of desirability and guessed at possible results, users have a greater stake in and a framework for looking at the actual findings. When real results are presented, the evaluator facilitates discussion on the implications of the data falling below, at, or above the desired response, and why the actual findings were different from or the same as what they guessed. In facilitating this exercise, the outcomes data presented must be highly focused and limited to major issues. In my experience, animated interactions among users follow as they fully engage and interpret the results. Figuring out what findings mean and how to apply them engages us in that most human of processes: making sense of the world. Utilization-focused evaluators invite users along on the whole journey, alternatively exciting and treacherous, from determining what's worth knowing to interpreting the results and following through with action.

I find that, given the time and encouragement, stakeholders with virtually no methods or statistics training can readily identify the strengths, weaknesses, and implications of the findings. The trick is to move people from passive reception—from audience status—to active involvement and participation. This active engagement of primary intended users is distinct from the job of presenting the findings in a formal report. We turn in Step 15 to increasing the utility of formal evaluation reporting and dissemination of findings. Before doing so, let me close this chapter by emphasizing the skills involved in facilitating users' discussion, interpretation, and sense-making of findings. The challenge, as always, is staying focused on what is useful. That's where the evaluator adds value. An old and oft-told consulting story illustrates this point.

A company's furnace broke down in the midst of winter. Given the urgency of the situation, the chief operating officer authorized calling in a furnace expert who was known to be the best in the business. He agreed to come immediately. Upon arrival, he carefully examined the furnace, testing pipe connections, examining electrical wires, and cleaning away soot-laden areas. He asked questions about the furnace's history and recent functioning. When his questions had been answered and he had completed his inspection, he drew a red X on one side of the furnace. Using a large hammer, he hit the mark hard, the sound reverberating throughout the building. The furnace started working.

The furnace expert presented his bill. The maintenance director looked at the invoice and said, "I can't ask our financial officer to approve a bill of $1,000 for a 15-minute inspection and then hitting a furnace with a hammer." Sputtering he said, "I need to see a detailed invoice."

The furnace expert took the invoice, added a couple of lines, and handed it back to the maintenance director. Detailed invoice: "Hitting the boiler: $50. Knowing where to hit the boiler: $950."

The value added by a utilization-focused evaluation facilitator isn't just getting users to talk about the findings. It's getting them to talk about, reflect on, and reach conclusions about the right things.

Checklist details about what is involved in each step are provided in the summary *U-FE Checklist* in the concluding chapter. See pages 420–421 for the checklist items for Step 14 discussed in this chapter.

PRACTICE EXERCISES

1. Locate an evaluation report on some program of interest to you. Examine how the report handles the distinctions between analysis, interpretation, judgment, and recommendations (see Exhibits 14.1 and14.5). Give examples of these distinctions from the report. Comment on and critique the extent to which these distinctions are adhered to in the evaluation.
2. Locate an evaluation report that includes recommendations. Examine the connection between findings and recommendations. To what extent can you connect the recommendations to the findings? Looking at the findings on your own, what additional recommendations, if any, occur to you?
3. Locate an evaluation report that includes comparisons. Analyze and discuss what comparisons were made. Generate additional potential comparisons using all the comparison alternatives in Menu 14.1 (Menu of Program Comparisons). You may have to make up data for some comparisons.

15

Prepare an Evaluation Report to Facilitate Use and Disseminate Significant Findings to Expand Influence

The single biggest problem with communication is the illusion that it has taken place.

George Bernard Shaw (1856–1950),
1925 Nobel Prize for Literature

The data from our study of federal health evaluations revealed that much important sharing of and discussion about findings and their significance is interpersonal and informal. In hallway conversations, over coffee, before and after meetings, over the telephone, and through informal networks, the word gets passed along when something useful and important has been found. Knowing this, evaluators can strategize about how to inject findings into important informal networks. This is not to diminish the importance of formal reports and oral briefings which, presented with thoughtful preparation and skill, can sometimes have an immediate and dramatic impact. But the increasing importance of networked communications in the Information Age carries a caution that *evaluators should not confuse producing a report with having communicated findings.*

In all cases, reporting is driven by intended evaluation purpose and the information needs of primary intended users. Formative reporting is different from a summative report. A lessons-learned report is distinct from an accountability report. When a single report serves multiple purposes (and audiences), clear distinctions should be made between sections of the report. Bottom line: *Communicating and reporting should be strategic* (Torres, Preskill, & Piontek, 1996), which means honed and adapted to achieve use by targeted users. Dissemination to larger audiences then follows.

Formally Communicating Evaluation Findings: Report Menu

In logic model terms, an evaluation report is an output, not an outcome. It can *feel* like an outcome because so much work goes into producing a major evaluation report. But, alas, it is a means to an end, not the end itself, the end being use. Indeed, reports can hinder use when they are poorly written, too long, overly obtuse, and in countless ways anything but user friendly.

As with other stages in utilization-focused evaluation, the reporting stage offers a smorgasbord of options. Menu 15.1 displays alternatives for reporting format and style, content, contributors, and perspectives. Selecting from the menu is affected by the purpose of the evaluation. A summative report will highlight an overall judgment of merit or worth with supporting data. A knowledge-generating report aimed at policy enlightenment may follow

MENU 15.1

Evaluation Reporting Menu

Style and Format Options: Written Report

- Traditional academic research monograph
- Executive summary followed by a full report
- Executive summary followed by a few key tables, graphs, and data summaries
- Executive summary only (data available to those interested)
- Different reports (or formats) for different targeted users
- Newsletter article for dissemination
- Press release
- Brochure (well crafted, professionally done)
- No written report; only oral presentations

Style and Format Options: Oral and Creative

- Oral briefing with charts
- Short summary followed by questions (e.g., at a board meeting or legislative hearing)
- Discussion groups based on prepared handouts that focus issues for interpretation and judgment based on data

Half-day or full-day retreat-like work session with primary intended users

Videotape or audiotape presentation

Dramatic, creative presentation (e.g., role-playing perspectives)

Involvement of select primary users in reporting and facilitating any of the above

Advocacy–adversary debate or court for and against certain conclusions and judgments

Written and oral combinations

Content Options

Major findings only; focus on data, patterns, themes, and results

Findings and interpretations with judgments of merit or worth (no recommendations)

(a) Summative judgment about overall program
(b) Judgments about program components

Recommendations backed up by judgments, findings, and interpretations

(a) Single, best-option recommendations
(b) Multiple options with analysis of strengths, weaknesses, costs, and benefits of each
(c) Options based on future scenarios with monitoring and contingency suggestions
(d) Different recommendations for different intended users

Authors of and Contributors to the Report

Evaluator's report; evaluator as sole and independent author
Collaborative report coauthored by evaluator with others involved in the process
Report from primary users, written on their behalf by the evaluator as facilitator and adviser, but report ownership resides with others.

Combinations:

(a) Evaluator generates findings; collaborators generate judgments and recommendations
(b) Evaluator generates findings and makes judgments; primary users generate recommendations
(c) Separate conclusions, judgments, and recommendations by the evaluator and others in the same report

Perspectives Included

Evaluator's perspective as independent and neutral judge

Primary intended users only

Effort to represent all major stakeholder perspectives (may or may not be the same as primary intended users)

Program staff or administrators respond formally to the evaluation findings (written independently by the evaluator); GAO approach

Review of the evaluation by an external panel—*metaevaluation*: Formatively and summatively evaluate the evaluation using evaluation standards to elucidate strengths and weaknesses a traditional academic format. A formative report may take the form of an internal memorandum with circulation limited to staff. I am often asked by students to show them the standard or best format for an evaluation report. The point of Menu 15.1 is that there can be no standard report format, *and the best format is the one that fulfills the purposes of the evaluation and meets the needs of specific intended users in a specific situation.* In many cases, multiple reporting strategies can be pursued to reach different intended users and dissemination audiences.

E. Jane Davidson, an independent evaluation consultant working out of New Zealand and author of the very useful *Evaluation Methodology Basics* featuring the nuts and bolts of sound evaluation (Davidson, 2005), has emphasized that evaluation reports should be structured around the demand for "actionable questions" (Davidson, 2010c, p. 13). My experience mirrors Jane's. Her reflections are so insightful and her voice so powerful that I want you to experience her thoughts on writing reports in her own words. In reviewing countless evaluation reports, she often found that they were "plagued with the structure of a Master's thesis," which made it quite difficult to figure out what results were important. This academic report format typically begins with a lengthy Executive Summary that presents "lots of introductory information, methodology, sampling, random snippets of findings that fail to give a clear sense of the program's quality or value, plus something incomprehensible about moderator variables." This is followed by

> an Introduction, Literature Review, a theoretical model and detailed explanation of the relevant social science theory explaining the links among some variables (unfortunately not a program logic model, and not even remotely linked to an evaluation question—this part contributed by a university faculty member with no evaluation expertise), Methodology, Findings (about 20 pages of raw data, all presented separately by source and data type with virtually no explanatory narrative, none of it linked back to the questions), Conclusions (some glimmers of hope in here, but by now we are 37 pages into the report and have lost most of our audience), Appendices. (Davidson, 2007, pp. v–vi)

She goes on to note that "for the client, reading a report like this feels like wading through mud. Page after page of graphs and interview quotes, but not a hint of whether or how they were used to answer any question of value. When, oh when, are they going to get to the point?" (p. vi).

In an effort to make reports more sensible and user friendly, Davidson recommends an alternative to the traditional research monograph format.

> One strategy I use is to structure the *Findings* part of the evaluation report into 7 +/– 2 sections, one for each of the 'big picture' evaluation questions used to frame the evaluation. In each section, all data pertaining to that question (qualitative, quantitative, interviews, surveys, observations, document analyses, from different people and perspectives) are presented, interpreted as they are presented, and woven together to form a direct answer to the question.

Next, I write a 2-page executive summary using the same structure: 7 +/– 2 questions with straight-to-the- point and explicitly evaluative answers of 1–2 paragraphs each.

If the client has seven or so major questions about the program that need to be answered, then the first two pages he or she reads (perhaps the only two pages!) should contain direct answers to those questions. And if the client wants to know on what basis those conclusions were drawn, it should be a simple matter to turn to the relevant section of the report and see clearly how 'quality' and 'value' were defined for that particular question, what data were used to answer it, and how they were interpreted together, relative to those definitions of quality/value. (Davidson, 2007, p. vi)

The 1:3:25 Format for Report Writing

The Canadian Health Services Research Foundation has pioneered a user-friendly approach to report writing that is becoming widely used as a way of communicating with focus. The 1:3:25 format specifies:

- One page for main messages and conclusions relevant to the reader
- A three-page executive summary of the main findings, and
- A 25-page comprehensive, plain-language report

Canadian Health Services Research Foundation (2008)

Another resource on structuring an evaluation report and making sure it contains all essential elements is the Evaluation Report Checklist (Miron, 2004). The thing to remember is that, while a report is only one part of the overall process, it is a concrete documentation of what has occurred and a visible representation of major findings. The quality of the report reflects on both the evaluator and the primary intended users. A great report won't ensure use, though it can help, while a lousy report can undermine not only use but future interest in evaluation among those who receive and read it. Take the time to do it well. Nothing undermines producing a quality report more assuredly than treating it like cramming for a final exam and spending an all-nighter just to get it done. Such reports are easy to spot—and undermine both credibility and utility, not to mention stress they induce and the toll they can take on the evaluator's mental health.

Utilization-Focused Reporting Principles

I've found the following principles helpful in thinking about how to make reporting useful:

1. Be intentional about reporting; that is, know the purpose of a report and stay true to that purpose.
2. Stay user focused: Focus the report on the priorities of primary intended users and answer their questions.

3. Use graphics and other visuals to communicate findings succinctly and powerfully.

4. Prepare users to engage with and learn from "negative" findings.

5. Distinguish dissemination from use.

Let me elaborate each of these principles.

1. Be intentional and purposeful about reporting.

Being intentional means negotiating a shared understanding of what it's going to mean to close-out the evaluation, that is, to achieve use. You need to communicate at every step in the evaluation your commitment to utility. One way to emphasize this point during early negotiations is to ask if a final report is expected. This question commands attention.

"Will you want a final report?" I ask.

They look at me and they say, "Come again?"

I repeat. "Will you want a final report?"

They respond, "Of course. That's why we're doing this, to get a report." And I respond. "I see it a little differently. I think we've agreed that we're doing this evaluation to get useful information to improve your programming and decision making. A final written report is one way of communicating findings, but there's substantial evidence now that it's not always the most effective way. Full evaluation reports don't seem to get read much and it's very costly to write final reports. A third or more of the budget of an evaluation can be consumed by report writing. Let's talk about how to get the evaluation used, then we can see if a full written report is the most cost-effective way to do that." Then I share Menu 15.1 and we start talking about reporting options.

Often I find that, with this kind of interaction, my primary intended users really start to understand what utilization-focused evaluation means. They start to comprehend that evaluation doesn't have to mean producing a thick report that they can file under "has been evaluated." They start to think about use. Caveat: Whatever is agreed on, especially if there's agreement not to produce a traditional academic monograph, get the agreement in writing and remind them of it often. A commitment to alternative reporting approaches may need reinforcement, especially among stakeholders used to traditional formats.

2. Focus reports on primary intended users and their priority questions.

A dominant theme running throughout this book is that use is integrally intertwined with users. That's the thrust of the personal factor. The style, format, content, and process of reporting should all be geared toward *intended use by intended users*. For example, we know that busy, big-picture policy makers and funders are more likely to read concise executive summaries than full reports, but detail-oriented users want—what else?—details.

Some users prefer recommendations right up front at the beginning of the report; others want them at the end; and I had one group of users who wanted the recommendations in a separate document so that readers of the report had to reach their own conclusions without interpreting everything in terms of recommendations. Methods sections may be put in the body of the report, in an appendix, or omitted and shared only with the methodologically interested. Sometimes users can't articulate what they want until they see a draft. Then they know what they don't want and the responsive evaluator will have to do some rewriting.

Beyond Generating a Report to Providing an Information Experience™

Information Experience™ is what *Juice Analytics* calls "the intersection between user experience and information-intensive applications, where success is how effectively a user can consume, understand, and apply that information."

Like sitting behind the wheel of a BMW or my two-year-old flipping through photos on an iPhone, great Information Experiences have less to do with features and more to do with an intimate connection between human and device. Great information experiences tell stories where data is the primary medium for communication. The information appears when it is needed and the device or application seems to anticipate the next question or action. These are the objectives that we apply to the solutions we design and build.

1. **Support the achievement of organizational objectives.** How can the information experience fit into users' existing decision-making and work processes? How can we influence decision making with the right information at the right time?
2. **Direct the user to likely actions in order to "get it done."** What are the important questions a user is trying to answer or tasks the user wants to accomplish? How can the application make it as easy and intuitive as possible to get to results? Does the navigation and user flow feel like an extension of users' thought process?
3. **Present only the information that needs to be seen.** For any given view of data and situational context, what is the most critical information to share with the user? How can information be progressively revealed to give the user what he or she needs to know at any given time?
4. **Present the information in a way that produces understanding and action.** For any given data and situational context, what is the most effective information visualization? What are the best ways to present information given users' experience and sophistication with interpreting information? What is the appropriate level of detail to be displayed given the context and user needs? (Juice Analytics, 2010, p. 1)

Consider this story from an evaluator in our federal use study.

Let me tell you the essence of the thing. I had almost no direction from the government [about the final report] except that the project officer kept saying, "Point 8 is really important. You've got to do point 8 on the contract."

So, when I turned in the draft of the report, I put points 1 through 9, without 8, in the first part of the report. Then I essentially wrote another report after that just on point 8 and made that the last half of the report. It was a detailed description of the activities of the program that came to very specific conclusions. It wasn't what had been asked for in the proposal I responded to, but it was what they needed to answer their questions. The project officer read it and the comment back was, "It's a good report except for all that crap in the front."

OK, so I turned it around in the final version, and moved all that "crap" in the front into an appendix. If you look at the report, it has several big appendices. All of that, if you compare it carefully to the contract, all that "crap" in the appendix is what I was asked to do in the original request and contract. All the stuff that constitutes the body of the report was above and beyond the call, but that's what he wanted and that's what got used.

"Boring! Not a single story in the whole thing."

3. Use graphics and other visuals to communicate findings succinctly and powerfully.

Mike Hendricks (1994) has studied effective techniques for executive summaries and oral briefings. The key, he has found, is good charts and graphics to capture attention and communicate quickly. A trend line, for example, can be portrayed more powerfully in graphic form than in a table, as Exhibit 15.1 shows. Hendricks trains evaluators on reporting and he asserts emphatically: "Evaluators have got to learn graphics. I'm amazed at how bad the charts and graphics are that I see in reports. You can't emphasize it too much. Reporting means GRAPHICS! GRAPHICS! GRAPHICS!" This involves "visible thinking," which includes causal mapping and other data displays (Bryson, Ackermann, Eden, & Finn, 2004).

The *Extreme Presentation™ Method* (2010) provides a set of tools for enhancing visual presentations including guidance on effective choice of visual formats and chart options for conveying different kinds of information. The *Periodic Table of Visualization Methods* (2010; Lengler & Eppler, n.d.) offers 100 examples of data visualization options, arranged thematically as a periodic table that you can interact with online. Nancy Duarte (2010) has assembled a set of videos on effective presentations that includes enhancing PowerPoint presentations (Duarte, 2008) as well as a range of techniques to more effectively engage audiences. Susan Kistler (2010a, 2010b), the executive director of the American Evaluation Association, is a leader in monitoring new developments in data visualization, like those cited here, and bringing them to the attention of evaluators.

Skilled visual facilitators can work with evaluators to facilitate, record, and represent the ideas of a group and map relationships between ideas and concepts shared by individuals in a group. California-based evaluator Terry Uyeki (2010) reports that "using graphic facilitation or recording often opens up thinking about patterns, themes, and a sense of the 'big picture' emerging from participant input processes. It is particularly effective when used with culturally diverse groups."

Journalist David McCandless (2010a), reflecting on "the beauty of data visualization," has asserted that *data is the new oil* in terms of its potential power in the Knowledge Age, or the new soil for growing knowledge—but only if it can be effectively accessed and displayed for appropriate understanding and use. Visualization, he explains and demonstrates, is a form of knowledge compression in which "the dataset can change your mindset." His "information is beautiful" website aims to do just that (McCandless, 2010b). No one has illustrated this phenomenon better than Swedish scholar Hans Rosling (2010), who animates statistical trends and graphically illustrates global development in 200 countries over the last 200 years in 4 minutes. His visualizations point the way to the future for evaluation presentations.

EXHIBIT 15.1

The Power of Graphics

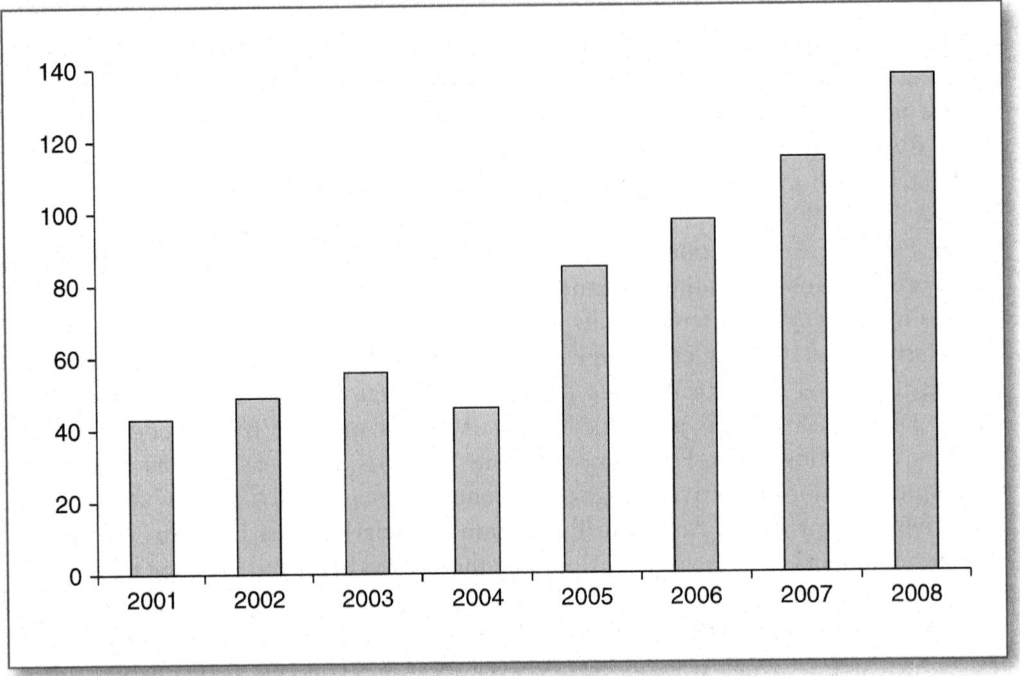

4. Prepare users to engage with and learn from "negative" findings.

> *There is nothing either good or bad, but thinking makes it so.*
>
> *Hamlet,* Act 2, Scene 2, 239–251
>
> *William Shakespeare*

The program staff's fear of negative results can undermine an evaluation. On the other hand, the absence of negative findings can call into question the evaluator's independence, integrity, and credibility. Here, then, is where evaluation use can take a back seat to other agendas. Staff will resist being made to look bad and will often treat the mildest suggestions for improvements as deep criticisms. Evaluators, worried about accusations that they've lost their independence, emphasize negative findings. As we grapple with these tensions, two points are worth remembering: (1) one person's negative is another person's positive; and (2) evaluators can do much to increase staff receptivity by shifting the focus of reporting to learning and use rather than simply being judged as good or bad.

Few evaluations are all negative or all positive. It's helpful to move beyond a dichotomous win/lose, pass/fail, success/failure, and positive/negative construct on evaluation results. This tendency to label evaluation findings as either positive or negative seems born of a tendency I find common among evaluators and decision makers: to think of evaluation findings in monolithic, absolute, and purely summative terms. This becomes especially true when evaluation findings get into the media—which tends to exaggerate the negative because negative findings make more compelling and attention-grabbing headlines. I reiterate that, in my experience, evaluation findings are seldom either completely positive or completely negative. Furthermore, whether findings are interpreted as positive or negative depends on who is using and interpreting the findings. As the old adage observes: *Whether the glass is half empty or half full depends on whether you're drinking or pouring.* Evaluators can shape the environment and context in which findings are reviewed so that the focus is on learning and improvement rather than absolute judgment. This is part of our overall responsibility to strive for balance.

5. Distinguish dissemination from use.

Dissemination of findings to audiences beyond intended users is distinct from the kind of use that has been the focus of this book. Studies can have an impact on all kinds of audiences in all kinds of ways. As a social scientist, I value and want to encourage the full and free dissemination of evaluation findings. Each of us ought to be permitted to indulge in the fantasy that our evaluation reports will have impact across the land and through the years. But only a handful of studies will ever enjoy (or suffer) such widespread dissemination.

Dissemination takes us beyond intended use by intended users into the broader concept of *evaluation influence* (Kirkhart, 2000), both intended and unintended, and longer-term *evaluation consequences* generally (Mark, 2006). This includes instances where planned dissemination *hopes for* broader influence but can't be sure if or where this will occur.

Dissemination efforts will vary greatly from study to study. The nature of dissemination, like everything else, is a matter for negotiation between evaluators and decision makers. In such negotiations, dissemination costs and benefits should be estimated. The questions addressed in an evaluation will have different meanings for people not directly involved in the painstaking process of focusing the evaluation. Different individuals and audiences will be interested in a given evaluation for reasons not always possible to anticipate. Effective dissemination involves skills in extrapolating the evaluation specifics of a particular study for use by readers in a different setting (raising issues of external validity and generalizability).

The problematic utility of trying to design an evaluation relevant to multiple audiences, each conceptualized in vague and general terms, was what has led to the emphasis in utilization-focused evaluation on identification and organization of primary intended users. Dissemination can broaden and enlarge the impact of a study in important ways, but the nature of those long-term impacts is largely beyond the control of the evaluator.

What the evaluator can control is the degree to which findings address the concerns of specific intended users. That is the use for which I take responsibility: intended use by intended users. Dissemination is not use, though it can be useful.

Exhibit 15.2 depicts the complex, dynamic relationship between use and diverse strategies for dissemination and influence. At the center, as the bull's-eye, is intended uses by intended users. The utilization-focused evaluator works with intended users to plan formal dissemination and influence strategies if the findings are of sufficient import to merit sharing more widely; these formal pathways are depicted by the solid box on the left. At the same time, informal networks can be energized for dissemination, as shown in the dotted-line box to the right. Informal networks are likely to generate some unexpected and emergent opportunities for further dissemination and influence. Moreover, in a complex dynamic system, some formal pathways will manifest links to informal networks, as shown in the feedback arrow at the bottom of the diagram, even as some informal dissemination networks may generate and lead to formal dissemination strategies, like publications and conference presentations. The dynamic links that begin informally and opportunistically but then morph into formal and planned strategies are represented by the meandering arrows at the top. The intended uses by intended users can further generate unanticipated but important new opportunities for dissemination and influence. As Exhibit 15.2 shows, dissemination can be a multifaceted, many-splendored phenomenon, like the diffusion of birth control pills, mobile phone applications, and the uses of the Internet for information dissemination, but always at the core, always in the spotlight, always in high-definition focus, is *intended uses by intended users.*

Use Is a Process, Not a Report

Analyzing and interpreting results can be exciting processes. Many nights have turned into morning before evaluators have finished trying new computer runs to tease out the nuances in some data set. The work of months, sometimes years, finally comes to fruition as data are analyzed and interpreted, conclusions drawn, recommendations considered, and the evaluation report finalized. Great relief comes in finishing an evaluation report, so much relief that it can seem like the report was the purpose. But use is the purpose and, as this book has emphasized throughout, use is a process, not a report or single event.

I remember fondly the final days of an evaluation when my co-evaluators and I were on the phone with program staff two or three times a day as we analyzed data on an educational project to inform a major decision about whether it met criteria as a valid model for federal dissemination funding. Program staff shared with us the process of watching the findings take final shape. Preliminary analyses appeared negative; as the sample became more complete, the findings looked more positive to staff; finally, a mixed picture of positive and negative conclusions emerged. Because the primary users had been intimately involved in designing the evaluation, we encountered no last-minute attacks on methods to

EXHIBIT 15.2

Complex, Dynamic Relationship Between Use and Dissemination Approaches, Both Planned and Unplanned

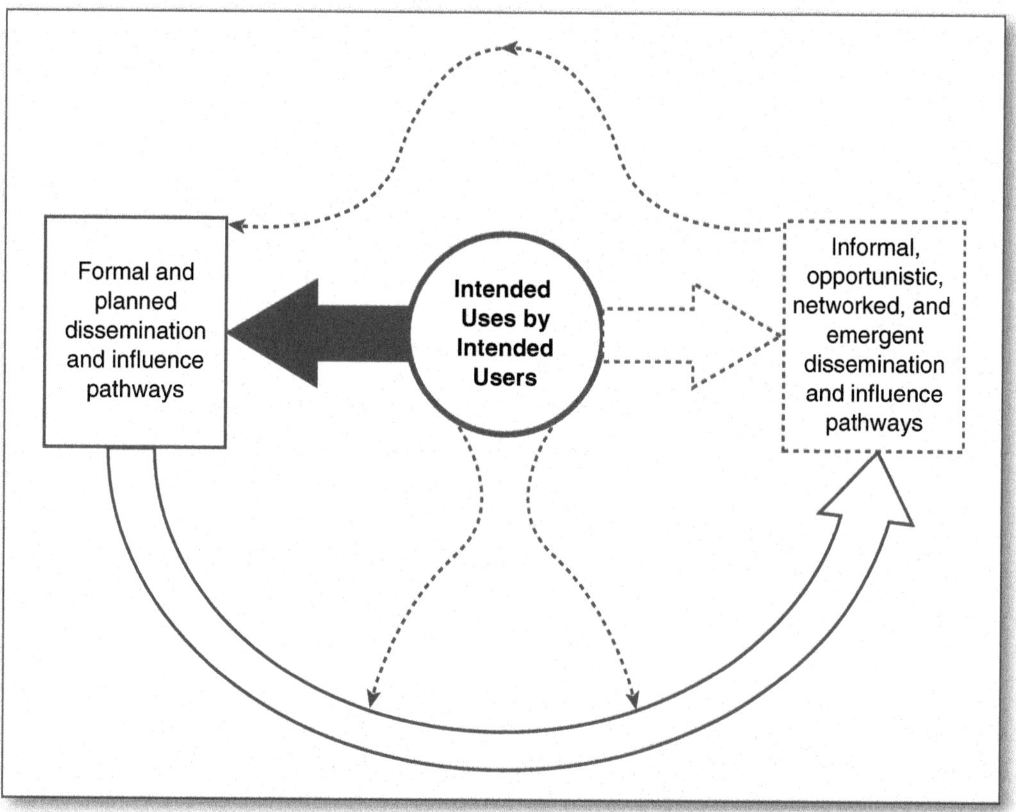

explain away negative findings. The program staff understood the data, from whence it came, what it revealed, and how it could be used for program development. They didn't get the dissemination grant that year, but they got direction about how to implement the program more consistently and increase its impact. Two years later, with new findings, they did win recognition as a "best practices" exemplar, an award that came with a dissemination grant. The highly polished summative evaluation report made that recognition possible and was a central part of the dissemination process. One intended use of the evaluation was to influence thinking and practices generally, but to achieve that dissemination and influence purpose, the evaluation first had to be useful to the primary intended users who funded, developed, implemented, and adapted the program in the years leading up to the final summative evaluation findings and report.

Ultimately, of course, utility is linked to accuracy. As reports get disseminated, any inaccuracies will take the spotlight and subject the report to potential ridicule. One of the most obvious examples of this phenomenon is premature obituary reports, as when the *New York Journal* published the obituary of American humorist Mark Twain. Upon hearing the news, Twain famously replied: "The reports of my death are greatly exaggerated." A more recent example is that of Dave Swarbrick, a British folk-rock violinist, who was killed off mistakenly by the *Daily Telegraph* in April 1999. The newspaper reported that he had been hospitalized in Coventry, where he subsequently died. His witty response to the news: "It's not the first time I have died in Coventry."

And what have these obituary examples to do with evaluation reports? Just this: In the Internet age, reports have a long life. Inaccurate reports seem especially hard to kill, as fake news, fabricated statistics, and distorted findings circulate round and round, generating affirmation by repetition rather than rigor. As *New Yorker* journalist Jonah Lehrer (2010a) found in a recent review of scientific publishing, "Many scientific theories continue to be considered true even after failing numerous experimental tests. . . . Although many scientific ideas generate conflicting results and suffer from falling effect sizes, they continue to get cited in the textbooks and drive standard medical practice" (p. 57). The long life expectancy of widely disseminated evaluation reports in the Internet age raises the stakes for determining what findings deserve a wide audience.

Taking Report Writing Seriously

Report writing is serious business, often with high stakes, and typically consuming considerable time and resources—which is why evaluation conferences often include a lot of self-deprecating humor about report writing, like this advice:

> Remember that people don't actually want to read an evaluation report. The purpose of reports is to decorate offices, not inform readers. So the most important things are cover color and size. Don't ask intended users about content and substance. Ask their preferences about cover color and size so that the report will nicely match their office décor and therefore be more likely to be prominently displayed. That's a *best practice* dissemination strategy.

Or this, on writing annual accountability reports:

> Those that think you do good work don't need to know your warts. Those that think you are a waste of space are not going to be convinced otherwise. So write for the great mass in between who just don't want to know. Help them not know. Nurture them.

> The safest path is to appear to have said a good deal, without having said anything at all. With a little practice, you can incorporate the ideas presented to produce impeccable annual reports that will confuse people so badly they won't even know they are confused. Look for the knowing nods of people when they read your report. That will tell you you have succeeded. (Bacal, 2009, p. 1)

Skepticism about the value of reports notwithstanding, effective report writing is an essential evaluator competence. Work at writing. Take time to do it well. Get feedback on how well you do. Evaluate use.

In doing so, you will be engaging in "utilization focused communication"—which is not an oxymoron according to international communications expert Ricardo Ramírez. He further asserts that "*communication focused evaluation* is not an oxymoron." These observations flow from reflections in which "evaluation and communication approaches and methods keep on interconnecting in my mind" (Ramírez, 2011). In essence, when thinking evaluation, think communications; when thinking communications, think evaluation. And make both utilization-focused.

Checklist details about what is involved in each step are provided in the summary *U-FE Checklist* in the concluding chapter. See pages 421–422 for the checklist items for Step 15 discussed in this chapter. (See pp. 375–376 for discussion of this distinction.)

PRACTICE EXERCISES

1. Using Menu 15.1, discuss the reporting situation that would be appropriate for each of the Style and Format Options (both Written and Oral). Show that you can match the reporting option to a situation for which that option is a good match. Make it clear how the situation you describe lends itself to each reporting option.
2. Find an evaluation report on the Internet. See if you can distinguish use (intended use by intended users) from dissemination. Discuss the implications of the distinction between use and dissemination using the particular example you've found to illustrate the implications you generate.

16

Follow Up With Primary Intended Users to Facilitate and Enhance Use

It ain't over till it's over.

Yogi Berra,
former New York Yankees baseball manager

Reporting evaluation findings is not use. That was the central message of Step 15. Producing findings and a report are outputs. Use is the desired outcome. Achieving that outcome means working with primary intended users after the findings and report are presented to facilitate use—*acting on the findings.*

In a 2006 online survey of members of the American Evaluation Association (Fleischer, 2007), 991 respondents rated which factors were most influential in facilitating use. Most highly rated were:

1. Planning for use at the beginning of the evaluation
2. Identifying and prioritizing intended uses of the evaluation
3. Developing a communicating and reporting plan

A communicating and reporting plan should extend beyond the report. Indeed, the evaluation design and contract should extend beyond producing a report. One of the greatest barriers to working with intended users to actually apply and act on findings and recommendations is that evaluation designs, work plans, and contracts typically end with production of the report. That means that no time and money has been allocated to the critical processes of following up with primary intended users to facilitate action and ongoing use.

Evaluators should not be expected to engage in follow-up work as a matter of goodwill. Follow-up to facilitate use is the payoff for months of work. No matter how good the report nor how clear the recommendations, utilization is served by working with primary intended users to monitor what happens to the findings and recommendations, and to watch for additional opportunities to apply findings, which can include opportunities for broader dissemination discussed in Step 15. Consider this example.

I completed an evaluation of an innovative adult reading program that integrated individualized computer instruction with personal tutoring. Following the summative report, which was largely positive but also indicated areas of potential program redesign, the following work took place to facilitate use.

- A presentation to the school board 2 months after the report, to inform a funding decision on the program and discuss with board members possible expansion of the program; this led to three subsequent meetings with a board committee. Follow-up time: 12 hours.
- A half-day session at the program's summer staff retreat to revisit the findings and discuss their implications for redesign and improvement; this led to work with a redesign team. Follow-up time: 3 days.
- A joint presentation with the program director at a national reading conference. Follow-up time to plan and make the presentation: 6 hours.
- An article for a monthly newsletter addressed to adult literacy specialists. Follow-up time: 3 hours.
- An in-person interview with a local newspaper journalist who wrote a news article on the findings, followed by some e-mail clarifications. Follow-up time, 2 ½ hours.
- A presentation at a statewide literacy education conference. Follow-up time: 4 ½ hours.
- Four meetings with the evaluation task force of primary intended users after the evaluation was completed. These were the people who had been involved in initially focusing evaluation questions, selecting methods, interpreting findings, and generating recommendations.

  Meeting 1: Developing the dissemination plan.

  Meeting 2: Focusing the presentation to the school board.

  Meeting 3: Three-month follow-up on how the findings were being discussed in various places and what actions had been taken on recommendations.

  Meeting 4: Discussing a new evaluation proposal for the refunded program.

  Follow-up time for these 4 meetings: 5 days (which included planning interactions for each meeting with the task force chair, developing materials for the meetings, and carrying out agreed-upon tasks after the meetings).

Over a period of 4 months following completion of the evaluation report, follow-up to enhance and facilitate use involved 11 ½ days of work. The original contract had included funds for a week of follow-up (5 days). A contract addendum was negotiated to fund the additional days of follow-up. These follow-up activities were critical to the ultimate high level of use attained.

Lessons About the Importance of Follow-Up to Enhance Use

1. *Plan for follow-up.* Develop a follow-up plan with primary intended users. Intentionality is a foundational value that undergirds utilization-focused evaluation. Use doesn't happen naturally or by chance. Use is more likely to occur if planned. The plan should include being alert to unanticipated and emergent opportunities.

2. *Budget for follow-up.* Follow-up by evaluators should not be a *pro bono,* goodwill effort. It is the culmination of the work. At the same time, primary intended users may need to rethink their commitment. They may have thought their work was over when the report was produced. Follow-up involves time from them to monitor what happens to findings and recommendations. This may require a formal recommitment beyond what they had originally expected.

3. *Adapt findings for different audiences.* Follow-up includes adapting and reformatting the findings for use with different potential user groups; for example

- ✓ A newsletter article
- ✓ Reporting sessions back to community people or those who provided data during the evaluation (e.g., interviewees)
- ✓ A PowerPoint presentation
- ✓ A workshop or staff retreat handout
- ✓ Conference presentations
- ✓ A press release
- ✓ A refereed journal article

In adapting findings for presentations to various user groups, pay particular attention to effective presentation techniques (Atkinson, 2007; Kistler, 2010a, 2010b; Reynolds, 2008; Torres, Preskill, & Piontek, 2004). Boring or poorly done evaluation presentations can hinder use.

4. *Keep findings in front of those who can use them.* People get busy. Despite the best of intentions, they lose track of findings and recommendations. Follow-up reminds intended users of their use commitments and helps them follow through.

5. *Watch for emergent opportunities to reinforce the relevance of findings.* The significance of findings can change over time, sometimes quickly. As people react to the results, new opportunities may emerge to connect the evaluation findings to unanticipated events, new decisions, emergent research, or other evaluation findings. Some of this is likely to be done in the report, but new opportunities for making these connections will often emerge after a report is completed.

6. *Deal with resistance.* Some types of resistance can be anticipated, but when findings start to attract serious attention, they can also attract serious criticism, some of which may be inaccurate or unfair. A meeting with primary intended users a month after a report has been released and disseminated can be a chance to assess what kinds of opposition have emerged and what, if anything, should be done about them.

7. *Watch for and guard against misuse.* As evaluation findings are used, the opportunities—and temptations—for misuse increase. "Misuse occurs when stakeholders modify, misstate, or inappropriately excerpt from the evaluation report. You have an important responsibility for assuring that your evaluation is conveying the information intended and not being misapplied in ways not justified by your evaluation" (Alkin, 2011, pp. 211–212).

8. *Champion use of the findings, but don't become a champion for the program.* Evaluator credibility is a major factor in whether findings are used. We can and should advocate for evaluation excellence and use. But, as former AEA President Eleanor Chelimsky (2010) has consistently warned, evaluators must avoid advocating for "individual groups, particular outcomes, partisans, lobbyists, the policy makers who give us grants and contracts, in short, stakeholders in general. The problem is that once the question of evaluative honesty—that paramount value—is raised, it will tend to vitiate the persuasiveness of our work. But this is not the case when we advocate for excellence in evaluation" (p. 1).

EXHIBIT 16.1

Lessons About the Importance of Follow-Up to Enhance Use

1. Plan for follow-up.
2. Budget for follow-up.
3. Adapt findings for different audiences.
4. Keep findings in front of those who can use them.
5. Watch for emergent opportunities to reinforce the relevance of findings.
6. Deal with resistance.
7. Watch for and guard against misuse.
8. Champion use of the findings, but don't become a champion for the program.
9. Continue to build evaluation capacity throughout the follow-up process.
10. Consider the future implications of all you do in follow-up, including interest in a new round of evaluation to address longer-term impact questions, or design of an evaluation for the next phase of an intervention.

9. *Continue to build evaluation capacity for use throughout the follow-up process.* A consistent theme of utilization-focused evaluation concerns the importance of training evaluation users. This is especially important during the ultimate pay-off processes of follow-up when key stakeholders are most directly engaged in going from findings to action, from reflection to decision, and from possible use to actual use. For example, it is rarely sufficient to just ask primary intended users how they want to monitor and reinforce use of findings and recommendations, or how the findings should be adapted for presentation to different audiences. In the active-reactive-interactive-adaptive process of evaluation facilitation, the evaluator will typically need to present primary intended users with options and possibilities, and help them consider the costs and benefit of various proactive approaches to enhancing use. This facilitates action in the moment but also builds capacity for future evaluation use.

10. *Consider the future implications of all you do in follow-up.* The follow-up period is also a transition period to future evaluation efforts. This may involve a new design for the next phase of a program, an evaluation approach for diffusing a successful program ("taking it to scale"), or interest in long-term follow-up of program participants for which there was not sufficient interest or funds originally; positive short-term results can give rise to new

opportunities for longitudinal follow-up. Many evaluations I have completed, *or thought I had completed,* led to revision of the design to include longer-term follow-up as questions of longer-term impact became more relevant and urgent given positive short-term findings.

- "Yes, the participants got and held jobs for 6 months, but what happened over the next 2 years?"
- "So test scores went up between pre- and posttest, but were those gains maintained the next year?"
- "Ahh, the community indicators have improved the past 2 years, but what will happen over the next year?"

The original evaluation design did not include these questions. Often initial evaluation budgets aren't sufficient to include longer-term data collection. Or unless there are positive short-term gains there would be no perceived value in a longitudinal design. Or the original design may have suffered from inadequate vision about what was possible. Whatever the reasons, once the findings are known, new evaluation questions can take center stage.

Negative findings can also generate additional follow-up. Will changes in the program lead to better outcomes? Will short-term negatives become longer-term positives, as when behavior changes take longer to manifest; for example, an initial lack of behavior change (end-of-program results) may turn positive 3 months later when participants have had the opportunity to use what they've learned. I found this to be the case in an early childhood parent education program where short-term behavioral changes were minimal but longer-term changes (6 months later) were significant.

Exhibit 16.1 lists these 10 lessons about the importance of follow-up to enhance use.

Checklist details about what is involved in each step are provided in the summary *U-FE Checklist* in the concluding chapter. See pages 422–423 for the checklist items for Step 16 discussed in this chapter.

PRACTICE EXERCISE

Take some actual evaluation findings and recommendations from a report you locate and consider potential follow-up steps that could be taken with those findings and recommendations. See how many of the 10 follow-up actions from Exhibit 16.1 you can apply to this concrete example you've located. You'll have to speculate and simulate possibilities, but that's how you get better and more creative at follow-up.

INTERLUDE, INTERCONNECTIONS AMONG STEPS 14–16. U-FE AS A COMPLEX DYNAMIC SYSTEM

Facilitating Use

As I've noted throughout, the actual utilization-focused evaluation process unfolds as a complex dynamic system of relationships with the steps interacting. Actions lead to reactions, interactions, feedback loops, and adaptations. This between-chapters interlude offers a graphic depiction of the interactions among Steps 14, 15, and 16. The concluding chapter offers a graphic that shows all 17 U-FE steps as a complex dynamic system (See pages 425–426.)

Interdependence of and Interactions Among Steps 14, 15, and 16

Step 14, organizing and presenting the data for use by primary intended users and others leads to Step 15, reporting findings to facilitate use and disseminate major findings to increase influence. But reactions to the draft report (feedback) may lead to additional analyses and reorganizing the data (back to Step 14). Step 15, reporting, leads to Step 16, following up to facilitate use of findings. That follow-up process, however, may lead to adaptations of the report for new audiences (back to Step 15), or even back to Step 14 for additional analysis. Thus, these processes are interdependent and interconnected rather than simply linear and sequential.

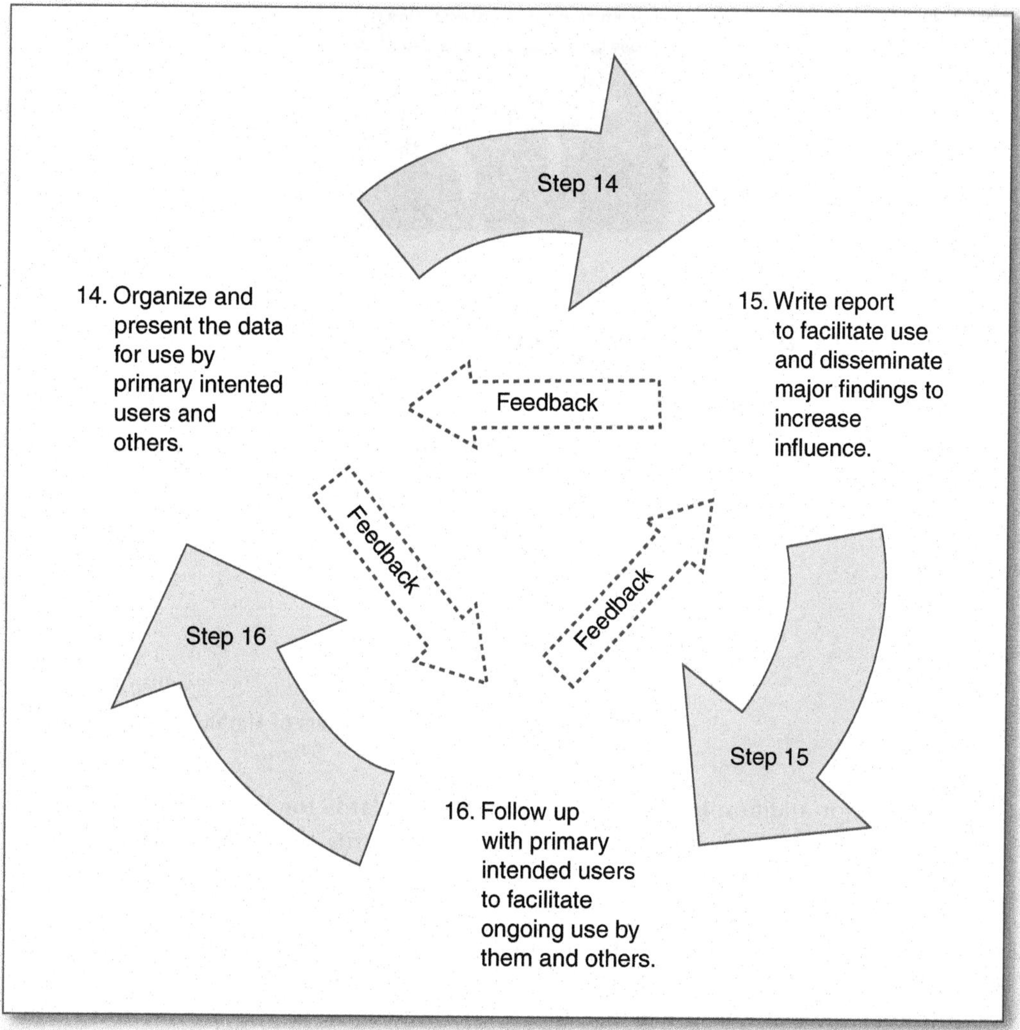
Step 14
14. Organize and present the data for use by primary intented users and others.
15. Write report to facilitate use and disseminate major findings to increase influence.
Feedback
Feedback
Feedback
Step 16
Step 15
16. Follow up with primary intended users to facilitate ongoing use by them and others.

Metaevaluation of Use

Be Accountable, Learn, and Improve

Accountability breeds response-ability.

Stephen R. Covey,
author of The Seven Habits of Highly Effective People

The major addition to the Joint Committee Standards for Evaluation in 2010 was the addition of "Evaluation Accountability Standards" focused on metaevaluation. *Metaevaluation* is evaluation of evaluation. "Metaevaluation is a professional obligation of evaluators. Achieving and sustaining the status of the profession requires subjecting one's work to evaluation and using the findings to serve clients well and over time to strengthen services" (Stufflebeam & Shinkfield, 2007, p. 649).

Utilization-focused metaevaluation focuses on evaluation of use and the factors that affect use, which includes the three standards in addition to utility and accountability: feasibility, propriety, and accuracy. The introductory chapter discussed and presented the standards as the context for the importance of and commitment to utility as a professional standard of excellence. During the 7 years of systematic review of the Joint Committee standards, considerable debate centered around whether to change the order of the categories, making accuracy first instead of utility. Dan Stufflebeam, the visionary chair of the committee that generated and published the first edition of standards in 1981, wrote to the revision committee articulating why the original order should be maintained. A portion of his letter is included in this chapter as Exhibit 17.1. It is well worth reading. I joined him

EXHIBIT 17.1

Why Utility Should Be Retained as First in Sequencing the Evaluation Standards

Daniel L. Stufflebeam

First Chair of the Joint Committee on Standards for Educational Evaluation (Joint Committee, 1994)

The new sequencing of the categories of standards is illogical and a counterproductive break with both the JC Standards' historic rationale and the rationale's position in mainstream evaluation thinking and literature.

The [proposed] new sequencing of the categories of *Standards* that places Accuracy ahead of Utility would, I believe, help return evaluation practice to the days, especially in the 1960s and 1970s, when evaluators produced many technically sound reports that only gathered dust on shelves. This would be a setback for the evaluation field in terms of wasting resources for evaluations in conducting many evaluations that make no difference. Such a return to producing technically elegant but irrelevant evaluation findings would also impair the credibility of professional evaluators.

The re-sequencing of categories of standards ignores the historic case for the original sequencing of categories of standards, as Utility, Feasibility, Propriety, and Accuracy. Originally, that sequencing was recommended by Lee Cronbach and his Stanford U. colleagues. They argued that an evaluation's potential utility should be the first concern of evaluator and constituents, because evaluators should not waste time and money in designing, conducting, and reporting studies that would not be used. Once a study's potential utility is established, then it makes sense, in turn, to assure that the study is feasible to conduct in the particular setting, to subsequently make sure it can meet requirements for propriety, and ultimately to design it to produce accurate findings. The Joint Committee endorsed this rationale, particularly because it was a step toward assuring that scarce evaluation resources would be used to conduct sound evaluations that make a positive difference. Clearly, it makes no sense to engage in extensive technical planning of an evaluation before determining that the evaluation is worth doing.

The above rationale has been well accepted by those who are clients and users of evaluation studies, as seen in the influence by JC representatives of teachers, administrators, and policy makers on the first two editions of the Standards. I would be surprised and disappointed if such representatives on the JC go along with the new sequencing of the categories of standards. . . .

If the JC leads the evaluation field back to where it was in the 1960's, with initial higher order concern for accuracy over utility, I fear we will again see thick reports—based on sophisticated, rigorous methodology—gathering dust on shelves and having only the negative outcomes of wasting effort and resources on studies that make no impact. Given the scarcity of resources for evaluation, studies should be conducted only if they will be used. Moreover, the ones that are done should be squarely focused on the intended users' intended uses and most important questions.

Addressing in order the present Standards' sequence of utility, feasibility, propriety, and accuracy has proved very functional in my evaluations and, I think, in those of others. Here is an example. In approaching the next evaluation I have been asked to conduct, I have set aside questions of feasibility (also, propriety and accuracy) until the client and I can work out questions of intended users and uses. I have convinced the client to give me a small planning grant to clarify the intended users, intended uses, and information requirements and on that basis to prepare a plan and budget for what is needed. It would make no sense for me first to ask this Foundation how much money they can afford, where the political sensitivities are, or even what procedures might not work in the given setting. Consistent with the present Standards, to me it makes eminently more sense to first reach consensus with the client about the users, intended uses, and desired value of the study. Then—given a convincing case for collecting pertinent, relevant information—the client and I will be prepared to engage in meaningful exchange, planning, and contracting concerning aspects of the projected evaluation's feasibility, propriety, and accuracy. . . .

I speak as one who has made extensive use of the *Standards* in a wide range of evaluation and metaevaluation applications. The *Standards* have proved to be an incredibly useful guide in my evaluation work.

Daniel L. Stufflebeam
September 10, 2008

Excerpt from letter to the Joint Committee on Standards for Educational Evaluation
(quoted with permission)

---

in advocating that utility remain first among equals. After extensive debate and review, including "the involvement of more than 400 stakeholders in national and international reviews, field trials, and national hearings" (Joint Committee, 2010), the first revision of the standards in 17 years was published retaining the categories in their original order with utility first (Yarbrough, Shulha, Hopson, & Caruthers, 2010). What the revised edition did add is the new category on "Evaluation Accountability" that includes three standards highlighting the importance of metaevaluation (see Exhibit 17.2).

Utilization-Focused Evaluation Metaevaluation

The Joint Committee Standards are not sufficient for a utilization-focused evaluation metaevaluation. Why? I'm glad you asked. Let me explain. Exhibit 17.3 cross-references the Joint Committee standards with the steps in utilization-focused evaluation as presented in this book. That exhibit reviews all eight Utility Standards and the general categories of Feasibility, Propriety, and Accuracy. The Utility Standards cover Evaluator Credibility, Attention to Stakeholders, Negotiated Purposes, Explicit Values, Relevant Information, Meaningful

EXHIBIT 17.2

Evaluation Accountability Standards

E1 Evaluation Documentation Evaluations should fully document their negotiated purposes and implemented designs, procedures, data, and outcomes.

E2 Internal Metaevaluation Evaluators should use these and other applicable standards to examine the accountability of the evaluation design, procedures employed, information collected, and outcomes.

E3 External Metaevaluation Program evaluation sponsors, clients, evaluators, and other stakeholders should encourage the conduct of external metaevaluations using these and other applicable standards. (Joint Committee, 2010; Yarbrough et al., 2010)

EXHIBIT 17.3

Standards and Steps in Utilization-Focused Evaluation (U-FE)

The utility standards are intended to ensure that an evaluation will serve the information needs of intended users. Utilization-focused evaluation aims to achieve intended use by intended users.

Utility standards (Joint Committee, 2010)	*Specific quality criterion*	*U-FE step focused on this criterion*
U1 Evaluator Credibility	Evaluations should devote attention to the full range of individuals and groups invested in the program and affected by its evaluation.	Step 2
U2 Attention to Stakeholders	Evaluations should devote attention to the full range of individuals and groups invested in the program and affected by its evaluation.	Step 3
U3 Negotiated Purposes	Evaluation purposes should be identified and continually negotiated based on the needs of stakeholders.	Steps 5 & 7

(Continued)

(Continued)

Utility standards (Joint Committee, 2010)	*Specific quality criterion*	*U-FE step focused on this criterion*
U4 Explicit Values	Evaluations should clarify and specify the individual and cultural values underpinning purposes, processes, and judgments.	Steps 1 & 14
U5 Relevant Information	Evaluation information should serve the identified and emergent needs of stakeholders.	Steps 3, 4, 5, 6, 7, 8, & 9
U6 Meaningful Processes and Products	Evaluations should construct activities, descriptions, and judgments in ways that encourage participants to rediscover, reinterpret, or revise their understandings and behaviors.	Steps 6, 14, 15, & 16
U7 Timely and Appropriate Communicating and Reporting	Evaluations should attend to the continuing information needs of their multiple audiences.	Steps 15 & 16
U8 Concern for Consequences and Influence	Evaluations should promote responsible and adaptive use while guarding against unintended negative consequences and misuse.	Steps 1, 4, 5, 6, 14, 15, & 16
	Additional Standards	
Feasibility Standards	The feasibility standards are intended to ensure that an evaluation will be realistic, prudent, diplomatic, and frugal.	Steps 1, 4, 5, 6 & 7
Propriety Standards	The propriety standards are intended to ensure that an evaluation will be conducted legally, ethically, and with due regard for the welfare of those involved in the evaluation, as well as those affected by its results.	Steps 2, 3, 4, 5, & 6
Accuracy Standards	The accuracy standards are intended to ensure that an evaluation will reveal and convey technically adequate information about the features that determine worth or merit of the program being evaluated.	Steps 8, 9, 10, 11, 12, 13, 14, & 15.

SOURCE: Joint Committee on Standards, 2010; Yarbrough, Shulha, Hopson, & Caruthers, 2010.

Processes and Products, Timely and Appropriate Communicating and Reporting, and Concern for Consequences and Influence. These are all important as factors contributing to use, but *the glaring gap in these criteria is actual use.* Did the intended users use the evaluation in intended ways? That is the essential criterion for utilization-focused metaevaluation.

The standard on Concern for Consequences and Influence comes close but stops short of calling for metaevaluation of actual use. It says, "Evaluations should promote responsible and adaptive use while guarding against unintended negative consequences and misuse" (U8). That's fine as far as it goes, "promoting use," but the bottom-line metaevaluation question should be whether and how the evaluation was actually used, not whether use was promoted. When evaluating a program, we don't just ask whether participant outcomes were promoted. We evaluate whether those outcomes were attained.

Utility Versus Use

Utilization-focused evaluation begins with the premise that evaluations should be judged by their utility—*and* actual use. The distinction between utility and use is important, and it was the focus of a debate I had with distinguished evaluation philosopher Michael Scriven in 2009 (Patton & Scriven, 2010). Use concerns how real people in the real world apply

"I envy your confidence. Even after decades of evaluations, these metaevalutions still make me feel naked."

evaluation findings and experience the evaluation process. In contrast, in Scriven's checklist for evaluation, he asserts that "Utility is usability and not actual use, the latter—or its absence—being at best a probabilistically sufficient but not necessary condition for the former, since it may have been very hard to use the results of the evaluation, and utility/usability means (reasonable) ease of use" (Scriven, 2007, p. 21). There is, then, a fundamental difference of opinion here about judging evaluations on their actual use versus their potential utility and possible ease of use.

This is a critical metaevaluation issue. To me, this is the equivalent, on the program side, of the program people saying, "We've developed a tremendous curriculum. The experts have reviewed this curriculum. It has high potential utility. The fact that kids aren't learning from it is their problem, not ours." This is the classic problem of confusing the output with the outcome. As evaluators, we don't let programs get away with just evaluating outputs and ignoring outcomes. We have to hold ourselves to at least that same standard.

Let's get very clear about this because it is central to the message of this entire book: A "utilizable" report is an output—and an important one. But the intended outcome is actual use. A metaevaluation that affirms that the report has high potential utility has evaluated an output. To conduct a metaevaluation on actual use requires going beyond assessing the potential utility of the report to finding out whether primary intended users actually used the evaluation in intended ways. So, yes, by all means include usability and potential utility as metaevaluation criteria, but the higher metaevaluation standard is whether and how an evaluation is actually used.

Follow-Up Support as a Metaevaluation Criterion

Now, where Scriven and I agree is about the importance of Step 16 in utilization-focused evaluation: going beyond producing a report to actually facilitating use. "Help with utilization beyond submitting the report should at least have been offered" (Scriven, 2007, p. 21). This adds the nature and quality of follow-up facilitation as a metaevaluation criterion, a position with which I heartily agree. As Scriven has elaborated:

> I encourage very strongly the idea that evaluators must stay with a whole phase beyond submitting a report, into interpretation and decisionmaking, if it's accessible. In my checklist for all evaluation designs, that point is called *Report and Support,* not just Report; the support is at least support in interpretation of the report *and its real implications.* (Patton & Scriven, 2010, p. 31)

Follow-up support is also a checkpoint in Stufflebeam's *Metaevaluation Checklist.* To ensure Evaluation Impact:

- Encourage and support stakeholders' use of the findings
- Show stakeholders how they might use the findings in their work

- Forecast and address potential uses of findings
- Conduct feedback workshops to go over and apply findings
- Make arrangements to provide follow-up assistance in interpreting and applying the findings. (Stufflebeam, 1999b, p. 3)

Stufflebeam offers detailed checkpoints for evaluating the report's potential utility by ensuring clarity and timeliness (p. 2), but he makes it clear that impact (actual use) is different from and requires action beyond reporting, namely, "make arrangements to provide follow-up assistance in interpreting and applying the findings."

International Metaevaluation Criteria: DAC Standards

The Development Assistance Committee of the Organisation for Economic Co-operation and Development (OECD) established its own standards for evaluation in 2010 (DAC, 2010). A Network on Development Evaluation supports implementation of the standards. Exhibit 17.4 presents the issues addressed by the DAC Standards. Of particular interest for our purposes is the fourth of the four categories: Follow-up, Use and Learning. Here the DAC standards go beyond utility to address actual use. In so doing, processes of interaction and engagement are offered to support actual use that go well beyond anything in the Joint Committee Standards.

EXHIBIT 17.4

DAC Quality Standards for Development Evaluation

1. *Overarching considerations*
   - 1.1 Development evaluation
   - 1.2 Free and open evaluation process
   - 1.3 Evaluation ethics
   - 1.4 Partnership approach
   - 1.5 Co-ordination and alignment
   - 1.6 Capacity development
   - 1.7 Quality control
2. *Purpose, planning and design*
   - 2.1 Rationale and purpose of the evaluation
   - 2.2 Specific objectives of the evaluation

- 2.3 Evaluation object and scope
- 2.4 Evaluability
- 2.5 Stakeholder involvement
- 2.6 Systematic consideration of joint evaluation
- 2.7 Evaluation questions
- 2.8 Selection and application of evaluation criteria
- 2.9 Selection of approach and methodology
- 2.10 Resources
- 2.11 Governance and management structures
- 2.12 Document defining purpose and expectations

3. *Implementation and reporting*

- 3.1 Evaluation team
- 3.2 Independence of evaluators vis-à-vis stakeholders
- 3.3 Consultation and protection of stakeholders
- 3.4 Implementation of evaluation within allotted time and budget
- 3.5 Evaluation report
- 3.6 Clarity and representativeness of summary
- 3.7 Context of the development intervention
- 3.8 Intervention logic
- 3.9 Validity and reliability of information sources
- 3.10 Explanation of the methodology used
- 3.11 Clarity of analysis
- 3.12 Evaluation questions answered
- 3.13 Acknowledgement of changes and limitations of the evaluation
- 3.14 Acknowledgement of disagreements within the evaluation team
- 3.15 Incorporation of stakeholders' comments

4. *Follow-up, use and learning*

- 4.1 Timeliness, relevance and use of the evaluation
- 4.2 Systematic response to and follow-up on recommendations
- 4.3 Dissemination

SOURCE: OECD, 2010.

DAC Standard Supporting Actual Use

Standard 4.1, on *timeliness, relevance, and use of the evaluation*, begins: "The evaluation is designed, conducted and reported to meet the needs of the intended users" (p. 15). That, in essence, is the overarching criterion of utilization-focused evaluation. It goes on: "Conclusions, recommendations and lessons are clear, relevant, targeted and actionable so that the evaluation can be used to achieve its intended learning and accountability objectives." These are basically *potential* utility criteria, as is the standard that "the evaluation is delivered in time to ensure optimal use of the results." Standard 4.1 concludes by requiring that "Systematic dissemination, storage and management of the evaluation report is ensured to provide easy access to all development partners, to reach target audiences, and to maximize the learning benefits of the evaluation" (p. 15). But here's where it gets interesting. Standard 4.2 moves from potential utility to actual use:

> *4.2 Systematic response to and follow-up on recommendations*
>
> Recommendations are systematically responded to and action taken by the person(s)/body targeted in each recommendation. This includes a formal management response and follow-up. All agreed follow-up actions are tracked to ensure accountability for their implementation. (OECD, 2010, p. 15)

This standard creates an interaction around the evaluation findings and recommendations. The evaluator offers findings and recommendations; then those who are supposed to act on findings and implement recommendations are asked for a formal response. They are then asked to report on what follow-up actions are taken. And this *coup de grâce:* **All agreed follow-up actions are tracked to ensure accountability for their implementation.** Actual use is an explicit metaevaluation criterion. *Bravo!*

Making Metaevaluation Utilization-Focused

How does one conduct a utilization-focused metaevaluation? The answer is straightforward: the same way you conduct a utilization-focused evaluation, by focusing on intended use by intended users. Who is the metaevaluation for? What is its purpose?

The Joint Committee Evaluation Accountability Standards (Exhibit 17.2) distinguish internal from external metaevaluation. Internal metaevaluation involves ongoing attention to quality assurance standards as the evaluation is being designed, conducted, and reported. External metaevaluation is done when the stakes are high and use is enhanced by ensuring the evaluation's credibility through independent, external evaluation of the evaluation. All the steps of utilization-focused evaluation presented in this book apply to metaevaluation, though in abbreviated and condensed form because of the narrower window of time in which a metaevaluation must be conducted to be timely and therefore useful.

Metaevaluation of Potential Utility and Actual Use

One implication of distinguishing utility versus use in the standards, and therefore in metaevaluation, is that the time lines are likely to be different. A metaevaluation of how the evaluation was conducted, including the quality of the report, can and should be done close to the completion of the report. The metaevaluation of actual use will have to be done some time later, when there has been an opportunity for use to occur.

For example, as this is written, I have begun a metaevaluation of the evaluation of implementation of the Paris Declaration on development aid. The Paris Declaration, endorsed on March 2, 2005, committed more than 100 government leaders, heads of agencies, and other senior officials to increase efforts to harmonize and align aid initiatives, and manage aid for results with a set of "monitorable actions and indicators" (OECD, 2005). The Accra Agenda for Action in 2008 added specific criteria for a more collaborative approach focused on developing countries' own development objectives.

The evaluation of the implementation of the Paris Declaration will be completed and the report submitted in mid-2011. That report will be aimed at the next major High Level Forum on Aid Effectiveness that take place in Busan, South Korea, in December 2011. The metaevaluation I submit will be completed in time to be used in conjunction with the evaluation report. That metaevaluation can only assess *potential utility* as well as adherence to other DAC Quality Standards (Exhibit 17.4). Any metaevaluation of *actual use* of the overall synthesis evaluation report can only be done during and after the High Level Forum since participants and decision makers in that Forum are the primary intended users. However, metaevaluation of the actual uses of individual country and agency reports that make up the overall synthesis report can and is being done sooner since those reports were completed by the end of 2010 and the primary intended users of those reports are decision makers in the countries and agencies. The point here is that a metaevaluation, like any utilization-focused evaluation, must be guided by strategic decisions about supporting intended uses by intended users. When, as in the case of the metaevaluation of the Paris Declaration, there are different intended users with different intended uses, the metaevaluation has to be conducted in distinct phases and delivered under different time lines to meet the needs of different stakeholders.

Reflective Practice and Learning

> *We now accept the fact that learning is a lifelong process of keeping abreast of change. And the most pressing task is to teach people how to learn.*
>
> *Peter Drucker (1909–2005)*
> management consultant and author,
> known as the "Father of Modern Management"

"I can honestly say that not a day goes by when we don't use those evaluations in one way or another."

Step 2 focused on assessing evaluator readiness by examining essential competencies for utilization-focused evaluators. Exhibit 17.5 summarizes the six categories of evaluator competence. These are used to guide professional development as the Canadian Evaluation Society is doing in its Professional Designations Program initiative (CES, 2010). The competencies also aim to ensure that evaluators will have the skills and knowledge necessary to effectively and credibly conduct an evaluation, basically a front-end assessment, which is why it is Step 2 in this book. But here I want to highlight the competencies as a metaevaluation framework for use *after an evaluation* to set priorities for ongoing professional improvement. I want to focus especially *on Reflective Practice* as a useful and important metaevaluation commitment.

EXHIBIT 17.5

Essential Evaluator Competencies as a Metaevaluation Framework

1. *Professional practice:* knowing and observing professional norms and values, including evaluation standards and principles.
2. *Systematic inquiry:* expertise in the technical aspects of evaluations, such as design, measurement, data analysis, interpretation, and sharing results.
3. *Situational analysis:* understanding and attending to the contextual and political issues of an evaluation, including determining evaluability, addressing conflicts, and attending to issues of evaluation use.
4. *Project management:* the nuts and bolts of managing an evaluation from beginning to end, including negotiating contracts, budgeting, identifying and coordinating needed resources, and conducting the evaluation in a timely manner.
5. *Reflective practice:* an awareness of one's program evaluation expertise as well as the needs for professional growth.
6. *Interpersonal competence:* the people skills needed to work with diverse groups of stakeholders to conduct program evaluations, including written and oral communication, negotiation, and cross-cultural skills.

SOURCES: Ghere, King, Stevahn, & Minnema, 2006; King, Stevahn, Ghere, & Minnema, 2001; Stevahn, King, Ghere, & Minnema, 2005, 2006.

While the Joint Committee Standards focus on metaevaluation as an accountability exercise, it can also be a learning exercise. We need to pause after an evaluation to reflect on what has gone well, what hasn't gone well, and how we can improve our work in the future. But we are busy and, despite the best of intentions, seldom do this. In speeches and workshops at professional evaluation association meetings I like to ask for a show of hands of those who systematically reflect on evaluations they have conducted for learning and further professional development. Few hands go up; typically, in fact, no one raises a hand.

The Institute of Management Consultants (2010) has found that effective consultants work at deepening their skills and updating their knowledge: "The most successful consultants, and the ones their clients value most, are created by making the commitment to hard learning and active professional development" (p. 251). All utilization-focused evaluators are consultants. As the essential competencies make clear, we all need effective interpersonal skills, up-to-date knowledge of methods and technology (like the latest in making visually effective presentations discussed in Step 15), better ways of doing situation analysis, efficient project management techniques, and engagement with innovative professional practices like incorporating complexity thinking and social networking into evaluations (Patton, 2011). Yes, attending professional evaluation conferences, taking workshops, and reading the latest journals and evaluation books are part of ongoing professional development, but the most personalized and individualized professional development comes from rigorous and systematic reflection on your own practice. And that means evaluating your evaluations.

The greatest influence on my thinking and practice has come from client feedback and follow-up utilization reviews of evaluations I've conducted. When I established the Minnesota Center for Social Research in the mid-1970s, I began the practice of following up every evaluation we conducted to find out how it was used. Those evaluations are the basis for many of the stories in my writings. Part of my preparation for doing a new edition of *Utilization-Focused Evaluation* (2008) is reviewing client feedback from evaluations and participant evaluations from workshops. When in the mid-1990s I went to prepare the third edition of the book and began reflecting on what had happened in the field in the 10 years since the previous edition, I was struck by something that my own myopia had not allowed me to see before. When I have followed up my own evaluations over the years, I have enquired from intended users about actual use. What I would typically hear was something like: Yes, the findings were helpful in this way and that, and here's what we did with them. If there had been recommendations, I would ask what subsequent actions, if any, followed. But, beyond the focus on findings and recommendations, what they almost inevitably added was something to the effect that "it wasn't really the findings that were so important in the end, it was going through the process." And I would reply: "That's nice. I'm glad you appreciated the process, but what did you do with the findings?" In reflecting on these interactions, I came to realize that *the entire field had narrowly defined use as use of findings*. We had thus not had ways to conceptualize or talk about what happens to people and organizations as a result of being involved in an evaluation process: what I have come to call "process use," attention to which is Step 6 in this book.

Likewise, I became involved in applying complexity concepts to evaluation (Patton, 2011) in response to requests from clients and metaevaluation reflective practice with clients and colleagues about the inadequacies of the linear models used in specific evaluations. Reflective practice itself, as a rigorous way of learning, was an approach I first used with evaluation clients to systematically and regularly capture developments in a program over time. That led me to conceptualize the steps in undertaking reflective practice for evaluation purposes (Patton, 2011, pp. 266–269). Thus it was as part of using reflective practice with clients that I learned to use it to improve my own evaluation practice. Reflective practice is more than spending 10 minutes at the end of an evaluation congratulating oneself on getting the damn thing done. It is systematic inquiry into what worked well, what didn't work so well, what was useful, what was not useful, and evaluating the evaluation against the criteria in the standards and the essential competencies. This is best done collaboratively with the primary intended users who were involved throughout the evaluation.

Commitment to Ongoing Professional Development

As evaluators, we are *knowledge workers,* a term coined a half century ago by eminent management consultant and scholar Peter Drucker to describe people who work primarily with information, developing and applying knowledge for improvement. He devoted his extensive career to enhancing knowledge use for organizational development and concluded:

> Understanding our strengths, articulating our values, knowing where we belong—these are also essential to addressing one of the great challenges of organizations: improving the abysmally low productivity of knowledge workers. (Drucker, 1999, p. 157)

Evaluators are by no means exempt from this observation and judgment. Metaevaluation, including serious reflective practice, is a commitment to get better at what we do and adapt to new challenges with innovative approaches as the world changes—and evaluation changes accordingly, or dies.

Checklist details about what is involved in each step are provided in the summary *U-FE Checklist* in the next and last chapter of this book. See pages 423–424 for the checklist items for Step 17 discussed in this chapter.

PRACTICE EXERCISE

Locate an evaluation report. Based on the purpose of the evaluation, the context in which it took place, and what you can glean about its intended users and intended uses, propose a metaevaluation of that evaluation.

Summary and Conclusion

I opened the preface of this book with reference to Janus, the Roman god depicted with two faces looking in opposite directions. The two directions I wanted to evoke were (1) linear step-by-step progression and (2) complex dynamic and nonlinear interactions. First then, throughout this book I have presented utilization-focused evaluation (U-FE) as a series of steps.

Utilization-Focused Evaluation Steps

Step 1.	Assess and build program and organizational readiness for utilization-focused evaluation
Step 2.	Assess and enhance evaluator readiness and competence to undertake a utilization-focused evaluation
Step 3.	Identify, organize, and engage primary intended users
Step 4.	Situation analysis conducted jointly with primary intended users
Step 5.	Identify and prioritize primary intended uses by determining priority purposes
Step 6.	Consider and build in process uses if and as appropriate
Step 7.	Focus priority evaluation questions
Step 8.	Check that fundamental areas for evaluation inquiry are being adequately addressed
Step 9.	Determine what intervention model or theory of change is being evaluated
Step 10.	Negotiate appropriate methods to generate credible findings that support intended use by intended users
Step 11.	Make sure intended users understand potential methods controversies and their implications
Step 12.	Simulate use of findings

(Continued)

(Continued)

Step 13.	Gather data with ongoing attention to use
Step 14.	Organize and present the data for interpretation and use by primary intended users
Step 15.	Prepare an evaluation report to facilitate use and disseminate significant findings to expand influence
Step 16.	Follow up with primary intended users to facilitate and enhance use
Step 17.	Metaevaluation of use: Be accountable, learn, and improve

Complete U-FE Checklist

This concluding chapter presents the full, detailed 17-step utilization-focused checklist that describes the primary tasks and major facilitation challenges of each step. That is followed, on p. 426, with a final and complete complex dynamic systems graphic depicting the interactions and interdependencies among the steps. These are the Janus-like two faces of U-FE, looking in opposite directions, but also looking at the same thing. Each alternative and contrasting depiction of the U-FE process is accurate yet distorted in some ways. The checklist steps portray an overly linear and sequential process but can be helpful in proposing, planning, and managing a utilization-focused evaluation and understanding the work involved in fulfilling each step. The complex dynamic systems graphic shows the interdependencies and interactions among the steps but can feel overwhelming in its complexity. Use the one that works for you and your personality type, or use both together, or each in turn. And, along the way, engage in some reflective practice on your uses and preferences.

Controlled Folly and Use

There's another sense in which the dual perspectives of Janus are relevant to utilization-focused evaluation: namely, by approaching use with a sense of controlled folly.

The sorcerer Don Juan, teaching anthropologist Carlos Castenada (1971) the *Yaqui Way of Knowledge,* introduced him to the idea of *controlled folly.* Controlled folly is quintessential Janus, acting within two perspectives at once and, in so doing, embracing paradox. One perspective is control. The other is chaos. In Don Juan's teaching, controlled folly required acting at every moment as if you are in complete control of your life while simultaneously knowing at the deepest level of knowing that our actions are all folly because larger forces are at work over which we ultimately have no control. What does this have to do with utilization-focused evaluation?

In my 2009 Claremont debate with Michael Scriven (Patton & Scriven, 2010), he worried about assigning blame for whether an evaluation gets used. It isn't automatically the evaluator's fault if use doesn't occur, he insisted. Many factors come into play, including resistant program managers, mistaken interpretations (misuse), and decision-maker incorrigibility, so . . .

> It's really important to be prepared to insulate the evaluator from unfair criticism due to nonuse when that's unfair criticism. If there's the slightest grounds for it being fair criticism, for example, that the report is full of technical jargon that you didn't need to use, or should have been translated, or that the authors keep getting off into academic sidetracks about the interesting issues that are not really relevant to the need of the decision maker—then, of course, the blame must fall on them. But if the mistake was not made at your point, and you wrote a highly usable set of recommendations and evaluations, and it wasn't used through somebody else making a mistake—that's not your fault. (p. 31)

Teachers worry about being blamed for low achievement when it's really parents' fault. Police worry about being blamed for crimes committed by repeat offenders when it's really judges' fault for not imposing harsher sentences. Doctors worry about being blamed for deaths—and sued—when it's really the patient's fault, or the blame resides with inadequate knowledge, or underfunded research, or hospital rules, or the unfairness of life. And evaluators worry about being blamed about nonuse when it's really the intended users' fault for not acting on the findings, actions that lie well beyond the evaluator's control. I hear this regularly from participants in utilization-focused evaluation workshops. "There's only so much we can do."

But this isn't about blaming, or escaping blame. It's about doing the best we can in an uncertain world. Utilization-focused evaluation comes with no guarantees. Far from it. The odds are often stacked against use. Many factors affect use, most of them out of the evaluator's control. Utilization-focused evaluation is just trying to improve the odds a bit, tilt the scale in the direction of greater and more meaningful use. So what does controlled folly have to do with this?

"There's only so much we can do." True enough. Then do that—and do it ferociously. Controlled folly points us to acting as if we are in control even when we know we aren't. Integrity lies in doing all we can do. Sorcerer, jester, and, yes, evaluator Don Juan asserts:

A person of knowledge chooses any act, and acts it out as if what is done matters, so when the action is fulfilled, peace follows. The utilization-focused evaluator acts as if what is done, when it is well done, with a focus on use, will lead to use, so when the evaluation is completed, peace follows.

Peace be with you.

In that spirit, I leave you with this thought from my philosophical alter ego, Halcolm:

A society that aspires to greatness will ultimately
be known by how it values evaluation—and evaluators.

UTILIZATION-FOCUSED EVALUATION CHECKLIST

17 Steps to Evaluations That Are Useful—and Actually Used

Each chapter describes a step in utilization-focused evaluation (U-FE). This checklist provides a summary of the steps. The checklist has two columns. Primary *U-FE tasks* are in the column on the left. Because of the emphasis on facilitation in U-FE, particular facilitation challenges are identified in the column on the right. Basic premises are presented for each step to provide a context for the primary tasks and special facilitation challenges.

Step 1. Assess and build program and organizational readiness for utilization-focused evaluation	
Premises: • Programs and organizations that are ready to seriously engage in evaluation are more likely to participate in ways that enhance use. • Use is more likely if key people who will be involved in and affected by the evaluation become interested in evidence-based reality testing, evaluative thinking, and use.	**Premises:** • The U-FE evaluator must engage those involved in an evaluation in ways that will deepen their understanding of evaluation and commitment to use. • Evaluability assessment includes examining if the program and organizational cultures are receptive to and ready for evaluation.
Primary tasks	*Evaluation facilitation challenges*
❑ Assess the commitment of those commissioning and funding the evaluation to doing useful evaluation.	Explaining U-FE and assessing readiness for evaluation generally and U-FE specifically
❑ Assess the evaluation context: ✓ Review important documents and interview key stakeholders. ✓ Conduct a baseline assessment of past evaluation use. ✓ Find out current perceptions about evaluation.	• Conducting individual and/or focus group interviews to get baseline information • Building trust for honest discussions about how evaluation is viewed
❑ When ready to engage, plan a launch workshop that will involve key stakeholders to both assess and build readiness for evaluation.	• Agreeing on what diverse stakeholders to involve in the launch workshop • Planning the launch workshop to deepen the commitment to reality testing and use

✓ Work with key stakeholders to launch the evaluation. ✓ Make the launch workshop an opportunity to further assess readiness for evaluation as well as enhance readiness.	• Creating a positive vision for evaluation and assessing incentives for and barriers to engaging in evaluation • Generating specific norms to guide the evaluation process • Other exercises that build capacity to engage in evaluation (See Menu 1.1.)
❑ Introduce the standards for evaluation as the framework within which the evaluation will be conducted (Joint Committee, 2010).	• Explaining the evaluation standards and their relevance to this evaluation • Facilitating the group to add their own norms for the evaluation
❑ Based on the initial experience working with key stakeholders, assess what needs to be done next to further enhance readiness, build capacity, and move the evaluation forward.	• Planning, negotiating, and facilitating the commitment of key stakeholders to move forward with evaluation • Generating commitment to strengthen evaluation capacity, as needed
Step 2. Assess and enhance evaluator readiness and competence to undertake a utilization-focused evaluation	
Premise: Facilitating and conducting a utilization-focused evaluation requires a particular philosophy and special skills.	**Premise:** Evaluation facilitators need to know their strengths and limitations and develop the skills needed to facilitate utilization-focused evaluations.
Primary tasks	*Evaluation facilitation challenges*
❑ Assess the *evaluator's* essential competencies: 1. Professional practice knowledge 2. Systematic inquiry skills 3. Situation analysis skills 4. Project management skills 5. Reflective practice competence 6. Interpersonal competence 7. Cultural competence	• As an evaluator, being rigorously reflexive about your strengths and weaknesses • In working with primary intended users, being forthright about those strengths and weaknesses • Engaging in ongoing professional development to build on strengths and reduce weaknesses
❑ Assess the match between the *evaluator's commitment* and the likely challenges of the situation.	Matching the evaluator's competencies with what is needed to work effectively with a particular group of primary intended users, evaluation situation, and set of challenges

(Continued)

(Continued)

❑ Assess the match between the *evaluator's substantive knowledge* and what will be needed in the evaluation.	Demonstrating sufficient substantive knowledge of the program being evaluated to have credibility with key stakeholders and be able to facilitate discussions on substantive issues
❑ Adapt the evaluation as the process unfolds.	Working with primary intended users in an active-reactive-interactive-adaptive style
❑ Assess whether a single evaluator or a team is needed, and the combination of competencies that will be needed in a team approach.	Working together as a team offers opportunity for mutual support and greater diversity of competencies brought to the evaluation but adds the complication of integrating team members into an effective working group
❑ Assure that the evaluators are prepared to have their effectiveness judged by the use of the evaluation by primary intended users.	Keeping the whole evaluation process focused on the outcome of intended use by intended users
Step 3. Identify, organize, and engage primary intended users	
Premise: Identifying, organizing, and engaging primary intended users optimizes the *personal factor,* which emphasizes that an evaluation is more likely to be used if intended users are involved in ways they find meaningful, feel ownership of the evaluation, find the questions relevant, and care about the findings. Primary intended users are people who have a direct, identifiable stake in the evaluation.	**Premise:** The U-FE facilitator has a stake in evaluation use and therefore an interest in identifying and working with primary intended users to enhance use.
Primary tasks	*Evaluation facilitation challenges*
❑ Find and involve primary intended users who are: ✓ Interested ✓ Knowledgeable ✓ Open ✓ Connected to important stakeholder constituencies ✓ Credible ✓ Teachable ✓ Committed and available for interaction throughout the evaluation process	• Determining real interest; building interest as needed; sustaining interest throughout the U-FE process • Determining knowledge of users; increasing knowledge as needed • Facilitating an evaluation climate of openness • Working with primary intended users to examine stakeholder connections and their implications for use • Building and sustaining credibility of the evaluation working group made up of primary intended users

	• Outlining and facilitating a process that intended users want to be part of and will commit to
❑ Explain the role of primary intended users throughout the evaluation process.	Helping primary intended users understand and commit to a utilization-focused evaluation
❑ Organize primary intended users into a working group for decision making and involvement.	Facilitating group identity, trust, and willingness to work together to plan the evaluation and negotiate key issues that will affect the evaluation's credibility and use
❑ Involve intended users throughout all steps of the U-FE process.	Building and enhancing the capacity of primary intended users to prioritize evaluation questions, make good design decisions, interpret data, and follow through to get findings used
❑ Monitor ongoing availability, interest, and participation of primary intended users to keep the process energized and anticipate turnover of primary intended users.	• Getting feedback about how intended users are experiencing the U-FE process • At the first indication of turnover, assessing the implications and planning to replace any primary intended users
❑ Orient any new intended users added to the evaluation working group along the way.	Facilitating understanding, commitment, and buy-in by new intended users added to the working group. In some cases, this may involve tweaking the design or data collection plan to incorporate and show responsiveness to their priority concerns.
Step 4. Situation analysis conducted jointly with primary intended users	
Premises: • Evaluation use is people- and context-dependent. • Use is likely to be enhanced when the evaluation takes into account and is adapted to crucial situational factors.	**Premises:** • The evaluator has responsibility to work with primary intended users to identify, assess, understand, and act on situational factors that may affect use. • Situation analysis is ongoing.
Primary tasks	*Evaluation facilitation challenges*
❑ Examine the program's prior experiences with evaluation and other factors that are important to understand the situation and context. (See Exhibits 4.1, 4.4, and 4.5.)	Working with intended users to identify and strategize about critical factors that can affect the priority questions, evaluation design, and evaluation use
❑ Identify factors that may support and facilitate use. (Force field analysis, Exhibits 4.2 and 4.3)	Distinguishing and strategizing about enabling factors that may enhance use

(Continued)

(Continued)

❑ Look for possible barriers or resistance to use. (Force field analysis, Exhibits 4.2 and 4.3)	Looking honestly for and assessing potential barriers to use
❑ Get clear about resources available for evaluation.	Including in the budget resources beyond analysis and reporting to facilitate use
❑ Identify any upcoming decisions, deadlines, or time lines that the evaluation should meet to be useful.	Being realistic about time lines; knowing about and meeting critical deadlines
❑ Assess leadership support for and openness to the evaluation.	Engaging leadership in a way that makes the evaluation meaningful and relevant (See Exhibit 4.7.)
❑ Understand the political context for the evaluation, and calculate how political factors may affect use.	Including attention to and being sophisticated about both potential uses and potential misuses of the evaluation politically
❑ Assess the implications for use of the evaluator's location internal or external to the program being evaluated; assess how internal-external combinations might enhance use. (See Exhibit 4.6.)	Assessing factors that can affect the evaluation's credibility and relevance, and therefore utility, like the advantages and disadvantages of internal and external evaluator locations and combinations
❑ Assess the appropriate evaluation team composition to ensure needed expertise, credibility, and cultural competence.	Finding the right mix of team members that can work together to produce a high-quality, useful evaluation
❑ Attend to both: ✓ Tasks that must be completed, and ✓ Relationship dynamics that support getting tasks done.	Finding and facilitating an appropriate balance between tasks and relationships (outcomes and process)
❑ Risk analysis: Assess ✓ idea risks, ✓ implementation risks, and ✓ evidence risks. (See Exhibit 4.8.)	Developing *contingency thinking* to be able to anticipate risks, identify risks as they emerge, and respond to challenges as they develop
❑ Continue assessing the evaluation knowledge, commitment, and experiences of primary intended users.	Building into the evaluation process opportunities to increase the capacity, knowledge, and commitment of primary intended users
❑ *Steps 1 to 4 interim outcomes check and complex systems interconnections review.*	• Understanding and taking into account system dynamics and interrelationships as the evaluation unfolds

Overall situation analysis: ✓ How good is the match between the evaluation team's capacity, the organization's readiness and evaluation needs, and the primary intended user's readiness to move forward with the evaluation?	• Being attentive to and adapting to complex system dynamics as they emerge • Staying active-reactive-interactive-adaptive throughout the evaluation
Step 5. Identify and prioritize primary intended uses by determining priority purposes	
Premise: *Intended use by primary intended users* is the U-FE goal. Use flows from clarity about purpose.	**Premise:** The menu of evaluation options should be reviewed, screened, and prioritized by primary intended users to clarify the primary purposes and uses of the evaluation.
Primary tasks	*Evaluation facilitation challenges*
❑ Review alternative purpose options with primary intended users.	Helping primary intended users understand evaluation purpose options and the importance of prioritizing the evaluation's purpose
✓ Consider how evaluation could contribute to **program improvement.**	Guiding primary intended users in reviewing potential formative evaluation uses
✓ Consider how summative evaluation judgments could contribute to **making major decisions** about the program.	Guiding primary intended users in reviewing summative evaluation opportunities to inform major decisions based on judgments of merit, worth, and significance
✓ Consider **accountability** uses.	Guiding users in assessing oversight and compliance issues, and the accountability context for the evaluation
✓ Consider **monitoring** uses.	Guiding users in examining the relationship between monitoring and evaluation
✓ Consider **developmental** uses.	Guiding users in distinguishing developmental evaluation from other uses, especially program improvement (i.e., the difference between improvement and *development*)
✓ Consider how evaluation could contribute by **generating knowledge.**	Guiding primary intended users in considering the possibility of using evaluation to generate lessons learned and evidence-based practices that might apply beyond the program being evaluated

(Continued)

(Continued)

❑ Prioritize the evaluation's purpose.	• Working with primary intended users to establish priorities and resolve conflicts over competing purposes, avoiding ambiguity or confusion about priorities • Avoiding the temptation to dabble in a little bit of everything
Step 6. Consider and build in process uses if and as appropriate	
Premise: The processes undertaken in how an evaluation is conducted have impacts on those involved with the evaluation.	**Premise:** The menu of *process use* options should be reviewed, screened, and prioritized by primary intended users to determine any appropriate process uses of the evaluation.
Primary tasks	*Evaluation facilitation challenges*
❑ Review alternative process use options with primary intended users.	Helping primary intended users understand process use options and the potential importance of process uses as intentional, thereby adding value to the evaluation
✓ Consider how **evaluative thinking might be infused into the organization culture** as part of doing the evaluation.	Guiding primary intended users in reviewing potential program and organizational culture impacts of evaluation, and whether to enhance and make then intentional
✓ Consider how the way in which the evaluation is conducted and who is involved **can enhance shared understandings.**	Guiding primary intended users in considering communication issues and areas where shared understandings could be enhanced through involvement in the evaluation process
✓ Consider possibilities for using evaluation processes to **support and reinforce the program intervention.**	Examining the potential interaction effects between how the evaluation is conducted, including how data are gathered, and attaining the desired outcomes of the intervention
✓ Consider **potential instrumentation effects and reactivity** as process uses to be made explicit and enhanced.	Facilitating examination of the potential effects of measurement as exemplified in the adage: "what gets measured gets done"
✓ Consider how the evaluation might be conducted in ways that **increase skills, knowledge, confidence, self-determination, and a sense of ownership** among those	Guiding users in considering evaluation approaches that are participatory, collaborative, empowering, inclusive, and democratic-deliberative in which evaluation processes have the goal of building

involved in the evaluation, included the program's staff and intended beneficiaries.	capacity, enhancing skills, and giving voice to those whose voices are less often heard
✓ Consider how evaluation could contribute to **program and organizational development.**	Considering the option of the evaluator becoming part of a development team involved in innovation and ongoing adaptation based on developmental evaluation (Patton, 2011)
❑ Review concerns, cautions, controversies, costs, and potential positive and negative effects of making process use a priority in the evaluation.	• Guiding users through the controversies surrounding various types of process uses • Examining potential pluses and minuses, including potential effects on the evaluation's credibility • Reviewing time and cost implications
❑ Examine the relationship and interconnections between potential process uses and findings use (Step 5).	Facilitating a complex systems understanding of how process uses and findings uses may be interconnected, interactive, and mutually interdependent
❑ Prioritize any intended process uses of the evaluation and plan for their incorporation into the design and conduct of the evaluation.	Having reviewed process options, work with primary intended users to establish priorities; resolve conflicts over competing purposes; avoid dabbling in a little bit of everything; avoid ambiguity or confusion about priorities.
Step 7. Focus priority evaluation questions	
Premise: No evaluation can look at everything. Priorities have to be determined. Focusing is the process for establishing priorities.	**Premise:** The menu of options for specifically focusing the evaluation should be reviewed, screened, and prioritized by primary intended users to determine their priorities.
Primary tasks	*Evaluation facilitation challenges*
❑ Apply criteria for good utilization-focused evaluation questions: ✓ Questions can be answered sufficiently well to inform understanding and support action. ✓ Questions can be answered in a timely manner and at reasonable cost. ✓ Data can be brought to bear on the questions; that is, they aren't primarily philosophical, religious, or moral questions.	Helping primary intended users create a culture of inquiry and learning: • Facilitating discussion of the connections between asking questions, getting answers, and taking action • Guiding primary intended users in considering resource and time line realities • Guiding users in understanding what kinds of questions can and cannot be answered with data

(Continued)

(Continued)

✓ The answer is not predetermined by the phrasing or framing of the question. ✓ The primary intended users want the question answered; they have identified it as important and can say why. ✓ The answer is actionable; intended users can indicate how they would use the answer to the question for future decision making and action.	• Guiding users in being open to genuine empirical inquiry: aiming to learn and find out rather than prove predetermined ideas or bias the results • Guiding users in surfacing what they care most about, what is most relevant • Guiding primary intended users in keeping intended use by intended users at the forefront of their focusing process
✓ Listen carefully to the priority concerns of primary intended users to help them identify important questions.	• Staying tuned into the concerns of primary intended users and not letting the evaluator's interest dominate or control the priority-setting process
✓ Connect priority questions to the intended purpose and uses of the evaluation to assure that they match.	• Facilitating a review of the interconnections between primary intended uses (Step 5) and specific, more detailed evaluation questions
✓ Offer a menu of focus options. (See Menu 7.1.)	• Doing a reasonably thorough review of options without overwhelming intended users
Step 8. Check that fundamental areas for evaluation inquiry are being adequately addressed	
Premise: Implementation, outcomes, and attribution questions are fundamental.	**Premise:** Evaluators should be sure that primary intended users have considered the issues and options involved in evaluating program implementation, outcomes, and attribution.
Primary tasks	*Evaluation facilitation challenges*
❑ Consider options for implementation evaluation that address the question: What happens in the program? ✓ Effort and input evaluation ✓ Process evaluation ✓ Component evaluation ✓ Treatment specification and intervention dosage	Helping primary intended users determine what implementation evaluation questions should have priority given the stage of the program's development, the priority decisions the evaluation will inform, and the resources available for evaluation
❑ Consider options for *outcomes* evaluation to answer the questions: ✓ What results from the program?	Facilitation challenges include: • Evaluability assessment: Are the program's goals sufficiently specific, measurable,

✓ How are participants changed, if at all, as a result of program participation? ✓ To what extent are the program's goals achieved? ✓ What unanticipated outcomes occur? ✓ To what extent are participants' needs met by the program?	achievable, relevant, and timebound (SMART) to be ready for evaluation of outcomes? • Determining which outcomes among the many a program may have are the priority for evaluation; what outcomes evaluation questions will yield the most useful findings? • Completing the utilization-focused evaluation framework for outcomes evaluation that differentiates target subgroup, desired outcome, outcome indicator, data collection, performance target, and intended use of the outcomes data
❑ Determine the importance and relative priority of the attribution issue: To what extent can outcomes be attributed to the program intervention?	Helping primary intended users understand the conceptual and methodological issues involved in asking questions about causality and generating credible evidence to support judgments about attribution
Step 9. Determine what intervention model or theory of change is being evaluated	
Premises: A program or intervention can usefully be conceptualized as a model or theory which describes how intended outcomes will be produced. Evaluation can include testing the model or theory.	**Premises:** Evaluators should be sure that primary intended users have considered the issues and options involved in evaluating the program's model or theory of change. How a theory of change is conceptualized will have important implications for how the evaluation is designed and conducted.
Primary tasks	*Evaluation facilitation challenges*
❑ Determine if logic modeling or theory of change work will provide an important and useful framework for the evaluation.	• Helping intended users understand the purposes of a logic model or theory of change for evaluation • Explaining the differences between a logic model and theory of change • Assessing the costs and benefits of using a logic model or theory of change to frame the evaluation
❑ Consider options for conceptualizing a program or intervention, or different elements of a program or change initiative: ✓ A linear logic model ✓ A map of systems relationships ✓ A complex adaptive system	Helping primary intended users understand and engage the differences among different conceptual approaches: logic models, systems thinking, and complex adaptive systems

(Continued)

(Continued)

<table>
<tr><td>❑ Appropriately match the evaluation design and measurement approach to how the program or intervention is conceptualized, understanding that linear logic models, systems maps, and complex nonlinear conceptualizations of interventions have both conceptual and methodological implications.</td><td>Facilitation challenges involve helping intended users understand the implications of conceptualizing the intervention in different ways:
• Designing an evaluation to test causal attribution hypotheses by specifying a linear model in which the connections are clear, logical, sequential, plausible–and testable
• Creating a meaningful systems map that provides insights into relationships and constitutes a baseline of systems interrelationships for purposes of evaluation
• Generating shared understandings around the evaluation implications of complex situations characterized by high uncertainty about how to produce desired outcomes, high disagreement among key stakeholders about what to do, and unpredictable and uncontrollable causality</td></tr>
<tr><td colspan="2">Step 10. Negotiate appropriate methods to generate credible findings that support intended use by intended users</td></tr>
<tr><td>Premises: The evaluation should be designed to lead to useful findings. Methods should be selected and the evaluation designed to support and achieve intended use by primary intended users.</td><td>Premises: Involving primary intended users in methods decisions increases their understanding of the strengths and weaknesses of the methods used and deepens their understanding of data collection decisions, which supports the commitment to use the resultant findings.</td></tr>
<tr><td>Primary tasks</td><td>Evaluation facilitation challenges</td></tr>
<tr><td>❑ Select methods to answer users' priority questions so that the results obtained will be credible to primary intended users.</td><td>Making sure that primary intended users play an active role in reviewing methods to examine their appropriateness and credibility</td></tr>
<tr><td>❑ Assure that the proposed methods and measurements are:
✓ Appropriate
✓ Practical
✓ Cost-effective
✓ Ethical</td><td>❑ Taking time to think through methods choices and their implications with intended users</td></tr>
</table>

❑ Assure that the results obtained from the chosen methods will be able to be used as intended.	Finding the right level of engagement with intended users, the "sweet spot," neither overly technical, nor overly simplistic
❑ Negotiate trade-offs between design and methods ideals and what can actually be implemented given inevitable constraints of resources and time.	• Negotiating criteria for methodological quality and what constitutes credible evidence among key stakeholders • Making the evaluator's own stake in a quality evaluation explicit and part of the negotiations without allowing the evaluator to become the unilateral decision maker about methods
❑ Identify and attend to threats to data quality, credibility, and utility.	Helping intended users consider the implications for use of methods and measurement decisions
❑ Adapt methods in response to changing conditions as the evaluation unfolds, dealing with the emergent dynamics of actual fieldwork.	Keeping primary intended users engaged with and informed about necessary changes and adaptations in methods as the evaluation unfolds
Step 11. Make sure intended users understand potential methods controversies and their implications	
Premises: The methodological gold standard is methodological appropriateness. Appropriate methods are those that answer users' priority questions. Involving intended users in methods decisions means that evaluators and intended users need to understand paradigm-based methods debates and their implications for the credibility and utility of a particular evaluation.	**Premises:** Evaluators need to be able to facilitate choices that are appropriate to a particular evaluation's purpose. This means educating primary stakeholders about the legitimate options available, the strengths and weaknesses of various approaches, the potential advantages and costs of using multiple and mixed methods, and the controversies that surround such choices.
Primary tasks	*Evaluation facilitation challenges*
❑ Select methods appropriate to the questions being asked.	Making sure that methods are selected jointly by primary intended users and the evaluator(s) based on appropriateness
❑ Discuss with intended users relevant methods debates that affect the methods choices in a particular evaluation, if appropriate and helpful to support decision making about methods. Issues to consider include: ✓ Quantitative versus qualitative data	• Helping primary intended users understand and consider how broader methodological debates may affect the credibility and utility of the particular evaluation being designed • Keeping the discussion about methodological debates practical and useful rather than academic and pedantic

(Continued)

(Continued)

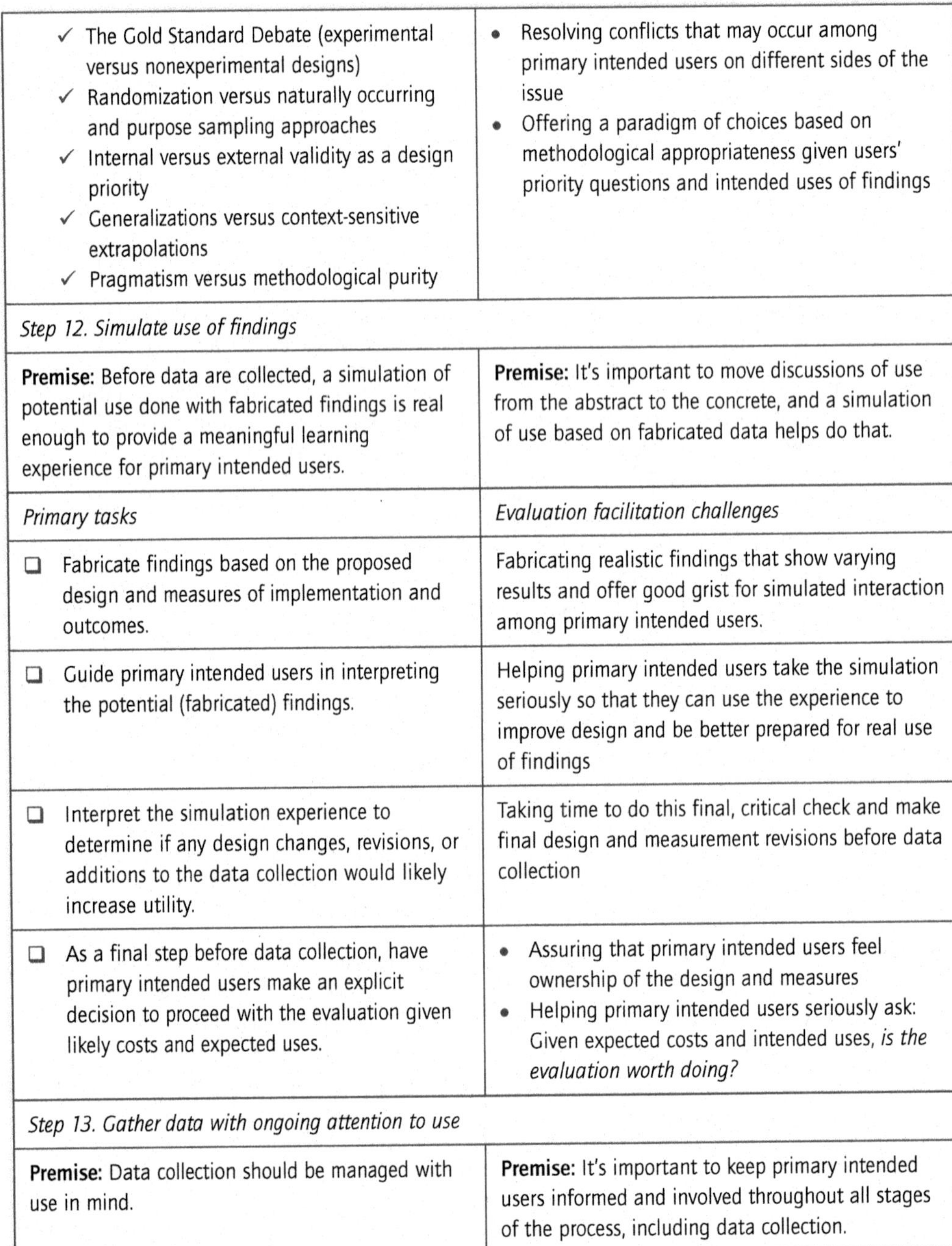

✓ The Gold Standard Debate (experimental versus nonexperimental designs) ✓ Randomization versus naturally occurring and purpose sampling approaches ✓ Internal versus external validity as a design priority ✓ Generalizations versus context-sensitive extrapolations ✓ Pragmatism versus methodological purity	• Resolving conflicts that may occur among primary intended users on different sides of the issue • Offering a paradigm of choices based on methodological appropriateness given users' priority questions and intended uses of findings
Step 12. Simulate use of findings	
Premise: Before data are collected, a simulation of potential use done with fabricated findings is real enough to provide a meaningful learning experience for primary intended users.	**Premise:** It's important to move discussions of use from the abstract to the concrete, and a simulation of use based on fabricated data helps do that.
Primary tasks	*Evaluation facilitation challenges*
❑ Fabricate findings based on the proposed design and measures of implementation and outcomes.	Fabricating realistic findings that show varying results and offer good grist for simulated interaction among primary intended users.
❑ Guide primary intended users in interpreting the potential (fabricated) findings.	Helping primary intended users take the simulation seriously so that they can use the experience to improve design and be better prepared for real use of findings
❑ Interpret the simulation experience to determine if any design changes, revisions, or additions to the data collection would likely increase utility.	Taking time to do this final, critical check and make final design and measurement revisions before data collection
❑ As a final step before data collection, have primary intended users make an explicit decision to proceed with the evaluation given likely costs and expected uses.	• Assuring that primary intended users feel ownership of the design and measures • Helping primary intended users seriously ask: Given expected costs and intended uses, *is the evaluation worth doing?*
Step 13. Gather data with ongoing attention to use	
Premise: Data collection should be managed with use in mind.	**Premise:** It's important to keep primary intended users informed and involved throughout all stages of the process, including data collection.

Primary tasks	*Evaluation facilitation challenges*
❑ Effectively manage data collection to ensure data quality and evaluation credibility.	• Staying on top of data collection problems and taking corrective steps before small issues become major ones • Being transparent with intended users about how data collection is unfolding and alerting them to any important deviations from the planned design
❑ Effectively implement any agreed-on participatory approaches to data collection that build capacity and support process uses.	• Working with, training and coaching nonresearchers in the basics of data collection • Ensuring quality data when using nonresearchers for data collection • Keeping primary intended users informed about issues that emerge in participatory data collection processes
❑ Keep primary intended users informed about how things are going in data collection.	• Providing just enough information to maintain interest without getting intended users bogged down in too much detail • Meeting diverse interest and needs as different key stakeholders may want different amounts of information along the way • Avoiding inappropriate micromanaging by primary intended users
❑ Offer appropriate feedback to those providing data; for example ✓ Let interviewees know that their responses are helpful. ✓ Provide program staff and leadership with a debriefing of site visits and evaluation observations.	• Providing feedback to enhance data collection without inappropriately affecting responses or evaluation credibility • Alleviating inappropriate anxiety among those providing data or among program staff receiving early feedback about the evaluation findings • Finding the right amount and nature of timely feedback to offer
❑ Report emergent and interim findings to primary intended users to keep them interested and engaged. ✓ Avoid surprises through early alerts about results. ✓ Match the nature and frequency of interim reports to the purpose, time line of the evaluation, and duration of data collection.	• Ensuring that interim findings are treated as interim and therefore not disseminated • Maintaining the confidentiality of interim findings reported • Providing enough feedback to maintain interest but not so much as to be annoying or intrusive

(Continued)

(Continued)

❑ Watch for and deal with turnover in primary intended users. ✓ Bring replacement key stakeholders up to date quickly. ✓ Connect new intended users with those involved all along the way. ✓ Facilitate understanding, engagement, and buy-in among any new primary intended users.	• Integrating new key stakeholders into an ongoing group of primary intended users • Taking into account the potentially divergent views and different priorities of a new primary intended user when data collection is already under way
Step 14: Organize and present the data for interpretation and use by primary intended users	
Premises: • Findings should be organized and presented to facilitate use by primary intended users. • Analysis, interpretation, judgment, and recommendations should be distinguished.	**Premise:** Facilitating data interpretation among primary intended users increases their understanding of the findings, their sense of ownership of the evaluation, and their commitment to use the findings.
Primary tasks	*Evaluation facilitation challenges*
❑ Organize data to be understandable and relevant to primary intended users. ✓ Organize the findings to answer priority questions. ✓ Keep presentations simple and understandable. ✓ Provide balance. ✓ Be clear about definitions. ✓ Make comparisons carefully and appropriately. ✓ Decide what is significant. ✓ Be sure that major claims are supported by rigorous evidence. ✓ Distinguish facts from opinion.	• Organizing the raw data into an understandable and usable format that addresses and illuminates priority evaluation questions • Keeping the initial interactions focused on what the data reveal before moving into interpretations and judgments
❑ Actively involve users in interpreting findings. ✓ Triangulate evaluation findings with research findings. ✓ Consider and compare alternative interpretations and explanations.	• Helping users distinguish between findings and interpretations • Working with users to think about what is significant and consider alternative explanations for the findings before drawing definitive conclusions • Taking time to fully engage the findings before generating action recommendations

❑ Actively involve users in making evaluative judgments. ✓ Be clear about the values that undergird judgments.	Helping users distinguish between interpretations and judgments, and making explicit the *values* on which judgments are made
❑ Actively involve users in generating recommendations, if appropriate and expected. ✓ Distinguish different kinds of recommendations. ✓ Discuss the costs, benefits, and challenges of implementing recommendations. ✓ Focus on actions within the control of intended users and those they can influence.	• Helping users distinguish between findings, interpretations, judgments, and recommendations • Making sure that recommendations follow from and are supported by the findings • Allowing time to do a good job on recommendations
❑ Examine the findings and their implications from various perspectives.	• Offering opportunities and taking the time to reflect on the analytical process and learn from it • Helping users distinguish varying degrees of certainty in the findings • Being open and explicit about data strengths and limitations
Step 15: Prepare an evaluation report to facilitate use and disseminate significant findings to expand influence	
Premise: Different kinds and formats of reports are needed for different evaluation purposes. Reports should be focused on serving priority intended uses of primary intended users.	**Premise:** Working with primary intended users to review reporting and dissemination options increases the likelihood of appropriate and meaningful use as well as the possibility of wider influence.
Primary tasks	*Evaluation facilitation challenges*
❑ Determine what kinds of reporting formats, styles, and venues are appropriate. ✓ Consider both formal written reports and less formal oral reports. ✓ Adapt different report approaches for different audiences and uses. ✓ Focus the report on answering priority questions and providing the evidence for those answers. ✓ Be prepared to help users maintain balance and deal with "negative" findings.	• Helping primary intended users calculate the comparative costs and uses of various evaluation reporting approaches • Involving primary intended users in some reporting opportunities • Strategizing with intended users about creative ways of reporting findings that may enhance their utility • Facilitating openness to learning from and appropriately using "negative" findings

(Continued)

(Continued)

<table>
<tr><td>❑ Deliver reports in time to affect important decisions.</td><td>Managing the tension between in-depth involvement of intended users and getting the report done on time</td></tr>
<tr><td>❑ Decide if the findings merit wider dissemination.
✓ Consider both formal and informal pathways for dissemination.
✓ Be alert to unanticipated pathways of influence that emerge as use and dissemination processes unfold.</td><td>• Helping users distinguish between use and dissemination
• Keeping users engaged as dissemination unfolds so that emergent opportunities can be grasped as appropriate</td></tr>
<tr><td colspan="2">Step 16. Follow up with primary intended users to facilitate and enhance use</td></tr>
<tr><td>Premise: The report is not the end of the evaluation. Use is enhanced by following up and working with primary intended users to apply the findings and implement recommendations.</td><td>Premise: Facilitating use includes follow-up with primary intended users to support taking action on findings and monitoring what happens to recommendations.</td></tr>
<tr><td>Primary tasks</td><td>Evaluation facilitation challenges</td></tr>
<tr><td>❑ Plan for follow-up. Develop a follow-up plan with primary intended users.</td><td>Helping primary intended users calculate the comparative benefits and uses of various follow-up possibilities</td></tr>
<tr><td>❑ Budget for follow-up.</td><td>Encouraging primary intended users to find adequate time and resources to do a good job of following up findings to enhance use. This involves both user and evaluator time and resources.</td></tr>
<tr><td>❑ Proactively pursue utilization:
✓ Adapt findings for different audiences.
✓ Keep findings in front of those who can use them.
✓ Watch for emergent opportunities to reinforce the relevance of findings.
✓ Deal with resistance.
✓ Watch for and guard against misuse.</td><td>• Helping users make strategic choices about where to focus follow-up efforts
• Keeping users engaged after the report has been disseminated
• Being a champion for use of the findings without becoming perceived as a champion for the program</td></tr>
<tr><td>❑ Look for opportunities to add to the evaluation.
✓ Opportunities may arise to add data to answer emergent or previously unanswered questions.</td><td>Helping primary intended users and other stakeholders see evaluation as an ongoing process rather than a one-time event or moment-in-time report. Findings often give rise to new questions.</td></tr>
</table>

✓ Longer-term follow-up of program participants may become more valued and important to see if short-term outcomes are maintained over time. ✓ Designing an evaluation for the next stage of the program may emerge as an opportunity.	Questions considered less important at an earlier time can take on new importance once findings have emerged.
Step 17: Metaevaluation of use: Be accountable, learn, and improve	
Premises: • Metaevaluation is a professional obligation of evaluators. • Utilization-focused metaevaluation places particular emphasis on an evaluation's utility *and* actual use.	**Premise:** To be meaningful and useful, metaevaluation must be undertaken seriously and systematically, with time devoted to it.
Primary tasks	*Evaluation facilitation challenges*
❑ Determine the primary intended users for the metaevaluation.	Determining primary intended users: The primary intended users of an evaluation may, or may not, be the same as the primary intended users for the metaevaluation.
❑ Determine the primary purpose and uses of the metaevaluation.	Distinguishing accountability purposes from learning uses, and distinguishing internal metaevaluation from external metaevaluation
❑ Determine the primary standards and criteria to be applied in the metaevaluation. ✓ Joint Committee Standards (2010) ✓ DAC standards for development evaluation (OECD, 2010)	Distinguishing potential utility and usability from actual use. Metaevaluation of potential utility may occur earlier than metaevaluation of actual use.
❑ Budget time and resources for the metaevaluation.	Taking time to do a good job of metaevaluation. This involves time and resources from both intended users and evaluators.
❑ Follow the steps for conducting a utilization-focused evaluation in conducting the utilization-focused metaevaluation.	• Helping users make strategic choices about where to focus follow-up efforts • Keeping users engaged after the report has been disseminated • Being a champion for use of the findings without becoming perceived as a champion for the program

(Continued)

(Continued)

❑ Engage in systematic reflective practice about the evaluation, its processes and uses, with primary intended users.	• Involving the evaluation's primary intended users in reflective practice as a metaevaluation exercise to further enhance their own capacities, provide feedback to the evaluator to deepen his or her own reflective practice, and bring closure to the evaluation process
❑ Engage in personal reflective practice to support ongoing professional development. ✓ Reflect on what went well, and not so well, throughout the evaluation. ✓ Assess your essential competencies and skills as an evaluator. ✓ Use what you learn to improve your practice and increase use.	• Following up evaluations to learn what worked and didn't work, what was useful and not useful. • Committing time to serious reflective practice and learning for ongoing professional development

U-FE COMPLEX DYNAMIC AND ADAPTIVE SYSTEMS GRAPHIC: INTERACTIONS AMONG ALL 17 STEPS

As noted throughout this book and at the beginning of this chapter, the steps in the U-FE checklist are necessarily linear and sequential. One step comes before the next. But the actual utilization-focused evaluation process unfolds as a complex, dynamic, and iterative system of relationships with the various elements and steps interacting. Actions lead to reactions, interactions, feedback loops, and adaptations. To depict utilization-focused evaluation as a complex dynamic and adaptive system, this graphic on the next page (and which also appears on the inside front cover) depicts the interactions and interdependencies among the steps of the checklist, a reminder of the complex nonlinear dynamics of real-world utilization-focused evaluation practice and engagement.

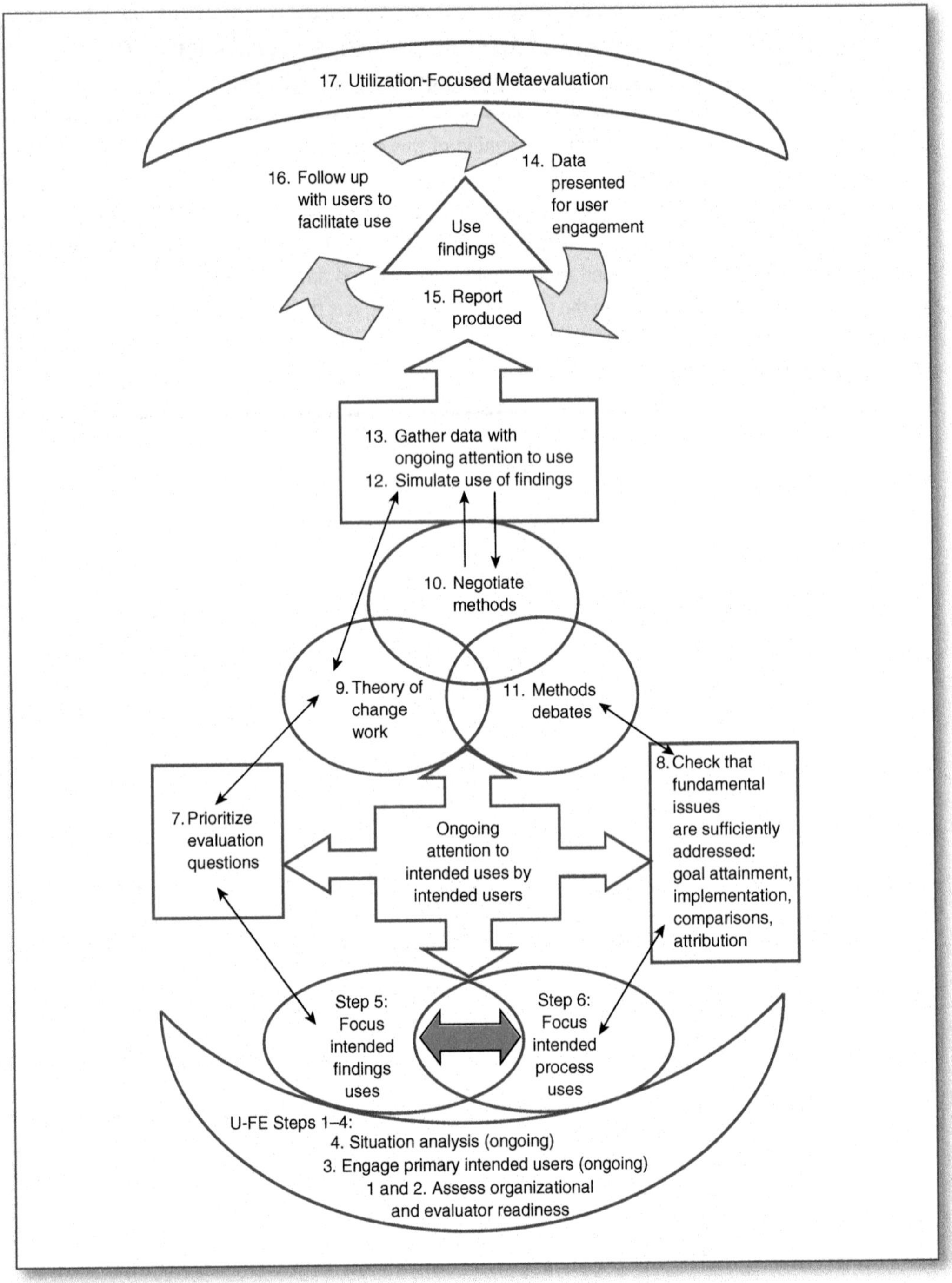

17. Utilization-Focused Metaevaluation

16. Follow up with users to facilitate use

Use findings

14. Data presented for user engagement

15. Report produced

13. Gather data with ongoing attention to use

12. Simulate use of findings

10. Negotiate methods

9. Theory of change work

11. Methods debates

7. Prioritize evaluation questions

Ongoing attention to intended uses by intended users

8. Check that fundamental issues are sufficiently addressed: goal attainment, implementation, comparisons, attribution

Step 5: Focus intended findings uses

Step 6: Focus intended process uses

U-FE Steps 1–4:

4. Situation analysis (ongoing)

3. Engage primary intended users (ongoing)

1 and 2. Assess organizational and evaluator readiness

References

Abma, T. (2006). The practice and politics of responsive evaluation. *American Journal of Evaluation, 27*(1), 31–43.

Adler, F. S. (1975). *Sisters in crime: The rise of the new female criminal.* New York: McGraw-Hill.

AEA (American Evaluation Association). (2004). *Guiding principles for evaluators.* http://www.eval.org/Publications/GuidingPrinciples.asp

AEA (American Evaluation Association). (2009). *Context and evaluation.* Theme of the 2009 American Evaluation Association annual conference, November 11–14 in Orlando, FL.

AEA (American Evaluation Association) Diversity Committee. (2004). A cultural reading of the *Program Evaluation Standards* (2nd ed.), Cultural Reading Task Force. http://www.eval.org/CRExecSum.htm

Alkin, M. C. (1985). *A guide for evaluation decision makers.* Beverly Hills, CA: Sage.

Alkin, M. C. (2011). *Evaluation essentials: From A to Z.* New York: Guilford.

Altschuld, J., & Kumar, D. (2005). Needs assessment. In S. Mathison (Ed.), *Encyclopedia of evaluation* (pp. 276–277). Thousand Oaks, CA: Sage.

Ames, D. R., & Kammrath, L. K. (2004). Mind-reading and metacognition: Narcissism, not actual competence, predicts self-estimated ability. *Journal of Nonverbal Behavior, 28*(3), 187–209.

Argyris, C. (1980). *Inner contradictions of rigorous research.* New York: Academic Press.

Atkinson, C. (2008). *Beyond bullet points.* Redmond, WA: Microsoft Press.

Bacal, R. (2009). Writing an annual report for government. http://work911.com/articles/humorgovernmentreports.htm

Bamberger, M., & Podems, D. (2002). Feminist evaluation in the international development context. *New Directions for Evaluation, 96,* 83–96.

Bamberger, M., Rugh, J., & Mabry, L. (2006). RealWorld evaluation: Working under budget, time, data, and political constraints. Thousand Oaks, CA: Sage.

Berk, R. A. (2007). What would Pete say? *American Journal of Evaluation, 28*(2), 203–206.

Bickman, L. (1985). Improving established statewide programs: A component theory of evaluation. *Evaluation Review, 9*(2), 189–208.

Bossidy, L., & Charan, R. (2002). Execution: The discipline of getting things done. New York: Crown Business.

Brandon, P. R., Smith, N. L., Trenholm, C., & Devaney, B. (2010). Evaluation exemplar: The critical importance of stakeholder relations in a national, experimental abstinence education evaluation. *American Journal of Evaluation, 31*(4), 517–531.

Brinkerhoff, R. (2003). *The success case method.* San Francisco: Berrett Koehler.

Author's Note: All web citations were current as of May 2011.

Brinkerhoff, R. (2005). *Success case method.* In S. Mathison (Ed.), *Encyclopedia of evaluation* (pp. 401–402). Thousand Oaks, CA: Sage.

Brooks, D. (2010, November 25). Description is prescription. *New York Times,* A37. http://www.nytimes.com

Bryson, J., Ackermann, F., Eden, C., & Finn, C. (2004). Visible thinking: Unlocking causal mapping for practical business results. West Sussex, England: John Wiley & Sons.

Buck, C. (1995, January 23). The world according to Soros. *The New Yorker,* pp. 54–78.

Burson, K. A., Larrick, R. P., & Klayman, J. (2006). Skilled or unskilled, but still unaware of it: How perceptions of difficulty drive miscalibration in relative comparisons. *Journal of Personality and Social Psychology, 90*(1), 60–77.

Campbell, D. T., & Stanley, J. C. (1963). *Experimental and quasi-experimental designs for research.* Chicago: Rand McNally.

Campbell-Patton, C. E., & Patton, M. Q. (2010). Conceptualizing and evaluating the complexities of youth civic engagement. In L. R. Sherrod, J. Torney-Purta, & C. A. Flanagan (Eds.), *Handbook of research on civic engagement in youth* (pp. 593–620). Hoboken, NJ: John Wiley & Sons.

Canadian Health Services Research Foundation, The. (2008, January). A handbook on knowledge sharing: Strategies and recommendations for researchers, policymakers, and service providers. *Insight and Action,* 28. http://www.chsrf.ca/Migrated/PDF/InsightAction/insight_action28_e.pdf

Carden, F., & Earl, S. (2007). Infusing evaluative thinking as process use: The case of the International Development Research Centre (IDRC). *New Directions for Evaluation. 116,* 61–74.

Castaneda, C. (1971). *A separate reality.* New York: Pocket Books. http://www.seattle-ts.org/controlled_folly.htm

Center for Effective Philanthropy. (2010, March 22). Funders make significant change based on grantee feedback. *Effective Matters,* 6(1). http://www.effectivephilanthropy.org/index.php?page=newsletter-6-1

Centers for Disease Control and Prevention. (2010). Logic model resources. http://www.cdc.gov/eval/resources.htm#logic model

CES (Canadian Evaluation Society). (2010). *Professional designations program: Credentialed evaluator (CE).* http://www.evaluationcanada.ca/site.cgi?en:5:6

Chapman, J. (2004). *System failure: Why governments must learn to think differently.* London: Demos.

Chelimsky, E. (2007). Factors influencing the choice of methods in federal evaluation practice. *New Directions for Program Evaluation, 113,* 13–33.

Chelimsky, E. (2010). AEA Thought Leaders Forum, December 19, 2010.

Chen, H. T. (2005). Theory-driven evaluation. In S. Mathison (Ed.), *Encyclopedia of evaluation* (pp. 415–419). Thousand Oaks, CA: Sage.

Chen, H. T. (2010). The bottom-up approach to integrative validity: A new perspective for program evaluation. *Evaluation and Program Planning, 33*(3), 205–214.

Christie, C. A. (2003). What guides evaluation? A study of how evaluation practice maps onto evaluation theory. *New Directions for Evaluation, 97,* 7–36.

Christie, C. (2005). A conversation with Ross Connor. *American Journal of Evaluation, 26*(3), 369–377.

Christie, C. (2007). Reported influence of evaluation data on decision makers' actions: An empirical examination. *American Journal of Evaluation, 28*(1), 8–25.

Clayson, Z., Castaneda, C. X., Sanchez, E., & Brindis, C. (2002). Unequal power—changing landscapes: Negotiations between evaluation stakeholders in Latino communities. *American Journal of Evaluation, 23*(1), 33–44.

Connor, R. (2004). Developing and implementing culturally competent evaluation: A discussion of multicultural validity in two HIV prevention programs for Latinos. *New Directions for Evaluation, 102,* 51–66.

Connor, R. (2005). The Colorado Healthy Communities Initiative. *American Journal of Evaluation, 26*(3), 363–377.

Council on Foundations. (1993). *Evaluation for foundations: Concepts, cases, guidelines, and resources.* San Francisco: Jossey-Bass.

Cousins, J. B. (2001). Do evaluator and program practitioner perspectives converge in collaborative evaluation? *The Canadian Journal of Evaluation, 16*(2), 113–133.

Cousins, J. B. (Ed.). (2007). Process use in theory, research, and practice. *New Directions for Evaluation, 116.*

Cousins, J. B., Donohue, J. J., & Bloom, G. A. (1996). Collaborative evaluation in North America: Evaluators' self-reported opinions, practices and consequences. *Evaluation Practice, 17*(3), 207–225.

Cousins, J. B., & Shulha, L. M. (2006). A comparative analysis of evaluation utilization and its cognate fields of inquiry: Current issues and trends. In I. F. Shaw, J. C. Greene, & M. M. Mark (Eds.), *The SAGE handbook of evaluation: Policies, programs and practices* (pp. 266–291). London: Sage.

Cronbach, L. J. (1975). Beyond the two disciplines of scientific psychology. *American Psychologist, 30,* 116–117.

Cronbach, L. J. (1982). *Designing evaluations of educational and social programs.* San Francisco: Jossey-Bass.

Cronbach, L. J., & Associates. (1980). *Toward reform of program evaluation.* San Francisco: Jossey-Bass.

DARE. (2011). http://www.dare.com/home/default.asp

Datta, L. (2005). Judicial model of evaluation. In S. Mathison (Ed.), *Encyclopedia of evaluation* (pp. 214–217). Thousand Oaks, CA: Sage.

Darwin, C. (1871). Introduction. *The descent of man.* London: Elibron Classics.

Davidson, E. J. (2005). *Evaluation methodology basics: The nuts and bolts of sound evaluation.* Thousand Oaks, CA: Sage.

Davidson, E. J. (2007, October). Unlearning some of our social scientist habits. *Journal of MultiDisciplinary Evaluation, 4*(8), iii–vi. http://survey.ate.wmich.edu/jmde/index.php/jmde_1/article/view/68/71

Davidson, E. J. (2010a). Language; translators; and cultural, context and other expertise on an evaluation team. Thought leader discussion series, *President's Forum,* January 20, 2010, American Evaluation Association. http://www.eval.org/thought_leaders.asp

Davidson, E. J. (2010b). Objectivity, the delusion of. Thought leader discussion series, *President's Forum,* February 11, 2010. American Evaluation Association. http://www.eval.org/thought_leaders.asp

Davidson, E. J. (2010c). XGEMS: Extreme genuine evaluation makeovers. Keynote address, Australasian Evaluation Society, September 3. http://realevaluation.com/pres/xgemsAES10.pdf

Davis, H., & Salasin, S. (1975). The utilization of evaluation. In E. Struening & M. Guttentag (Eds.), *Handbook of evaluation research, Vol. 1.* Beverly Hills, CA: Sage.

Deaton, A. (2010). Instruments, randomization, and learning about development. *Journal of Economic Literature, 48,* 424–455. http://www.aeaweb.org/articles.php?doi=10.1257/je1.48.2.424

Development Assistance Committee. (2010). *The DAC quality standards for development evaluation.* DAC Network on Development Evaluation, Organisation for Economic Co-operation and Development. http://www.oecd.org/document/30/0,3746,en_21571361_34047972_38903582_1_1_1_1,00.html

Dickson, P. (2010). *Paul Dickson quotes.* http://www.gigausa.com/quotes/authors/paul_dickson_a001.htm

Donaldson, S., Gooler, L., & Scriven, M. (2002). Strategies for managing evaluation anxiety: Toward a psychology of program evaluation. *American Journal of Evaluation, 23*(3), 261–273.

Donmoyer, R. (1996). Educational research in an era of paradigm proliferation: What's a journal editor to do? *Educational Researcher, 25*(2), 19–25.

Donmoyer, R. (2005). Connoisseurship. In S. Mathison (Ed.), *Encyclopedia of evaluation* (pp. 76–80). Thousand Oaks, CA: Sage.

Drucker, P. F. (1999). Knowledge worker productivity. *Management challenges of the 21st century.* New York: HarperBusiness. http://www.afterquotes.com/great/quotes/knowledge.htm See also: http://www.knowledgeworkerperformance.com/Knowledge-Worker-Management/Drucker-Knowledge-Worker-Productivity/default.aspx

Drucker, P. F. (2000). *Wisdom from Peter Drucker: His four greatest lessons.* Annual Conference of the Peter F. Drucker Foundation for Nonprofit Management, November 6, New York City. http://www.leadnet.org/epubarchive.asp?id=41&db=archive_explorer#wisdom

Duarte, N. (2008). slide:ology: The art and science of creating great presentations. Sebastopol, CA: O'Reilly Media.

Duarte, N. (2010). Duarte design's videos. http://vimeo.com/dartedesign/videos

Duignan, P. (2010). DOVUE, Visualizing outcomes. http://www.doview.com/

Dunbar, K., & Fugelsang, J. (2005). Scientific thinking and reasoning. In K. J. Holyoak & R. Morrison (Eds.), *Cambridge handbook of thinking & reasoning* (pp. 705–726). New York: Cambridge University Press. http://www.utsc.utoronto.ca/~dunbarlab/pubpdfs/Cambridgehandbook2005.pdf

Dunning, D., & Kruger, J. (1999). Unskilled and unaware of it: How difficulties in recognizing one's own incompetence lead to inflated self-assessments. *Journal of Personality and Social Psychology, 77*(6), 1121–1134.

Earl, S., Carden, F., & Smutylo, T. (2001). *Outcome mapping.* Ottawa: IDRC. http://www.idrc.ca/en/ev-9330-201-1-DO_TOPIC.html

Eden, C., & Ackermann, F. (1998). *Making strategy.* Thousand Oaks, CA: Sage.

Eoyang, G. H. (2006). Human systems dynamics: Complexity-based approach to a complex evaluation. In B. Williams & I. Iman (Eds.), *Systems concepts in evaluation: An expert anthology* (pp. 123–139). Point Reynes, CA: Edgepress of Inverness.

Eoyang, G. H., & Berkas, T. (1998). *Evaluation in a complex adaptive system (CAS).* Circle Pines, MN: Chaos Ltd. http://www.chaos-limited.com/EvalinCAS.pdf

Extreme Presentation™ Method. (2010). http://extremepresentation.typepad.com/blog/tools.html

Eyle, A. (Ed.). (2002). The education issue. *ReconsiDer: Forum on Drug Policy, 1*(4). http://www.drugpolicy.org/docUploads/education.pdf

Fadiman, C., & Bernard, A. (2000). *Bartlett's book of anecdotes.* Boston: Little, Brown.

Feldman, S. (2010, September 13). Dr. Sim: Jushua Epstein solves real problems using artificial worlds. *Forbes,* 20–23. http://www.forbes.com/forbes/2010/0913/opinions-computer-simulations-vaccinations-ideas-opinions.html

Fetterman, D., & Wandersman, A. (Ed.). (2005). *Empowerment evaluation principles in practice.* New York: Guilford.

Fink, A. (2004). *Evaluation fundamentals: Insights into the outcomes, effectiveness, and quality of health programs.* Thousand Oaks, CA: Sage.

Fisher, D., Imm, P., Chinman, M., & Wandersman, A. (2006). *Getting to outcomes with developmental assets: Ten steps to measuring success in youth programs and communities.* Minneapolis, MN: Search Institute.

Fitzpatrick, J. (2000). Conversation with Gary Henry. *American Journal of Evaluation, 21*(1), 108–117.

Fitzpatrick, J. (2004). Exemplars as case studies: Reflections on the links between theory, practice, and context. *American Journal of Evaluation, 25*(4), 541–559.

Fleischer, D. (2007). Evaluation use: A survey of U.S. American Evaluation Association members. Unpublished master's thesis, Claremont Graduate University, Claremont, CA.

Flores, K. S. (Ed.). (2003). Youth participatory evaluation: A field in the making. *New Directions for Evaluation,* No. 98. San Francisco: Jossey-Bass.

Flores, K. S. (2007). Youth participatory evaluation: Strategies for engaging young people. San Francisco: Jossey-Bass.

Fournier, D. M. (2005). Evaluation. In S. Mathison (Ed.), *Encyclopedia of evaluation* (pp. 139–140). Thousand Oaks, CA: Sage.

Fujita, N. (2010). Beyond Logframe: Using systems concepts in evaluation. Tokyo: Foundation for Advanced Studies on International Development. http://mande.co.uk/2010/uncategorized/beyond-logframe-using-systems-concepts-in-evaluation/

Funnell, S. C., & Rogers, P. J. (2011). *Purposeful program theory: Making effective use of theories of change and logic models.* San Francisco: Jossey-Bass.

GAO (Government Accountability Office). (1991). *Designing evaluations,* GAO/PEMD-10.1.4. Washington, DC: GAO.

GAO (Government Accountability Office). (1995). *Program evaluation: Improving the flow of information to the congress,* GAO/PEMPD-95–1. Washington, DC: GAO.

GAO (Government Accountability Office). (2003). *Youth illicit drug use prevention: DARE* long-term evaluations and federal efforts to identify effective programs. GAO-03–172R Youth Illicit Drug Use Prevention. Washington, DC: U.S. General Accounting Office.

GAO (Government Accountability Office). (2009). *A variety of rigorous methods can help identify effective interventions.* GAO-10–30. Washington, DC: GAO. http://www.gao.gov/new.items/d1030.pdf

Gawande, A. (2002). *Complications: A surgeon's notes on an imperfect science.* New York: Metropolitan Books.

Gawande, A. (2007, December 10). Annals of medicine: The checklist. *The New Yorker Magazine.* http://www.newyorker.com/reporting/2007/12/10/071210fa_fact_gawande

Gawande, A. (2009). *The checklist manifesto: How to get things right.* New York: Metropolitan Books.

Ghere, G., King, J., Stevahn, L., & Minnema, J. (2006). A professional development unit for reflecting on program evaluation competencies. *American Journal of Evaluation, 27*(1), 108–123.

Gigerenzer, G., Todd, P. M., & the ABC Research Group (1999). *Simple heuristics that make us smart.* New York: Oxford University Press.

Gladwell, M. (2002). *The tipping point: How little things can make a big difference.* Boston: Little, Brown.

Glasmeier, A. K. (2010). *Living wage calculator.* The Pennsylvania State University. http://www.livingwage.geog.psu.edu/

Grasso, P. (2003). What makes an evaluation useful? Reflections from experience in large organizations. *American Journal of Evaluation, 24*(4), 507–514.

Greene, J. (1990). Technical quality versus user responsiveness in evaluation practice. *Evaluation and Program Planning, 13*(3), 267–274.

Greene, J. (2006). Stakeholders. In S. Mathison (Ed.), *Encyclopedia of evaluation* (pp. 397–398). Thousand Oaks, CA: Sage.

Grob, G. (2003). A truly useful bat is one found in the hands of a slugger. *American Journal of Evaluation, 24*(4), 499–505.

Groopman, J. (2007, January 29). What's the trouble? How doctors think. *The New Yorker,* 36–41.

Guba, E. (1977). *Overcoming resistance to evaluation.* Keynote speech at the Second Annual Conference on Evaluation, University of North Dakota.

Guba, E., & Lincoln, Y. (1981). *Effective evaluation: Improving the usefulness and evaluation* results through responsive and naturalistic approaches. San Francisco: Jossey-Bass.

Hammond, S. A., & Mayfield, A. (2004). *Naming elephants: How to surface undiscussables for greater organizational success.* Bend, OR: Thin Book Publishing.

Hanson, D. J. (2007). Drug abuse resistance education: The effectiveness of DARE. http://alcohol facts.org/DARE.html

Harpst, G. (2008). *Execution revolution: Solving the one business problem that makes solving all other problems easier.* Findlay, Ohio: Six Disciplines Publishing.

Harris, R. (2009, November 18). *Reef conservation strategy backfires.* Washington, DC: National Public Radio. http://www.npr.org/templates/story/story.php?storyId=120536304

Hattie, J. (2008). *Visible learning: A synthesis of over 800 meta-analyses relating to achievement.* New York: Routledge.

Heckman, J. J., & Smith, J. A. (1995). Assessing the case for social experiments. *Journal of Economic Perspectives, 9*(2), 85–110.

Hendricks, M. (1994). Making a splash: Reporting evaluation results effectively. In J. S. Wholey, H. P. Hatry, & K. E. Newcomer (Eds.), *Handbook of practical program evaluation* (pp. 549–575). San Francisco: Jossey-Bass.

Hinton, B. (1988, Spring). *Audit tales: Kansas intrigue.* Legislative Program Evaluation Society (LPES) Newsletter, p. 3.

Hofstetter, C. H., & Alkin, M. (2003). Evaluation use revisited. In T. Kellaghan, D. L. Stufflebeam, & L. Wingate (Eds.), *International handbook of education evaluation* (pp. 189–196). Boston: Kluwer.

Hopson, R. (1999). Minority issues in evaluation revisited. *American Journal of Evaluation, 20*(3), 433–437.

Hopson, R. (Ed.). (2000). How and why language matters in evaluation. *New Directions for Evaluation,* 86.

House, E. R. (1980). *Evaluating with validity.* Beverly Hills, CA: Sage.

House, E. R. (1999). Evaluation and people of color. *American Journal of Evaluation, 20*(3), 433–437.

House, E. R. (2004). Intellectual history in evaluation. In M. C. Alkin, *Evaluation roots: Tracing theorists' views and influences* (pp. 218–224). Thousand Oaks, CA: Sage.

House, E. R. (2005a). Deliberative democratic evaluation. In S. Mathison (Ed.), *Encyclopedia of evaluation* (pp. 104–108). Thousand Oaks, CA: Sage.

House, E. R. (2005b). Social justice, 6. In S. Mathison (Ed.), *Encyclopedia of evaluation* (pp. 393–396). Thousand Oaks, CA: Sage.

House, E. R., & Howe, K. (1999). *Values in evaluation and social research.* Thousand Oaks, CA: Sage.

House, E. R., & Howe, K. (2000). Deliberative democratic evaluation: Evaluation as a democratic process. *New Directions for Evaluation, 85,* 3–12.

IDRC (International Development Research Centre). (2010). *Outcome mapping.* Ottawa, Canada: IDRC. http://www.idrc.ca/en/ev-26586-201-1-DO_TOPIC.html

Imas, L. G. M., & Rist, R. C. (2009). *The road to results: Designing and conducting effective development evaluations.* Washington, DC: The World Bank.

Inbar, M. (1979). *Routine decision-making.* Beverly Hills, CA: Sage.

Institute of Management Consultants. (2010, March 1). Putting your consulting skills to the test. Consultant's Tip #251. http://www.imcusa.org/members/blog_view.asp?id=334056&post=93327&hhSearchTerms=251

Jacobs, F. H. (1988). The five-tiered approach to evaluation. In H. B. Weiss & F. Jacobs (Eds.), *Evaluating family programs* (pp. 37–68). Hawthorne, NY: Aldine.

Joint Committee on Standards for Educational Evaluation. (1994). *The program evaluation standards.* Thousand Oaks, CA: Sage. http://www.wmich.edu/evalctr/jc/

Joint Committee on Standards for Educational Evaluation. (2010). *The program evaluation standards.* http://www.jcsee.org/program-evaluation-standards

Juice Analytics. (2010). Information experiences.™ http://www.juiceanalytics.com/writing/information-experiences/

Julnes, G., & Rog, D. (2007). Current federal policies and controversies over methodology in evaluation. *New Directions for Program Evaluation,* No. 113.

Kahneman, D., & Tversky, A. (Eds.). (2000a). *Choices, values, and frames.* Boston: Cambridge University Press.

Kahneman, D., & Tversky, A. (2000b). Prospect theory: An analysis of decision under risk. In D. Kahneman & A. Tversky (Eds.), *Choices, values, and frames* (pp.17–43). Boston: Cambridge University Press.

Kaplan, R. S., & Norton, D. P. (2008). *Execution premium: Linking strategy to operations for competitive advantage.* Boston: Harvard Business Press.

Kellogg Foundation, W. K. (2005). *Logic model development guide: Using logic models to bring together planning, evaluation & action.* Battle Creek, MI: Author. http://www.wkkf.org/knowledge-center/resources/2010/Logic-Model-Development-Guide.aspx

King, J. (2005). Participatory evaluation. In S. Mathison (Ed.). *Encyclopedia of evaluation* (pp. 291–294). Thousand Oaks, CA: Sage.

King, J. A., Morris, L. L., & Fitz-Gibbon, C. T. (1987). *How to assess program implementation.* Newbury Park, CA: Sage.

King, J., Stevahn, L. Ghere, G., & Minnema, J. (2001). Toward a taxonomy of essential program evaluator competencies. *American Journal of Evaluation, 22*(2), 229–247.

Kirkhart, K. E. (2000). Reconceptualizing evaluation use: An integrated theory of influence. *New Directions for Evaluation, 88,* 5–23.

Kirkhart, K. (2005). Through a cultural lens: Reflections on validity and theory in evaluation. In S. Hood, R. K. Hopson, & H. T. Frierson (Eds.), *The role of culture and cultural context: A mandate for inclusion, the discovery of truth, and understanding in evaluative theory and practice* (pp. 21–29). Greenwich, CT: Information Age Publishing.

Kirkhart, K. (2010). Review of utilization-focused evaluation. *American Journal of Evaluation, 31*(4), 588–596.

Kistler, S. (2010a, January 2). Susan Kistler on data visualization [Web log post]. http://www.aea365.org/blog/

Kistler, S. (2010b). Susan Kistler on data visualization part II [Web log post]. http://www.aea365.org/blog/

Klein, G. (1999). *Sources of power: How people make decisions.* Cambridge, MA: MIT Press.

Kristof, N. (2007, July 2). Attack of the worms. *New York Times,* p. A19.

Kruger, J., & Dunning, D. (1999). Unskilled and unaware of it: How difficulties in recognizing one's own incompetence lead to inflated self-assessments. *Journal of Personality and Social Psychology, 77,* 1121–1134.

Kuhn, T. (1970). *The structure of scientific revolutions.* Chicago: University of Chicago Press.

Kusek, J. Z., & Rist, R. C. (2004). *Ten steps to a results-based monitoring and evaluation system.* Washington, DC: The World Bank.

Kushner, S. (2000). *Personalizing evaluation.* London: Sage.

Le Guin, U. K. (1969). *The left hand of darkness.* New York: Ace Books.

Lehrer, J. (2010a). The neuroscience of screwing up. *Wired,* January, 80–85, 121.

Lehrer, J. (2010b, December 13). The truth wears off. *The New Yorker,* 52–56.

Lengler, R., & Eppler, M. J. (n.d.). *Towards a periodic table of visualization methods for Management.* http://www.visual-literacy.org/periodic_table/periodic_table.pdf

Mark, M. (2006, November 2). The consequences of evaluation: Theory, research, and practice. Presidential plenary address, American Evaluation Association Annual Conference. Portland, OR.

Mark, M., Henry, G., & Julnes, G. (2000). *Evaluation: An integrated framework for understanding, guiding, and improving public and nonprofit policies and programs.* San Francisco: Jossey-Bass.

Mathison, S. (Ed.). (2005). *Encyclopedia of evaluation.* Thousand Oaks, CA: Sage.

Mayer, S. (1993). Common barriers to effectiveness in the independent sector. In S. T. Gray (Ed.), *A vision of evaluation* (pp. 7–11). Washington, DC: Independent Sector.

Mayne, J. (2008). *Contribution analysis: An approach to exploring cause and effect.* ILAC (Institutional Learning and Change) Brief. http://www.outcomemapping.ca/download.php?file=/resource/files/csette_en_ILAC_Brief16_Contribution_Analysis.pdf

Mayne, J. (2011). Exploring cause-effect questions using contribution analysis. In K. Forss, M. Marra, & R. Schwartz (Eds.), *Evaluating the complex: Attribution, contribution and beyond.* New Brunswick, NJ: Transaction Books.

McCabe, A., & Horsley, K. (2008). *The evaluator's cookbook: Exercises for participatory evaluation with children and young people.* New York: Routledge.

McCandless, D. (2010a). *The beauty of data visualization.* TEDGlobal lecture. http://www.ted.com/talks/david_mccandless_the_beauty_of_data_visualization.html

McCandless, D. (2010b). Debtris US. *Information is beautiful.* http://www.informationisbeautiful.net/

McGarvey, C. (2006). *Making measures work for you: Outcomes and evaluation.* New York: GrantCraft, Ford Foundation.

McKegg, K. (2003). From margins to mainstream: The importance of people and context in evaluation utilization (pp. 214–234). In N. Lunt, C. Davidson, & K. McKegg (Eds.), *Evaluating policy and practice: A New Zealand reader.* Auckland, New Zealand: Pearson Prentice Hall.

McKegg, K. (2010). *Evaluation competencies project.* Aotearoa New Zealand Evaluation Association. http://www.anzea.org.nz/index.php?option=com_content&view=article&id=91&Itemid=99

McLaughlin, M. (1976). Implementation as mutual adaption. In W. Williams & R. F. Elmore (Eds.), *Social program implementation* (pp. 167–180). New York: Academic Press.

Mertens, D. M. (2005). Inclusive evaluation. In S. Mathison (Ed.), *Encyclopedia of evaluation* (pp. 195–198). Thousand Oaks, CA: Sage.

Mertens, D. M. (2007). *Transformative research and evaluation.* New York: Guilford.

Miron. G. (2004). *The evaluation report checklist.* Western Michigan University. http://www.wmich.edu/evalctr/checklists/evaluation-management/

Mizumoto, A., & Lim, Y. (2010, October 28). *Reflections on the utilization-focused evaluation (UFE) process: Strengthening ICTD research capacity in Asia.* Evaluation Conclave 2010, New Delhi. http://evaluationinpractice.files.wordpress.com/2010/12/sirca_conclave-2010-presentation-3_yl.pdf

Moncur, M. (2004). *The way of Lao-tzu.* http://www.quotationspage.com/quote/24004.html

Moore, G. (2000). An interview with Gordon Moore. In L. Schmitt (Ed.), *Ingenuity, 5*(2), 1–3.

Morell, J. A. (2010). *Evaluation in the face of uncertainty: Anticipating surprise and responding to the inevitable.* New York: Guilford.

Morell, J. A., Hilscher, R., Magura, S., & Ford, J. (2010). Integrating evaluation and agent-based modeling: Rationale and an example for adopting evidence-based practices. *Journal of Multi-Disciplinary Evaluation,* 6(2), 32–56. http://survey.ate.wmich.edu/jmde/index.php/jmde_1/article/view/275/264

National Network for Collaboration. (2010). *Training manual.* http://crs.uvm.edu/nnco/cd/index.htm

O'Connor, D. (1997, July 25). Humphrey gives DARE qualified endorsement. *St. Paul Pioneer Press,* A1, A5.

OECD. (2005). Paris declaration and Accra agenda for action. http://www.oecd.org/document/18/0,2340,en_2649_3236398_35401554_1_1_1_1,00.html

OECD. (2010). The DAC quality standards for development evaluation. http://www.oecd.org/document/30/0,3746,en_21571361_34047972_38903582_1_1_1_1,00.html

Office on Smoking and Health. (2007). *Introduction to process evaluation in tobacco use prevention and control.* Atlanta, GA: Centers for Disease Control and Prevention.

Pandolfini, B. (1998). *The winning way: The how, what and why of opening strategems.* Palmer, AK: Fireside.

Patrizi, P., & Patton, M. Q. (Eds.). (2010). *Evaluating strategy. New Directions for Evaluation, 128.*

Patton, M. Q. (1978). *Utilization-focused evaluation.* Beverly Hills, CA: Sage.

Patton, M. Q. (1994). Developmental evaluation. *Evaluation Practice, 15,* 311–320.

Patton, M. Q. (2002). *Qualitative research and evaluation methods* (3rd ed.). Thousand Oaks, CA: Sage.

Patton, M. Q. (2007). Process use as a usefulism. *New Directions for Evaluation. 116,* 99–112.

Patton, M. Q. (2008). *Utilization-focused evaluation* (4th ed.). Thousand Oaks, CA: Sage.

Patton, M. Q. (2010). *Evaluation models: Utilization-focused evaluation checklist.* Kalamazoo, MI: Center for Evaluation, Western Michigan University. http://www.wmich.edu/evalctr/checklists/

Patton, M. Q. (2011). *Developmental evaluation: Applying complexity concepts to enhance innovation and use.* New York: Guilford.

Patton, M. Q., Grimes, P., Guthrie, K., Brennan, N., French, B., & Blyth, D. (1977). In search of impact: An analysis of the utilization of federal health evaluation research. In C. H. Weiss (Ed.), *Using social research in public policy making* (pp. 141–164). Lexington, MA: D. C. Heath.

Patton, M. Q., & Scriven, M. (2010, February). The promise and pitfalls of utilization-focused evaluation. In S. I. Donaldson, M. Q. Patton, D. M. Fetterman, & M. Scriven, The 2009 Claremont debates. *Journal of MultiDisciplinary Evaluation,* 6(13), 15–57. http://survey.ate.wmich.edu/jmde/index.php/jmde_1/article/view/260/250

Pawson, R. (2002a). Evidence-based policy: In search of a method. *Evaluation, 8*(2), 157–181.

Pawson, R. (2002b). Evidence-based policy: The promise of 'realist synthesis.' *Evaluation, 8*(3), 340–358.

Pawson, R., & Tilley, N. (1997). *Realistic evaluation.* Thousand Oaks, CA: Sage.

Pawson, R., & Tilley, N. (2005). Realistic evaluation. In S. Mathison (Ed.), *Encyclopedia of evaluation* (pp. 362–367). Thousand Oaks, CA: Sage.

Peltz, M. (1999, February). Winner's choice. *WORTH, 8*(2), 103–105.

Periodic Table of Visualization Methods (2010). http://www.visualliteracy.org/periodic_table/periodic_table.html#. Also, you may want to look at the research behind it all via this academic paper about the Development of the Periodic Table: http://www.visual-literacy.org/periodic_table/periodic_table.pdf

Perrin, B. (1998). Effective use and misuse of performance measurement. *American Journal of Evaluation, 19*(3), 367–379.

Perrin, B. (2007). Towards a new view of accountability. In M.-L. Bemelmans-Videc, J. Lonsdale, & B. Perrin (Eds.), *Making accountability work: Dilemmas for evaluation and for audit* (pp. 41–62). London: Transaction Books.

Podems, D. R. (2010, August). Feminist evaluation and gender approaches: There's a difference? *Journal of MultiDisciplinary Evaluation, 6*(14).

Poister, T. H. (2004). Performance monitoring. In J. S. Whorler, H. P. Hatry, & K. E. Newcome (Eds.), *Handbook of practical evaluations* (pp. 98–125). San Francisco: Jossey-Bass.

Positive Deviance Initiative. (2009). http://www.positivedeviance.org/

Preskill, H. (2005). Appreciative inquiry. In S. Mathison (Ed.), *Encyclopedia of evaluation* (pp. 18–19). Thousand Oaks, CA: Sage.

Preskill, H. (2007, November). Evaluation's second act: A spotlight on learning." Presidential Address, 21st annual conference of the American Evaluation Association, Baltimore, MD.

Preskill, H., & Caracelli, V. (1997). Current and developing conceptions of use: Evaluation use TIG survey results. *American Journal of Evaluation, 18*(3), 209–226.

Preskill, H., & Jones, N. (2009). *A practical guide for engaging stakeholders in developing evaluation questions*. Princeton, NJ: Robert Wood Johnson Foundation. http://www.rwjf.org/pr/product.jsp?id=49951

Preskill, H., & Russ-Eft, D. (2005). *Building evaluation capacity: 72 activities for teaching and training*. Thousand Oaks, CA: Sage.

Quarry, W., & Ramírez, R. (2009). *Communication for another development: Listening before telling*. New York: Zed Books.

Ramírez, R. (2011, January 19). Why 'utilization focused communication' is not an oxymoron [Web log post]. http://www.comminit.com/en/node/329198/bbc

Ramírez, R., & Brodhead, D. (2010). DECI—lessons from year 1. *Evaluation Conclave 2010*, New Delhi, 28 October. http://evaluationinpractice.files.wordpress.com/2010/12/deci_panel_ramirez.pdf

Ravallion, M. (2009). Should the randomistas rule? *Economists' Voice, 6*(2), 1–5.

Reynolds, G. (2008). *Presentation Zen*. Berkeley, CA: New Riders.

Rist, R. C. (2006). The 'E' in monitoring and evaluation: Using evaluative knowledge to support a results-based management system. In R. C. Rist & N. Stame (Eds.), *From studies to streams: Managing evaluative systems* (pp. 3–22). New Brunswick, NJ: Transaction Books.

Rist, R. C., & Stame, N. (Eds.). (2006). *From studies to streams: Managing evaluative systems*. New Brunswick, NJ: Transaction Books.

Rog, D. J. (1985). A methodological assessment of evaluability assessment. Doctoral dissertation, Vanderbilt University, Nashville, TN.

Rogers, P. J. (2005). Accountability. In S. Mathison (Ed.), *Encyclopedia of evaluation* (pp. 2–4). Thousand Oaks, CA: Sage.

Rosling, H. (2010). 200 countries, 200 years, 4 minutes. http://www.flixxy.com/200-countries-200-years-4-minutes.htm

Russell, B. (1998). *The triumph of stupidity in Mortals and others: Bertrand Russell's American essays*. New York: Routledge.

Russon, C. (2005). Cluster evaluation. In S. Mathison (Ed.), *Encyclopedia of evaluation,* (pp. 66–67). Thousand Oaks, CA: Sage.

Russon, C., & Russon, G. (Eds.). (2004). International perspectives on evaluation standards. *New Directions for Evaluation, 104*.

Russon, C., & Russon, K. (2010). How the I Ching or Book of Changes can inform Western notions of theory of change, *Journal of MultiDisciplinary Evaluation, 6*(13), 87–93.

Rutman, L. (1977). *Barriers to the utilization of evaluation research.* Presented at the 27th Annual Meeting of the Society for the Study of Social Problems, Chicago.

Safire, W. (2006, October 8). On language: Bridge to nowhere. *New York Times Sunday Magazine.* http://www.nytimes.com/2006/10/08/magazine/08wwln_safire.html.

Safire, W. (2007, May 6). Halfway humanity. (On Language). *Sunday New York Times Magazine.* http://www.nytimes.com/2007/05/06/magazine/06wwln-safire-t.html

Salganik, M. J., & Watts, D. J. (2008). Leading the herd astray: An experimental study of self-fulfilling prophecies in an artificial cultural market. *Social Psychology Quarterly, 71,* 338–355.

Salmen, L., & Kane, E. (2006). *Bridging diversity: Participatory learning for responsive development.* Washington, DC: The World Bank.

Sanders, J. (2002). Presidential address: On mainstreaming evaluation. *American Journal of Evaluation, 23*(3), 253–273.

Schorr, L. (1988). *Within our reach: Breaking the cycle of disadvantage.* New York: Doubleday.

Schroeder, S. (2002). Execution trumps strategy every time. Speech to the Evaluation Roundtable, Robert Wood Johnson Foundation, Princeton, NJ.

Schwandt, T. A. (2001). *Dictionary of qualitative inquiry* (2nd ed.). Thousand Oaks, CA: Sage.

Scriven, M. (1967). The methodology of evaluation. In R. W. Tyler, R. M. Gagne, & M. Scriven (Eds.), *Perspective of curriculum evaluation* (pp. 39–83). AERA Monograph Series on Curriculum Evaluation, No. 1. Chicago: Rand McNally.

Scriven, M. (1972a). Objectivity and subjectivity in educational research. In L. G. Thomas (Ed.), *Philosophical redirection of educational research: The seventy-first yearbook of the National Society for the Study of Education* (pp. 94–142). Chicago: University of Chicago Press.

Scriven, M. (1972b). Prose and cons about goal-free evaluation. Evaluation Comment: *The Journal of Educational Evaluation, 3*(4), 1–7.

Scriven, M. (1980). *The logic of evaluation.* Iverness, CA: Edgepress.

Scriven, M. (1991). *Evaluation thesaurus* (4th ed.). Newbury Park, CA: Sage.

Scriven, M. (1993). Hard-won lessons in program evaluation. *New Directions for Program Evaluation, 58.*

Scriven, M. (2007). *Key evaluation checklist.* http://www.wmich.edu/evalctr/archive_checklists/kec_feb07.pdf

Seigart, D., & Brisolara, S. (Eds.). (2002). Feminist evaluation: Explorations and experiences. *New Directions for Evaluation,* No. 96.

Shadish, W. R., Jr., Newman, D. L., Scheirer, M. A., & Wye, C. (1995). Guiding principles for evaluators. *New Directions for Program Evaluation, 66.*

Shah, I. (1964). *The Sufis.* Garden City, NY: Doubleday.

Shea, M., & Love, A. (2007). *Self-assessment of stage of internal evaluation organizational capacity development.* Toronto, Canada: Unpublished manuscript.

Shepard, E. (2002). We wasted billions on D.A.R.E. *ReconsiDer Quarterly, 1*(4). http://www.drugpolicy.org/docUploads/education.pdf

Sherrod, L. R., Torney-Purta, J., & Flanagan, C. A. (Eds.). (2010). *Handbook of research on civic engagement in youth.* Hoboken, NJ: John Wiley & Sons.

Sherwood, K. (2005). Evaluating home visitation: A case study of evaluation at The David and Lucile Packard Foundation. *New Directions for Evaluation, 105,* 59–81.

Simon, H. (1957). *Administrative behavior.* New York: Macmillan.

Simon, H. (1978). On how we decide what to do. *Bell Journal of Economics, 9,* 494–507.

Smith, G. C. S., & Pell, J. P. (2003, December 18). Parachute use to prevent death and major trauma related to gravitational challenge: Systematic review of randomized controlled trials. *British Medical Journal, 327,* 1459–1461.

Smith, M. F. (2005). Evaluability assessment. In S. Mathison (Ed.), *Encyclopedia of evaluation* (pp. 136–139). Thousand Oaks, CA: Sage.

Smith, N. (1980, Winter). Studying evaluation assumptions. *Evaluation Network Newsletter,* pp. 39–40.

Stake, R. E. (1975). *Evaluating the arts in education: A responsive approach.* Columbus, OH: Charles E. Merrill.

Stake, R. E. (1996, June 25). Beyond responsive evaluation. Minnesota Evaluation Studies Institute keynote, University of Minnesota, Minneapolis.

Stake, R. E. (2005). *Multiple case study analysis.* New York: Guilford.

Stake, R., & Abma, T. (2005). Responsive evaluation. In S. Mathison (Ed.), *Encyclopedia of evaluation* (pp. 376–379). Thousand Oaks, CA: Sage.

Stevahn, L., King, J., Ghere, G., & Minnema, J. (2005). Establishing essential program evaluator competencies. *American Journal of Evaluation, 26*(1), 43–59.

Stevahn, L., King, J., Ghere, G., & Minnema, J. (2006). Evaluator competencies in university-based evaluation training programs. *Canadian Journal of Program Evaluation, 20,* 101–123.

Stockdill, S. H., Duhon-Sells, R. M., Olson, R. A., & Patton, M. Q. (1992). Voice in the design and evaluation of a multicultural education program: a developmental approach. *Minority Issues in Program Evaluation, New Directions in Program Evaluation, 53,* 17–34.

Stufflebeam, D. L. (1994). Empowerment evaluation, objectivist evaluation, and evaluation standards: Where the future of evaluation should not go and where it needs to go. *Evaluation Practice, 15*(3), 321–338.

Stufflebeam, D. L. (1999a). *Evaluation plans and operations checklist.* Kalamazoo, MI: Center for Evaluation, Western Michigan University. http://www.wmich.edu/evalctr/wp-content/uploads/2010/05/plansoperations1.pdf

Stufflebeam, D. L. (1999b). Metaevaluation checklist. Kalamazoo, MI: Center for Evaluation, Western Michigan University. http://www.wmich.edu/evalctr/archive_checklists/program_metaeval_10point.pdf

Stufflebeam, D. L. (2000). *Guidelines for developing evaluation checklists: The checklists development checklist.* Kalamazoo, MI: Center for Evaluation, Western Michigan University. http://www.wmich.edu/evalctr/checklists/guidelines_cdc.pdf

Stufflebeam, D. L. (2005). CIPP Model. In S. Mathison (Ed.), *Encyclopedia of evaluation* (pp. 60–65). Thousand Oaks, CA: Sage.

Stufflebeam, D. L., & Shinkfield, A. J. (2007). Metaevaluation: Evaluating evaluations. In *Evaluation theory, models, and applications* (Chapter 27). San Francisco: Jossey-Bass.

Suchman, E. A. (1967). *Evaluative research: Principles and practice in public service and social action programs.* New York: Russell Sage.

Sutcliffe, K., & Weber, K. (2003, May). The high cost of accurate knowledge. *Harvard Business Review, 81,* 74–84.

Symonette, H. (2004). Walking pathways toward becoming a culturally competent evaluator: Boundaries, borderlands, and border crossings. *New Directions for Evaluation,* No. 102, 95–110.

Torres, R., Preskill, H., & Piontek, M. (1996). *Evaluation strategies for communicating and reporting: Enhancing learning in organizations.* Thousand Oaks, CA: Sage.

Torres, R., Preskill, H., & Piontek, M. (2004). *Evaluation strategies for communicating and reporting: Enhancing learning in organizations* (2nd ed.). Thousand Oaks, CA: Sage.

Treasury Board of Canada. (2002). *Case studies on the uses and drivers of effective evaluations in the government of Canada.* Ottawa: Treasury Board of Canada. http://www.tbs-sct.gc.ca/eval/tools_outils/impact/impact_e.asp#5.0

Tuan, Y.-F. (2000). *Escapism.* Baltimore, MD: The Johns Hopkins University Press.

Tversky, A., & Fox, C. (2000). Weighing risk and uncertainty. In D. Kahneman & A. Tversky (Eds.), *Choices, values, and frames* (pp. 93–117). Boston: Cambridge University Press.

Tversky, A., & Kahneman, D. (2000). Advances in prospect theory: Cumulative representation of uncertainty. In D. Kahneman & A. Tversky (Eds.), *Choices, values, and frames* (pp. 44–65). Boston: Cambridge University Press.

Twenge, J. M., & Campbell, W. K. (2009). *The narcissism epidemic: Living in the age of entitlement.* New York: Free Press.

University of Wisconsin Cooperative Extension. (2010). Program development and evaluation. Madison, WI: U.W. Cooperative Extension. http://www.uwex.edu/ces/pdande/evaluation/evallogicmodel.html

Uphoff, N. (1991). A field methodology for participatory self-evaluation. *Community Development Journal, 26*(4), 271–285.

Urban J. B., & Trochim, W. (2009). The role of evaluation in research-practice integration: Working toward the "Golden Spike." *American Journal of Evaluation, 30*(4), 538–553.

Uyeki, T. (2010, December 13). Using visual methods in evaluation [Web log post]. http://www.aea365.org/blog/

Vernooy, R. (Ed.). (2010). Collaborative learning in practice: Examples from natural resource management in Asia. Ottawa: IDRC. http://publicwebsite.idrc.ca/EN/Resources/Publications/Pages/IDRCBookDetails.aspx?PublicationID=44

Wadsworth, Y. (2010). *Building in research and evaluation: Human inquiry in living systems.* Victoria, Australia: Allen & Unwin.

Wageningen International UR. (2006). Participatory planning, monitoring and evaluation. Wageningen, The Netherlands: IAC. http://portals.wi.wur.nl/ppme/?Home

Waller, J. (2004). *Fabulous science: Fact and fiction in the history of scientific discovery.* New York: Oxford University Press.

Walsh, S. (2009). Linking coral reef health and human welfare. Doctoral thesis. San Diego: University of California.

Wargo, M. J. (1995). The impact of federal government reinvention on federal evaluation activity. *Evaluation Practice, 16*(3), 227–237.

Wehipeihana, N., Davidson, E. J., McKegg, K., & Shanker, V. (2010). What does it take to do evaluation in communities and cultural contexts other than our own? *Journal of MultiDisciplinary Evaluation, 13,* 182–192.

Weiss, C. H. (Ed.). (1977). *Using social research in public policy making.* Lexington, MA: D. C. Heath.

Weiss, C. H. (1980). Knowledge creep and decision accretion. *Knowledge: Creation, Diffusion, Utilization, 1*(3), 381–404.

Weiss, C. H. (2000). Which links in which theories shall we evaluate? Program theory in evaluation: Challenges and opportunities. *New Directions for Evaluation, 87,* 35–45.

Weiss, C. H., & Bucuvalas, M. (1980, April). Truth tests and utility tests: Decision makers' frame of reference for social science research. *American Sociological Review, 45,* 302–313.

Weiss, C. H., Murphy-Graham, E., & Birkeland, S. (2005). An alternate route to policy influence: How evaluations affect DARE. *American Journal of Evaluation*, *26*(1), 12–30.

Weiss, H. B., & Greene, J. C. (1992). An empowerment partnership for family support and education programs and evaluations. *Family Science Review, 5*(1, 2), 145–163.

Westley, F., Zimmerman, B., & Patton, M. Q. (2006). *Getting to maybe: How the world is changed.* Toronto, Canada: Random House Canada.

Whitmore, E. (Ed.). (1998). Understanding and practicing participatory evaluation. *New Directions for Evaluation, 75.*

Wholey, J. (2005). Joseph S. Wholey. In S. Mathison (Ed.), *Encyclopedia of evaluation* (pp. 450–451). Thousand Oaks, CA: Sage.

Williams, B. (2003). Getting the stuff used. In N. Lunt, C. Davidson, & K. McKegg (Eds.), *Evaluating policy and practice: A New Zealand reader* (pp. 196–213). Auckland, New Zealand: Pearson Prentice Hall.

Williams, B. (2005). Systems and systems thinking. In S. Mathison (Ed.), *Encyclopedia of evaluation* (pp. 405–412). Thousand Oaks, CA: Sage.

Williams, B., & Hummelbrunner, R. (2011). *Systems concepts in action: A practitioner's toolkit.* Stanford, CA: Stanford University Press.

Williams, B., & Iman, I. (2006). *Systems concepts in evaluation: An expert anthology.* AEA Monograph. Point Reynes, CA: Edgepress.

World Bank, The. (2004). Influential evaluations: Evaluations that improved performance and impacts of development programs. Washington DC: The World Bank. http://lnweb90.worldbank.org/oed/oeddoclib.nsf/24cc3bb1f94ae11c85256808006a0046/67433ec6c181c22385256e7f0073ba1c/$FILE/influential_evaluations_ecd.pdf

World Bank, The. (2005). Maintaining momentum to 2015? An impact evaluation of interventions to improve maternal and child health and nutrition in Bangladesh. Washington, DC: Operations Evaluation Department, The World Bank.

World Bank, The. (2006). Reducing poverty on a global scale: Learning and innovating for development. Washington DC: The World Bank.

Yarbrough, D. B., Shulha, L. M., Hopson, R. K., & Caruthers, F.A. (2010). *The program evaluation standards: A guide for evaluators and evaluation users* (3rd ed.), Thousand Oaks, CA: Sage.

Author Index

Subject Index